PHILIPPIANS,
COLOSSIANS,
AND PHILEMON

PREACHING THE WORD
Edited by R. Kent Hughes

PHILIPPIANS, COLOSSIANS, AND PHILEMON

The Fellowship *of the* Gospel *and the* Supremacy *of* Christ

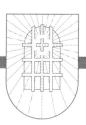

R. KENT HUGHES

CROSSWAY

WHEATON, ILLINOIS

Philippians, Colossians, and Philemon

Copyright © 2013 by R. Kent Hughes

Published by Crossway
  1300 Crescent Street
  Wheaton, Illinois 60187

Previously published as: *Philippians* © 2007 by R. Kent Hughes and *Colossians and Philemon* © 1989 by R. Kent Hughes.

Cover design: John McGrath, Simplicated Studio

Cover image: Adam Greene, illustrator

First printing 2013

Printed in the United States of America

ISBN-13: 978-1-4335-3630-4
ISBN-10: 1-4335-3630-7
PDF ISBN: 978-1-4335-3631-1
Mobipocket ISBN: 978-1-4335-3632-8
ePub ISBN: 978-1-4335-3633-5

Library of Congress Cataloging-in-Publication Data

Hughes, R. Kent.
 Philippians, Colossians, and Philemon : the fellowship of the gospel and the supremacy of Christ / R. Kent Hughes.
  pages cm. — (Preaching the Word)
 Includes bibliographical references and index.
 ISBN 978-1-4335-3630-4 (hc)
 1. Bible. Philippians—Commentaries. 2. Bible. Colossians—Commentaries. 3. Bible. Philemon—Commentaries. I. Title.
BS2705.53.H84   2013
227'.07—dc23   2013026506

From *Philippians*:
For Barbara,
my best friend and lifelong comrade
in the Fellowship of the Gospel

From *Colossians and Philemon*:
For David Hamilton MacDonald,
friend of friends

Paul and Timothy, servants of Christ Jesus,
To all the saints in Christ Jesus who are at Philippi,
with the overseers and deacons: Grace to you and
peace from God our Father and the Lord Jesus Christ.

PHILIPPIANS 1:1, 2

. . . that in everything he might be preeminent.

COLOSSIANS 1:18b

Table of Contents

COLOSSIANS
The Supremacy of Christ

PHILEMON

A Word to Those Who Preach the Word

There are times when I am preaching that I have especially sensed the pleasure of God. I usually become aware of it through the unnatural silence. The ever-present coughing ceases, and the pews stop creaking, bringing an almost physical quiet to the sanctuary—through which my words sail like arrows. I experience a heightened eloquence, so that the cadence and volume of my voice intensify the truth I am preaching.

There is nothing quite like it—the Holy Spirit filling one's sails, the sense of his pleasure, and the awareness that something is happening among one's hearers. This experience is, of course, not unique, for thousands of preachers have similar experiences, even greater ones.

What has happened when this takes place? How do we account for this sense of his smile? The answer for me has come from the ancient rhetorical categories of *logos*, *ethos*, and *pathos*.

The first reason for his smile is the *logos*—in terms of preaching, God's Word. This means that as we stand before God's people to proclaim his Word, we have done our homework. We have exegeted the passage, mined the significance of its words in their context, and applied sound hermeneutical principles in interpreting the text so that we understand what its words meant to its hearers. And it means that we have labored long until we can express in a sentence what the theme of the text is—so that our outline springs from the text. Then our preparation will be such that as we preach, we will not be preaching our own thoughts about God's Word, but God's actual Word, his *logos*. This is fundamental to pleasing him in preaching.

The second element in knowing God's smile in preaching is *ethos*—what you are as a person. There is a danger endemic to preaching, which is having your hands and heart cauterized by holy things. Phillips Brooks illustrated it by the analogy of a train conductor who comes to believe that he has been to the places he announces because of his long and loud heralding of them. And that is why Brooks insisted that preaching must be "the bringing of truth through personality." Though we can never perfectly embody the truth we preach, we must be subject to it, long for it, and make it as much a part of our ethos as possible. As the Puritan William Ames said, "Next to the Scriptures, nothing makes a sermon more to pierce, than when it comes out of the inward affection of the heart without any affectation." When a preacher's *ethos* backs up his *logos*, there will be the pleasure of God.

Last, there is *pathos*—personal passion and conviction. David Hume, the Scottish philosopher and skeptic, was once challenged as he was seen going to hear George Whitefield preach: "I thought you do not believe in the gospel." Hume replied, "I don't, but he does." Just so! When a preacher believes what he preaches, there will be passion. And this belief and requisite passion will know the smile of God.

The pleasure of God is a matter of *logos* (the Word), *ethos* (what you are), and *pathos* (your passion). As you preach the Word may you experience his smile—the Holy Spirit in your sails!

R. Kent Hughes
Wheaton, Illinois

Acknowledgments

From *Philippians*

This is my thirteenth contribution to the Preaching the Word commentary series. And over the years I have become increasingly aware of how much I owe to those who have supported my work. My talented administrative assistants have been, respectively, Mrs. Lillian Smith, Mrs. Sharon Fritz, and Mrs. Pauline Epps—all very competent and committed to improving the shape and substance of my work. Mr. Herbert Carlburg has had his hand in every volume, checking all references and correcting my grammar. And then, of course, I have had the deft and wise services of Crossway's senior editor Ted Griffin, whose theological acumen has sharpened my expression of important truths.

Lastly, any preacher knows that the congregation adds to or detracts from the pulpit ministry. And happily, in my case, the people of College Church have vastly contributed to this volume by their expectations, criticisms, suggestions, and prayers—for which I am so grateful.

Now, in respect to this volume, special thanks to Pauline, Herb, Ted, and my wife, Barbara, for their singular contributions.

From *Colossians and Philemon*

I must express appreciation to my secretary, Mrs. Sharon Fritz, for her patience and care in typing the manuscripts of these studies; also to Mr. Herb Carlburg for his cheerful, weekly proofreading, and Rev. Jeff Buikema, pastor of Covenant Presbyterian Church, LaCrosse, Wisconsin, for his reading of the manuscript and helpful suggestions. Lastly, special thanks to Dr. Lane Dennis, president of Crossway Books, for his vision for this undertaking and consistent encouragement.

PHILIPPIANS

The Fellowship of the Gospel

Paul and Timothy, servants of Christ Jesus, To all the saints in Christ Jesus who are at Philippi, with the overseers and deacons: Grace to you and peace from God our Father and the Lord Jesus Christ.

1:1, 2

1

A Particular Joy

PHILIPPIANS 1:1, 2

THIS IS ADMITTEDLY SUBJECTIVE, but it seems to me that the four chapters of Philippians have provided more favorite quotes and sound bites than any other section of Scripture of similar length—certainly it has done that for me. Here are some of my favorites:

- "For to me to live is Christ, and to die is gain." (1:21)
- "I am hard pressed between the two. My desire is to depart and be with Christ, for that is far better." (1:23)
- "Only let your manner of life be worthy of the gospel of Christ." (1:27)
- "Do nothing from selfish ambition or conceit, but in humility count others more significant than yourselves. Let each of you look not only to his own interests, but also the interests of others." (2:3, 4)
- "Have this mind among yourselves, which is yours in Christ Jesus, who, though he was in the form of God, did not count equality with God a thing to be grasped, but emptied himself, by taking the form of a servant, being born in the likeness of men. And being found in human form, he humbled himself by becoming obedient to the point of death, even death on a cross. Therefore God has highly exalted him and bestowed on him the name that is above every name, so that at the name of Jesus every knee should bow, in heaven and on earth and under the earth, and every tongue confess that Jesus Christ is Lord, to the glory of God the Father." (2:5–11)
- "Work out your own salvation with fear and trembling, for it is God who works in you, both to will and to work for his good pleasure." (2:12, 13)
- "That I may gain Christ and be found in him, not having a righteousness of my own that comes from the law, but that which comes through faith in Christ." (3:8, 9)
- "But one thing I do: forgetting what lies behind and straining forward to what lies ahead, I press on toward the goal for the prize of the upward call of God in Christ Jesus." (3:13, 14)

- "But our citizenship is in heaven, and from it we await a Savior, the Lord Jesus Christ." (3:20)
- "Rejoice in the Lord always; again I will say, rejoice." (4:4)
- "Do not be anxious about anything, but in everything by prayer and supplication with thanksgiving let your requests be made known to God. And the peace of God, which surpasses all understanding, will guard your hearts and your minds in Christ Jesus." (4:6, 7)
- "Finally, brothers, whatever is true, whatever is honorable . . . " (4:8)
- "I have learned in whatever situation I am to be content." (4:11)
- "I can do all things through him who strengthens me." (4:13)

You can see that I love this Bible book. But there is a danger in knowing these lines so well: they can take on a life of their own apart from their context and become sentimentalized and emptied of their depth.[1] For example, "Rejoice in the Lord always" (4:4) has become for some within the church and outside it a motto for merely willing a superficial happiness, rather than the deep, theologically grounded command that it is.

As a matter of fact, Philippians is not (as is commonly thought) the "Epistle of Joy." But joy is a motif in Philippians, and when it flashes forth, as it does sixteen times, it is sparked by the deeper themes of Paul's letter. Philippians calls us to a particular joy, the joy experienced by Paul in Roman captivity facing a capital charge while his leadership was being contested by usurpers within the church. So as we journey through Philippians it is my hope that these favorite verses and other familiar lines of this amazing letter will take on their first-century depth and power.

Paul's Journey to Philippi

The background of Philippians is this: Paul and Barnabas had returned victoriously from the famous Council in Jerusalem, with the Council's decisive ruling that Gentile believers did not have to be circumcised or adopt Jewish customs to be saved. It was a watershed ruling. Gentile evangelism was given a mighty, liberating boost. But then Paul and Barnabas separated, and Paul took Silas and set out on his second missionary journey (cf. Acts 15:36–40). Timothy joined them in Lystra (cf. Acts 16:1–5).

Paul's plan was to retrace the steps of his first missionary journey and encourage the churches. As they traveled west, the trio attempted to go back down to Ephesus, but the Holy Spirit checked them. Then they tried to go north to Bithynia by the Black Sea, and again the Spirit of Jesus did not allow it (cf. Acts 16:6, 7). Thus Paul, Silas, and Timothy were effectively funneled west to Troas and the mouth of the Dardanelle Straits, the gateway to Europe. There Dr. Luke joined them, forming a dynamic foursome.

It was there at the Dardanelles that Paul beheld standing before him in a night vision a man from Macedonia (a European from what today is northern Greece), urging him and saying, as Luke tells it, "'Come over to Macedonia and help us.' And when Paul had seen the vision, immediately we sought to go on into Macedonia, concluding that God had called us to preach the gospel to them" (Acts 16:9, 10). In an instant came one of the great turning points in history as Paul and company made a two-day crossing to Neapolis and walked nine miles along the Egnatian Way to Philippi. Rome did not know it, but the flag of Christianity was unfurled in the empire that day.

Philippi was not a big city, no more than 10,000 at the most, and rested on a narrow shoulder of land, crowned by an acropolis guarding the *Via Egnatia*, the famous highway between Rome and her eastern empire. Philippi had been founded by Greeks in the fourth century B.C. Phillip of Macedonia, the father of Alexander the Great, had named it after himself.[2]

But now it was a Roman colony because in 42 B.C. Philippi achieved note as the place where Mark Anthony and Octavian (Augustus) fought the forces of Brutus and Cassius, the assassins of Julius Caesar, defeating Cassius. Later in 31 B.C. when Augustus defeated Mark Anthony in the battle of Actium, Augustus renamed the colony after himself—*Colonia Iulia Augusta Philippensis*.[3] As a Roman town it was governed by Roman law. Roman expatriates made up the citizenry. Latin became the official language, and the citizens wore Roman dress. The public inscriptions in the forum and on all the buildings were exclusively Latin. So the leadership and aristocracy of Philippi were completely Roman and Latin. This naturally created a Greek-speaking underclass that made up the local populace. These were the construction workers and tradesmen and merchants.[4] It is to this social group that Paul initially came.

Paul's custom when entering a town was to go first to the Jews, to the synagogue (cf. Acts 14:1). But there were so few Jews in the city that the necessary quorum to form a synagogue of ten men did not exist.[5] However, after a few days Paul did discover a Sabbath congregation meeting alongside a river outside the city walls. It was a group of God-fearing Gentile women meeting in "a place of prayer" (16:13). Today there is a general agreement that the exact site of that "place of prayer" was just outside the southern gate at the bank of the Gangites River, which still flows only fifty meters from the old city wall.[6] That was likely where Paul and Silas made initial contact with Gentile women worshiping the God of Israel—women who would soon become the first Christians of Philippi.

Paul's Reception in Philippi

The first of these women was a merchant named Lydia. As Luke tells it, "One who heard us was a woman named Lydia, from the city of Thyatira, a seller of purple goods, who was a worshiper of God. The Lord opened her heart to pay attention to what was said by Paul" (Acts 16:14). The man in the Macedonian vision turned out to be a woman! Lydia believed, her entire household believed, and they were all baptized on the spot in the Gangites (v. 15).

Spiritual opposition was almost immediate in the form of a girl who had "a spirit of divination" (v. 16; literally "a pythonic spirit," referencing demonic control). The girl's loud, incessant heralding of the truth about Paul and company—"These men are servants of the Most High God, who proclaim to you the way of salvation" (v. 17)—was a demonic attempt to co-opt the gospel and destroy it. Paul exorcised the spirit on the spot—and found himself in deep trouble because he had driven out the girl's owners' source of income! Paul and Silas were seized and were taken to the "Roman" magistrates, were identified as "Jews" (appealing to the Romanness of the officials and their anti-Semitic prejudices), and were savagely beaten by the *lictors*—they got their licks!

We all know the story. As the bruised and bleeding duo sat in stocks in the bowels of the prison and sang songs in the night, "hymns to God" (v. 25), a great earthquake freed them from their stocks and opened the prison doors. And the gospel further invaded Europe when the jailer cried out, "'Sirs, what must I do to be saved?' And they said, 'Believe in the Lord Jesus, and you will be saved, you and your household'" (vv. 30, 31). Then came another round of baptisms!

When the magistrates learned that Paul and Silas were Roman citizens, their arrogance turned to quaking fear and profuse apologies as they urged them to quietly leave town. They did leave, but not before visiting Lydia. There were undoubtedly tears and maybe even some laughter and hoots in Lydia's home. Possibly they sang a few "prison songs." Certainly there were praise and thanksgiving to God and prayers for the new church—Lydia and her household, the jailer and his household, perhaps other God-fearing women from the riverbank, maybe even the ex-pythoness. The flag of the gospel had been raised on a new continent. We should take note in this day of the science of church growth and the promotion of the homogeneous unit principle that this was not a homogeneous church plant but rather the Body of Christ in glorious diversity.

It is important to understand here that the church in Philippi would become Paul's favorite church.[7] Paul enjoyed a unique closeness to the Philippians, which we see in exceptionally warm and friendly expressions in this letter. Paul makes this clear right after his greeting as he says, "I thank my God in all my remembrance of you, always in every prayer of mine for you all making my prayer with joy, because of your partnership in the gospel from the first day until now" (vv. 3–5). The word "partnership" is the Greek word *koinonia*, "fellowship"—Paul feels a warm "fellowship in the gospel" with the Philippians. As we will see in our next study, the same word (fellowship, partnership) or its derivatives appear in six verses in Philippians (cf. 1:5, 7; 2:1; 3:10; 4:14, 15 [twice]). And we shall see that this is not a church social fellowship as Christians today often think of the word, but a robust fellowship that rides on their mutual commitment to the gospel. This gospel fellowship grew from their commitment to support Paul's mission spiritually and materially (cf. 4:15, 16).

What we must understand as we go through Philippians is that while there are various reasons for Paul's writing, this letter comes from the depth of fellowship that Paul and the Philippians shared in the gospel. This accounts for the feel of this letter and is the basis for what Paul said to the Philippians and how he said it.

This is why this commentary has the subtitle "The Fellowship of the Gospel"—it is an epic fellowship as suggested by Tolkien's title *The Fellowship of the Ring*. No punch and cookies here. This is the fellowship of compatriots bound together in a great cause. You will not understand the letter if you do not understand this.

Paul's Letter to the Philippians (vv. 1, 2)

The occasion for Paul's letter to the Philippians came years after the founding of the church and sprang from their financial support of him as a prisoner in Rome (cf. 4:18). Their monetary gift had been carried to him by a church member named Epaphroditus, who had nearly died during its delivery (cf. 2:27). And when Epaphroditus recovered and prepared to return, Paul asked him to carry the letter home. So the letter arrived late in Paul's imprisonment, after A.D. 60 and probably after A.D. 62.[8]

Paul's letter reveals many purposes: to express gratitude for their generosity, to explain why he sent Epaphroditus back so quickly, to catch them up, to inform them that he would shortly be sending Timothy, to warn them of Judaizers, to urge them to stand firm and be united.[9] But under and around all these purposes was the reality of their fellowship in the gospel.

The very words of Paul's greeting evoke his attitude of partnership with the Philippians as he tailors his greeting for the occasion. Most noticeably he omits the use of the title "apostle" and begins, "Paul and Timothy, servants of Christ Jesus" (v. 1). The disuse of his title evidences the familiar warmth that existed between him and the Philippian believers.[10] And his inclusion of Timothy as coauthor indicates that Paul would share his authority with those in the "partnership [fellowship] in the gospel" (v. 5). As Karl Barth put it, "A hero, a genius, a 'religious personality' stands alone; an apostle has others beside him like himself and sets them on his own level."[11] Even more, Paul identifies himself and Timothy as "servants [literal translation, "slaves"] of Christ Jesus" (v. 1)—a term that in its Philippian/Roman context carried negative connotations that were just as repugnant to the fashionable middle class of the first century as today.[12] Paul knew exactly what he was saying because the only other use of "slave" in this letter will come in 2:7, used of Christ, who "took the form of a servant [*slave*]."

Along with these careful self-designations Paul identifies his recipients as "all the saints in Christ Jesus who are at Philippi, with the overseers and deacons" (1:1). Thus while he recognized the church leaders, he emphasized that he was writing to *all* those in Christ. Paul was not playing favorites. His emphasis on "all" foreshadows the call to unity that he would powerfully voice.

Paul and the Philippians' fellowship in the gospel, their gospel partnership, gives the theological and relational context and texture for his major themes. At the very heart of the letter is Paul's call to the Philippians to let their "manner of life be worthy of the gospel of Christ" (1:27), and as such, living a gospel-worthy life becomes the theme that extends to the end of chapter 2. Thus, to live worthy of the gospel there must be *unity*—"standing firm in one spirit, with one mind striving side by side for the faith of the gospel" (1:27)—in gospel partnership. They must be "of the same mind" (2:2). They must "look . . . to the interests of others" (2:4). They must have the mind of Christ (cf. 2:5–8). They must "work out [their] own salvation" as Christ works in them (2:12, 13). They must live like Timothy and Epaphroditus (2:19–30)—men who walked worthy of the gospel.

This said, Christ is the center of the letter. No other noun occurs more in Philippians than his name. The Christology of the hymn of Christ in 2:6–11 can be said to underpin the thinking of everything else in Philippians.[13] Philippians is about Christ. Philippians is about people in Christ Jesus (cf. 2:29; 3:1; 4:4, 10). Philippians is about people who are in the fellowship of the gospel because they are in Christ. Philippians is about people whose "citizenship is in heaven" (3:20).

Such grand themes and purposes! And understand this—the motif that sparkles and effervesces throughout them is joy.

- 1:4b: "making my prayer with joy."
- 1:18b: "Christ is proclaimed, and in that I rejoice. Yes, and I will rejoice."
- 1:25b: "your . . . joy in the faith."
- 2:2: "complete my joy."
- 2:17, 18: "Even if I am to be poured out as a drink offering upon the sacrificial offering of your faith, I am glad and rejoice with you all. Likewise you also should be glad and rejoice with me."
- 2:28: "that you may rejoice."
- 2:29: "So receive him in the Lord with all joy."
- 3:1: "Finally, my brothers, rejoice in the Lord."
- 4:4: "Rejoice in the Lord always; again I will say, rejoice."
- 4:10: "I rejoiced in the Lord greatly."

Philippians evokes a particular joy. It is the joy *of* Christ and joy *from* Christ. It is a joy that effervesces in the dark places of life. It is available for those "in Christ" (3:3), who stand together as they partner in the fellowship of the gospel. Our studies in Philippians will enhance our experience of this particular joy.

I thank my God in all my remembrance of you, always in every prayer of mine for you all making my prayer with joy, because of your partnership in the gospel from the first day until now. And I am sure of this, that he who began a good work in you will bring it to completion at the day of Jesus Christ.

1:3–6

2

Paul's Joyous Thanksgiving

PHILIPPIANS 1:3–6

WHEN THEOLOGIAN BROUGHTON KNOX was serving as a young chaplain in the British navy on a ship preparing for D-day and the invasion of Normandy, he noted that the minds of all hands on board, regardless of rank, were focused on the invasion's success. No one thought of his own interests, but only on how he could help his shipmates in their commonly shared task. He says, "I remember noting in my mind how I had never been happier."[1]

After the invasion and return to England, everyone noticed a difference in the atmosphere on ship. It was still friendly because it was a well-run ship. But several of the sailors, sensing the difference, asked the young chaplain why things had changed. Knox reflects, "The answer was quite simple. During those months that preceded and followed D-day, our thoughts had a minimum of self-centeredness in them. We gave ourselves to our shared activity and objective. . . . Once the undertaking was over we reverted to our own purposes, as we do normally."[2] Broughton Knox was, of course, reflecting on his ship's experience of the fellowship that people experience in pursuing a common goal. Human friendship is a wonderful thing, but fellowship goes beyond friendship. Fellowship occurs among friends committed to a common cause or goal and flourishes through their common pursuit of it.

J. R. R. Tolkien's *Fellowship of the Ring* rides upon this reality. The fellowship of the Ring is made up of individuals of disparate origin and ridiculous diversity that exceed any of our ethnic or social differences: four hobbits, tiny beings with large, hairy, shoeless feet—Frodo Baggins and his friends Merry, Sam, and Pippin; two men, warriors of the first rank always dressed for battle—Boromir of Gondor and Aragorn, son of Arathorn II, King of Gondor; one wizard, Gandalf, the ancient nemesis of evil and a repository of wisdom and supernatural power; an elf, Legolas, from a fair race of archers of the forest with pointed ears; and a dwarf, Gimli, a stout, hairy, axe-wielding creature from the dark chambers under the mountains.

The nine members of the fellowship bore few affinities. The elves and the dwarves were like the English and the French because both had an unspoken agreement to feel superior to the other. However, the nine very different individuals, bound together by their great mission to defeat the forces of darkness and save Middle-Earth, became inseparable and their covenant indissoluble. The man Boromir, despite his lapses, gave his life for the hobbits. And the elf and the dwarf came to form a great friendship, so great that Gimli was inducted into an honored order reserved only for elves.

Such can be earthly human fellowship when the conditions are right. But here in Philippians our text has at its heart a depth of fellowship that exceeds any earthly fellowship—"your partnership [fellowship] in the gospel" (v. 5)—which is rooted in God and is a quest that can only be described as eternal.

The theme of verses 3–6 is that of joyous apostolic thanksgiving ringing from Paul's prison cell in Rome—a thanksgiving grounded in three things: (1) Paul's remembrance of the Philippians, (2) the Philippians' participation (fellowship) in the gospel, and (3) Paul's confidence in their future.

Thankful Remembrance (vv. 3, 4)

Paul's Gratitude

As Paul mused in his Roman cell, his mind ranged across Italy and the Adriatic to Macedonia and over the *Via Egnatia* to "little Rome," the pretentious Roman colony of Philippi—and the beloved faces of Lydia and her clan, the jailer and his family, Euodia and Syntyche and Clement and scores of others who had been added to the church. And Paul smiled as he wrote, "I thank my God in all my remembrance of you, always in every prayer of mine for you all making my prayer with joy" (vv. 3, 4). This is so typical of Paul because, in truth, Paul rarely thanked God for *things*. Paul thanked God for *people* who, despite whatever trouble they may have been to him, remained a source of joy and thanksgiving.[3]

The Apostle Paul is frankly astonishing in this respect. On an earlier occasion when he had not yet been to Rome but was writing his conclusion to his famous epistle to the Romans, he listed no less than thirty-three names in his concluding greetings (Romans 16). Most of those people he had met on his journeys through Asia and Asia Minor and had subsequently taken up residence in Rome. The great theologian was a people person first and foremost. Imagine the heart and the energy that went into such ministry. Paul was always inquiring and making note of his people's whereabouts and condition and was thanking God in all his remembrance of them.

Joyful Prayer

And the outcome was not only thankfulness to God but joyous petition— "always in every prayer of mine for you all making my prayer with joy" (v. 4). This was an intensely emotional matter for Paul as the inclusive words "always," "every," and "all" convey.[4] When he thought of their names, he automatically prayed for them—and that included *all* of them, not just a favored few. But what is most noteworthy is that here in verse 4 Paul begins to sound the note of joy that rings fifteen more times in this letter as it builds to its ringing crescendo in chapter 4: "Rejoice in the Lord always; again I will say, rejoice" (v. 4).

This early joy note is very significant for two reasons. First, the Macedonian churches, among which the Philippian church was prominent, had been noted for their joy amidst affliction. Paul even challenged the Corinthians with their example:

> We want you to know, brothers, about the grace of God that has been given among the churches of Macedonia, for in a severe test of affliction, their abundance of joy and their extreme poverty have overflowed in a wealth of generosity on their part. (2 Corinthians 8:1, 2; cf. Acts 16:34)

Perhaps the Philippians, due to the ongoing hostility of their opponents, had begun to lose their abundance of joy. So Paul sounds an early opening note of joy.

Second, Paul himself was in prison, awaiting possible death. This means that joy is not a result of pleasant circumstances or prosperity or success. Joy for Paul (and the Biblical writers) was not an emotion or a mood or a feeling but an *attitude*. And thus it can be commanded, whereas an emotion cannot.[5] So here in Philippians Paul will command, "Finally, my brothers, rejoice in the Lord" (3:1), and a few verses later, "Rejoice in the Lord always; again I will say, rejoice" (4:4). He even tells them that if he is executed he will rejoice, and so should they (cf. 2:17, 18). He does not urge a feeling but an attitude.

The source of joy is outside itself. It is "in the Lord" (cf. 2:29; 3:1; 4:4, 10). It can be commanded because they are "in the Lord" who gives it.[6] What Paul does with this early joy note and its fifteen echoes is to assure his close friends who are so burdened about his imprisonment that being in prison has not robbed him of his joy. Paul consciously models the joy that he will command the Philippians to have.[7] What a standard Paul's remembrance from his jail sets as it evokes thanksgiving and prayer and joy in his soul. What a call to those of us charged with the care of souls to remember all our people always with thanksgiving and joyful prayer.

Thankful for Fellowship (v. 5)

Paul's thankful, backward look was based on the long-standing reality of the Philippians' "partnership [fellowship] in the gospel from the first day until now" (v. 5), which is the center of verses 3–6.[8] As we have mentioned, the depth of the fellowship that Paul celebrated here exceeds that of any earthly fellowship. The great reason for this is that there was, as Gordon Fee says, a "three-way bond" between Paul, the Philippians, and Christ.[9] This provided the spiritual glue of their fellowship. Even more, it infused their fellowship in the gospel with the "other-person-centeredness" that exists between the Father and the Son and the Holy Spirit—the full and perfect fellowship within the Trinity.[10] Elsewhere the Apostle John writes, "and indeed our fellowship is with the Father and with his Son Jesus Christ" (1 John 1:3). Thus the fact that they were in Christ provided their fellowship with a cohesion and others-directedness that focused them away from self-interest toward the interests of the fellowship (cf. Philippians 2:4).

The intense, pulsating spirituality at the center of the Philippians' fellowship is obvious in the occurrences of the *koinon* word group (fellowship, partnership, share) in Philippians. It was a fellowship of grace as Paul indicates in 1:7: "for you are all partakers [fellowshipers] with me of grace, both in my imprisonment and in the defense and confirmation of the gospel." It was a fellowship in the Holy Spirit, as is seen in 2:1: "So if there is any encouragement in Christ, any comfort from love, any participation [fellowship] in the Spirit . . ." It was a fellowship in Christ's sufferings as seen in Paul's prayer in 3:10: "that I may know him and the power of his resurrection, and may share his sufferings [literally, the fellowship of his sufferings]." And, finally, it was a costly fellowship because the Philippians gave to Paul generously, as is seen in verses 14, 15 of chapter 4: "Yet it was kind of you to share [fellowship in] my trouble. And you Philippians yourselves know that in the beginning of the gospel, when I left Macedonia, no church entered into partnership [fellowship] with me in giving and receiving, except you only." Thus the mentions of the *koinon* word group in Philippians indicates that their fellowship was rooted in divine grace and in the Holy Spirit and involved sacrifice and suffering.

Bearing in mind that the Philippians' fellowship rested on a three-way bond in Christ and was infused with the others-directedness of the Trinity and as such was a fellowship of grace and the Spirit and was, further, a costly fellowship—bearing all this in mind, the thing that made Paul's heart sing with thanksgiving was the Philippians' "partnership [fellowship] in the gospel from the first day until now" (v. 5).

From day one the Philippians had been gospel partners. Upon their salvation Lydia and her household and the jailer and his household and those saved over the years became stalwarts in the fellowship of the gospel. And from prison Paul gave thanks for "every word spoken and every deed done in behalf of the gospel from the moment of their conversion(s) to the present, including their gift" (Fee).[11]

What a fellowship it was! Brothers and sisters in Christ's three-way bond, bound together in a great quest—nothing less than the evangelization of the Gentile world, sharing the gospel with all who would hear, reaching out to those in need, living out a divine others-directedness, looking not to their own interests but to the interests of others, suffering in fellowship with Christ, giving in such a way that the astonished apostle would recount how that

> in a severe test of affliction, their abundance of joy and their extreme poverty have overflowed in a wealth of generosity on their part. For they gave according to their means, as I can testify, and beyond their means, of their own accord, begging us earnestly for the favor of taking part in the relief of the saints—and this, not as we expected, but they gave themselves first to the Lord and then by the will of God to us. (2 Corinthians 8:2–5)

How Paul loved them, and how they loved him! Now verses 3–5 of Philippians 1 come alive: "I thank my God in all my remembrance of you, always in every prayer of mine for you all making my prayer with joy, because of your partnership in the gospel from the first day until now." Joyous thanksgiving rings out over the "fellowship of the gospel."

I recall several years ago a man in the church I was then pastoring musing after his return from a short-term missions project about the wonderful fellowship he had experienced on the trip and wishing that he could experience the same at home. Since then I have reflected that his ten days with a band of brothers and sisters serving in South America united in laboring for the gospel was a happy experience like that of the first-century fellowship of the gospel. Further, I think that when Christians go from church to church looking for good fellowship, they are looking for an illusion.

What do I mean? Fellowship over coffee after a church service is good, but it is not Christian fellowship. It is fellowship among Christians, but not the fellowship that Paul celebrated. Don't misunderstand—having coffee and meals together is one of our great pleasures. I love a cup of coffee with friends. I will eat anything and all that is placed in front of me, relishing it all the more in the company of good friends and conversation!

But if you are looking for true fellowship, give yourself to the gospel at home and around the world. Serve together with others in women's Bible studies, children's ministries, youth ministries. Do short-term missions. Join mercy work to alleviate suffering in places like the vast area devastated by disasters like Hurricane Katrina. Take the good news to the poor. Join a band of brothers and sisters to pray for the world. That is how you will experience genuine Christian fellowship.

Thankful Confidence (v. 6)

Paul's thankful recollections from prison for the Philippians themselves and then for their fellowship in the gospel is freighted with joyful confidence: "And I am sure of this, that he who began a good work in you will bring it to completion at the day of Jesus Christ" (v. 6). Philippians 1:6 may well be the first verse I memorized as a newborn Christian over fifty years ago when, on the night I believed, I underlined this verse in red pencil by flashlight. In fact, I still have that tiny Bible with its fine leaves of India paper. I went to sleep that night secure in the astonishing thought that what God had begun would be continued to the day of Christ.

I was right to do so, though my assurance was embedded in a larger promise because, in terms of the context, Paul was assuring the Philippians that the work of the long-term fellowship of the gospel that God had begun in them would be brought to glorious consummation when Christ returns. Though Paul was in prison, he was absolutely confident that the good work of their gospel partnership would succeed gloriously.

How could this bring such assurance to a twelve-year-old boy reading his Bible by flashlight? The answer is that the fellowship of the gospel in Philippi began *individually* with God's sovereign choice of Lydia as the first convert in Europe. Of Lydia, Luke writes, "The Lord opened her heart to pay attention to what was said by Paul" (Acts 16:14). God chose Lydia in Christ before the foundation of the world (cf. Ephesians 1:4). God had begun his "good work" in her, and her salvation was part and parcel of the great work in Philippi. God's sovereign initiative and sovereign faithfulness would see them both through to the end. That is why my assurance under the illumination of my flashlight was not misplaced.

Paul's confidence was in the "Godness of God."[12] Moisés Silva writes,

"Theologians who speak of salvation as being God's from beginning to end are not using mere rhetoric, for this is precisely Paul's conception as he addresses the Philippians regarding their share in the gospel."[13] Everything is from God!

As I reflect on my fifty plus years in Christ it is indeed God who has kept me. It is not my grip on God that has made the difference, but his grip on me. I am not confident in my goodness. I am not confident in my character. I am not confident in my history. I am not confident in my "reverend" persona. I am not confident in my perseverance.

But I am confident in God. I am confident in this word to Lydia and to the jailor and to all the saints in Philippi—and to me: "he who began a good work in you will bring it to completion at the day of Jesus Christ" (v. 6). This is a promise for every man, woman, and child who turns to Christ, and it is a promise for the great fellowship of the gospel!

The Apostle Paul looked through the bars of his confinement and remembered the Philippians with a smile and with prayers laced with joy as he thanked God in all his remembrances of them. His joy was real—not a futile willing but the attitude of a man who knows God is in control. He thanked God for their awesome fellowship in the gospel from the very first day he met them. No church social here, but rather a deep partnership grounded in Christ and the Holy Trinity and in grace and in the Spirit and in suffering and in sacrifice—a robust band of brothers and sisters in a quest for the souls of the world.

And he was confident that when Jesus returned, the work that Jesus inaugurated, he would complete.

Joy pealed from that prison cell in Rome.

It is right for me to feel this way about you all, because I hold you in my heart, for you are all partakers with me of grace, both in my imprisonment and in the defense and confirmation of the gospel. For God is my witness, how I yearn for you all with the affection of Christ Jesus.

1:7, 8

3

Paul's Joyful Affection

PHILIPPIANS 1:7, 8

I HAD ONE OF THE sweetest honors of my life when I spoke at the fiftieth anniversary celebration of the Granada Heights Friends Church, the church in which I grew up. The memories of that weekend—the faces of old friends (the old faces of friends!)—the faces of loved ones and colleagues and mentors and teachers and youth sponsors and the students under my ministry—will be with me until I no longer know their names and the beloved geography of their faces.

I was there as an almost thirteen-year-old when it all began. I was one of the first three in the "youth group." I was the lone junior high student, all one hundred pounds of me. I was there in the Sunny Hills American Legion Hall on Sunday mornings when the beer cans were swept out so church could begin. I saw the first spade of earth ceremonially turned in the lemon grove on the corner of Leffingwell and Granada in La Mirada, California. I sat with my mother and younger brother in tie and sport coat listening to the pastor unfold to my uncomprehending but awed soul the glories of the gospel.

Granada Heights was the womb that warmed my young soul until it was ready for birth when Pastor Verl Lindley led me to Christ the summer before my freshman year in high school. At that same time I was called to the gospel ministry under his winsome, manly way. He has been my lifelong example and mentor.

I was lovingly nurtured by my twentysomething youth sponsors Howard and Ruby Busse—young, energetic, positive big thinkers—who were astonishingly hospitable. As I think back, I remain amazed by their forbearance—for example, when I and my buddies Dave and Jack woke the Busses up because we wanted to talk, and Howard invited us into their bedroom, climbed back in bed, and cheerfully engaged three dopey boys.

The church gave me the milk of the Word through the strong teaching of my college group teacher Robert Seelye. My education was this: My freshman year Robert taught us through the book of Romans. My sophomore year he began with chapter 1 of Romans, and by June we were in chapter 16. My junior year, you guessed it—Romans! Robert Seelye not only gave me a theological grounding, but the lifelong conviction that God's Word is wholly inerrant, totally sufficient, and massively potent. He gave me the foundation for a life of Biblical exposition. I also must say, as I have said before, that this man remains the most effective personal evangelist I have ever met. He and his wife Barbara are Pauline and apostolic in their worldwide care of souls.

My home church saw me through hard times through the prayers of spiritual mothers like Roselva Taylor, who, as I well remember, when I came to church with cuts and a black eye from a fight at a party, took me aside and let me know of her commitment to pray for me—and did so for years. Of course, I have had many fathers and mothers of the church, many of whom are now part of the Church Triumphant.

Granada Heights is where I learned ministry from Verl and Lois Lindley. Verl, now in his eighties, still functions for me like the face in a ubiquitous television monitor to whom I look for advice. *What would Verl do?* And his wife, Lois, tiny and lovely with a musical voice, a Bible teacher par excellence, is the reason, I think, I married Barbara, who is so much like her. I served as their high school and college pastor for nearly a decade, and many of my students, now middle aged (including Rick Hicks, the president of Operation Mobilization USA), have been lifelong friends.

So I can relate to Paul's joyous thanksgiving from faraway Rome for the Philippian church.

> I thank my God in all my remembrance of you, always in every prayer of mine for you all making my prayer with joy, because of your partnership in the gospel from the first day until now. And I am sure of this, that he who began a good work in you will bring it to completion at the day of Jesus Christ. (vv. 3–6)

How assuring and triumphant it is to know beyond a shadow of a doubt that God has in Christ blessed the ministry of my home church and guaranteed its future until the day of Jesus Christ.

I can also relate to Paul's emotional expression of affection for the Philippians, which so naturally flows from his thankfulness as he continues in verses 7, 8, saying:

> It is right for me to feel this way about you all, because I hold you in my heart, for you are all partakers with me of grace, both in my imprisonment and in the defense and confirmation of the gospel. For God is my witness, how I yearn for you all with the affection of Christ Jesus.

Here Paul's outpouring of affection for the Philippian church is stronger than in any of his other letters.[1]

Affection from the Heart (v. 7a)

Paul begins with an intensely personal declaration: "It is right for me to feel this way about you all, because I hold you in my heart" (v. 7a). My experience has taught me that it is virtually a law of spiritual relationships that you will hold very dear to your heart those who have come to Christ under your influence or have grown and benefited from your ministry. Paul's first convert in Europe, Lydia, the extraordinary woman merchant, a seller of purple—a mother of the church—was surely a recurrent face on Paul's spiritual landscape and was dear to his heart. From his jail cell, thoughts of Lydia and her family and the Philippian jailer's clan and the excellent women Euodia and Syntyche warmed his soul, despite their feuding. Paul cherished the thought of them.

The extraordinary depth of his affection rests in the fact that he held them in his heart. This was not a casual aside, as we so often glibly refer to our hearts as a vague pleasantry. Paul had no hearts on his underwear! He never mailed a pink valentine. Paul truly meant he had all of them in the very center of his being, the source of his physical and inner life—his thought processes and emotions and will[2]—the center of his consciousness.[3]

An experience from the fiftieth anniversary celebration I mentioned is suggestive of Paul's heart affection. In the early seventies a college student named Jody, a serious Christian as a high school student under my ministry, lost her virginity and became pregnant as the result of a single instance with another counselor at one of the famed West Coast Christian camps. When she came to me, she was being pressured by the young man and his parents to get an abortion. The situation was complicated because the boy's father was a leading elder in one of the prominent evangelical churches of Southern California. I called the pastor, and you can imagine the flap. Jody became a single mom to a beautiful little girl. Fourteen years later in the mid-eighties her lovely daughter became one of the top-ranked tennis players in California.

I thought then about how the girl so full of life and promise could have well become refuse to be tossed out at the end of a business day in an abortion clinic. Jody and her daughter have been in my heart for over thirty years. You can imagine my emotion when, after speaking at the evening service of the church's fiftieth anniversary, I turned around to see Jody and her husband standing there along with her daughter and her husband carrying Jody's grandson—three generations! What a celebration of life!

Paul, the great apostle, had all the believers in his heart. The Philippians' physical and spiritual geography was at the center of his life—such was the scope of his affection.

Affection from Fellowship (v. 7b)

Paul's affection likewise rose out of a fellowship of grace that was supercharged with action, as we can see in reading all of verse 7: "It is right for me to feel this way about you all, because I hold you in my heart, for you are all partakers with me of grace, both in my imprisonment and in the defense and confirmation of the gospel." Here we have the same *koinon* or fellowship word as in verse 5 where it is rendered "partnership"; here it is rendered "partakers." You can hear the same sound or assonance in the Greek. In verse 5 we have *koinonia* and in verse 7 *synkoinonoi*, which could be rendered "fellowshipers"—"for you are all fellowshipers with me of grace." Again the sense here is Tolkienesque because the partakers of grace are action bound like those in *The Fellowship of the Ring*.

This is a revelatory moment in Paul's writings because "grace" here is not just saving grace. Rather Paul considers suffering and sacrifice and struggling for the gospel all to be grace. Proof of this can be seen in 1:29 where the verbal form of *charis* ("grace") is used: "For it has been granted [graced] to you that for the sake of Christ you should not only believe in him but also suffer for his sake." Suffering because of the gospel is a grace in Paul's thinking and theology. Few concepts could have been more revolutionary in the Greco-Roman world. Pagans did not think this way![4]

But Paul exults in this grace of gospel struggle and affliction that produces and sustains their affection. "My imprisonment" (v. 7) is literally "my chains" because he was actually chained between two guards and was understandably smarting under the oppressive arrangement of never being alone.[5] But the Philippians fellowshiped with him in his chains by virtue of their prayers and financial gifts (cf. 4:14, 15). They remembered Paul in prison as though in prison with him (cf. Hebrews 13:3). Though so far away, he could sense that their hearts beat pulse for pulse with his. The Philippians were also there to support Paul in his defending the gospel and then confirming it with positive proofs and testimony.[6] Again, it was the Philippians' love and commitment to the gospel that bound them in their fellowship with Paul. Significantly, the word "gospel" appears more times per line in Philippians than in any book in the New Testament, some nine times (cf. 1:5, 7, 12, 16, 27 [twice]; 2:22; 4:3, 15).

So it was that the richness of the fellowship from the grace of Paul's sufferings for the gospel became the ground of deep affection. How true to my experience. Drawing again upon that distant ministry in California, I recall a spring break at the height of the sixties when a band of my young high-schoolers joined with me to share the gospel. It was 1968, and the place was a fourteen-mile stretch of the Colorado River outside Parker, Arizona, where thousands of students gathered to party with little fear of the meager police force. That, besides the Arizona sun, was the big draw. The going was tough, and my students took their lumps. One even got tossed into the river for his witness! But there was a memorable reward in five students who did come to Christ, several of whom went on to become committed Christians. But above all this there is the affectionate memory of a group of grimy, sunburned students praying together, nursing their wounds, and bravely attempting to share the most important news in the world—partakers of grace in the afflictions and joys that are part and parcel of the defense and confirmation of the gospel. We remain to this day bound with a special affection, which is only a hint of the affection that rose out of Paul's partnership of grace with the Philippians.

What must tie Christians together is this passion for the gospel, this fellowship in the gospel. Nothing else is strong enough to hold us all together. The gospel—this good news that in Jesus, God himself has reconciled us to himself—brings about a precious God-centeredness that we share with other believers.

Christ's Affection (v. 8)

From his prison in Rome, Paul so welled up with emotion that he called God as witness to the depth of his affection: "For God is my witness, how I yearn for you all with the affection of Christ Jesus." Such an oath was rare in Paul's letters, but he wanted to drive the truth of his longing and affection for the Philippians deep into their hearts by calling God as witness because God alone knew the contours of his inner life. The God-attested truth is that Paul yearned (longed) for all of them. Toward the end of the book (in 4:1) Paul will use the same word amidst mounting expressions of affection: "Therefore, my brothers, whom I love and long for, my joy and crown . . ."

But what he wanted them to see most of all was that his God-attested affection for them was "the affection of Christ Jesus." The word "affection" literally is "the inward parts," referring to what we call the viscera. Alec Motyer, the esteemed preacher and commentator, explains:

> It expresses a yearning that is as much physical as mental, a longing love which moves the whole inner being. But what a remarkable expression Paul uses! He loves them "in the inner being of Christ Jesus." Certainly this means that he patterns his love for them on that of Christ (*cf.* Eph. 5:1), but the wording demands something more than the notion of "imitation." Paul is saying that he has so advanced in union with Christ that it is as if Christ were expressing His love through Paul. Two hearts are beating as one—indeed one heart, the greater, has taken over and the emotional constitution of Christ Himself has taken possession of His servant.[7]

This was so incredible that Paul felt it necessary, as he wrote from his cell, to call God as witness that it was true. So we see in this culminating expression of affection the standard that we all must pursue—the very affection of Christ Jesus. This is possible because of the three-way bond that exists between us individually, our fellow believers, and Christ—a bond that is charged with the other-person-centeredness of the Holy Trinity as we have fellowship with the Father and the Son and the Holy Spirit.

Paul's affection for the Philippians overflowed here because (1) he held the Philippians in his heart, and (2) they shared in the hardships of the ministry of the gospel, and (3) Paul truly longed for them with the affection of Christ Jesus.

Time is flying by for all of us, and over the years we will be separated by distance and time. But whether near or far, may the bonds of our affection be such that we hold each other in our hearts, remembering with fond affection our fellowship together in the grace of gospel ministry—longing for all with the affection of Christ Jesus.

And it is my prayer that your love may abound more and more, with knowledge and all discernment, so that you may approve what is excellent, and so be pure and blameless for the day of Christ, filled with the fruit of righteousness that comes through Jesus Christ, to the glory and praise of God.

1:9–11

4

Paul's Prayer

PHILIPPIANS 1:9–11

VERSES 3–11 OF THE opening chapter of Philippians form a single paragraph that functions as an introduction to the whole book and as such introduces many of the themes and motifs of the letter. Although this is a cohesive unit, I have chosen to divide verses 3–11 into three studies because they are so theologically packed.

"Paul's Joyous Thanksgiving" is the title I gave to the study on verses 3–6 because as Paul's thoughts from his prison cell drifted across the Adriatic into northern Macedonia and Philippi he wrote, "I thank my God in all my remembrance of you, always in every prayer of mine for you all making my prayer with joy." Paul's deep thanksgiving for the Philippian church then evoked "Paul's Joyful Affection," the title of our study on verses 7, 8. Though the apostle was in chains in Rome his heart wasn't chained, and it was in his unfettered heart that Paul held every last one of the Philippians—at the very center of his being. This was not hyperbole but spiritual reality. Paul's oath "For God is my witness, how I yearn for you all with the affection of Christ Jesus" (v. 8) was a declaration that the very affection of Christ himself was controlling him. This affection would effervesce again later in 4:1 when he called them "my brothers, whom I love and long for, my joy and crown."

Now, having the breadth of Paul's thanksgiving for the Philippians before us, along with the depth of Paul's astonishing affection, we come to Paul's prayer for the Philippian believers in verses 9–11. Here Paul builds on the mention of his joyful prayer in verse 4 and makes prayer the rising emotional climax to his introduction. Paul's opening words—"And it is my prayer"—informed the Philippians, and us, that this is *how* and *what* Paul prayed when he prayed for them. This brief text is both humbling and elevating. That is what it has been for me. Do we pray like this? Have we ever prayed like this? Paul tells us that there are things more important than our day-to-day needs.

Prayer for Abounding Love (v. 9a)

Paul opens with a statement that is stunning in itself: "And it is my prayer that your love may abound more and more" (v. 9a)—stunning because "love" here has no object. He doesn't say "that your love *for God* may abound more and more," nor does he say "that your love *for one another* may abound more and more."[1] This is because Paul prayed that love would overflow up to God and out to each other in limitless abundance. Paul, always rooted in the Old Testament, knew that the two tables of the Ten Commandments were structured in just this way. The first four command love for God, and the last six command love for others. Vertical love first, horizontal love second. Thus Paul prayed that the Philippians' love would overflow all dimensions in a lavish, ongoing, limitless love—an unremitting geyser of love up to God and a flood of love out to others. The old Latin commentator Bengel says, "The fire in the apostle never says, It is enough."[2] Paul is passionate here—*more love, more love!*

Prayer for Knowledge and Insight (v. 9b)

At the same time, we know that Paul was not praying for a shapeless, uninformed overflow of love because the whole of verse 9 reads, "And it is my prayer that your love may abound more and more, with knowledge and all discernment."

Knowledge

Our existential, postmodern culture is very sentimental about love. We have heard from the sixties on, "All you need is love," as if other-directed goodwill is the answer to life. A modern proverb says, "Love is blind," suggesting that blissful ignorance is part and parcel of love. Frank Sheed gives us a prophetic word for such foolishness:

> A virtuous man may be ignorant, but ignorance is not a virtue. It would be a strange God Who could be loved better by being known less. Love of God is not the same thing as knowledge of God; love of God is immeasurably more important than knowledge of God; but if a man loves God knowing a little about Him, he should love God more from knowing more about Him: for every new thing known about God is a new reason for loving Him.[3]

The more we know of God, the more reason we will have to love him.

The word that Paul uses here to urge that our overflow of love be "with knowledge" (*epignosis*) is used by Paul in all fifteen occurrences in his letters to mean the knowledge of God and of Christ.[4] It is a personal knowledge. It is "profoundly existential, relational and responsive" (Bockmuehl).[5] And Paul was super-passionate that his converts increase in this knowledge. In fact all four of the "Prison Epistles" pray for this at the end of his introductions.

- Ephesians 1:17: "that the God of our Lord Jesus Christ, the Father of glory, may give you the Spirit of wisdom and of revelation in the knowledge of him."
- Philippians 1:9: "And it is my prayer that your love may abound more and more, with knowledge and all discernment."
- Colossians 1:9, 10: "And so, from the day we heard, we have not ceased to pray for you, asking that you may be filled with the knowledge of his will in all spiritual wisdom and understanding, so as to walk in a manner worthy of the Lord, fully pleasing to him, bearing fruit in every good work and increasing in the knowledge of God."
- Philemon 6: "[A]nd I pray that the sharing of your faith may become effective for the full knowledge of every good thing that is in us for the sake of Christ."

We must understand that Christian love is never a matter of sentimentality. Christian love comes from a work of the Holy Spirit bringing the revelation of Christ through the Word of God. And the more you are in the Word, the more your knowledge of God and Christ will increase, and the more your love will overflow. All the Scriptures speak of Christ (cf. John 5:46)! And each new thing you learn of him will become a fresh reason for loving him.

Remember this: a superficial love for God is a sure sign of a superficial knowledge of God. This is why we must give priority to gathered worship with our Bibles and hearts open to God. This is why we must daily open the Scriptures for ourselves and teach them to our children. This is why we must read both the Old and New Testaments with our eyes wide open to Christ, whom God has made known (cf. John 1:18). This is why the Gospels and Epistles must be in our souls. The more you know of him, the more your love will rush up to him and out to the world! This is why Paul prayed that their "love [would] abound more and more, with knowledge" (Philippians 1:9).

Insight

There is, of course, another important word here because "knowledge" is coupled with "all discernment" or more precisely, "all insight." This Greek word appears only here in the New Testament, but it is used twenty-two times in the Greek translation of the Old Testament book of Proverbs, where it means practical insight, the insight that informs conduct—practical conduct.[6]

What remarkable movement we have in Paul's prayer for his beloved church—a limitless overflow of love to God and others, coupled with a growing knowledge of Christ and God (both reciprocally increasing the other), and all of this producing practical insight for living. Several years ago Dr. Kyung Chik Han, pastor of the Young Nak Presbyterian Church in Seoul, Korea, was honored at a fifty-year class reunion at Princeton Theological Seminary. He answered several questions at that banquet. Dr. Earl Palmer was there and remembers:

> At one point he explained the theological examination process for elders in the Young Nak Church, which with a membership of 50,000 communicants is the largest Presbyterian church in the world. He said that each prospective elder was examined in 'Bible, Theology, Church History and Common Sense.' Yes, of course, I thought to myself when I heard his remarks—common sense should be added to Theology, Church History and Bible![7]

Indeed. We see that right here in Paul's prayer invoking practical insight for day-to-day living for his dearest friends. Who says theology is irrelevant? Again, overflowing love coupled to a growing personal knowledge of God leads to practical insight for common everyday living—the kind of quality essential for eldership in that vast Korean church and for any success in Christian living. This is what we all so desperately long for as we seek to lead our families and the church.

Prayer for Assessing What Is Best (v. 10a)

What benefits! But there is more as Paul's line of prayer thought extends to a further result—"so that you may approve what is excellent" (v. 10a).

The idea here is intensely practical: it is to examine or test what is before us so as to determine what is excellent or the best. Originally this was applied to determining the best, for example, among metals or livestock. Here it has to do with our lives as Christians. Markus Bockmuehl describes this as "the Spirit-bred ability to discern that which God has already marked off as essential or 'superlative' regarding life in Christ."[8] This ability includes not only distinguishing right from wrong but also the best from second best.[9]

Life for everyone, and especially believers, is a series of choices. What we choose day to day will shape the course of our lives. Foolish choices will leave us unprepared for the coming King. It is the little choices that determine our spiritual vitality because they in turn govern bigger choices. Most of us have little trouble distinguishing the big issues. We know that theft and murder are wrong and that generosity and justice are right. But in the gray area, choices involve a range of options that are not so clearly moral or clear cut. It is here that we find difficulty in discerning the best. What confused lives so many Christians lead because they do not have the wherewithal to discern what is best.

To see falsely is worse than blindness. A man who is so blind that he cannot distinguish the ditch from the road still may be able to feel which is which. But if he sees the ditch as the road and the road as the ditch, he is in big trouble. And many today are in big trouble.

However, if God's children overflow with love to God and others, along with a growing personal knowledge of God and Christ and practical insight, they will be able to discern and choose what is superlative—the best over the second best—the best over the good—the best in knowledge of God—the best in priorities—the best in habits—the best in pleasures—the best in pursuits— the best course of action for themselves and for their families.

What a beautiful prayer Paul prays for his beloved! May our prayers for one another be that we will be able to discern what God has marked off as best. That's what you need, fathers. That's what you need, mothers. That's what you need, leaders. And that is what Paul prays for.

Prayer for the Day of Christ (vv. 10b, 11)

Paul's brief account of how he prays concludes with his ultimate purpose for the Philippians, which is readiness for the coming of Christ: ". . . and so be pure and blameless for the day of Christ, filled with the fruit of righteousness that comes through Jesus Christ, to the glory and praise of God" (vv. 10b, 11). This is the second mention of "the day of Christ," as Paul already referred to it in the famous words of verse 6. Paul wanted the Philippians to be prepared. You can sense the urgency in the Greek, which literally reads "*against* the day of Christ"[10]—Paul wants them to stand well under the divine scrutiny. "Preparation for the day of the Lord was for Paul neither a pious platitude nor a millenarian obsession, but a way of life" (Bockmuehl).[11] Christian growth was not an end in itself but had an eye to the grand goal of standing before Christ. Paul was sublimely obsessed with the coming of that day,[12] and this graced obsession controlled his prayer for his beloved Philippians.

Pure and Blameless

His prayer was that they would be "pure and blameless" against that great day (cf. v. 10b). "Pure" means "unmixed," as in unmixed substances. It denotes transparency of heart, a heart with pure and unmixed desires.[13] Paul prays for their moral transparency—that "what you see is what you get" with the Philippians, and it is good.

"Blameless" is literally "without stumbling," "not stumbling."[14] And this metaphorical sense enhances the picture. Paul's prayer is that the Philippians will live pure, morally transparent lives, free from stumbling—and thus stand upright and pure on that day in the dazzling presence of Christ who knows all. Oh, to pray like this for each other!

Filled with the Fruit of Righteousness

But Paul wants more than that the Philippians stand pure and tall and acquitted before Christ, because he further prays that they may be filled with the fruit of godly deeds[15]—"filled with the fruit of righteousness that comes through Jesus Christ"—that the righteousness of Christ would be evident in righteous, fruitful living. This means first that the heart qualities Paul calls the fruit of the Spirit—"love, joy, peace, patience, kindness, goodness, faithfulness, gentleness, self-control" (Galatians 5:22, 23)—would work themselves out in the substantive fruit of godly deeds.

A tree that bears fruit is alive. But a tree that is filled with fruit glorifies the gardener's care! "Whoever abides in me and I in him, he it is that bears much fruit" (John 15:5). "By this my Father is glorified, that you bear much fruit" (John 15:8). When Christ returns, Paul wants the Philippians to be like fruit trees at harvest, their branches hung low, laden with the good deeds that Christ has worked in and through them.

For the Praise and Glory of God

Predictably, Paul concludes with a doxology. All this is for "the glory and praise of God" (v. 11b). This is a fitting conclusion not only to the prayer but to the whole paragraph. The truth is, as John Piper says, "All who cast themselves on God find that they are carried into endless joy by God's omnipotent commitment to his own glory."[16]

Paul reveled in the thought of God's glory. At the climax of the Christ hymn later in Philippians we read, "so that at the name of Jesus every knee should bow, in heaven and on earth and under the earth, and every tongue confess that Jesus Christ is Lord, to the glory of God the Father" (2:10). And then there will be the climactic doxology at the letter's end: "To our God and Father be glory forever and ever. Amen" (4:20). Such elation! Such joy!

This magnificent introductory paragraph that began with Paul's thanksgiving for the Philippians and then moved to his affection for them has now concluded with Paul's description of how he prayed for them. This is the substance of real prayers, repeatedly offered in real time and space and history by a real man. This is not pious spiritual musing. This is *how* and *what* Paul prayed.

What the apostle has outlined has relevance for those of us who care at all for our families and the Body of Christ. Certainly we must pray for our jobs and our finances and our health and our children's grades and friendships. But if that is it, we have missed it. We need love to overflow in a limitless geyser up to God and out to others. We need to have our love ride and expand upon an increasing knowledge of God as revealed in Christ Jesus—because the more we know of him, the more we will love him.

We need to grow in all discernment—practiced insight and common sense for living. We need to be able to weigh the choices before us and choose what is excellent, the best. We need to be ready for the day of Christ. We need to be transparently pure and stand upright before Christ in that day. And as we stand tall, our lives need to be hung heavy with the fruit of the righteousness that comes through Jesus. We need our lives to be a doxology to the glory and praise of God as part of the endless, joyous commitment to God's glory.

And more, this is what we need to pray for each other. Parents, this is what we must pray for our children and grandchildren. This is a call for real prayers for real people in real space and real time.

I want you to know, brothers, that what has happened to me has really served to advance the gospel, so that it has become known throughout the whole imperial guard and to all the rest that my imprisonment is for Christ. And most of the brothers, having become confident in the Lord by my imprisonment, are much more bold to speak the word without fear. Some indeed preach Christ from envy and rivalry, but others from good will. The latter do it out of love, knowing that I am put here for the defense of the gospel. The former proclaim Christ out of selfish ambition, not sincerely but thinking to afflict me in my imprisonment. What then? Only that in every way, whether in pretense or in truth, Christ is proclaimed, and in that I rejoice.

1:12–18a

5

The Gospel First!

THE APOSTLE PAUL lists his extensive sufferings in 2 Corinthians 11. Has anyone in recorded history suffered so much over the course of years—multiple near-death floggings—gruesome stoning—frequent shipwrecks—dangers on the road from both places and people—great suffering over an extended period of time? Is there an equal to Paul's suffering? Probably not. The annals of the world's epic lives and journeys contain nothing to rival the courage and endurance and love of the Apostle Paul. He is not only the church's great hero but the world's great hero.

You would think that Paul's unparalleled sufferings and endurance would elevate him above criticism. In fact, he suggested just that at the end of his letter to the Galatians: "From now on let no one cause me trouble, for I bear on my body the marks of Jesus" (6:17).

But that was not to be because as Paul sat in chains in Rome, some in the church were apparently bitter toward him, feeling that his appeal to the emperor would bring harder times upon them. They reasoned that if Paul hadn't gone up to Jerusalem in the first place, he likely wouldn't have been arrested. He knew the establishment in Jerusalem hated him. He should have anticipated the outcome. Now, as a prisoner of Rome, he was bringing unwanted attention on the church. Paul was too headstrong, they said. Cooler heads must prevail. Besides, the fact that Paul was in chains, and his ministry therefore confined, seemed evidence enough that God's validating hand had been lifted from him.

But Paul, the old gospel warhorse, was not impressed or intimidated by such thinking and forcefully set the record straight for the Philippians and all history. "I want you to know, brothers, that what has happened to me has really served to advance the gospel" (v. 12). With the barest allusion to his circumstances, Paul exulted in the advancement of the gospel, which for him was the main thing, the great thing, his abiding passion—especially in this short book as the noun "gospel" appears nine times (cf. 1:5, 7, 12, 16, 27 [twice]; 2:22; 4:3, 15). By "gospel" he means the preaching of Christ (his death, resurrection, and present lordship) rather than the results of preaching.[1] Paul's imprisonment meant that the preaching of the gospel advanced in Rome.

Paul's utter fixation on the proclamation of the gospel is evidenced by the two mentions of the gospel in our text (vv. 12, 16) plus the recurrent synonymous phrases "to speak the word" (v. 14), "preach Christ" (v. 15), "proclaim Christ" (v. 17).

For Paul, the advance of the gospel overrides all else. Everything in Paul's life is subsumed to this end. If we fail to understand this, we fail to understand Paul.

Advance through Imprisonment (vv. 12–14)

Paul leaves no doubt as to the gospel's progress both among pagans and among Christians.

Among Pagans

As to the gospel's furtherance in pagan Rome, he explains, "so that it has become known throughout the whole imperial guard and to all the rest that my imprisonment is for Christ" (v. 13). The imperial guard, the Praetorian, consisted of 9,000 handpicked soldiers who were honored with double pay, good pensions, and special duties. Among their not-so-special duties was that of guarding imperial prisoners by an attached chain. So Paul experienced a shuffle of soldiers manacled to him. Certainly few of the 9,000 *praetoriani*[2] were chained to Paul, but the gospel effect was exponential. As soldier after soldier was chained to him in successive watches, they heard the gospel both directly and from Paul's conversations with his visitors. My imagination hears the apostle's silent prayer as a new soldier is chained to him—"Thank you, Lord. Here's another one to tell about Jesus." So as the *praetoriani* observed and listened to the great apostle, they heard the astonishing story of the long-promised Jewish Messiah, who was crucified as the Jewish Scriptures predicted and was resurrected as their Scriptures predicted and, amazingly, forgives sins through his death and resurrection.

Ironically (sublimely!), Paul's imprisonment brought the gospel to the very heart of secular political power in Rome. As to how many believed, we

do not know. But we do know that the gospel was preached among the Prae-
torian Guard and that some believed, because Paul closes this letter saying,
"Greet every saint in Christ Jesus. The brothers who are with me greet you.
All the saints greet you, especially those of Caesar's household" (4:21, 22).

Among Christians

The gospel advanced into paganism, and it likewise made an advance in the
Christian community: "And most of the brothers, having become confident in
the Lord by my imprisonment, are much more bold to speak the word without
fear" (v. 14). Persecution has regularly been just what the doctor ordered for
fearful Christians. I cannot forget turning the pages of the February 1956 issue
of *Life* magazine and tremulously viewing the photos that *Life's* famous pho-
tographer Cornell Capa had taken of the scene where five young missionaries
had died at the hands of the primitive Aucas and the striking photos of their
wives and children, and then some months later staying up far into the night
reading Elisabeth Elliot's *Through Gates of Splendor* and *The Shadow of the
Almighty* as I took to heart her husband's words: "He is no fool who gives
what he cannot keep to gain that which he cannot lose."[3]

My wife, Barbara, and I never imagined we would meet Elisabeth Elliot,
much less get to know her. But decades later Barbara, along with several others, was invited to Elisabeth's seaside home north of Boston where Elisabeth
spent several days sharing her life with them as she recounted those storied
events and her long walk with God.

The wholehearted commitment of the five young missionary couples has
remained in my heart. And today whenever I see those haunting black-and-
white photos and read the account, it evokes the springtime of my growing
commitment to the gospel, just as it has done for tens of thousands.

Paul's imprisonment had issued in a springtime of commitment in the
Roman church. Previously timid believers began "to speak the word without
fear." And it was not a "baker's dozen" but most of the Christian community.
It was gospel time in the Eternal City!

I wonder, will it take the same experience to drive away our fears and
make us bold with the gospel?

Advance through Ill Will and Goodwill (vv. 15–18a)

All was not well in the Roman church despite the fact that the vast majority
had the courage to speak the word. There were actually two groups of preach-

ers in the church who proclaimed Christ but from different motives: "Some indeed preach Christ from envy and rivalry, but others from good will" (v. 15).

On the one hand, Paul was suffering from the classic malady known as the hatred of theologians, termed by the Latin doctors *odium theologicum*—evidenced here in "envy and rivalry," ugly terms that pop up elsewhere in Paul's lists of vices (cf. Galatians 5:20ff. and Romans 1:29). The Greek historian Xenophon said, "The envious are those annoyed only at their friends' successes."[4] So envy is more set on depriving the other person of the desired thing than on gaining it.[5] John of the Cross explained its pathology in the church: "As far as envy is concerned, many experience displeasure when they see others in possession of spiritual goods. They feel sensibly hurt because others surpass them on this road, and they resent it when others are praised."[6] Paul had come to Rome with a long list of ministerial successes to his credit. Notwithstanding his unimpressive appearance, the gifts Paul possessed were immense, unique apostolic endowments. He had taken the gospel to Asia Minor and on into Europe, fighting Judaizers and heretics all the way—and had won. When Paul arrived in Rome, the focus of the church turned naturally to the apostle, and some of the leadership turned green with envy and began a contentious gospel rivalry.

On the other hand, the majority preached Christ "from good will." And Paul explains of them, "The latter do it out of love, knowing that I am put here for the defense of the gospel" (v. 16). They understood that Paul was under orders issued by God[7] and that his captivity was part of his defense of the gospel. So those in the majority were motivated to preach Christ by their love for God and their love for his apostle.

Thus there were two opposing groups in Rome who preached the gospel. We understand those who did it out of love. But who were those who did it from ill will? For starters, they were not heretics or apostates. They were not preaching another gospel or another Christ. If they had been, Paul would have said, as he did to the Galatians, "let him be accursed" (cf. Galatians 1:8, 9). Paul's detractors were preaching the Biblical Jesus. They were not anti-Christ but anti-Paul.

They preached the true gospel motivated by a warped amalgam of perversity. Again, they preached Christ "out of selfish ambition" (v. 17) or rivalry. These preachers were petty, territorial, calculating, and focused on self-promotion.[8] Paul's diminution could mean their elevation. John Claypool said in his 1979 Yale Lecture on Preaching that even while in seminary he experienced jealous jockeying for position and that his experience in the parish ministry had not been much different. He writes:

I can still recall going to state and national conventions in our denomination and coming home feeling drained and unclean, because most of the conversation in the hotel rooms and the halls was characterized either by envy of those who were doing well or scarcely concealed delight for those who were doing poorly. For did that not mean that someone was about to fall, and thus create an opening higher up the ladder?[9]

Such men's twisted perversity evoked not only rivalry but insincerity (mixed motives) in their proclamation of Christ. So along with the exalted motive of glorifying Christ by preaching the cross and bringing sinners to him, they preached, as Paul says, "not sincerely but thinking to afflict me in my imprisonment" (v. 17). The sheer cussedness of this is astonishing. The literal sense of "to afflict me" is "to raise up affliction," so that "The meaning is . . . to stir up some inward annoyance, some trouble of spirit" (O'Brien).[10] They actually preached Christ with the hope that it would rub salt in Paul's wounds. How small! How perverse! There can be no doubt that their actions did hurt him and made his imprisonment worse.

The Apostle Paul had ample reason to feel down. He was the missionary general of the early church, a type A personality if there ever was one. Confinement was tough on his activist soul. He knew the gospel as did no other. He was the preeminent theologian of the apostolic church. He had more knowledge in his little finger than his detractors had in their combined IQs. He had the right stuff. He could take a beating like no one else. No one could gainsay his experience. But Paul refused to have a pity party. There was no "Why me?" from Paul.

Rather, Paul voiced an astonishing attitude: "What then? Only that in every way, whether in pretense or in truth, Christ is proclaimed, and in that I rejoice" (v. 18). Paul was so gospel intoxicated, so centered on getting the good news of Christ out to the lost in Rome, that his feelings and aspirations were subsumed and subject to the gospel.

Don Carson writes:

Paul's example is impressive and clear: Put the advance of the gospel at the center of your aspirations. Our own comfort, our bruised feelings, our reputations, our misunderstood motives—all of these are insignificant in comparison with the advance and splendor of the gospel. As Christians, we are called upon to put the advance of the gospel at the very center of our aspirations.

What are your aspirations? To make money? To get married? To travel? To see your grandchildren grow up? To find a new job? To retire early? None of these is inadmissible; none is to be despised. The question is whether these aspirations become so devouring that the Christian's central aspiration is squeezed to the periphery or choked out of existence entirely.[11]

So the centrality of the gospel is the great question and challenge for us. Is the gospel first and foremost in our lives and in our church? The answer will determine our future.

The history of some of the mainline Protestant denominations in our country serves to make the point. There were generations that believed the gospel and held that there were certain accompanying social and political entailments. Then came a generation that assumed the gospel but identified with the entailments. The next generation denied the gospel but made the entailments everything. This is a caricature that is simplistic and reductionist. Nevertheless, in broad swaths it describes Protestant liberalism in America.[12]

When the gospel is no longer the main thing, when it becomes assumed, the next generation may be lost. As evangelicals we must take note. All kinds of issues cry for our attention—abortion, pornography, media bias, economic justice, racial discrimination, classism, sexism, to name a few. And we need to be alert and involved in certain of them. But if any of them become the main thing so that the gospel is marginalized, beware!

Am I advocating an insular, privatized faith? Not at all. The gospel preached by gospel-first people led the way in the abolition of slavery, prison reform, child labor laws, and the protection of women, as the writings of Charles Colson and Marvin Olasky attest.[13]

We each have our calling in life, as electrician or teacher or mother or plumber or analyst or lawyer or mechanic or musician or fireman. But whatever our calling, the gospel must be first.

Life will have its ups and downs for all of us. There will be times when we will feel metaphorically chained by the circumstances of life—misunderstood, maligned, ignored, spitefully used. But if the gospel is first in our life, we will be able to say with Paul, "What then? Only that in every way, whether in pretense or in truth, Christ is proclaimed, and in that I rejoice" (v. 18).

Yes, and I will rejoice, for I know that through your prayers and the help of the Spirit of Jesus Christ this will turn out for my deliverance, as it is my eager expectation and hope that I will not be at all ashamed, but that with full courage now as always Christ will be honored in my body, whether by life or by death. For to me to live is Christ, and to die is gain. If I am to live in the flesh, that means fruitful labor for me. Yet which I shall choose I cannot tell. I am hard pressed between the two. My desire is to depart and be with Christ, for that is far better. But to remain in the flesh is more necessary on your account. Convinced of this, I know that I will remain and continue with you all, for your progress and joy in the faith, so that in me you may have ample cause to glory in Christ Jesus, because of my coming to you again.

1:18b–26

6

Paul's Joyous Confidence

PHILIPPIANS 1:18b–26

SEVERAL WEEKS BEFORE Andrew Chong, a beloved physician and a former elder in the church I pastored for many years, passed away, he was taken to Northwestern Hospital in Chicago to have a stent cleared of blockage. The procedure was invasive, and after some time the surgeon came out and indicated that he could not go on because there was too much bleeding. He said, "You'd better get your family here. He may not make it through the night." So all the children were rushed to Andrew's bedside, where they gathered weeping and saying their good-byes.

Andrew had just come out of the anesthetic and was in intense pain and unable to speak. Seeing his family's distress, he made a curious motion with his finger, which they finally understood as a request for a pen. Of late he had been unable to write in a straight line. But now, very slowly and with intense deliberation, he wrote twelve words in a single column.

> For to me
> to live
> is Christ,
> and
> to die
> is gain.

Andrew anchored the column with "Hallelujah." The writing of that last word took him a full minute as he made sure he spelled it correctly (always the precise surgeon). And then he spoke: "Nothing has changed. Nothing has changed."

It was his soul's spontaneous last will and testament. These beautiful words, of course, were not original with Dr. Chong but were penned by the Apostle Paul, who was himself in difficult circumstances as a prisoner of Rome. In fact, Paul alluded to his own possible death, saying, "Even if I am to be poured out as a drink offering upon the sacrificial offering of your faith, I am glad and rejoice with you all" (Philippians 2:17). Andrew had reached back to Paul's victorious declaration in the midst of a world ostensibly falling apart and made it his own. Andrew Chong's subscript—"Hallelujah," which means "Praise the Lord"—was the careful signature of his soul's joyous confidence and submission to the will of God.

This famous aphorism—"For to me to live is Christ, and to die is gain" (v. 21)—perhaps the most often quoted line from Philippians, stands at the spiritual center of the paragraph before us—a section in which Paul dynamically affirms his joyous confidence in God. May our consideration of Paul's words from prison both ground and spike our confidence in Christ as we live through the difficulties of life.

Confidence in Final Vindication (vv. 18b–20)

Paul is affirming his joy amidst the chains of his present imprisonment. "What then? Only that in every way, whether in pretense or in truth, Christ is proclaimed, and in that I rejoice" (v. 18a).

Confident in Deliverance

As Paul looks to the future, he opens with a remarkable declaration of joy-filled confidence in his personal deliverance: "Yes, and I will rejoice, for I know that through your prayers and the help of the Spirit of Jesus Christ this will turn out for my deliverance" (vv. 18b, 19).

This is a notable assertion because Paul is not referring to physical deliverance. The word he uses here for "deliverance" is *soterian*, which is generally translated "salvation" and usually refers to the final deliverance of believers at the last judgment when they stand vindicated before God.[1] Paul was confident of this ultimate deliverance, whatever Caesar decided to do with him. The same confidence was expressed from prison by Paul to Timothy at the end of his second letter to his young assistant: "The Lord will rescue me from every evil deed and bring me safely into his heavenly kingdom" (2 Timothy 4:18). Thus Paul was entirely confident in his ultimate deliverance.

At the same time he was not confident in his self-contained spiritual resources. Rather, his confidence in deliverance rested upon the prayers of the Philippians, which then would bring on the supply of the Spirit of Christ in his life. ". . . for I know that through your prayers and the help of the Spirit of Jesus Christ this will turn out for my deliverance" (v. 19). More accurately the word "help" should read "supply," referring to the Spirit himself whom God supplies.[2] So the Philippians' prayers would bring about God's supplying the Spirit to Paul.

How was this? After all, Paul was already indwelt by the Holy Spirit, as are all believers, as Paul had explained earlier to the Romans: "Anyone who does not have the Spirit of Christ does not belong to him" (8:9b). Furthermore, all believers have all of the Spirit all the time. However, there are apparently times when believers experience more of the Spirit's fullness and power. The dramatic encounters of the book of Acts affirm this repeatedly. As the Apostle Peter stood before Caiaphas and the Sanhedrin, he was "filled with the Holy Spirit" and spoke (4:8). When the apostles were released by the Sanhedrin, we read that "they were all filled with the Holy Spirit and continued to speak the word of God with boldness" (4:31b). Next, prior to Stephen's stoning, we read, "But he, full of the Holy Spirit, gazed into heaven and saw the glory of God, and Jesus standing at the right hand of God" (7:55). Later, when Paul confronted Elymas the magician, Paul was "filled with the Holy Spirit" and judged him (13:9). And, lastly, when Paul and Barnabas were driven from Pisidian Antioch, we read of those left behind, "And the disciples were filled with joy and with the Holy Spirit" (13:52). So we see that the book of Acts repeatedly demonstrates that God's servants regularly receive special supplies of the Spirit's filling during times of trial.[3]

Thus as Paul sat in Roman custody he was confident that as the Philippians prayed, fresh supplies of the Spirit of Jesus Christ would be poured into his heart, empowering him for every trial and securing his ultimate deliverance. Paul knew that his converts in Philippi, those who shared in the fellowship of the gospel (1:5), prayed for him, and that is why he naturally solicited their prayers, knowing that they would pray. This fueled his towering confidence in his difficult situation. In fact, his declaration "this will turn out for my deliverance" (v. 19) was a conscious echo of Job amidst his troubles when that man of God said, "Even this will turn out for my deliverance" (Job 13:16, LXX).[4]

Paul had massive confidence. But there was not a hint of self-confidence or self-sufficiency. He was dependent upon his friends' prayers for the supply of the Spirit. Their prayers would actually give him fresh fillings of the Spirit for each new challenge. It is the same today. We must practice this as we pray for each other, and especially for those undergoing challenging times. Our prayers can effect not only the confidence but the deliverance of our brothers and sisters.

Confident That Christ Will Be Honored

Paul's confidence in his deliverance was matched by his confidence that Christ would be honored, "as it is my eager expectation and hope that I will not be at all ashamed, but that with full courage now as always Christ will be honored in my body, whether by life or by death" (v. 20).

The apostle's confidence pulsates. To understand it, we must set aside our normal English usage of *hope* with its note of uncertainty, as in "I hope the Bears will beat the San Francisco 49ers" or as with crossed fingers we say, "Let's hope it won't rain." In contrast to this, Biblical hope brims with certainty because it is based upon the fact that "God is God and has underwritten the future" (Bockmuehl).[5]

Paul's "hope" radiated with confidence. Here Biblical hope is coupled with "eager expectation," an expression that appears only here and in Romans 8:19 where it describes physical creation's "eager longing" for ultimate redemption that will come with "the revealing of the sons of God." Thus, Paul's statement "it is my eager expectation and hope" referred to his intense expectation of what is sure to happen[6]—his breathless confidence and certitude. Paul's intense confidence was that "I will not be at all ashamed" because the progress of the gospel would not and could not be thwarted by even the worst outcome of his trial before Caesar.

The apostle's confident, breathless expectation was that "with full courage now as always Christ will be honored in my body, whether by life or by death" (v. 20b). Paul fully expected to be courageous and bold in holding forth the gospel before Caesar, so that Christ would be honored whether he lived or died. In effect he confidently said, "My body will be the theatre in which Christ's glory is displayed" (Ellicott).[7]

Paul, the veteran of hundreds of lashes and a thousand indignities, did not know what pains and humiliations awaited him. Yet there was no fear in Paul. Rather, there was bounding, eager confidence that whatever happened, Christ would be surely glorified.

Confidence in Life or Death (vv. 21–24)

Confident Ideal

With this, Paul gave the Philippians his triumphant aphorism—a proverb for the church universal—an ideal for every believing soul: "For to me to live is

Christ, and to die is gain" (v. 21). When the Philippians heard this read, the effect must have been stunning because of its parallelism, tonal assonance, and compactness (in the original Greek there are no verbs, which is normal, good Greek grammar; but these distinctions together make the statement epigrammatic): "For to me to live Christ, and to die gain."

How could Paul say "For to me to live is Christ"? At the deepest level it was because Christ was in him and he was in Christ—a description used more than any other in the New Testament to describe the believer's living, saving union with Christ. The classic expression of this "in Christ" truth is in another verb-less Greek sentence: "Therefore, if anyone is in Christ, he is a new creation. The old has passed away; behold, the new has come" (2 Corinthians 5:17). The Greek is explosive: "If anyone in Christ—new creation!" The miracle of mutual "in-ness" with the divine Christ lay at the root of Paul's astonishing confidence—"for to me to live is Christ."

Along with this, Paul could say, "For to me to live is Christ" because he had taken up the cross of the suffering Christ. As Paul explained to the Galatians, "I have been crucified with Christ. It is no longer I who live, but Christ who lives in me" (Galatians 2:20). We must understand that "For to me to live is Christ" is not the triumphant sentimentality of a trouble-free life but the joyous embrace of the burdens of the cross of Christ.

In effect, altogether this meant that Christ was at the conscious center of everything—so that Paul had a Christ-centered ministry, a Christ-powered ministry, and a Christ-exalting ministry. Paul would have lauded the declaration of Count Nikolaus von Zinzendorf, the father of German Protestant missions: "I have but one enthusiasm; it is He, only He."[8]

This was utterly true for Paul, as he said later in this letter: "that I may know him and the power of his resurrection, and may share his sufferings, becoming like him in his death" (3:10).

All for Jesus! All for Jesus!
All my being's ransomed powers;
All my thoughts and words and doings,
All my days and all my hours.

Mary D. James
"All for Jesus," 1889[9]

"For to me to live is Christ"—Paul's confidence in this life extended into death—"and to die is gain." To borrow the Apostle John's words, "we know that when he appears we shall be like him, because we shall see him as he is" (1 John 3:2b). Paul's death would also mean that his righteousness in Christ (cf. Philippians 3:9) would have its full effect. In this world Paul was still beset with his own sins—as Luther would say, "At the same time justified, yet a sinner." But in death, the battle would be over, and the apostle would repose in all righteousness. Such gain! In this world Paul experienced pain after pain and trauma upon trauma, but come death it would all be over—no "mourning, nor crying, nor pain anymore, for the former things have passed away" (Revelation 21:4b).

The clarity and sanity of Paul's confident dictum "For to me to live is Christ, and to die is gain" show up the shallow tragedy of so many in Paul's day and now. Among the ruins of ancient Carthage there is an inscription carved by a Roman soldier: "To laugh, to hunt, to bathe, to game—that is life."[10] "For to me to live is to hunt, go to the baths, and party!" As the Looney Tunes finis says, "That's all, folks!" It is the same today because most will fill in the blank of "For to me to live is—" with anything but Christ.

According to the tabloids and celebrity magazines, "for to me to live is" to fornicate, to accumulate, to dine well. Or on a more prosaic level, "for to me to live is" to golf, to work, to garden, to travel, to watch TV, to ski, to shop 'til I drop. Of course, if this be our life, then death is the loss of everything. When Queen Elizabeth I, the idol of European fashion, was dying, she turned to her lady-in-waiting and said, "O my God! It is over. I have come to the end of it—the end, the end."[11]

But when Dr. Andrew Chong came to the end, he wrote, "For to me to live is Christ, and to die is gain. Hallelujah" and confidently said, "Nothing has changed. Nothing has changed." Now he lives in eternal gain.

Confident Deliberations

Having given voice to that stunning aphorism, Paul paused to talk to himself and knowingly invited the Philippians to witness the inner deliberations of his heart. He debated for their benefit what he would do as to life and death if it were up to him. "If I am to live in the flesh, that means fruitful labor for me. Yet which I shall choose I cannot tell. I am hard pressed between the two. My desire is to depart and be with Christ, for that is far better. But to remain in the flesh is more necessary on your account" (vv. 22–24). For Paul, "Death is a glorious possession of Christ; life is a glorious bearing of fruit" (Motyer).[12] Some choice! His options hemmed him in like ever-narrowing walls of rock on either side. He was literally "hard pressed" to choose between two marvelous possibilities.

But here pleasant thoughts of death tipped the scales: "My desire is to depart and be with Christ, for that is far better" (v. 23). Paul's confidence about the delight of death was unbounded. The word he used for "depart" is an inviting metaphor suggesting a ship's moorings being cast off, weighing anchor, rising on the tide, and sailing toward the shore of home.[13] This image appears with great effect in C. S. Lewis's *Chronicles of Narnia*.

In modern terms I imagined this gentle transition from here to Heaven when Barbara and I took a train from Interlaken, Switzerland, to Domodossola, Italy. After a brief glimpse of the Swiss countryside, our train hurtled through a dark tunnel under the Alps where, after a brief journey, we burst into the sunshine of Italy and Domodossola! Paul passionately longed to be able to pull out of the station and be in the light of Christ's presence. Paul's citizenship was already there (cf. 3:20). He longed for the "far better." He had earlier been to the third heaven and its paradise, to the abode of God, where he heard words that he was not permitted to speak (cf. 2 Corinthians 12:4). But he had glimpsed the "far better." So for Paul, death would be "far better" than anything that could happen or be imagined.

Death for the Christian is always far better. I believe that with all my heart—whether you are nine months, nine years, or ninety-nine years old! Death was especially inviting for this man who had been beaten with hundreds of stripes, left for dead, and was now imprisoned in Rome. Later he would tell Timothy:

> For I am already being poured out as a drink offering, and the time of my departure has come. I have fought the good fight, I have finished the race, I have kept the faith. Henceforth there is laid up for me the crown of righteousness, which the Lord, the righteous judge, will award to me on that Day, and not only to me but also to all who have loved his appearing. (2 Timothy 4:6–8)

Such confident longing. But Paul was not into himself or instant gratification, but others. So he concluded amiably, "But to remain in the flesh is more necessary on your account" (Philippians 1:24). What grips us here is that the apostle's deep longing for Heaven and the face of Christ was subordinated to what was best for his converts.

Paul was not only a gospel-first man (cf. vv. 12–18a), but he was an others-first man! Frank Thielman writes:

> Every major feature of his life at the time when he wrote the letter—his physical comfort, the opinions others have about him, his position with respect to the secular authorities, and the question of whether he lives or dies—are molded by his commitment to the advancement of the gospel.[14]

Paul's deliberations modeled for the Philippians what he would clearly teach in 2:4: "Let each of you look not only to his own interests, but also to the interests of others." Christ was more important to him than life itself, and others were more important to him than being in Heaven with Christ. What a needed message for the church as it stands amidst a me-first culture that makes self-fulfillment into entitlement.

Confident of Reunion (vv. 25, 26)

The realization that remaining alive for the present is more important than his ultimate desire gives Paul the confidence that he will live beyond his present imprisonment. "Convinced of this, I know that I will remain and continue with you all, for your progress and joy in the faith, so that in me you may have ample cause to glory in Christ Jesus, because of my coming to you again" (vv. 25, 26). Paul had no divine word about his staying alive, but given his apostolic calling and the need for his ministry to the Philippians, he felt sure that he had more life ahead of him—and that they would glory not in him but in Christ Jesus.

This is the fourth sounding of the joy-note in Philippians, and the third and fourth notes bracket this passage (cf. vv. 18b, 25). Paul overflowed with joyous confidence, whatever life held for him.

Paul's grand epigram of confidence informed everything. Let us invite it to detonate in our souls as it did for Andrew Chong. Slowly say the seven words as Dr. Chong stacked them vertically for his family.

> For to me
> to live
> is Christ

Can we say this? Do we know him? Is he in us? Have we taken up his cross?

Then we can say it from our hearts: *For—to—me—to—live—is—Christ*. And if we can say that, we can confidently embrace the five-word result:

> and
> to die
> is gain.

And if we can do that, we can joyously write over our souls,

> Hallelujah!

Only let your manner of life be worthy of the gospel of Christ, so that whether I come and see you or am absent, I may hear of you that you are standing firm in one spirit, with one mind striving side by side for the faith of the gospel, and not frightened in anything by your opponents. This is a clear sign to them of their destruction, but of your salvation, and that from God. For it has been granted to you that for the sake of Christ you should not only believe in him but also suffer for his sake, engaged in the same conflict that you saw I had and now hear that I still have.

1:27–30

7

Worthy Citizens

PHILIPPIANS 1:27–30

SHAKESPEARE'S SEVERAL PLAYS involving King Henry V begin with young Prince Henry as a vain, dissolute young man who spends his time drinking and carousing with old John Falstaff. But when Henry's father, the king, dies, Henry changes. Prince Henry realizes his unworthiness and that the crown will be his through no virtue of his own. So he confesses to his dying father, "You won it, wore it, kept it, gave it me." Then, upon the crown being given to him, Henry vows to live a worthy life:

> The tide of blood in me
> Hath proudly flowed in vanity till now.
> Now doth it turn and ebb back to the sea,
> Where it shall mingle with the state of floods,
> And flow henceforth in formal majesty.[1]

And from then on Henry V becomes one of the worthiest and noblest kings of England—his noble heritage flowed from him with majesty.

There is something of this idea in the opening lines of our text, though it may not be readily apparent. The line reads, "Only let your manner of life be worthy of the gospel of Christ" (v. 27)—which in effect is a call to individually say, "Let the tide of blood in me (the life of Christ) flow henceforth in formal majesty." This will become clear as we unpack the treasures of this opening line.

The Call to Live as Worthy Citizens (v. 27a)

Citizenship

At the center of the treasure is the fact that "Only let your manner of life" under-translates the Greek, which better reads, "Only let your manner of life *as citizens* be worthy of the gospel of Christ." The Greek verb is *politeues-thai*, which shares its root with the cognate noun *polis* or "city" as well as with another noun, *politeuma*, which is translated "citizenship" in 3:20 ("But our citizenship is in heaven"). So here in verse 27 it means "live as citizens." Thus Paul purposely uses language evocative of citizenship because he has in mind the ultimate citizenship of the Philippians. As Gordon Fee explains, "Paul now uses the verb metaphorically, not meaning 'live as citizens of Rome'—although that is not irrelevant—but rather 'live in the Roman colony of Philippi as worthy citizens of your heavenly homeland.'" Fee adds, "As Philippi was a colony of Rome in Macedonia, so the church was a 'colony of heaven' in Philippi, whose members were to live as its citizens in Philippi."[2]

Paul could not have more carefully chosen and crafted his words to impress and encourage his Philippian brothers and sisters as they struggled in that self-consciously prideful, elitist little Roman colony that was so pre-occupied with the coveted citizenship of Rome. Here Paul challenges his beloved Philippians with a "counter-citizenship whose capital and seat of power are not earthly but heavenly, whose guarantor is not Nero but Christ" (Bockmuehl).[3] The town of Philippi was enjoying the personal patronage and benefactions of Lord (*Kyrios*) Caesar, but the Philippians were subjects of the One who alone is *Kyrios* and to whom every knee (including "Lord" Nero's) will bow.[4]

The Philippians were to live out what they were—like an unbowed African slave who towered above his manacled comrades—the son of a king, and he could not forget it! "Philippians, live out your blood-bought, heavenly citizenship."

Gospel

The evidence of living well as citizens of Heaven is a life "worthy of the gospel of Christ." Paul's emphasis on worthiness can be heard in the original's word order: "Only worthy of the gospel of Christ live as citizens." The gospel was to be adorned by the way the Philippians lived out their heavenly citizenship. Their partnership (or fellowship) in the gospel from the first day had evoked Paul's initial note of joy in this letter (cf. 1:4, 5). Paul and the Philippians shared a special gospel bond sealed with the adhesive of their blood, sweat, and tears.

For Paul the gospel was first! His jailhouse joy rested in the fact that the gospel went out to pagan soldiers, then through his encouraged brothers, and was even preached by his competitors who were trying to afflict him. "What then?" asked Paul. "Only that in every way, whether in pretense or in truth, Christ is proclaimed, and in that I rejoice" (v. 18).

This gospel-first ethic was what Paul enjoined of the Philippians. There had never ever been a congenial environment for the gospel in Philippi. The little Roman *polis* declared war on Paul and his converts from day one when the Roman lictors beat him and Silas (cf. Acts 16:22). The battle was cosmic. Those believers, as citizens of Heaven and subjects of the Lord of lords, were engaged in mortal combat. And their weapons were the good news—the preaching of Christ—and lives that proved "worthy of the gospel."

The Distinctives of Worthy Citizens (vv. 27b, 28)

The Philippians' commitment to Jesus Christ as Lord was a threat to the civic-minded, patriotic Romans who ran Philippi. The Philippians' allegiance to another "Lord" than Caesar bordered on treason as it challenged the political establishment. At times Christians were tarred with the (amazing to us!) opprobrium "atheist" because their loyalty to Christ challenged the divinity of Caesar. The Roman citizens of Philippi, who customarily honored the emperor at every public gathering, pressured the church to conform. Christians were a political embarrassment with their *Kyrios* Jesus. And more, Christians who had the temerity to declare with Paul that their citizenship was in Heaven (cf. 3:20) were thought to be "un-Roman" and thus enemies to public order.[5]

Because of this there was widespread persecution in Philippi and through-out the other churches of Macedonia, about whom we have these sound bites: "a severe test of affliction . . . extreme poverty" (2 Corinthians 8:2), "in much affliction" (1 Thessalonians 1:6), "your steadfastness and faith in all your persecutions and in the afflictions that you are enduring" (2 Thessalonians 1:4). Heavenly citizenship worthy of the gospel was costly and demanding.

Spiritual Steadfastness

This demanded steadfastness, as Paul says: "so that whether I come and see you or am absent, I may hear of you that you are standing firm in one spirit" (v. 27b). Here we must understand that the "one spirit" is the Holy Spirit because in every other use of this wording in Paul's writings it refers to the Holy Spirit.[6]

Therefore the Philippians' ability to stand firm was supernaturally based on the Holy Spirit's work in giving them new life, indwelling them, and incorporating them into the church (cf. Romans 8:11; 1 Corinthians 12:13; Titus 3:5). The Philippians were called to stand firm against attacks on the gospel as they drew on the inner work of the Holy Spirit in their lives. There is nothing here of bootstrap resolve. The Philippians were not asked to reach down deep in their inner person and will to pull themselves together. Their "No!" to Roman culture's demands to compromise the gospel rested in what God had accomplished in their lives.

At the same time this standing firm in the unity of the Holy Spirit produces action. God's great work is the ground of everything.

Teamwork

The immediate and concomitant effect of their "standing firm in one spirit [Spirit]" that Paul called for was profound cooperation—"with one mind striving side by side for the faith of the gospel" (v. 27c). "Striving side by side" is the teamwork vocabulary of athletes or soldiers. It is at the heart of winning teams. Stephen Ambrose in his book *Comrades*, which includes the story of Lewis and Clark, describes this as the secret of their epic accomplishments: "What Lewis and Clark had done, first of all, was to demonstrate that there is nothing that men cannot do if they get themselves together and act as a team."[7]

Paul knew that the success of the church in Philippi depended on such teamwork, but, of course, the stakes were far higher than the exploration of the American West. It was "the faith of the gospel" (v. 27c). It was *the* faith—its spread and growth—everything for which Paul was spending and being spent.

Fearlessness

Living as citizens worthy of the gospel first requires that we stand together, grounded immovably in the work of the Holy Spirit, and then that we strive together side by side like athletes determined to win the game. Of course, there is more if we are to live worthily, and that is to "not [be] frightened in anything by your opponents. This is a clear sign to them of their destruction, but of your salvation, and that from God" (v. 28). Some of us can remember high school or college athletics when we stepped onto the field or court or mat against daunting opponents and tried our best to look cool and unintimidated, hoping that would be a sign of their destruction and our victory. Of course, our opponents affected the same nonchalance and cool. The bottom line was, it didn't make a whole lot of difference because as the event progressed they found out what we had, or more likely what we didn't have!

But in Philippi it wasn't a game, and the stakes were more than a win or a loss. The opponents in Philippi came both from the ranks of the Roman establishment who despised the believers' un-Romanness and from those who found the lives of the Philippians to be living rebukes to their pagan way of life. Together these meant that the threat of violence was always there and was sometimes activated.

Certainly this was something to naturally fear. But Paul tells the Philippians to "not [be] frightened in anything by your opponents." How could they not be afraid? The rare Greek word used here was employed elsewhere for startling horses into a stampede. It describes a panic reaction.[8] Don't panic, advises Paul. Keep your head. You're a citizen of Heaven. God is in control. Don't be intimidated.

But unlike the bravado and posturing at the onset of an athletic event, this will be "a clear sign to them of their destruction, but of your salvation, and that from God" (v. 28b). This doesn't mean that their adversaries would recognize their own doom, though they might have a dim awareness of it, but that it is nevertheless a sign of their destruction, their judgment. Of course, believers see it all, including their own salvation. D.A. Carson explains:

> Your change in character, your united stand in defense of the gospel, your ability to withstand with meekness and without fear the opposition that you must endure, constitutes a sign. That sign speaks volumes, both to the outside world and the Christian community. It is a sign of judgment against the world that is mounting the opposition; it is a sign of assurance that these believers really are the people of God and will be saved on the last day.[9]

In 1984 Mehdi Dibaj was imprisoned by the government of Iran on charges of "apostasy" for converting from Islam to Christianity. He languished in prison for ten years until his case was tried in 1994. Some of the last lines of his written defense read:

> [Jesus Christ] is our Saviour and He is the Son of God. To know Him means to know eternal life. I, a useless sinner, have believed in His beloved person and all His words and miracles recorded in the Gospel, and I have committed my life into His hands. Life for me is an opportunity to serve Him, and death is a better opportunity to be with Christ. Therefore I am not only satisfied to be in prison for the honour of His Holy Name, but am ready to give my life for the sake of Jesus my Lord. . . .

Mehdi Dibaj was sentenced to execution but was released under pressure from the U.S. State Department—only to be found dead in a Tehran park, the third Christian murdered in Iran after release from prison.[10] Dibaj's measured conduct as he calmly stood his ground for the gospel was a sure sign of his enemies' coming judgment and his salvation, which perhaps some of those who knew him, due to God's grace, began to see.

> The tide of blood in Mehdi Dibaj
> Did flow henceforth in formal majesty.

The Grace of Worthy Citizenship (vv. 29, 30)

The proofs that the Philippians' courageous stand was a sign of their salvation were the twin facts that they were graced with salvation and with suffering: "For it has been granted to you that for the sake of Christ you should not only believe in him but also suffer for his sake" (v. 29). The verb "granted" can be literally rendered "graced" because it means "to give freely or graciously as a favor."[11] And the passive voice means that the twin gifts are from God.

The gracious gift of believing in Christ is a magnificent blessing. It is the grand evidence that God looks on you with favor. "But to all who did receive him, who believed in his name, he gave the right to become children of God, who were born, not of blood nor of the will of the flesh nor of the will of man, but of God" (John 1:12, 13). It is the eternal boon of God. But with this there is also another magnificent boon, as Karl Barth explains: "The grace of being permitted to *believe* in Christ is surpassed by the grace of being permitted to *suffer* for him, of being permitted to walk the way of Christ with Christ himself to the perfection of fellowship with him."[12] The fellowship of Christ's sufferings moves the believer beyond the role of beneficiary of Christ's death to a sharer in his sufferings (cf. Colossians 1:24).

The suffering that comes to a Christian (as a Christian) is not a sign of God's neglect but rather a proof that grace is at work in his or her life. As Paul would tell Timothy, "Indeed, all who desire to live a godly life in Christ Jesus will be persecuted" (2 Timothy 3:12). To the Philippians, he later penned this astonishing prayer: "that I may know him and the power of his resurrection, and may share his sufferings, becoming like him in his death" (3:10). This attitude wasn't Paul's alone because we read in Acts that after the apostles had been beaten in the presence of the council of Israel, "they left the presence of the council, rejoicing that they were counted worthy to suffer dishonor for the name" (Acts 5:41).

Here, as a further word of encouragement and motivation to live as citizens "worthy of the gospel" (v. 27), Paul indicated that the Philippians shared in the same sufferings with him—"engaged in the same conflict that you saw

I had and now hear that I still have" (v. 30). They and Paul together made up the heroic fellowship of the gospel (cf. 1:5), which meant that they shared in the same "conflict" (*agôn*) with Paul. Their conflict, whether in Philippi or Rome, was one. What they saw Paul endure in Philippi (and what they themselves were enduring in Philippi) along with what they heard he was enduring in Rome was all part of the apostolic *agôn*.

Paul's point was that he and the Philippians were all recipients of grace as they had been given the gifts of salvation and suffering. Their mutual *agôn* was a testimony to the grace of God. Listen to John Calvin's passionate application:

> Oh, if this conviction were fixed in our minds, that persecutions are to be reckoned among God's benefits, what progress would be made in the doctrine of godliness! And yet, what is more certain than that it is the highest honour of the Divine grace, that we suffer for His name either reproach, or imprisonment, or miseries, or tortures, or even death, for in that case He decorates us with His insignia. But more will be found who will order God and His gifts to be gone, rather than embrace the cross readily when it is offered to them. Woe, then, to our stupidity![13]

The understanding that suffering and salvation are both gifts of grace is essential to discipleship and perseverance. Sadly, the misunderstanding or rejection of this has led to the spiritual demise of not a few.

The transcending call for all of us is to "Only let your manner of life [as citizens of Heaven] be worthy of the gospel of Christ" (v. 27a). We are recipients of the gospel. Our sins have been paid for by Christ himself. One day, along with Paul, we will receive "the crown of righteousness" from Christ the Lord (cf. 2 Timothy 4:8). And we will well be able to say, "You won it, wore it, kept it, gave it to me." All glory to God!

As benefactors of the gospel, we are charged to be like Paul—gospel-first people—living lives worthy of the gospel—"standing firm in one spirit" as we are planted firm by the work of the Holy Spirit in a graced unity—"with one mind striving side by side for the faith of the gospel" as we team together in mutual support and coordination to promote the authentic gospel (v. 27). This we are to do while "not [being] frightened in anything" (v. 28)—no panic but calm assurance. And we are to do all of this understanding that God's grace to us includes both salvation and suffering. If we imagine grace to be only pleasant benefits and blessings, then suffering is seen to be anything but grace. And many such confused souls have walked away from God and his Church and his grace.

Standing together—striving side by side—without fear—as full recipients of his dual graces of salvation and suffering—this is worthy of the gospel—this is full citizenship.

So if there is any encouragement in Christ, any comfort from love, any participation in the Spirit, any affection and sympathy, complete my joy by being of the same mind, having the same love, being in full accord and of one mind. Do nothing from selfish ambition or conceit, but in humility count others more significant than yourselves. Let each of you look not only to his own interests, but also to the interests of others.

2:1–4

8

Living Worthily
in the Church

PHILIPPIANS 2:1–4

WHEN A CERTAIN CHURCH IN DALLAS became divided, the rift was so bitter that each side instituted a lawsuit seeking to dispossess the other from the church's property—this despite Scripture's warnings about taking such matters before public courts (cf. 1 Corinthians 6:1–8). The story, of course, hit the Dallas newspapers and garnered considerable interest from the readers. The judge wisely ruled that it was not the province of the court to decide such matters until the case had been heard before the denomination's church court. So the dispute was remanded to the ecclesiastical court where, eventually, the decision was made to award the real estate and properties to one side.

The losers withdrew and formed another church nearby. Church growth the American way! It was reported in the Dallas newspapers (no doubt with some delight) that the church court had traced the trouble to its source—the trouble began when, at a church dinner, an elder had been served a smaller slice of ham than a child seated next to him.[1] Church hostesses, make sure you always serve heaping elder portions to the elders and deacons or you might come before Judge Judy!

Imagine the laugh that the good people of Dallas got out of that one! Of course, this is nothing new, nor is it confined to the exotics of American church culture. Leslie Flynn in his book with the dubious title *Great Church Fights* quotes a story from a Welsh newspaper about a church that was looking for a new pastor.

Yesterday the two opposition groups both sent ministers to the pulpit. Both spoke simultaneously, each trying to shout above the other. Both called for hymns, and the congregation sang two—each side trying to drown out the other. Then the groups began shouting at each other. Bibles were raised in anger. The Sunday morning service turned into a bedlam. Through it all, the two preachers continued to outshout each other with their sermons.

Eventually a deacon called a policeman. Two came in and began shouting for the congregation to be quiet. They advised the 40 persons in the church to return home. The rivals filed out, still arguing. Last night one of the group called a "let's-be-friends" meeting. It broke up in argument.

The newspaper article was headlined, "Hallelujah! Two Jacks in One Pulpit."[2]

Another good laugh for the good people of the UK. I'm not above smiling at the follies and absurdities of life. Both these events could make excellent sketch material for *Saturday Night Live* or British television—"Monty Python's Flying Circus Goes to Church."

The sad thing is that these stories actually happened and that they illustrate what is all too true—many of the gravest dangers to the church come from within. It's always been this way. As Karl Barth piquantly remarked, "There are no letters in the New Testament apart from the problems of the church."[3] This is clearly true of the letter to the Philippians, which is one of Paul's letters from prison, written when the dangers from without were immense.

In fact, Paul's command that opened the preceding paragraph in 1:27, 28 referenced the external dangers and called the Philippians to "hang tough": "Only let your manner of life be worthy of the gospel of Christ, so that whether I come and see you or am absent, I may hear of you that you are standing firm in one spirit, with one mind striving side by side for the faith of the gospel, and not frightened in anything by your opponents." This said, Paul knows that toughing it out in the face of external pressures will not be enough. If the Philippians are to live lives worthy of their heavenly citizenship, they must also not allow themselves to be undone from within the church.

The Philippians must be united not only against their common foes but also unified in heart and mind and in mutual regard for one another. Verses 1–4 of chapter 2 form a single sentence that is a passionate appeal for *unity* and *mutual care* within the church.

Fourfold Motivations (v. 1)

Paul began with a deliberately emotional appeal that was meant to move the Philippians to a fourfold remembrance of what happened to them when they came to Christ. "So if there is any encouragement in Christ, any comfort from love, any participation in the Spirit, any affection and sympathy . . ." (v. 1). Paul hoped these sweet recollections of the supernatural in their lives would move them to do what was necessary to ensure their unity and mutuality.

His first recollection, "So if there is any encouragement in Christ," summoned their experience of salvation when the Holy Spirit came alongside them and comforted and strengthened them. This is true of all our biographies if we have truly come to Christ. My memory as a boy was that I received a treasury of consolation and strength. Being in Christ and knowing beyond a shadow of a doubt that Christ was in me exceeded mere "atta boy!" encouragement as we normally think of it. I was consoled, and I was strengthened in Christ.

Paul's second recollection, "any comfort from love," referenced their experience of Christ's love. They realized that they were loved unconditionally by Christ, who gave his life for them. This is the love we sing about—the "love that will not let me go"—the lyrical consolations that ring from our souls in salvation. Every child of God understands this love. I well remember the new sense of security I felt as I drifted off to sleep.

The third recollection was "any participation in the Spirit." This is the *koinon* word, the *fellowship* word that is so embedded in the argument of Philippians, first appearing in 1:5 where Paul celebrated the Philippians' "partnership [fellowship] in the gospel." This fellowship in the Spirit came when, as Paul explained, "in one Spirit we were all baptized into one body—Jews or Greeks, slaves or free—and all were made to drink of one Spirit" (1 Corinthians 12:13). And now it rests as the lingering, final word of the sublime Trinitarian benediction that we repeatedly invoke: "The grace of the Lord Jesus Christ and the love of God and the fellowship of the Holy Spirit be with you all" (2 Corinthians 13:14). This is the enduring reality of our lives—fellowship in the Spirit.

The fourth recollection—"any affection and sympathy"—is more exactly the divine compassion and mercy that came from Christ himself to us at salvation and now passes through us to others. As Jesus said in the Sermon on the Mount, "Blessed are the merciful, for they shall receive mercy" (Matthew 5:7), indicating that a merciful heart is a sign of having received mercy. Compassion and mercy flow in the lives of those who have experienced them.

Paul is so emotionally compelling here. He has taken the Philippians back to the graced memories of the supernatural work of Christ in their souls at salvation. He has activated their spiritual camcorders. They all had experienced encouragement and comfort in Christ. They remembered the consolation of Christ's love when they became his. They, through Christ, had found fellowship in the Spirit. And the compassion and sympathy of Christ had not only graced their souls but had flowed from them to others. Thus, with all of this freshly replaying on their inner screens, the Philippians must heed the exhortation through their beloved apostle to maintain unity and mutual care in the church. And so must we. This is necessary if we are to live a life worthy of the gospel of Christ.

Living Worthily: Unity (v. 2)

As to unity, Paul says, "complete my joy by being of the same mind, having the same love, being in full accord and of one mind" (v. 2). This is, in short, a dynamic unity of mind. Note that the thought begins with the words "the same mind" and ends with the words "of one mind," both of which speak of a life intent on a unified purpose—a single goal. And what is the unified goal? The gospel! Paul mentioned the gospel five times in the first chapter, and in the fifth mention (verse 27) he declared, "Only let your manner of life be worthy of the gospel," which is the commanding theme all the way to 2:18. So the call here in 2:2 to be "of the same mind, having the same love, being in full accord and of one mind" is a plea that the Philippians be "gospel oriented as they relate to and care for one another."[4]

So the unity that Paul emotionally enjoins, by recalling the supernatural realities that the Philippians experienced when they received the gospel, is that they themselves be gospel-oriented men and women. How informing! The unity Paul wants is not a vacuous togetherness but a oneness fraught with dynamic purpose. This is important instruction for the church universal. It is cliché today to say that "the purpose of the church is worship" without understanding that if the gospel of Christ is not the center of everything (the unifying purpose), it is not New Testament worship. So if we attempt to take Paul seriously, the gospel must be in the center of our thinking and at every level of ministry.

Paul was so passionate about this that he cared little about himself as long as the church was getting it right. Though he was in prison on a capital charge, chained, guarded 24/7, afflicted by those who should be his friends, with execution at hand, he rested his joy in Christ and the gospel and insisted that his joy would be "complete" if they lived out their unity in the gospel. That's all the happiness Paul sought! Paul knew that a people so unified in purpose would not be concerned with who gets the extra biscuit at a church dinner. He knew that to be gospel oriented is to be others oriented.

Living Worthily: Mutual Care (vv. 3, 4)

Paul was explicit about mutual care within the church: "Do nothing from selfish ambition or conceit, but in humility count others more significant than yourselves" (v. 3).

Humility/Lowliness

"Selfish ambition" and "conceit" have always been part and parcel of the world and its systems. In the secular Greek literature of Jesus' day the words *humility* and *lowliness* were rarely used, and if they were used, it was in a derogatory sense of servile weakness or obsequious groveling or shameful lowliness.[5]

Conceit has definitely been more in vogue over the centuries. The seventeenth-century Frenchman Comte Aimery de La Rochefoucauld was noted for his aristocratic conceit. On one occasion, disgusted by the improper protocol in a certain household, he said to a friend of his own peerage, "Let us walk home together and talk of rank." And then speaking of the Duc du Luynes he remarked that his family was "mere nobodies in the year 1000."[6] Rousseau said, "I rejoice in myself. My consolations lie in my self esteem. . . . If there were a single enlightened government in Europe, it would have erected statues to me."[7] Egoism was seen across the channel too in the likes of Oscar Wilde who, when asked as he went through customs if he had anything to declare, answered, "Only my genius." Conceit is de jure in the world system. Conventional wisdom has it that you can't get anywhere without it. And there is some truth in that. But it is an abomination in the church.

The rule for the gospel-oriented church is, "but in humility count others more significant than yourselves." Several years ago I preached at Southern Seminary in Louisville. After the sermon I asked the president, Al Mohler, about A. T. Robertson, the famous Greek scholar. Robertson was the towering genius and masterful scholar of his day, as the nearly 1,400 pages of his *Grammar of the Greek New Testament* testify. He was also the son-in-law of John A. Broadus, New Testament scholar and one of the founding professors of the seminary. Mohler offered to take me to A. T. Robertson's grave and drove me to the Cave-Hill Cemetery grave site.

But first he pointed me to Broadus's grave, a towering monument erected by his relatives. As I gazed up at its granite inscription, he directed my attention down to a flat grave marker next to it—that of the great A. T. Robertson. Mohler remarked, "Robertson wanted to be buried in Broadus's shadow."

That is a beautiful sentiment. And whatever the realities of their relationship, it remains a remarkable expression of Paul's directive, "but in humility count others more significant than yourselves." The lowliness that was utterly despised by the Greeks and makes such little sense today has become the highest virtue for the child of God. Markus Bockmuehl writes:

> Instead of pursuing their own prestige, that strangely addictive and debasing cocktail of vanity and public opinion, the Philippians are called to humility (*tapeinophrosune*), the 'lowliness of heart' which agrees to treat and think of others preferentially. . . . The biblical view of humility is precisely *not* feigned or groveling, nor a sanctimonious or pathetic lack of self-esteem, but rather a mark of moral strength and integrity. It involves an unadorned acknowledgement of one's own creaturely inadequacies, and entrusting one's fortunes to God rather than to one's own abilities or resources.[8]

If we wonder how a person of superior abilities can regard others as more significant than himself or herself, the answer is to use those abilities for self-assessment by the light of the Scriptures. Then take to heart the words of the surpassing genius and Christian Blaise Pascal, who concluded after much thought, "what amazes me most is to see that everyone is not amazed at his weakness."[9] In the words of St. Chrysostom, "There is nothing so foreign to a Christian as arrogance."[10] When we actually see ourselves for what we are, our conceit and vainglory will recede, and we will begin to count others more significant than ourselves.

This is in fact the way Paul himself lived, as he earlier explained to the Corinthians: "I try to please everyone in everything I do, not seeking my own advantage, but that of many, that they may be saved. Be imitators of me, as I am of Christ" (1 Corinthians 10:33—11:1); "Let no one seek his own good, but the good of his neighbor" (1 Corinthians 10:24). This is living a life worthy of the gospel of Christ.

Others-Directed

Paul gives this others-oriented call classic expression in verse 4: "Let each of you look not only to his own interests, but also to the interests of others." Looking to the interests of others is at the heart of all godly parenting. This is what our godly mothers and fathers did, and we parents are called to live it out every day. No one can effectively parent who is into himself or herself. And friendship only flourishes in the flow of others-directedness, as the story of Jonathan and David's friendship poignantly reminds us.

As to Paul's great concern here, a healthy church that will survive the onslaught of a hostile and fracturing culture must be a place where each one looks "not only to his own interests, but also to the interests of others." In such a church every portion served at a church dinner will be "just right" regardless of the size, and only one Jack will be in the pulpit at a time. Hallelujah!

The conductor of a symphony orchestra was once asked what is the most difficult instrument to play. He responded, "Second violin. I can find plenty of first violinists, but to find someone who can play second violin with enthusiasm—that is a problem. And if we have no second violin, we have no harmony."

> It takes more grace than I can tell
> To play the second fiddle well.[11]

Paul's signature command—"Only let your manner of life [as citizens of Heaven] be worthy of the gospel of Christ" (1:27)—demanded that the Philippians both stand firm against the onslaughts from *outside* the church and attacks from *within* the church. As to the latter, the church will live in a manner "worthy of the gospel of Christ" when it has a unified focus on the gospel so that its people are "of the same mind, having the same love, being in full accord and of one mind" (2:2). This gospel-oriented unity will then show itself in care for others—counting others more significant than themselves and looking out for the interests of others.

Paul was not captive to the neo-pagan proposition that we cannot love others until we love ourselves.[12] Certainly he didn't hate himself. In fact Paul's theology celebrated the fact that Christ loved him and gave himself for Paul (cf. Galatians 2:20) and that he, and all Christians, were not only loved but had been given all things (cf. Romans 8:32).

Therefore the source of Paul's call to live lives worthy of the gospel through unity in the church and in other-directedness *is Christ himself*—this is all possible for those who are "in Christ" (2:1), a truth Paul celebrates with this matchless charge:

> Have this mind among yourselves, which is yours in Christ Jesus, who, though he was in the form of God, did not count equality with God a thing to be grasped, but emptied himself, by taking the form of a servant, being born in the likeness of men. And being found in human form, he humbled himself by becoming obedient to the point of death, even death on a cross. Therefore God has highly exalted him and bestowed on him the name that is above every name, so that at the name of Jesus every knee should bow, in heaven and on earth and under the earth, and every tongue confess that Jesus Christ is Lord, to the glory of God the Father. (2:5–11)

Have this mind among yourselves, which is yours in Christ Jesus, who, though he was in the form of God, did not count equality with God a thing to be grasped, but emptied himself, by taking the form of a servant, being born in the likeness of men. And being found in human form, he humbled himself by becoming obedient to the point of death, even death on a cross.

2:5–8

9

The Self-Humiliation
of Christ

PHILIPPIANS 2:5–8

THE APOSTLE MATTHEW reports that toward the end of Jesus' ministry an ugly, competitive spirit developed among the apostles when James and John (and their mother) attempted to get Jesus to promise them privileged thrones in the kingdom. "[W]hen the ten heard it, they were indignant at the two brothers" (20:24). Harsh words and angry gestures were exchanged among the Twelve. Tempers flared! So Jesus called them together and said:

> You know that the rulers of the Gentiles lord it over them, and their great ones exercise authority over them. It shall not be so among you. But whoever would be great among you must be your servant, and whoever would be first among you must be your slave, even as the Son of Man came not to be served but to serve, and to give his life as a ransom for many. (vv. 25–28)

It would seem that none could miss the point. However, as we all know, hearing the truth and making it part of our lives are not the same thing, even when we are devoted to Christ. Several days later, when the apostles arrived in Jerusalem to celebrate the Passover, they were still going at it. Peter and John had secured a room for Passover as Jesus had directed, but they had neglected to make arrangements for foot-washing. And as the apostles wandered in, no one would condescend to perform the humble task. Jesus' teaching (only a few days earlier), as direct as it was, had apparently had no effect. No one would volunteer for the lowly task. How very human they were. How like us.

As John's Gospel relates the account of what happened behind closed doors, the disciples were reclining at the table with their shamefully dirty feet stretching out behind them. The meal was in process, but the conversation was strained because of the tension. What a pleasant way to eat Passover! Then they became aware that the Teacher had risen from supper and was standing apart from them. As they watched he removed his outer garment. Next he took a towel and wrapped it around his body. And then he poured water into a basin and began slowly to move around the circle, washing each disciple's outstretched feet, wiping them with the towel with which he was wrapped.[1]

It was a breathtaking deed. The Midrash taught that no Hebrew, even a slave, could be commanded to wash feet.[2] Yet Jesus did it in the most humble way possible, clothed in a servant's towel. In the breathless silence of that upper room, the apostles heard the trickle of water as it was poured, the friction of the towel as their feet were wiped off, the sound of the Master breathing as he moved from one to another. The incarnate Son, God himself, had dressed like a servant and washed the feet of his prideful, arrogant creatures. Then he said, "If I then, your Lord and Teacher, have washed your feet, you also ought to wash one another's feet. For I have given you an example, that you also should do just as I have done to you. Truly, truly, I say to you, a servant is not greater than his master, nor is a messenger greater than the one who sent him" (John 13:14–16).

Jesus used the ancient logic, "If it is true for the greater (me), then it must be true for the lesser (you)." That is always a powerful argument. But coming from his infinitude, it is infinitely compelling. Yet, so often divine logic and compulsion stall in our hearts because we are so like the men at Jesus' table. In the words of poet Robert Raines:

> I am like James and John
> Lord, I size up other people
> in terms of what they can do for me;
> how they can further my program,
> feed my ego,
> satisfy my needs,
> give me strategic advantage.
> I exploit people,
> ostensibly for your sake,
> but really for my own sake.
> Lord, I turn to you
> to get the inside track
> and obtain special favors,
> your direction for my schemes,
> your power for my projects,
> your sanction for my ambitions,

your blank checks for whatever I want.
I am like James and John.[3]

Given our natural bent to be self-centered, it has always been difficult to live out Christ's directive—as Paul advises the Philippians in our present text, to "do nothing from selfish ambition or conceit, but in humility count others more significant than yourselves. Let each of you look not only to his own interests, but also to the interests of others" (2:3, 4). Humility and others-directedness are hard for us. We find it difficult in our most important relationships both in the home and in the household of faith.

And here in Philippians, as Paul calls God's people to live a "life . . . worthy of the gospel" (1:27), he turns to the ultimate example of Christ and his self-humiliation in 2:5–11, the theological, Christological centerpiece and jewel of the book. Many consider it the most exalted prose in the New Testament. One scholar has likened it to "the soaring, unanswerable language of a Bach cantata which is best understood by being heard out to the end—and then heard again."[4] And certainly it does serve us in this way. When we read and reread this passage, it takes us down in Christ's humiliation and then up in soaring exaltation. We will now consider the first movement in verses 5–8—the preexistent Christ's self-humiliation—as an example for our hearts.

Paul begins, "Have this mind among yourselves, which is yours in Christ Jesus"—literally, "Think this among yourselves, which also in Christ Jesus" (v. 5). Paul's concern for the Philippians was not so much for their minds as it was for their interactions (for the whole congregation), that they would live out in their mutual relationships the same humble attitude that characterized Jesus[5]—"Have this mind *among yourselves*." So as we take up the mind of Christ, it is "not for the satisfaction of our curiosity, but for the reformation of our lives" (Motyer).[6]

Christ's Humility in Heaven (v. 6)

Our Savior's humility in Heaven is described explicitly—"who, though he was in the form of God, did not count equality with God a thing to be grasped" (v. 6).

His Existence

Christ existed in the majestic "form of God" from all eternity as he shared in the glory of God. Jesus alluded to this in the upper room in his high-priestly prayer on the eve of his death: "And now, Father, glorify me in your own presence with the glory that I had with you before the world existed" (John

17:5). Calvin comments, "The form of God means here his majesty. For as man is known by the appearance of his form, so the majesty which shines forth in God is His figure."[7] The glory that Christ had before the world may seem unreal to our unreflective, distracted souls, but the reality behind these words is beyond our comprehension. We declare creedally that he is "Light of Light" as we reach for some expression of the glorious reality, but we know little of what we declare. This is among the persistent challenges in reading about Christ—to allow our minds to dwell upon the incomprehensible realities of his person so that our understanding is progressively elevated and our hearts are enlarged.

At the same time "form of God" does not refer simply to his external appearance, but to his being. Hebrews 1:3 tells us, "He is the radiance of the glory of God and the exact imprint of his nature." Note that Christ is not a mere *reflector* of God's glory. He is "the radiance," the one who radiates the glory of God! He shines forth his own essential glory along with that of the Father and the Spirit in the mystery of the Trinity.

His Attitude

Here the wonder increases because of his eternal humility in Heaven. Though he existed in the splendorous "form of God, [he] did not count equality with God a thing to be grasped" (v. 6b). The idea is that he did not hold on to his equality with God as something to use for his own advantage.[8] Here we need to look back to verses 3, 4—to Christians who vie as rivals as they seek their own interests. How unlike such people was the pre-incarnate Christ. Rather than viewing his equality with God as something to keep, he saw it as qualifying him for his humble descent to save his people.

Christ's eternal humility in Heaven is a thing of astonishing wonder.

Christ's Humility in Incarnation (v. 7)

Christ's humility in Heaven is next followed by his humility in incarnation—"but emptied himself, by taking the form of a servant, being born in the likeness of men" (v. 7).

His Emptying

During the early part of the twentieth century liberal theologians abused the meaning of this text by developing the *kenosis* theory (the title coming from the Greek word *kenao*, which means "to empty"). They thought that when Christ emptied himself, he ceased to be God or stripped himself of his attributes.

Today this theory is discredited by virtually all scholars of every persuasion. This is because four of the five uses of the verb "to empty" in the New Testament are metaphorical. Moreover, the emptying (or "making himself nothing," as some translations render it) is defined by the following two phrases of verse 7—namely, "taking the form of a servant" and "being born in the likeness of men."[9] The negative action of emptying is actually defined by Christ's positive action in the incarnation.

Emptying by taking—"taking the form of a servant." Here the word "form" has the same sense as in verse 6, where "form" signifies both the *appearance* and the *being* of God. So when Christ took on "the form of a servant [slave]," he adopted the *appearance* and *being* of a slave. This taking on was an emptying, as Christ so dramatically demonstrated when he stripped himself in the upper room and washed the disciples' feet. Christ did not *exchange* the form of God for the form of a slave. Rather he *manifested* the form of God in the form of a slave.[10]

Emptying by being born. The other phrase that further defines his emptying—"being born in the likeness of men"—describes his full identity with the human race. He fully participated in our human experience. Jesus was truly man, but not merely man.[11] Christ's eternal humility in Heaven is a thing of astounding wonder—Christ never *became* humble because he *was* humble. He is the genesis and apotheosis of humility. And beyond that, his humility in the incarnation is a thing of even greater wonder.

I remember from my boyhood my pastor sometimes reciting at Christmas J. B. Phillips's fanciful dialogue, "The Angels' Point of View." In an imaginary conversation a very young angel was being shown the splendors and glories of the universe by a senior and experienced angel.

> The little angel was beginning to be tired and a little bored. He had been shown whirling galaxies and blazing suns, infinite distances in the deathly cold of interstellar space, and to his mind there seemed to be an awful lot of it all. Finally, he was shown the galaxy of which our planetary system is but a small part. As the two of them drew near to the star which we call our sun and to its circling planets, the senior angel pointed to a small and rather insignificant sphere turning very slowly on its axis. It looked as dull as a dirty tennis ball to the little angel whose mind was filled with the size and glory of what he had seen.
>
> "I want you to watch that one particularly," said the senior angel, pointing with his finger.
>
> "Well, it looks very small and rather dirty to me," said the little angel. "What's special about that one?"
>
> "That," replied his senior solemnly, "is the Visited Planet."

"'Visited'?" said the little one. "You don't mean visited by—"

"Indeed I do. That ball, which I have no doubt looks to you small and insignificant and not perhaps overclean, has been visited by our young Prince of Glory."

And at these words he bowed his head reverently.[12]

From there, Phillips leads the junior angel through a series of revelations about Christ's incarnation that leaves him stunned and incredulous. Oh, to have fresh eyes and a tender heart as we revisit these astonishing truths—to live our lives in a spiritual springtime of wonder—to be perpetually knocked out by the realities of Christ!

Now the wonder deepens even more as Paul recounts Christ's self-humiliation in death.

Christ's Humility in Death (v. 8)

The descent bottoms out: "And being found in human form, he humbled himself by becoming obedient to the point of death, even death on a cross." His "human form" or more exactly his human shape was that of the visible appearance of a man. Those who saw Christ saw him as a man.

He fully identified himself with humanity. He was not a facsimile (cf. Luke 2:52; John 1:14; Romans 8:3; Galatians 4:4; Colossians 1:22; Hebrews 2:17; 4:15; 5:7, 8; 1 John 4:2, 3).[13]

His Self-Humbling

As a real man, "he humbled himself by becoming obedient to the point of death" (v. 8a). Note: no one humbled him! "He humbled *himself*." Kierkegaard commented on this verse:

> Christ humbled *himself—not*, he *was* humbled. O infinite sublimity, of which it must categorically be true that there was none in heaven or on earth or in the abyss that could humble him! He humbled himself. The infinite qualitative difference between Christ and every other man lies indeed in this, that in every humiliation which he suffers it is absolutely necessary that he himself should assent and confirm that he is willing to submit to that humiliation. This is infinite superiority over suffering, but at the same time also suffering infinitely more intense in kind.[14]

So at every level, his humbling was his own doing.

His not holding tightly to his equality with God—
his emptying—
his becoming a servant in body and soul—

his full entrance into humanity—
his humbling—were all of his own doing.

The message for the Philippians and all the rest of us who are prone to ambition and vainglory is clear: "in humility count others more significant than yourselves. Let each of you look not only to his own interests, but also to the interests of others" (vv. 3, 4). "He is lowly minded who humbles himself, not he who is lowly by necessity" (Chrysostom).[15]

Christ's self-humiliation brought ultimate obedience—"by becoming obedient to the point of death" (v. 8b). So we see Christ in Gethsemane overcome with fear because he knew what his death would entail—his becoming sin for us (cf. 2 Corinthians 5:21). He knew that he must propitiate the wrath of God (cf. 1 John 2:2). Thus we hear him say in the garden, "My soul is very sorrowful, even to death" (Mark 14:34). "And there appeared to him an angel from heaven, strengthening him. And being in an agony he prayed more earnestly; and his sweat became like great drops of blood falling down to the ground" (Luke 22:43, 44). Jesus prayed, "Father, if you are willing, remove this cup from me. Nevertheless, not my will, but yours, be done" (Luke 22:42). His self-humiliation meant full obedience.

His Death

And then he died the most scandalous of deaths—"even death on a cross" (v. 8c). Humanity had not created a more degrading or loathsome experience than this. Polite Roman society considered the mention of the cross to be an obscenity.[16] In fact, this may account for the relatively late appearance of the cross as a Christian symbol.[17] What sort of person would wear an obscenity as a necklace? "Even death on a cross" is the crowning shudder and an expression of humble obedience. Calvin remarks, "For by dying in this way He was not only covered with ignominy in the sight of men, but also accursed in the sight of God. It is assuredly such an example of humility as ought to absorb the attention of all men; it is impossible to explain it in words suitable to its greatness."[18] The humblest man who ever lived is Christ himself, the God-man.

Think of it:

- He was eternally humble in Heaven: "though he was in the form of God, [he] did not count equality with God a thing to be grasped" (v. 6).
- He was astonishingly self-humbling in the incarnation: "but emptied himself, by taking the form of a servant, being born in the likeness of men" (v. 7).

- He was infinitely self-humbling in his death: "And being found in human form, he humbled himself by becoming obedient to the point of death, even death on a cross" (v. 8).

What does Paul make of this plunging, self-humbling of Christ? Only this: "Do nothing from selfish ambition or conceit, but in humility count others more significant than yourselves. Let each of you look not only to his own interests, but also to the interests of others. Have this mind among yourselves, which is yours in Christ Jesus" (vv. 3–5). This is the divine call for everyone in the Body of Christ. This is the path for living a life worthy of the gospel of Christ.

Serving others is to be the vocation of every Christian, poor or rich. Counting others as more significant than ourselves is to be the constant and sincere attitude of our souls. Looking out for the interests of others is to be descriptive of all who are part of the Body of Christ. Jesus said:

If I then, your Lord and Teacher, have washed your feet, you also ought to wash one another's feet. For I have given you an example, that you also should do just as I have done to you. Truly, truly, I say to you, a servant is not greater than his master, nor is a messenger greater than the one who sent him. (John 13:14–16)

Therefore God has highly exalted him and bestowed on him the name that is above every name, so that at the name of Jesus every knee should bow, in heaven and on earth and under the earth, and every tongue confess that Jesus Christ is Lord, to the glory of God the Father.

2:9–11

10

Christ's Super-Exaltation

PHILIPPIANS 2:9–11

THERE IS A SENSE in which Christ wore the servant's towel from eternity because as the Lamb that was slain before the foundation of the world, he was eternally determined to redeem us (cf. Revelation 13:8). So we see that Christ's downward self-humiliation was due to his eternal resolve. First, there was *his humility in Heaven*—"who, though he was in the form of God, did not count equality with God a thing to be grasped" (2:6). Rather, Christ viewed his equality with God as qualifying him for his humble descent to save his people. Second, there was *his humility in incarnation*—"but emptied himself, by taking the form of a servant, being born in the likeness of men" (v. 7). Jesus fully identified with the human race and donned a towel as he took on the appearance and being of a slave. And, third, there was *his humility in death*—"And being found in human form, he humbled himself by becoming obedient to the point of death, even death on a cross" (v. 8). Nothing could be lower. He became a shame and scandal for us!

And it was all his own doing. No one humbled him! Herod did not humble him. Pilate did not humble him. The high priest did not humble him. The Romans did not humble him. Jesus "humbled himself." The humblest man who ever lived is Christ himself, the God-man. No other man or woman has even come close!

Of course, as we know from the flow of the text, Christ's self-humiliation was followed by his grand exaltation by God the Father. So the down, down, down of Christ's humiliation is followed by his soaring exaltation. To get the feel of this, picture the gears of a catapult being ratcheted down ever tighter with the three movements of his self-humiliation, so that the final groaning click of the gears creates an explosive tension, and then the gear is tripped, launching indescribable exaltation.

Christ's exaltation (his catapult upward) has two movements: his *past* exaltation and his *future* exaltation.

God's Past Exaltation of Christ (v. 9)

The exaltation that Christ now enjoys stretches our understanding as it is expressed in verse 9: "Therefore God has highly exalted him and bestowed upon him the name that is above every name."

Super-Exaltation

This is the ultimate illustration of Jesus' own axiom, delivered to those full of religious pride: "The greatest among you shall be your servant. Whoever exalts himself will be humbled, and whoever humbles himself will be exalted" (Matthew 23:11, 12). In keeping with his own spiritual law, Jesus' self-humiliation brought about his supreme exaltation.

Though Christ's exaltation was a once-and-for-all event, it was the culmination of a process that began with the resurrection. He had gone down, down, down through his incarnation and passion and death (which wrought such infinite spiritual compression), but then in a final, explosive upsurge the grave could no longer hold him. Thus we have that brilliant moment on Sunday morning when Jesus came right through his graveclothes in the sacred body of his humiliation, glorious and radiant. And in the following moments, says Matthew, "there was a great earthquake, for an angel of the Lord descended from heaven and came and rolled back the stone and sat on it" (28:2). *Look, world—Jesus has risen from the dead!* The great message of the resurrection is that he lives!

Following Jesus' resurrection he was on earth for forty days, repeatedly appearing and ministering especially to his apostles. On day forty he led them out to Bethany, "and lifting up his hands he blessed them. While he blessed them, he parted from them and was carried up into heaven" (Luke 24:50, 51). The great message of the ascension is that Jesus has gone back to Heaven and will return again in like manner, as the angels explained to the apostles: "This Jesus, who was taken up from you into heaven, will come in the same way as you saw him go into heaven" (Acts 1:11).

Jesus' resurrection and ascension were capped by his exaltation to the right hand of God the Father (cf. Acts 2:33). There he sat down at the right hand of the Majesty on high, where he now rules (cf. Hebrews 1:3). The great message of Christ's exaltation is that he reigns!

The Scriptures contain no account of the moment of his exaltation when the glory that he had with the Father "before the world existed" was restored to him (cf. John 17:5). Perhaps this is because it is beyond description. What joy! What triumph! We know now that Christ is in Heaven with myriads of angels who are singing, "Worthy is the Lamb who was slain, to receive power and wealth and wisdom and might and honor and glory and blessing!" (Revelation 5:12). Were there cosmic fireworks at Christ's exaltation? Astral explosions? Starbursts? We do not know. Certainly there were awesome fanfare and unrestrained celebration as the eternal Son reentered the glory that had always been his.

And here in Philippians Paul pulls out all the stops, using a word found nowhere else in the New Testament, as he says literally, "Therefore God *super-exalted* him" (v. 9a). Christ received the highest exaltation. This is incomprehensible. It is in a class by itself.

The awesome retrospect is that Christ's humiliation eventuated in his resurrection, his ascension, and now his super-exaltation and rule as he reigns forever. This is theological-historical fact.

His Name

The parallel and complementary component of Christ's super-exaltation is that he now has a new name because God has "bestowed on him the name that is above every name" (v. 9b). As we know, Christ Jesus has a lot of names. To highlight a few, he is called Immanuel, Wonderful Counselor, Prince of Peace, the Almighty, Ancient of Days, the Door, the Chief Shepherd, the Good Shepherd, the Great Shepherd, the Word, the Light, the Lamb, the Bread of Life, the Rock, the Bridegroom, and the Alpha and Omega.[1] So what, then, is the mysterious name in Philippians 2?

The clue lies in the fact that it is "above every name." It is greater than any other name conferred on Jesus. In fact, it is God's own name *kyrios* (Lord), which was used in the Greek Old Testament to represent Yahweh, the personal name of the God of Israel.[2] The name given to Jesus that is above every name is indeed Yahweh, God's name, which fills so much of the Old Testament. How can we be sure? Verse 11 identifies Jesus as "Lord" (*kyrios*), Yahweh[3]—"every tongue [will] confess that Jesus Christ is Lord, to the glory of God the Father." Giving Jesus the name "Lord" (Yahweh) is the ultimate of all honors because God says in Isaiah 42:8, "I am the LORD [Yahweh]; that is my name." It is no one else's name. Yahweh is the name that trumps all other titles—the awesome covenant name of the God of Israel—"the name that is above every name."

Does this suggest that God's Son, who is coeternal and coequal with the

Father and the Spirit from all eternity, experienced in his incarnation and death an increase in power and authority above that which he had before his humiliation? Absolutely not. Nothing could be higher than his being in "the form of God" (v. 6) and sharing "equality with God" (v. 6). Therefore the terms "super-exalted" and "the name that is above every name" must be understood as referring "to a position of recognizable superiority over all creation" and that Jesus' "resurrection and ascension to the Father's right hand make his superiority more fully evident to the creation over which he rules" (Thielman).[4] Jesus' super-exaltation and surpassing new name were a gain in *official* glory, not in *essential* glory.[5] The fact is, before his ascension Jesus gathered his disciples together and said, "All authority in heaven and on earth has been given to me" (Matthew 28:18).

What a moment it must have been those 2,000 years ago when Jesus entered Heaven and Paradise—to super-exaltation and a new name!

God's Future Exaltation of Christ (vv. 10, 11)

As wondrous as Christ's past and present exaltation is, the Father of glory has ordained further future exaltation for his Son—"so that at the name of Jesus every knee should bow, in heaven and on earth and under the earth, and every tongue confess that Jesus Christ is Lord, to the glory of God the Father" (vv. 10, 11). The scope and force of this declaration come from its being an echo of Isaiah 45:23, which is Yahweh's declaration that all will worship him: "By myself I have sworn; from my mouth has gone out in righteousness a word that shall not return: 'To me every knee shall bow, every tongue shall swear allegiance.'" Here in Philippians 2:10, 11 Paul applies this to Jesus.

As to how dynamic Paul's application is, we must understand that the forty-fifth chapter of Isaiah is the Old Testament's most forthright and force-ful statement of God's sovereign rule in history and salvation. Four times in Isaiah 45 the Lord declares his absolute sovereignty. Three times he says, "I am the LORD [Yahweh], and there is no other" (vv. 5, 6, 18), and once he says, "For I am God (*El*), and there is no other" (v. 22). And it is with this fourth declaration of sovereignty that we have Yahweh's call for utter allegiance: "Turn to me and be saved, all the ends of the earth! For I am God, and there is no other. By myself I have sworn; from my mouth has gone out in righteous-ness a word that shall not return: 'To me every knee shall bow, every tongue shall swear allegiance'" (vv. 22, 23).

Thus we can't miss Paul's connection: Jesus is the "LORD" (Yahweh) of Isa-iah 45, and because Yahweh is his "name that is above every name," "at the name of Jesus every knee [will] bow, in heaven and on earth and under the earth, and every tongue confess that Jesus Christ is Lord [Yahweh], to the glory of God the Father" (Philippians 2:10, 11). What a dazzling revelation! And what an answer to the liberal theologians of the late nineteenth and early twentieth centuries who rejected the God of the Old Testament in preference for the God of the New Testament. Paul teaches us that Jesus is the sovereign God of *both* Testaments!

Every Knee

"Every knee . . . in heaven and on earth and under the earth" refers to every rational being in the universe. "In heaven" signifies angelic beings. "On earth" designates earthly inhabitants, human beings. And "under the earth" refers to dead human beings and fallen spirits. No knee in the universe is excluded, be it human, angelic, or demonic. This means that some will bow with spontaneous ecstasy, and others with grudging mourning and shame.

The certainty of this was sealed with Yahweh's oath in Isaiah 45:23: "By myself I have sworn; from my mouth has gone out in righteousness a word that shall not return: 'To me every knee shall bow, every tongue shall swear allegiance.'" So, regardless of your spiritual state, regardless of your will, however steely and proud it may be, you will bow your knee to Jesus. The only question is, when? How much better to do it now!

Every Tongue

Confession with the tongue is the spoken counterpart to bowing the knee. So Paul concludes, "and every tongue confess that Jesus Christ is Lord, to the glory of God the Father" (v. 11). Remarkably, the threefold declaration "Jesus Christ is Lord" is apostolic shorthand for the gospel (cf. 2 Corinthians 4:5; cf. Romans 10:9).

First, "*Jesus*" (meaning "the Lord saves"), the name given to the Son of God at his incarnation, signifies that the Lord's salvation came when Jesus was born. This is why Simeon swept baby Jesus into his arms and declared, "Lord, now you are letting your servant depart in peace, according to your word; for my eyes have seen your salvation" (Luke 2:29, 30). Second, the title "*Christ*" (meaning "the Anointed," "the Messiah") speaks of his being the fulfillment of Old Testament prophecy—"that Christ died for our sins in accordance with the Scriptures, that he was buried, that he was raised on the third day in accordance with the Scriptures" (1 Corinthians 15:3, 4). Third, "*Lord*" is here understood to represent the divine name Yahweh, which is a public declaration of his sovereignty—"I am the LORD, and there is no other" (Isaiah 45:5, 6, 18; cf. 45:14, 22).[6]

This gospel triad, "Jesus Christ is Lord," is what we confess today when we gather for worship and confession. That is a shadow and anticipation of what will be ultimately offered by all the universe. Soon every tongue of every rational being in all creation will confess that Jesus Messiah is Yahweh! Every believing heart will cry it at the top of its lungs in voice and song, and we, with the angels, will do it over and over for all eternity. Every unbelieving heart will confess it too, in dismal submission and despair. Even Satan will do it. His knee and his tongue will not be excluded. Every fallen spirit will do it. Legion upon legion will do it. Caiaphas will confess that Jesus Messiah is Yahweh. Herod will do it. Pilate will do it. Nero will confess that Jesus Christ is Lord. Hitler will do it. Stalin will do it. Every soul from every age will confess that Jesus Messiah is Yahweh.

And this lordship of Christ Jesus will all be "to the glory of God the Father." Jesus' sovereign lordship was the Father's plan from the beginning. He super-exalted his Son and conferred upon him his own incomparable name. Jesus' lordship reveals God's glory as eternal Father, the Father of Christ.[7]

What are we to make of this astonishing Christology, this elegant nuanced theology of Christ?

Obviously it is meant to help us understand, in broad contours, Christ's self-humiliation and then his super-exaltation by God the Father. We are to understand that Jesus' self-humiliation began in Heaven when he "did not count equality with God a thing to be grasped" (v. 6). Then his self-humiliation moved further downward in his incarnation when he emptied himself by becoming a man and a servant. His self-humiliation reached the lowest point possible when he became obedient to death on the cross, a scandalous death.

Christ's self-humiliation was followed by his divine exaltation when God the Father super-exalted him to incomparable heights where he continues to reign, bearing the Father's own name that is above every name—Yahweh, Lord! Furthermore, there is a time yet coming when every knee of every rational being in the universe will bow, and every tongue will confess that Jesus Messiah is Yahweh to the glory of God the Father. It is important that these contours cycle and recycle through our minds, so that they become part of our perpetual regard of Christ.

But even more, it is of eternal importance that we believe them with all of our hearts. These thoughts are not the wild notions of Paul's rabbinic imagination, nor are they the playground of theologians. This is what Christ Jesus truly did for you and me. His self-humiliation really did happen—only it was far more wrenching then we can imagine. And likewise his super-exaltation is beyond wonder. Yet all of this is true and demands our belief. We must not simply think that we believe it. We must in fact believe it! Why? Because what we believe about Christ is the most important thing about us, and because what we believe about him determines the way in which we live. Do you believe what Paul teaches about Christ in Philippians 2:5–11?

This said, there is something else—Paul gave this stunning example of Christ's humiliation and exaltation to motivate the Philippian church to "do nothing from selfish ambition or conceit, but in humility count others more significant than yourselves. Let each of you look not only to his own interests, but also to the interests of others" (vv. 3, 4). In fact, this concern extends to later in the chapter where Paul remarks about Timothy, "For I have no one like him, who will be genuinely concerned for your welfare. For they all seek their own interests, not those of Jesus Christ" (vv. 20, 21). So we must understand that counting others as more significant than ourselves and looking out for the interests of others is directly related to what we understand about Christ and what we believe he did. We are, in fact, commanded to have the mind among ourselves that is in Christ Jesus (cf. v. 5).

Others first is both a sign that the gospel is well among us and a necessity for the health of the church. Others-directedness encapsulates the role of a good husband as defined in Ephesians 5. He counts his wife as more significant than himself and looks out for her interests before his. In fact, he dies for her and loves her flesh like he loves his own body. His soul is a thermometer monitoring the Fahrenheit of her soul. Others-directedness practically defines the role of parent, producing protective fathers and nurturing mothers who regard their children as more important than themselves.

In the church, others first effectively defines the role of pastors and elders. As Peter describes it:

> So I exhort the elders among you, as a fellow elder and a witness of the sufferings of Christ, as well as a partaker in the glory that is going to be revealed: shepherd the flock of God that is among you, exercising oversight, not under compulsion, but willingly, as God would have you; not for shameful gain, but eagerly; not domineering over those in your charge, but being examples to the flock. (1 Peter 5:1–3; cf. 1 Timothy 3:1–7; Titus 1:5–16)

Others-directedness is meant to characterize the exchange within the Body of Christ between brothers and sisters. We really are to regard each other as more important than ourselves. We really are to look out for the interests of others.

And we can do that because we have the example of Christ, who really did it. And we have his mind.

Therefore, my beloved, as you have always obeyed, so now, not only as in my presence but much more in my absence, work out your own salvation with fear and trembling, for it is God who works in you, both to will and to work for his good pleasure. Do all things without grumbling or disputing, that you may be blameless and innocent, children of God without blemish in the midst of a crooked and twisted generation, among whom you shine as lights in the world, holding fast to the word of life, so that in the day of Christ I may be proud that I did not run in vain or labor in vain. Even if I am to be poured out as a drink offering upon the sacrificial offering of your faith, I am glad and rejoice with you all. Likewise you also should be glad and rejoice with me.

2:12–18

11

On Common Salvation

PHILIPPIANS 2:12–18

THE DOWNWARD COMPRESSION OF Christ's self-humiliation followed by the explosive upward vault of his super-exaltation demands our awed contemplation. We do our souls well to meditate upon the measured descent of his downward steps: his humility in Heaven, his humiliation in the incarnation, and his humiliation in death. Our Savior really did this. He was not playacting. Nothing could be lower than his "death, even death on a cross" (v. 8b).

We will do our souls yet more good by contemplating his present super-exaltation, wherein he has been given the name Lord (Yahweh), a "name that is above every name" (v. 9), which will eventuate in his future exaltation when, at the name of Jesus, every knee in the universe will bow "and every tongue confess that Jesus Christ is Lord, to the glory of God the Father" (v. 11b). We will all be there (no exceptions!), and we will join every intelligent being in the universe in the full confession and contemplation that Jesus is Christ (Messiah) and the Lord (Yahweh). What a grace it is to be able to contemplate this even now as believers.

The grandeur of all of this is stunning. And knowing how Paul often follows theology with doxology, we might expect a song of praise or a glorious benediction. But not this time, because Paul has raised this high Christology with an eye to ground-level practicality, as is evidenced by the immediate "Therefore" of verse 12 that references everything that preceded in chapter 2. In effect Paul says, "You have heard me call you to humbly count others more important than yourselves and to look out for the interests of others (cf. vv. 3, 4). You have just heard me describe the example of the one who lived this out in his humiliation and the divine approval in his exaltation (cf. vv. 5–11). Now I am going to give you more explicit directives as to how you must live—'work out your own salvation with fear and trembling, for it is God who works in you, both to will and to work for his good pleasure' (vv. 12b, 13)."

Work Out Your Common Salvation (vv. 12, 13)

From boyhood this has been one of my favorite Scriptures, which I mentally filed alongside the encouraging words of Philippians 1:6, "And I am sure of this, that he who began a good work in you will bring it to completion at the day of Jesus Christ." In 1:6 I found confidence in God's work in my individual life, and here in 2:12, 13 I was powerfully challenged to give close attention to my personal conduct as I lived out my salvation in Christ.

I have also experienced much good from these texts together. From boyhood I have rightly believed that God would complete his work of grace in my life. And from boyhood I have believed that I must carefully work out my own salvation. Further, I have correctly understood that this was not a matter of synergism between me and God, in which he did his part and I did mine, and together we saved me! I clearly understood that everything was and is from God.

But what I did not see through my highly individualized lens is that this text with its command "work out your own salvation with fear and trembling" (v. 12) does not refer primarily to the salvation of individual believers but to working out our salvation within the church, the Body of Christ. The application of this text is first *corporate* (how the church must conduct itself) and then *individual*. This is a *both/and* text that focuses first on the communal conduct of the church, which, of course, includes individual behavior. The challenge to "work out your own salvation" to the Philippians was both to all of them as a body and to each of them as its members.

Our Work

That Paul's appeal is to the community of faith in Philippi is evident in his opening words: "Therefore, my beloved, as you have always obeyed . . ." (v. 12). The beloved Philippians, in fact, had been in the fellowship of the gospel from the initial day of their salvation to the present (cf. 1:5). And their obedience was not to Paul but to Christ and the gospel. It was "the obedience of faith," as Paul calls it in Romans, which comes from the gospel (see 1:5; 16:26; cf. 15:18).[1] Paul's beloved Philippians had a long history of obedience to Christ and the gospel. And now that some problems had arisen, he urged them to demonstrate their Christian obedience even more in his absence by working out their own salvation with fear and trembling as they attended to the problems.

Their attention to difficulties within the body was to be a matter of great reverence. Christ's super-exaltation meant that they, along with the whole universe, will one day not only confess him but give account for their conduct. Clearly, the responsibilities of Christian obedience and membership in Christ's body are not casual matters. The very sound of the Greek words for "fear and trembling" (*phobos* and *tromos*) are evocative of the tremulous awe that God demands as the church works out its own salvation.

God's Work

But as awesome as our call to work out our own salvation is, we are not left to our own devices, "for it is God who works in you, both to will and to work for his good pleasure" (v. 13). We know from common experience that there are two aspects to every conscious action: the hidden *will* and the outward *work*. But God does more than merely strengthen our willing and doing. Paul's explanation goes deeper. "God himself is working in us both to will and to act: he works in us at the level of our wills and at the level of our doing" (Carson).[2] God works *in* us, not merely *with* us. Again, the thought of synergism (my work plus God's work gets it done) shrinks the scope of what God actually does within us. The suggestion of synergism in this text is theologically absurd.

Pascal's approving quotation of Augustine will help our thinking along. Augustine wrote, "Our deeds are our own, because of the free will producing them, and they are also God's, because of his grace causing our free will to produce them." And he says elsewhere, "God makes us do what he pleases by making us desire what we might not desire."[3] The work that God does in us "both *to will* and *to work* for his good pleasure" is expansive and complete. Further, his "good pleasure" is, by virtue of his love for us, our great good. And here, in respect to the Philippian church, what pleases God is an end to the dissensions among them.

Paul's magnificent "therefore" sentence of verses 12, 13 is meant to be sweetly motivational: "Therefore, my beloved, as you have always obeyed, so now, not only as in my presence but much more in my absence, work out your own salvation with fear and trembling, for it is God who works in you, both to will and to work for his good pleasure." What an incentive this was to this beloved church to carry on.

How to Work Out Your Common Salvation (vv. 14–18)

Paul cuts to the chase with a second command that tells the Philippians in no uncertain terms what is crucial to their obedience in working out their own salvation: "Do all things without grumbling or disputing" (v. 14).

Don't Be Complainers

Paul's mention of murmuring and questioning conjures up the pathetic grousing and whining of ancient Israel in the wilderness (cf. Exodus 16:12). And his words are intentionally vivid. "Grumbling" (*goggusmon*) is an onomatopoeic word that sounds like what it means (you can hear the muffled complaints in the repetition of this word), and "disputing" (*dialogismon*) evokes to our English-speaking ears the petty dialoguing that calls everything into question. This is not a pretty picture. Moreover, the allusion to the wilderness episode tells us that the complaints were by and large toward the leadership. This may be why "overseers" and "deacons" are "mysteriously singled out" in Paul's introduction to the letter (cf. 1:1).[4] Perhaps such criticisms were the animus of the conflict between Euodia and Syntyche (cf. 4:2).

In any event, as Markus Bockmuehl astutely says, "These things, then, are not minor blemishes of morality, peripheral human weaknesses in an otherwise flawless Christian spectacle. Instead, they are part of what marks the watershed of the Christian life."[5]

Critical, complaining spirits are the historic bane of the church from Philippi to Peoria, Illinois to Philadelphia. They are found in every culture, like the nineteenth-century Scots who went to church to see if the gospel *was* preached. Or today's McChurch worshippers who leave their church to go down the street to find a church more to their liking.

If we are reading Paul correctly, "do[ing] all things without grumbling or disputing" is a watershed state of the soul. Those who persist in such murmuring are not obedient to Christ and his gospel and are rejecting the divine call to "work out your own salvation" (v. 12). They impede their own souls and the souls of their brothers and sisters in this matter. They are undertows to the Body of Christ. So if you are one of these people, understand that when you finally stand before your Savior, you will answer with shame.

Paul sees the New Testament church as the people of the new exodus who have been delivered from a spiritual Egypt by the blood of Christ, the Passover Lamb, and who are now on their way home to the ultimate promised land. And he wants us to get it right.[6]

Be Examples

If they get it right (by putting away their "grumbling" and "disputing"), they will become examples to the pagan culture of Philippi, and even to the world. Paul's full thought is, "Do all things without grumbling or disputing, that you may be blameless and innocent, children of God without blemish in the midst of a crooked and twisted generation, among whom you shine as lights in the world, holding fast to the word of life" (vv. 14–16a). The self-conscious, "wannabe" Roman culture of Philippi that gave devotion to Caesar as "Lord" was "crooked and twisted" indeed. The church's declaration that Jesus is Messiah and Yahweh was blasphemous to the imperial cult. Such twisted perversity! Yet amidst this perversity (if the Philippians repented of their grousing and murmuring), the church would be blameless and innocent toward God, and their kind conduct with one another as brothers and sisters would demonstrate that they were children of God to that "twisted" culture.

The sentence continues, "among whom you shine as lights in the world, holding fast to the word of life" (vv. 15b, 16a). This is an allusion to Daniel 12:3, which describes the resurrection age when "those who are wise shall shine like the brightness of the sky above; and those who turn many to righteousness, like the stars forever and ever." Thus Christians who live in humble harmony as they should, considering others more important than themselves, shine resurrection light in a dark world, especially as they are "holding fast to the word of life," the gospel of Christ.[7]

We are prone to think that the way we relate to our brothers and sisters in Christ is a matter of indifference and that we are entitled to a little grouchiness, *goggusmon*. Even more, we can convince ourselves that a critical spirit is a virtue. We have probably all met someone who claimed to have the gift of criticism. "After all, someone needs to have the courage to say what *I know* everyone is thinking. Besides, a little disdain for others will be good for them. We wouldn't want them to think too highly of themselves, would we? Some 'healthy' grumbling and questioning will help this ship sail right." But that is not what Paul says. In fact, such conduct impedes the working out of salvation in the church. In fact, it can ruin one's own soul or the soul of another in the church. It can make the church the cultural joke of "a crooked and twisted generation."

Our conduct in the church must be a matter of *phobos* and *tromos*—"fear and trembling." Jesus, who was obedient unto death (v. 8), bids us through Paul, "Therefore, my beloved, as you have always obeyed . . . work out your own salvation with fear and trembling, for it is God who works in you, both to will and to work for his good pleasure" (vv. 12, 13).

Be Positive and Joyous

Paul's next comment, which finishes his sentence, is surprising because it seems out of sync as he injects a personal note: "so that in the day of Christ I may be proud that I did not run in vain or labor in vain" (v. 16b). Gordon Fee remarks, "Most likely the sentence has gotten away from him a bit, and this final phrase is to be understood primarily in response to their 'shining as lights in the world as they hold firm the word of life.'"[8] However that may be, Paul tied the effectiveness of his apostolic ministry (as to whether it was "in vain") to the way those in the church in Philippi lived out their calling with one another. And this reference to "the day of Christ" moved him to thoughts of joy.

Paul's Joy

The apostle twice sounds the note of joy in verse 17: "Even if I am to be poured out as a drink offering upon the sacrificial offering of your faith, I am glad and rejoice with you all." The sacrificial image Paul evokes was common practice in both pagan and Jewish sacrifices. A priest would offer a sacrifice and then later pour out a sacrificial libation to complement it. So Paul saw the Philippians as priests offering a sacrificial offering of faith, followed by his pouring his own libation over it. Was Paul referring to his death? We do not know. But what is clear is that he viewed his service as a complement or contribution to their service. Paul's Christlike humility flashed bright here because he viewed himself as a complement to their sacrifice and not vice versa.[9] At this thought his joy peaked. Literally he said, "I rejoice and co-rejoice with you all."

The Philippians' Joy

Paul invites them to join his double-dose of joy with a double-dip of their own: "Likewise you also should be glad and rejoice with me" (v. 18).

The joy note sounds four times in the space of these two verses, and that is very significant. Up to now all mentions of joy (except 1:25) have referenced Paul's joy (cf. 1:4, 18 [twice]; 2:2, 17 [twice]).

But now with this imperative to rejoice, a shift takes place, and their joy will be commanded three times more (cf. 3:1; 4:4 [twice]). Also, this first imperative was totally meshed with Paul's joy and was a command to rejoice in the midst of suffering.[10] What we have here is a partaking of the fellowship of the gospel at its deepest level (cf. 1:5, 7)—a fellowship rooted in the three-way bond of Paul, Christ, and the Philippians.

In fact, the driving theological reality is Christ himself, whose self-humiliation (vv. 6–8) and super-exaltation (vv. 9–11) are the ground of assurance of future victory and the motivating example to "work out your own salvation with fear and trembling, for it is God who works in you, both to will and to work for his good pleasure" (vv. 12, 13).

I hope in the Lord Jesus to send Timothy to you soon, so that I too may be cheered by news of you. For I have no one like him, who will be genuinely concerned for your welfare. For they all seek their own interests, not those of Jesus Christ. But you know Timothy's proven worth, how as a son with a father he has served with me in the gospel. I hope therefore to send him just as soon as I see how it will go with me, and I trust in the Lord that shortly I myself will come also.

2:19–24

12

Timothy: One Who Seeks Others' Interests

PHILIPPIANS 2:19-24

ANTHONY TROLLOPE'S *Barchester Towers*, a novel about the mid-nineteenth-century Church of England, ends with a concluding word about the Reverend Mr. Harding, the humble pastor of the tiny church of St. Cuthbert. Trollope writes:

> The Author now leaves him in the hands of his readers; not as a hero, not as a man to be admired and talked of, not as a man who should be toasted at public dinners and spoken of with conventional absurdity as a perfect divine, but as a good man without guile, believing humbly in the religion which he has striven to teach, and guided by the precepts which he has striven to learn.[1]

This is a fitting tribute to the humble, selfless man of God that Trollope created in Mr. Harding, and in anticipation of the text before us, it makes a fitting tribute to Paul's humble disciple Timothy—with the exception that Timothy *is* "a man to be admired and talked of," as we shall see.

The Apostle Paul's brief references to Timothy and then Epaphroditus here in Philippians are not casual but rather are meant to capture our attention and top off Paul's train of thought that began in 1:27 with the charge, "Only let your manner of life [as citizens of the kingdom] be worthy of the gospel of Christ."

Paul's thought goes like this: In 1:27–30 he instructs the Philippians on how to live lives worthy of the gospel in relation to the surrounding pagan world—namely, by "standing firm in one spirit, with one mind striving side by side for the faith of the gospel" (v. 27). In doing this Paul tells them not to be "frightened in anything" (v. 28) and that it has been granted them to "not only believe in him but also suffer for his sake" (v. 29). This is the face and disposition with which the Philippians are to live in this world.

Next, in 2:1–4, Paul tells the Philippians how to live lives worthy of the gospel within the fellowship of the church. Very specifically, they were to treat each other with selfless humility: "Do nothing from selfish ambition or conceit, but in humility count others more significant than yourselves. Let each of you look not only to his own interests, but also to the interests of others" (vv. 3, 4).

Paul viewed all of this as so vital that in 2:5–11 he reached for the ultimate example of Christ, saying "Have this mind among yourselves, which is yours in Christ Jesus," and used the most exalted language to describe Christ's astonishing self-humiliation and super-exaltation (vv. 6–11).

Then, in verses 12–18, on the basis of Christ's example Paul again refocused his call for the church to walk worthy of the gospel of Christ: "work out your own salvation with fear and trembling, for it is God who works in you, both to will and to work for his good pleasure" (vv. 12, 13). If the church does this, its people will shine as lights amidst a crooked and twisted generation as they hold fast to the gospel. This will be cause for multiple and mutual rejoicings!

Now in verses 19–30 Paul gives flesh-and-blood examples of the selfless conduct to which he is calling the Philippian church. Here are men who live lives "worthy of the gospel of Christ" (1:27).

Travel Plans

Paul begins with Timothy: "I hope in the Lord Jesus to send Timothy to you soon, so that I too may be cheered by news of you" (v. 19). Remember, Paul is under arrest in Rome. And as always with Paul, there is no presumption in his planning as he hopes "in the Lord Jesus" to send Timothy their way. This is not a glib cliché. This is the way Paul lived, as other outtakes from his letters make clear: "if the Lord wills" (1 Corinthians 4:19) and "if the Lord permits" (1 Corinthians 16:7)—Deo volenti.

Paul bows to God's will, but at the same time he longs for Timothy to make that round-trip to Philippi and back to Rome because he felt sure that cheerful, heartening news would be coming from Philippi as the Philippians read his letter and took it to heart. Paul deeply loved this little church, as he said in the introduction of this letter: "I hold you in my heart . . . how I yearn for you all with the affection of Christ Jesus" (cf. 1:7, 8). As a result Paul had hitched his emotions to the ups and downs of the church. Certainly the apostle was a happy man, but his was not an unclouded happiness. The ministry brought new joys, but with those joys there were also new sorrows. As he had earlier written to the Corinthians, "And, apart from other things, there is the daily pressure on me of my anxiety for all the churches. Who is weak, and I am not weak? Who is made to fall, and I am not indignant?" (2 Corinthians 11:28, 29). Similarly, he wrote to the Thessalonians, "when I could bear it no longer, I sent to learn about your faith, for fear that somehow the tempter had tempted you and our labor would be in vain" (1 Thessalonians 3:5). Paul's heart rose and fell with his people. His greatest pains were heart pains over his people. But his greatest joys were heart palpitations over their advances. Paul anticipated that news from the Philippians would do his heart good.

Oh, that we would have such vulnerable hearts, that our emotions would be tied to the health of the church and the advance of the gospel. Modern culture isn't disposed this way. The cultural ideal is to make a place for yourself away from the ups and downs of life—a kind of Buddhist retreat. Our modern method is to do this through wealth, environment, and technology—plastic insulations. But that is not what God calls us to. The Christian life is meant to be a life of passion and commitment and vulnerability. The detached, benign smile is not divine; it is the face of false religion. The face of Christ is his visage on the cross and his radiant resurrection countenance. His smile is that of shalom amidst the storms of life. Tears and laughter are the divine meter.

Timothy's Caring Heart (vv. 20, 21)

At the moment of Paul's writing, the condition of the Roman church was bleak—even shocking—because young Timothy stood alone in Rome in his commitments.

Self-Centered Romans

The Roman church was afflicted with a pathetic self-centeredness, as is so clear from Paul's sad report: "For I have no one like him, who will be genuinely concerned for your welfare. For they all seek their own interests, not those of Jesus Christ" (vv. 20, 21). Literally Paul said, "I have no one equal in soul." As he spiritually surveyed the Christian community in Rome, Paul could not find anyone whom he deemed of like soul or mind.[2]

This seems an astonishing statement, but the rest of what Paul said will make it clear. Paul's assessment was that there was no one like Timothy, "who will be genuinely concerned for your welfare"—that is, one who, when he arrived on the scene in Philippi, would give the active interest and practical care that Paul desired be shown[3]—the kind of care he himself would give. But Timothy would prove to be the genuine article.

Ironically, the very self-centeredness that Paul had just warned the Philippians about in 2:4 ("Let each of you look not only to his own interests, but also to the interests of others") was part of everyday life in Rome—"For they all seek their own interests, not those of Jesus Christ" (v. 21). Paul has already told us that even while he was under arrest in Rome, "Some indeed preach Christ from envy and rivalry" (1:15; cf. v. 17). Thus many of the capable preachers in Rome were infused with a mean-spirited, selfish ambition. Certainly there were good Christians in Rome because once the others heard of Paul's plight, "most of the brothers, having become confident in the Lord by my imprisonment, are much more bold to speak the word without fear" (1:14).

What self-centered individuals was Paul referring to? Certainly not Epaphroditus, who had almost died in serving the gospel and was going to carry the letter back to Philippi. And certainly not the women in the Roman church because they were not candidates to make the dangerous trip to encourage the Philippians. And for similar reasons Paul's indictment did not apply to elderly men or the infirm.

Those whom Paul indicted were the able-bodied men in the church who had no concern about the church in Philippi or about the interests of Christ in the spread of the gospel. In a word, the able-bodied Christian men of Rome were infused with self and selfishness. Evidently the real men like Luke and Aristarchus were out of town, leaving only young Timothy to be the man. But how he shined!

Selfless Timothy

Paul knew that Timothy's concern for the welfare of the Philippians would be so genuine that when Timothy arrived in Philippi, his concern would look very much like "worry" because that is how the word "concerned" (v. 20) is often translated. Put positively, he would be wonderfully anxious about the Philippians' welfare.[4] Such godly, transparent interest in the welfare of others is a thing of beauty. It is said that when Henrietta Mears, one of the most effective American Christians of the twentieth century, would walk into a room, each person often had the feeling that she was saying to him or her, "Where have you been? I've been looking all over for you."[5] Miss Mears's genuine concern for others marked and elevated a whole generation of remarkable leaders.

Timothy had learned the art of putting others before himself. In a bygone day when a prominent soldier was returning from foreign duty, a newly hired driver was sent to the station to pick him up. When he asked how he would recognize the soldier, the soldier's aged mother said, "Look for somebody helping someone else." And sure enough, when the train pulled in, the driver saw a man assisting an old woman, and it was the soldier![6] So it was with Timothy.

Timothy was the only one left with Paul in Rome who was free enough from his own self-interests to devote himself to the welfare of others. May we, like Timothy, rise above the tow of our culture, even our "Christian culture." Lesslie Newbigin, theologian and missiologist, writes:

> I suddenly saw that someone could use all the language of evangelical Christianity, and yet the center was fundamentally the self, my need of salvation. And God is auxiliary to that. . . . I also saw that quite a lot of evangelical Christianity can easily slip, can become centered in me and my need of salvation, and not in the glory of God.[7]

What a strange irony—that the gospel could become the occasion for a profound self-absorption. We do live in an age of unprecedented self, of weightless souls consumed with their own gravity. And today many Christians actually believe that it is "Christian" to pursue self-fulfillment as an ultimate goal in life. I have witnessed this several times when I have sat listening to a preacher offer up the common bromide, "We cannot love others until we love ourselves" and have seen the congregation nod and murmur assent while I am inwardly saying, "Not!" What un-Biblical foolishness!

But Timothy's example trumps such self-delusion. As Dietrich Bonhoeffer writes:

> We must be ready to allow ourselves to be interrupted by God. God will be constantly crossing our paths and canceling our plans by sending us people with claims and petitions. We may pass them by, preoccupied with our more important tasks, as the priest passed by the man who had fallen among thieves, perhaps reading the Bible. When we do that, we pass by the visible sign of the Cross raised [in] our path to show us that, not our way, but God's way must be done. It is a strange fact that Christians frequently consider their work so important and urgent that they will allow nothing to disturb them. They think they are doing God a service in this, but actually they are disdaining God's "crooked yet straight path" (Gottfried Arnold). They do not want a life that is crossed and balked. But it is part of the discipline of humility that we must not spare our hand where it can perform a service and that we do not assume that our schedule is our own to manage, but allow it to be arranged by God.[8]

Timothy's Excellence of Character (v. 22)

Along with Timothy's caring heart, the second and parallel reason for Paul's dispatching Timothy to Philippi was his excellence of character.

His Worth

The Philippians were well aware of Timothy's character. Paul reminds them, "But you know Timothy's proven worth" (v. 22a). Timothy was there when Lydia, a seller of purple, became the first convert on the soil of Europe. He had witnessed the baptism of her and her entire household. Perhaps he assisted in the ceremony in the Gangetes (cf. Acts 16:11–15). Timothy had served as Paul's envoy to Macedonia a decade earlier (cf. 1 Thessalonians 3:2; Acts 17:14; 18:5; 19:22), to Corinth on several occasions (cf. 1 Corinthians 4:17; 16:10), and also to Ephesus (cf. 1 Timothy 1:2ff.).[9] Timothy had proven his mettle.

His Devotion

Furthermore, his devotion to the Apostle Paul was remarkable: "as a son with a father he has served with me in the gospel" (v. 22b). Paul was Timothy's spiritual father because Timothy, like so many others, had come to Christ under Paul's ministry.

But that was not Paul's point here. Rather, it was their father-son friendship. Stephen Ambrose, in his best-selling book *Comrades*, describes friendship:

> Friends never cheat each other, or take advantage, or lie. Friends do not spy on one another, yet they have no secrets. Friends glory in each other's successes and are downcast by the failures. Friends minister to each other, nurse each other. Friends give to each other, worry about each other, stand always ready to help. Perfect friendship is rarely achieved, but at its height it is an ecstasy.[10]

It certainly was that for Paul and Timothy. Their friendship had grown over the years on the ancient apprenticeship model. Timothy had learned by observing, listening to instruction, and doing. They had endured tumultuous times together, and young Timothy was ever the learner. The depth of their friendship is seen in the Pastoral Epistles, where Paul twice called Timothy "my child" (cf. 1 Timothy 1:18; 2 Timothy 2:1). Now Paul trusted Timothy to act just as he would.

But most of all, in Timothy's serving with Paul in the gospel, Timothy followed the servant role of Jesus, who "emptied himself, by taking the form of a servant" (Philippians 2:7). Timothy had followed the model of Christ.

Paul wanted the Philippians to observe, when Timothy came, a selfless, flesh-and-blood example of one who lives a life "worthy of the gospel of Christ" (1:27). Timid by nature, Timothy had stood firm in one spirit with Paul and the Philippians, fearlessly striving side by side for the gospel (1:27). He had set aside rivalry and conceit and counted others more significant than himself, while looking out for the interests of others. He had put on the mind of Christ. He had put on the towel of Christ. He had devoted his life to the church as the place to work out his and his fellow believers' salvation with fear and trembling. He had long put away grumbling and disputing. And he shined as a light in the dark world. Timothy effervesced with apostolic joy.

The apostle placed all his confidence in Timothy's caring *heart* and excellence of *character*. Timothy's life said to the Philippians and to us that we too, by God's grace, can live lives that are worthy of the gospel as citizens of the kingdom.

The sacred author now left Timothy in the hands of his readers as a hero, as a man to be admired and talked of, a good man without guile, believing humbly in the faith he had labored to teach, and guided by the precepts he sought to learn from his apostle-father.

I have thought it necessary to send to you Epaphroditus my brother and fellow worker and fellow soldier, and your messenger and minister to my need, for he has been longing for you all and has been distressed because you heard that he was ill. Indeed he was ill, near to death. But God had mercy on him, and not only on him but on me also, lest I should have sorrow upon sorrow. I am the more eager to send him, therefore, that you may rejoice at seeing him again, and that I may be less anxious. So receive him in the Lord with all joy, and honor such men, for he nearly died for the work of Christ, risking his life to complete what was lacking in your service to me.

2:25–30

13

A Man to Honor

PHILIPPIANS 2:25–30

AS WE HAVE SEEN, fellowship in the Philippian church was not of the ice cream social variety but was rather the fellowship of people bound together by a great spiritual quest. The Greek root word for *fellowship* occurs six times across the brief chapters of Philippians, rendered variously as "partnership" (twice), "partakers" (once), "participation" (once), and "share" (twice). And each occurrence emphasizes a different aspect of the Philippians' fellowship or participation with one another: 1:5 emphasizes "partnership in the gospel"; 1:7 describes the Philippians as "partakers . . . of grace"; 2:1 lists their "participation in the Spirit"; 3:10 records Paul's desire to "share" in Christ's sufferings; and 4:14, 15 employ the words "share" and "partnership" to stress fellowship in giving—"Yet it was kind of you to share my trouble. And you Philippians yourselves know that in the beginning of the gospel, when I left Macedonia, no church entered into partnership with me in giving and receiving, except you only" (4:14, 15). So fellowship involved participation in the gospel and grace and the Spirit and suffering and giving. In 2:25–30 we learn that the Philippians had decided to express and confirm their fellowship with Paul by taking up an offering for him and dispatching an envoy to make the 800-mile trek to Rome and pay Paul's prison expenses and minister to his needs. This was crucial because the Roman prison system didn't provide for food, clothing, or medical care.

So young, strong, healthy, godly Epaphroditus was chosen and was entrusted with a considerable sum of money. This meant that he was not traveling alone when he fell ill because Paul had established apostolic precedent in sending large gifts by group (cf. 2 Corinthians 8:16–22). The most likely scenario, therefore, is that when Epaphroditus fell ill, one of his traveling companions (or an acquaintance passing the other way) returned to Philippi with the alarming news, while another, or others, stayed with Epaphroditus and nursed him along so that he finally made it to Rome, very much worse for the wear.[1] But ever-faithful Epaphroditus delivered the goods and set himself, as he was able, to caring for Paul as the Philippians' surrogate.

However, it wasn't long until Paul decided that the young man should return to Philippi for reasons that the apostle would later explain. What is at once apparent from what Paul says here is that he was concerned that the Philippians give the young man a proper welcome. It was very possible that the little church's preoccupation with surviving in Philippi's obtrusive, oppressive, "little Rome" culture, coupled with their surprise at Epaphroditus' early return and the fact that he didn't remain with Paul as long as they expected, could have worked to make his "welcome" to be little more than a perfunctory acknowledgment of his return, without the church truly engaging him and hearing his story and expressing appreciation.

This is what happened to my generation after the Vietnam War when our men and women returned from an unpopular war that was fought a long way from home. There were no outpourings of public appreciation and no parades because most people wanted to forget. America's corporate amnesia was a sad thing. And it took years for a proper monument to be erected for those who gave everything.[2]

A church (like a culture) that does not recognize the sacrifice of its own for the sake of the gospel makes a big mistake. And the wise apostle simply would not let that happen. Moreover, Epaphroditus' selfless conduct was a living example of the mind of Christ in his serving the interests of others. So in verses 25–28 Paul prepares the way for a proper homecoming upon Epaphroditus' return to Philippi.

Preparing the Way Home (vv. 25–28)

Paul began with an unusually complimentary introductory fanfare. There was no drum roll, but it was definitely *"Here's Epaphroditus!"*: "I have thought it necessary to send to you Epaphroditus my brother and fellow worker and fellow soldier, and your messenger and minister to my need" (v. 25).

His Resumé

Epaphroditus' introductory resumé had five entries, three from Paul and two that referenced the Philippians. Paul called him "my brother and fellow worker and fellow soldier." In a world of imitations, "my brother" referred to the real thing—the theological reality that two who were truly brothers shared the same spiritual bloodline. "My brother" resounded with affection, the love of believer for believer—"my dear brother."

"Fellow worker" is intentionally elevating. Jesus would say of the church in Ephesus, "I know you are enduring patiently and bearing up for my name's sake, and you have not grown weary" (Revelation 2:3), and this was singularly true of Epaphroditus. He worked, but more, he was Paul's "*fellow worker*," the great apostle's coworker. Paul was the public, up-front apostle, and Epaphroditus was the behind-the-scenes servant. Yet the two were equally coworkers—one in work and dignity.

Next, the image that "fellow soldier" evokes lifts Epaphroditus high. Paul says elsewhere, "For we do not wrestle against flesh and blood, but against the rulers, against the authorities, against the cosmic powers over this present darkness, against the spiritual forces of evil in the heavenly places" (Ephesians 6:12). This was the battle. The two fought shoulder-to-shoulder in Rome. Perhaps Paul had in mind the trademark imperial soldiers' battle ethic of standing side by side, dug in with shields locked solid, swords drawn. The truth is, young Epaphroditus was a battle-tested warrior who had been wounded in combat and was being sent home for a rest.[3] This man was no weekend warrior. He had proven himself with distinction.

Beyond that, Epaphroditus had served the Philippians themselves in a twofold manner, as "your messenger and minister to my need" (v. 25b)—two titles of honor that rightfully belonged to the great Apostle Paul himself.[4] "Messenger" is literally "apostle." And though Paul did not use *apostle* here in the full technical sense of one who had seen the resurrection and had a special commission to preach the gospel (cf. Acts 1:21–23; Romans 1:1; 1 Corinthians 15:7), it was, nevertheless, a designation of intended dignity. Likewise, "minister" is also a title of dignity[5] that was evocative of priestly service as Epaphroditus ministered to Paul's needs.[6]

Here's the picture: Epaphroditus was a *layman* whom we would never have heard of were it not for Paul's brief reference here. Epaphroditus served in no public capacity. He did not shepherd a flock, as did Timothy. He did not take the gospel to an unreached area. He did not receive special revelation. And he wrote nothing.[7] All he did was faithfully discharge his duty by delivering a bag of money to Paul and then by looking after him. Yet he is called by Paul "brother . . . fellow worker . . . fellow soldier" and was identified to the Philippians as "apostle" and "minister." We must understand that to serve in some unnoticed, unrecognized place in the Body of Christ is as much the work of Christ as is public ministry. Paul teaches the same thing in

1 Corinthians 12 in his exposition of giftedness. Paul believed this implicitly, and so must we!

Epaphroditus was remarkable. He held himself responsible to God by the same standard of faithfulness that Paul used for himself. No wonder Paul singled the young man out as an example to the church in Philippi, where so many were looking out for themselves rather than others. Epaphroditus had put on the mind of Christ, taking on the humble life of an unsung servant. The Philippians needed to see the young man for the man he was and receive him as such.

His Homesickness

As a further motivation to properly welcome Epaphroditus back, Paul mentions Epaphroditus' homesickness: "for he has been longing for you all and has been distressed because you heard that he was ill" (v. 26). This was not a case of simple longing for a warm bed and some Aegean cuisine. It was a complex tension. Paul had used the same term in the introduction to this letter to describe his own personal longing for the Philippians "with the affection of Christ Jesus" (1:8). But what really distressed Epaphroditus was not the fact that he had been so ill, but the knowledge that news had gotten back to Philippi of how desperately sick he was. He was distressed because he feared they were distressed. This may be difficult to understand in this day of cell phones when while in England I can call a friend and have him answer on his cell as he walks out of a restaurant in France! However, longtime missionary families understand Epaphroditus well and can tell you of quite different days when it took weeks to communicate.

How intensely Epaphroditus mentally suffered is seen in that the only other use of the Greek word here translated "distressed" is used to describe Jesus' anguish in Gethsemane (cf. Mark 14:33).[8] The young man agonized as he imagined the prayers that were being offered for him by his brothers and sisters in the church. Some of them, he knew, had lost sleep over his plight. How he longed for them to know he was okay. What a sympathetic, empathetic soul Epaphroditus was! Again, the young man was like Christ in his lack of self-interest and focus upon others. "You Philippians, receive him properly."

His Illness

If that wasn't enough to convince them to give him a good welcome, Paul adds, "Indeed he was ill, near to death. But God had mercy on him, and not only on him but on me also, lest I should have sorrow upon sorrow" (v. 27). The gravity of Epaphroditus' trauma was such that it suggests that his fellow travelers had given up hope that he would live. Again the example of Christ-like servanthood is repeated. Just as Christ had died as a servant, just as Paul had faced death serving the gospel, so Epaphroditus had come near to death in Christ's service.

We who have the benefits of modern medicine may easily read right past "[b]ut God had mercy on him." But in Paul's day few people drew back from death's door. This wasn't a matter of the young man's simply getting better but of God's direct healing[9]—"the sovereign merciful act of God himself" (O'Brien).[10] Epaphroditus had been spared death by the merciful intervention of God himself. And, as the apostle was quick to mention, the mercy extended further, to Paul himself—"and not only on him but on me also, lest I should have sorrow upon sorrow" (v. 27b). Like Christ, Paul was "a man of sorrows" due to his calling (cf. Isaiah 53:3). He was also a man who, amidst sorrows, experienced a fountain of joy, as we note from the sixteen instances of forms of the word *joy* in Philippians. Among his present sorrows in Rome was the selfish rivalry of some Christian leaders. How thankful he was that the sorrow of Epaphroditus' death was not overlaid upon this sorrow. How grateful he was for the sovereign will of God and for divine mercy. But what Paul wanted the Philippians to know was that when they received Epaphroditus back again, they were receiving a man who, as it were, was back from the dead. So this was likewise a mercy to them.

For all these reasons—Paul's esteem for Epaphroditus as a brother, a fellow worker, a fellow soldier, an apostle, and a messenger who desperately longed for home and was distressed at their distress and who almost died carrying out their assignment—because of all of this Paul says, "I am the more eager to send him, therefore, that you may rejoice at seeing him again, and that I may be less anxious" (v. 28). When Epaphroditus arrived, the Philippians would be relieved to know he was safe, Epaphroditus would be relieved to be home, and Paul would be "less anxious" about him. Nothing would please Paul more than a proper reunion.

Paul Commands a Warm Welcome (vv. 29, 30)

Paul now urged, "So receive him in the Lord with all joy, and honor such men, for he nearly died for the work of Christ, risking his life to complete what was lacking in your service to me" (vv. 29, 30). During the long separation between Paul and the Philippian church (and especially since his imprisonment in Rome), the Philippians had been unable to fully express their fellowship/partnership in Paul's ministry—especially since they lacked a way to supply his needs. But Epaphroditus' heroics enabled them to complete their gospel obligation to Paul. They owed the young man big-time.

In effect, single-talented as Epaphroditus was, he was like Christ. Paul makes this very clear in the Greek because the phrase that tells us that Epaphroditus "nearly died" in verse 30 is exactly the same as the phrase in 2:8, which describes Christ coming "to the point of death." Epaphroditus' near death for Paul echoes Christ's real death for us. This young man had the mind of Christ.

Epaphroditus represents a category of people who are to be honored.[11] If we have read Paul correctly, it is not only the up-front people, those with the more public gifts, who are to be honored but also those who regardless of their gifts live out the example of Christ. By holding up Epaphroditus, Paul contradicted the Greco-Roman culture's, and also our modern culture's, rewarding those who seek prestige and position.[12] This ought to lay the ax to those of us who define success in the evangelical community as a kind of lordship: sitting in the honored seat, being the feted guest at luncheons, speaking to vast throngs, building monuments, naming buildings after ourselves, collecting honorary titles.

Over the course of chapter 2, Paul had taken great pains to get the Philippians outside themselves, beginning with the command in verses 3, 4: "Do nothing from selfish ambition or conceit, but in humility count others more significant than yourselves. Let each of you look not only to his own interests, but also to the interests of others." Paul had held up the supreme example of Christ in verses 5–11. He had raised the example of his protégé Timothy in verses 19–24, as a man who looked out for others' interests. He had lifted up the layman Epaphroditus as an unforgettable example in verses 25–30.

But what about Paul himself? As we would expect, we see that the great apostle practiced what he preached as he put the interests of others above his own in sending Timothy and Epaphroditus back to Philippi, leaving himself alone and unattended in Rome. Was Paul thinking about himself during those dark days in Rome? Hardly! He was willing to sacrifice his own interests for the well-being of others. Paul, the theologian, lived out every aspect of his theology in the most practical ways.

What about us? We know that public ministry gifts must be used to glorify Christ in looking out for the interests of others. We know that God sees all and will hold his leaders responsible. But what about the quiet, perhaps single-talented Christians like Epaphroditus? Will they get a pass? No! Rather, they should fear that if they bury their talent (thinking "it won't matter"), God will certainly see and hold them accountable. They should read what the master said to the lazy servant in Jesus' parable in Matthew 25:14–29.

Epaphroditus certainly wasn't Paul or Timothy. He was a "brother," a "fellow worker," a "fellow soldier," a "messenger [apostle]," a "minister" (v. 25)—*that's all!* He had the mind of Christ—*that's all!* He is honored today by both man and God—*that's all!*

Finally, my brothers, rejoice in the Lord. To write the same things to you is no trouble to me and is safe for you. Look out for the dogs, look out for the evildoers, look out for those who mutilate the flesh. For we are the circumcision, who worship by the Spirit of God and glory in Christ Jesus and put no confidence in the flesh. . . .

3:1–3

14

Rejoicing and Warning

PHILIPPIANS 3:1-3

AS MOST ENGLISH VERSIONS have rendered it, Paul begins chapter 3 with, "Finally, my brothers"—a phrase that has occasioned a lot of humor at the expense of preachers, as, for example when the little boy whispered to his father, "What does the preacher mean when he says 'finally'?" To which his father muttered, "Absolutely nothing, son."[1] Of course, we preachers could argue that we have apostolic precedent for this because right here, as the Apostle Paul concludes, he says "Finally" and then goes on for two more chapters!

Actually, however, most of our translations have made this more difficult than it is because there is evidence in postclassical Greek that the word functions as a transitional particle to introduce a fresh point in the progress of thought and could well be translated, "Well then, my brothers, rejoice" or "And so, my brothers, rejoice" or "Moreover, my brothers, rejoice."[2] This fits well with the fact that the occurrences of "rejoice" in the book of Philippians function like a hinge at the beginning or the end of the sections in which it appears. Paul uses "rejoice" first in 1:18 when he concludes, "What then? Only that in every way, whether in pretense or in truth, Christ is proclaimed, and in that I rejoice. Yes, and I will rejoice." Here in 3:1 he builds on the second occurrence of "rejoice" from 2:17, 18 where he had affirmed, "Even if I am to be poured out as a drink offering upon the sacrificial offering of your faith, I am glad and rejoice with you all. Likewise you also should be glad and rejoice with me." In the intervening verses Paul expresses his joy over the examples of Timothy and Epaphroditus, especially the latter who almost died for the gospel (cf. vv. 19–30, esp. vv. 28, 29).

So as Paul begins a new section that outlines the doctrinal troubles the

Philippians might soon face, he writes, "Finally, my brothers, rejoice in the Lord." And when he transitions to the following section in 4:4 he will hinge it with the command, "Rejoice in the Lord always; again I will say, rejoice."

Significantly, as Paul prefaces the warnings of chapter 3 with the call to rejoice, he couples it for the first time in Philippians with the qualifier "in the Lord" because the Lord himself is both the *occasion* and *source* of their joy. Such joy (because it is "in the Lord") is independent of adverse circumstances. The great John Wesley exuded his joy in the Lord on a three-week preaching mission with Rev. John Nelson during which the two slept on the hard floor with no padding. Wesley used Nelson's coat for a pillow, and Nelson used Burkitt's notes on the New Testament for his. As Nelson relates it, "One morning about three o'clock Mr. Wesley turned over, and, finding me awake, clapped me on the side saying: 'Brother Nelson, let us be of good cheer: I have one whole side yet, for the skin is off but one side!'"[3] Over the years I have seen this rejoicing in believers who manifested joy in the Lord during tragedy and physical pain. I can think of one man in particular who, though terminally ill, actually brought cheer to those who attended him in the hospital.

The whole of verse 1 reads, "Finally [And so], my brothers, rejoice in the Lord. To write the same things to you is no trouble to me and is safe for you." What are "the same things" of which he writes? They are Paul's frequent exhortations to rejoice during affliction, as we have already noted (cf. 2:28, 29; 3:1; 4:4). Paul doesn't mind repeating these exhortations—it's "no trouble."

Further, his call for rejoicing in the Lord is "safe" for them because it serves as a safeguard against the lures of those who would attempt to undermine their faith. The point is, "Paul understands joy in the Lord to be *inherently* 'safe' (*asphales*), by definition a bulwark against all manner of dangers" (Bockmuehl).[4] The often-quoted saying from Nehemiah 8:10 states this truth explicitly and memorably: "the joy of the LORD is your strength." Joy in or from the Lord is inherently strengthening. This is implicit in Psalm 81:1: "Sing aloud to God our strength; shout for joy to the God of Jacob!" The books of Chronicles tell us that after King David had installed the ark in Jerusalem, his song of thanks linked strength and joy: "Splendor and majesty are before him; strength and joy are in his place" (1 Chronicles 16:27).

There is safety for all believers in the joy of the Lord. Matthew Henry, the Puritan expositor, wrote, "The joy of the Lord will arm us against the assaults of our spiritual enemies and put our mouths out of taste for those pleasures with which the tempter baits his hooks."[5] The joy of the Lord is a divine armament. Those living in his joy are resistant to attacks that take others down.

Resiliency marks their steps. The taste of joy renders the tempter's offerings bland by comparison.

So we see why the apostle is happy to continually urge his followers to rejoice in the Lord—because rejoicing will serve as a safeguard through all of life. Are you safe, or are you in danger?

Threefold Warning against the Circumcision Party (v. 2)

We don't know what triggered Paul's explosive warning, "Look out for the dogs, look out for the evildoers, look out for those who mutilate the flesh" (v. 2). We do know that Paul had been fighting off the Judaizers for years. Judaizers were Jewish Christians (or ostensibly Christians) who insisted that Gentile Christians must submit to the Mosaic law, including circumcision.[6] In Acts 15 we first read of Paul and Barnabas withstanding them, and the resultant Council of Jerusalem backed Paul and Barnabas. Later when the Judaizers invaded the new church in Galatia, Paul pulled out his verbal flamethrower: "But even if we or an angel from heaven should preach to you a gospel contrary to the one we preached to you, let him be accursed. As we have said before, so now I say again: If anyone is preaching to you a gospel contrary to the one you received, let him be accursed" (Galatians 1:8, 9; cf. 3:1–14). Paul had no use for the circumcision party.

Perhaps as Paul was dictating his letter to the Philippians from his Roman confinement, he had become newly aware of some Judaizing activity in the Roman church. Whatever the exact incident, Paul here engages in searing rhetoric with three alliterated insults that all begin with the letter *kappa* (*k*): "Look out for the dogs" (*kunas*), "look out for the evildoers" (*kakous ergatas*), "look out for those who mutilate the flesh" (*katatome*) (v. 2). These fierce alliterated epithets would have had resounding effects on the ears of the listeners. But far more striking than their acoustical effects was that they were freighted with ironic sarcasm, as each of the three insults took a virtue that the Judaizers claimed for themselves and reversed it. Paul impaled the Judaizers on their own vocabulary.

Those Dogs!

Frankly, Paul's first warning, "Look out for the dogs" (v. 2), would hurt my dog's feelings if this could be translated into Canine because my dog has never done anything wrong. Daisy doesn't bark, she doesn't beg, she doesn't steal. All she does is flash a panting smile as she tries to figure out what I want her to do. Daisy is, well—perfect!

But first-century Israelites didn't have pets, and they had no use for dog food. Dogs were coyote-like scavengers who fed on roadkill, carrion, filth, and garbage—they were vivid images of the unclean. So for the Jews, a dog was a perfect metaphor for those who did not keep Israel's dietary laws, and thus a powerful metaphor for Gentiles and lapsed Jews. But here in Philippians, by warning Christians, "Look out for the dogs" Paul effected a stunning reversal, charging that the Judaizers were the unclean "dogs" who stood outside the covenant blessings.[7] As Karl Barth put it, "Like the lash of a whip comes Paul's term: dogs!—unclean."[8] Ouch!

Those Evildoers!

The second epithet, "look out for the evildoers" (v. 2), is likewise a barbed irony because it is a pun on the Judaizers' claim to be doing the works of the Law. "The works of the Law" was a pious slogan used to distinguish Jew from Gentile, or the observant Jew from the nonobservant.[9] Thus by Paul's calling the Judaizers "evildoers," Paul was saying that rather than doing the works of the Law, they were literally "evil workers" (*kakous ergatas*). The irony for the Judaizers was that all their attention to the works of the Law made them evil workers—and therefore spiritual Gentiles—dogs.

Those Mutilators!

The third epithet, "look out for those who mutilate the flesh" (v. 2), is particularly scathing because the word "mutilate" (*katatome*) is a sarcastic play on the word for "circumcision" (*peritome*).[10] Moreover, the same word for "mutilation" is used in 1 Kings 18 (LXX) to describe the self-mutilation of the prophets of Baal (cf. 1 Kings 18:28). Thus, as Peter T. O'Brien concludes, "Circumcision, their greatest source of pride, is interpreted by the apostle as mutilation—a sure sign that they have no part in God's people at all."[11]

So as we take a step back, what we see in Paul's three sharp warnings is that he took the Judaizers' rhetoric and slapped them hard with their own slogans. And he alliterated it so it would stick firm in the minds of the Philippians. What a warning to us if we should venture to add legalistic requirements to the gospel of grace.

A Threefold Description of the True Circumcision (v. 3)

The Old Testament prophets had long lamented the uncircumcised hearts of their people and called for spiritual circumcision (cf. Jeremiah 9:25). Indeed, as Paul argued in Romans 4:9–12 Abraham was justified by faith long before he was circumcised. Paul understood that those who have faith are the circumcised in heart. So Paul included himself emphatically in his declaration, "For we are the [real] circumcision" (Philippians 3:3). Thus Paul carried on his attack on the Judaizers with the "unequivocal assertion of the great spiritual reversal: Judaizers are the new Gentiles, while Christian believers have become true Jews" (Silva).[12] Paul was explicit: "For no one is a Jew who is merely one outwardly, nor is circumcision outward and physical. But a Jew is one inwardly, and circumcision is a matter of the heart, by the Spirit, not by the letter. His praise is not from man but from God" (Romans 2:28, 29). True circumcision is that of the heart and is a matter of faith and grace from beginning to end.

Here Paul selects three qualities of the true people of God.

Upward Service

The real circumcision is "worship by the Spirit of God" (v. 3). Those who are in Christ are part of a new order. "Therefore, if anyone is in Christ, he is a new creation. The old has passed away; behold, the new has come" (2 Corinthians 5:17). The newness of the new creation is the product of creation power (cf. 2 Corinthians 4:4–6). But the passing of the *old* and the coming of the *new* is also meant to call to mind the coming of the new covenant that Paul earlier described wherein we have been made "ministers of a new covenant, not of the letter but of the Spirit. For the letter kills, but the Spirit gives life" (2 Corinthians 3:6). The evidence of the new covenant and circumcision of the heart is the indwelling of the Holy Spirit (cf. Romans 8:8, 9).

This indwelling is a wonder, as John Donne so well says:

> Wilt thou love God as he thee? then digest,
> My soul, this wholesome meditation,
> How God the Spirit, by angels waited on
> In heaven, doth make his temple in thy breast.
>
> John Donne
> *Holy Sonnets*, XV, lines 1–4

And when God indwells us, he makes us worshippers. His Spirit takes our part before his own throne and helps us with our weaknesses, empowering acceptable worship and prayer (cf. Romans 8:26, 27). Worshipping by the Spirit of God frees us from bondage to any one place. All of life becomes worship.

Outward Boasting

Secondly, those who are the real circumcision "glory in Christ Jesus" (v. 3). This is because it is the work of the Holy Spirit to exalt Jesus (cf. John 16:14).

When we worship by the Spirit, we naturally glory in Christ Jesus. More exactly, "we *boast* in Christ Jesus." We boast because it is not our hold on Christ that saves us—it is Christ. We boast because it is not our joy in Christ that saves us—it is Christ. We boast because it is not even our faith that saves us—it is Christ. Christ becomes the Divine Obsession[13] of the real circumcision. Christ becomes the singular concern and focus of his people. The evidence of the fullness of the Spirit is a one-track mind and a one-theme tongue that speaks perpetually of Christ. Christ becomes the source of all satisfaction.

> Thou, O Christ, art all I want;
> More than all in Thee I find.
>
> Charles Wesley
> "Jesus, Lover of My Soul," 1740

Christ becomes the focus of our ongoing praise. We boast ever more in the cross. Christ is the center of all Heaven and the obsession of every son or daughter who worships him by the Spirit of God.

Inward Confidence

The spiritual corollary to boasting in Christ is the third characteristic of circumcised hearts: they "put no confidence in the flesh" (v. 3)—that is, they put no confidence in anything that is outside of Christ.[14] If your boast is in Christ, your confidence cannot be in yourself. And most certainly, as the mention of "flesh" is at least a passing glance at circumcision, we must never place our confidence in external religious observance, no matter what it may be.

We must be aware of false circumcision in whatever form it may come to us—in newly packaged legalisms, in glittering "give and get" promises of the prosperity gospel, or in the self-help formulas that flood the media. But beyond vigilance there is the safety of joy in the Lord—to be so full of joy that no other offers appeal to us, to have tasted what is good so deeply that we have no taste for the allurements of the tempter, for the joy of the Lord is our strength. And, lastly, joy is the currency of those who are the real circumcision, "who worship by the Spirit of God and glory in Christ Jesus and put no confidence in the flesh" (v. 3).

. . . though I myself have reason for confidence in the flesh also. If anyone else thinks he has reason for confidence in the flesh, I have more: circumcised on the eighth day, of the people of Israel, of the tribe of Benjamin, a Hebrew of Hebrews; as to the law, a Pharisee; as to zeal, a persecutor of the church; as to righteousness under the law, blameless. But whatever gain I had, I counted as loss for the sake of Christ. Indeed, I count everything as loss because of the surpassing worth of knowing Christ Jesus my Lord. For his sake I have suffered the loss of all things and count them as rubbish, in order that I may gain Christ and be found in him, not having a righteousness of my own that comes from the law, but that which comes through faith in Christ, the righteousness from God that depends on faith. . . .

3:4–9

15

From Reveling
to Revulsion

PHILIPPIANS 3:4-9

MIDWAY THROUGH PAUL'S composing this letter to his beloved church, something reminded the apostle that religious wolf packs were at that moment traveling the trade routes from Jerusalem toward Philippi and that they potentially could savage his tiny flock with their promise of a deeper and more complete faith through the adoption of circumcision and observance of the Law. Thus we saw Paul's fiery warning and declaration, "Look out for the dogs, look out for the evildoers, look out for those who mutilate the flesh. For we are the circumcision, who worship by the Spirit of God and glory in Christ Jesus and put no confidence in the flesh" (vv. 2, 3). This apparently further inspired and energized Paul to take on the Judaizers at their own fleshly game because he switched to the first person and added, "though I myself have reason for confidence in the flesh also" (v. 4).

What follows is the apostle's unparalleled description of his human achievements before he met Christ, which has been called "one of the most remarkable personal confessions that the ancient world has bequeathed to us."[1] As we know, this description of his fleshly accomplishments was really a masterful setup because Paul's boasting in his achievements paved the way for his remarkable rejection of them.

Paul's Dependence upon His Self-Righteousness (vv. 4–6)

We begin in verse 4 with Paul's self-perception when he was still Saul of Tarsus: "If anyone else thinks he has reason for confidence in the flesh, I have more." For starters, Paul declared without any qualifications that his ground for personal boasting exceeded that of any person in Judaism! In effect, he threw down the gauntlet, saying, "Top this if you can, you Judaizers." And then Paul deftly chronicled seven personal superiorities of which he could boast.

The first four are inherited privileges, followed by a trio of personal accomplishments.

Paul's Inherited Privileges

First, Paul was "circumcised on the eighth day" (v. 5), or literally "with respect to circumcision an eight day one." He was circumcised by his parents seven days after his birth (the Jewish eighth day) in strict compliance with the Abrahamic covenant (cf. Genesis 17:12; Leviticus 12:3). Most significantly, this meant that he was not a proselyte from paganism. He was no later-in-life convert. He was an eight-dayer—an insider from birth.

Second, Paul was "of the people of Israel" (v. 5), or more exactly "of the *race* of Israel." This meant that in addition to not being a proselyte he couldn't possibly be a child of proselytes. Racially he was a pure-blooded Israelite. *Israel* and *Israelite* were inside terms by which Jews referred to their own nation. Others might call them "Jews," but only they called themselves "the children of Israel."[2] Paul was a total insider.

Third, he was "of the tribe of Benjamin" (v. 5). Benjamin was the only son born in the promised land (cf. Genesis 35:16–18). And the tribe of Benjamin was the only tribe to remain faithful to Judah and the house of David after the death of Solomon (cf. 1 Kings 12:21). The tribe of Benjamin went into exile with the tribe of Judah and returned from exile with Judah to resettle Jerusalem (cf. Nehemiah 11:7–9, 31–36). Benjamin remained at the core of spirituality. King Saul, Israel's first king, was a Benjaminite (cf. 1 Samuel 9:1, 2). And the Apostle Paul's given name was Saul (cf. Acts 7:58; 13:9). Thus Paul's heritage radiated insider pride.

Fourth, the Apostle Paul was "a Hebrew of Hebrews" (v. 5). Though Paul had been born outside the Holy Land in Tarsus, he was a "Hebrew," and his parents were "Hebrews" before him. "Hebrew of Hebrews" also indicates that he spoke Hebrew and Aramaic (cf. Acts 21:40; 22:2; 26:14). Paul spoke Hebrew or Aramaic when so many Diaspora Jews knew only Greek, and he prayed and read the Scriptures in Hebrew (cf. Acts 6:1, 2). Though Paul was born in Cilicia, his parents made sure that he had the best education in Jerusalem under the famous Rabbi Gamaliel (cf. Acts 22:3). Paul was a private school insider.

So we see that the apostle had impeccable credentials before he ever lifted a hand! In effect, regarding prestige his upbringing was not unlike that of our New England blue bloods whose genealogies and education and position have been established facts for generations. But Paul didn't rest on his ancestry or name, as do so many of the privileged. His track record was phenomenal, as we see in his trio of achievements (superiorities #5, 6, and 7).

Paul's Personal Achievements

Fifth, we read, "as to the law, a Pharisee" (v. 5). Pharisaism was a lay movement that had its beginnings when the Jews returned from exile. The movement solidified during the Maccabean times, and by the first century the Pharisees were the most impressive and respected group in Israel. According to Josephus they numbered about 6,000[3]—an elite denomination within Israel. *Pharisee* means "separated one." The Pharisees distanced themselves from unclean persons and ate only with observant Jews.

Paul's ancestors were Pharisees, as he told the Sanhedrin (cf. Acts 23:6). However, Paul's Pharisaism was a matter of choice and deep conviction as he voluntarily bound himself to keep the hundreds of commandments of the oral law.[4] Paul was a brilliant, intransigent Pharisee, a heavyweight who could hold his own with anyone.

Sixth, we read "as to zeal, a persecutor of the church" (v. 6). Paul orchestrated a terror campaign against the church and had achieved a growing infamy as a Pharisaic terrorist. Luke chronicles this in Acts and, most notably, Paul's presence at the gruesome stoning of Stephen as he guarded the garments of the executioners while he gazed approvingly upon the execution (cf. Acts 7:58; 8:1; 9:1, 2). Most significantly, Jesus' opening words to Paul on the Damascus Road mentioned Paul's persecutions (cf. Acts 9:4, 5; 22:7, 8; 26:14, 15).[5] Paul's self-appointed zeal initiated and led the way in the pogrom against Jewish Christians. He saw himself as a latter-day Phinehas in his zeal for the Law (cf. Numbers 25:6–8) and was highly esteemed by his people for his actions.

Seventh, and lastly, "as to righteousness under the law, blameless" (v. 6). Notice that Paul did not say he was sinless or perfect but "blameless." The Pharisees assumed that a faithful Israelite could keep the Torah's 613 commandments because the Law provided rituals and procedures to receive forgiveness and purification.[6] Paul's conduct was "blameless" in the sense that "blameless" describes an exemplary way of life lived in accordance with Pharisaic interpretations. And this is how his peers saw him—wholly blameless. Peter T. O'Brien asserts that Paul "speaks of his blamelessness as an objective fact, as incontestable as his circumcision, his membership in the tribe of Benjamin, and his persecution of the church."[7] Paul (Saul of Tarsus) was "blameless" under the Law.

What an amazing accomplishment and claim. Paul was a spiritual athlete in a category by himself. What focus the man must have had—what confidence—what self-possession—what discipline—what an iron will!

No living soul could gainsay Paul's fourfold insider credentials. No one could excel his threefold performance. His sevenfold superiority put him in a class of his own. Paul's claim "If anyone else thinks he has reason for confidence in the flesh, I have more" was no empty boast. Listen well, Judaizers, those of you who would import the laws and strictures of the old covenant back into Christ and his church. Listen to what this spiritual superman has to say.

Paul's Radical Reversal (vv. 7–9)

Paul's Accounting Reversal

Paul astonished his readers (and us) by saying, "But whatever gain I had, I counted as loss for the sake of Christ" (v. 7). Paul is consciously precise here as he employs accounting terminology—"gain . . . loss." When the Victorian poet and pastor-theologian John Keble was a young don at Oxford, he served as his college's bursar (financial officer) for a brief period. Few pastors then, or now, are trained in balancing figures. During one embarrassing year Keble's balance was off by two thousand pounds, and nothing he did could resolve it—until someone solved the mystery by noting that Keble had written the year (around 1820) at the top of the column and then added it into the amount.[8]

As a checkbook-challenged pastor, I sympathize. But though Paul was not mathematically challenged (and uses careful accounting terms), his account balances in a very odd way. Everything was on the credit side and nothing on the debit side. However, in a flash he struck off everything in the credit column and inserted it in the debit column. Christ alone stands in the credit column. The apostle's language is explicit because "gain" is in the plural and "loss" is in the singular. One by one the apostle had carefully added up the individual items of merit as he looked to the judgment. They were real pluses. But in a blinding moment they became one great singular loss.[9] Jesus Christ became Paul's one and only credit!

Paul went on to emphatically explain why this was so: "Indeed, I count everything as loss because of the surpassing worth of knowing Christ Jesus my Lord" (v. 8a). This statement is uniquely personal and looks back to Paul's meeting the risen Christ on the Damascus Road. There the grace of the Lord Jesus found Paul the terrorist. And from that point Paul began a process of understanding, first in the house of Ananias and then in Tarsus and then during several years in Arabia (cf. Galatians 1:17, 18).

Now Paul's understanding has become stunning because it is only here in Paul's writings that we find the intensely personal "Christ Jesus my Lord." This is the only place Paul called God the Father or Christ "*my* Lord." The wonder of this increases when we realize that the Philippian hymn of 2:6–11 climaxes with Jesus being given God's name "Lord" (Yahweh), so that at the end "every tongue [will] confess that Jesus Christ [Messiah] is Lord [Yahweh], to the glory of God the Father" (2:11). Here Paul made the astonishing claim that the same Christ is "*my* Lord"—the awesome Yahweh of Scripture was Paul's Lord. No wonder all his credits slid to the debit column. Paul knew Christ Jesus in close intimate relationship, and that superseded everything.

The apostle summarized the accounting loss-gain thoughts in the next sentence: "For his sake I have suffered the loss of all things and count them as rubbish, in order that I may gain Christ" (v. 8b). Paul lost not only his incredible human assets but everything that went with it—his own view of himself, his status, his friendships, his wealth, his assured position in life. And on top of that, he embraced a life of epic hardship and abuse unique in the history of the world (cf. 2 Corinthians 11:23–29).

In truth, he counted it all as "rubbish"—using a crude expletive by first-century standards. Paul's former accomplishments had become abhorrent to him, not because they were bad (for they were not), but because they kept him from Christ.

And he had no regrets. John Calvin noted that when people battling a storm at sea cast their belongings overboard to lighten the ship, they wail afterward at the loss.[10] But Paul did not look back. There was no hidden longing. Why? Because he will gain Christ in that final great day when his goal is fully realized. To die will be gain (cf. 1:21)!

Paul's New Dependence

As Paul looked to the final day when he will gain Christ, he further desired to "be found in him, not having a righteousness of my own that comes from the law, but that which comes through faith in Christ, the righteousness from God that depends on faith" (v. 9). While Paul pursued a righteous life in everything, he had no desire for self-righteousness of his own making. He was done with that.

What he most desired was the righteousness that "comes through faith in Christ" (v. 9), or more accurately, "that comes through *the faithfulness of Christ*."[11] The righteousness that he possessed came from Christ's faithful obedience to the Father on the cross as he drank the cup of death to the full for our sins.[12] It is all grace because of Christ's faithful work. Paul was saying that "he [Christ] saved us, not because of works done by us in righteousness, but according to his own mercy" (Titus 3:5).

This righteousness is brought about by Christ's faithfulness but is appropriated by human faith—"the righteousness from God that depends on faith" (Philippians 3:9b). This is saving faith because it includes abandoning all those things with which we would credit ourselves, relying instead on the faithful work of Christ.

What a mercifully powerful message to those who may be tempted to mix a legalistic regimen with the gospel of grace. Paul's credentials were matchless and unassailable. He was born with it all! Even more, his accomplishments were stratospheric. He was actually "blameless" under the Pharisaic legal system. But his encounter with Christ showed it all to be loss. What about us, so far removed from the first-century church and the wolf packs treading the trade routes to their doorsteps? As Carson says:

> Most who read these pages, I suspect, will not be greatly tempted to boast about their Jewish ancestry and ancient rights of race and religious heritage. But we may be tempted to brag about still less important things: our wealth, our status, our education, our emotional stability, our families, our political or business successes, our denominational alignments, or even about which version of the Bible we use. Be careful of people like that. They tend to regard everyone who is outside their little group as somehow inferior. Somewhere along the way they inadvertently—or even intentionally and maliciously—imagine that faith in Christ Jesus and delight in him is a little less important than their personal accomplishments.
>
> Instead, look around for those whose constant confidence is Jesus Christ, whose constant boast is Jesus Christ, whose constant delight is Jesus Christ. Jesus is the center of their worship, the center of their gratitude, the center of their love, the center of their hope . . . emulate those whose constant confidence and boast is in Christ Jesus and in nothing else.[13]

Our only boast, our only confidence, our only hope must be in Christ. Paul went on to say, "that I may know him and the power of his resurrection, and may share his sufferings, becoming like him in his death, that by any means possible I may attain the resurrection from the dead" (3:10, 11). That's the passion that flows through this entire passage. We must emulate those whose constant confidence and boast is in Christ Jesus and in nothing else. He is our only hope.

. . . that I may know him and the power of his resurrection, and may share his sufferings, becoming like him in his death, that by any means possible I may attain the resurrection from the dead.

3:10, 11

16

Paul's Desire to Know Christ Fully

PHILIPPIANS 3:10–11

THE LONG PARAGRAPH that makes up Philippians 3:1–11 pulses with passion from beginning to end. It begins with Paul's heated warnings, "Look out for the dogs, look out for the evildoers, look out for those who mutilate the flesh" (v. 2). Then Paul listed his seven righteous superiorities that left him "blameless" under the Law, only to reject them with the emotional and indelicate expletive *skubala*—"rubbish" (v. 8). The paragraph concludes with the apostle's nearly explosive words over and against those who would attempt to bring the Philippians under the Law—"that I may know him and the power of his resurrection, and may share his sufferings, becoming like him in his death, that by any means possible I may attain the resurrection from the dead" (vv. 10, 11). Paul passionately asserted that the cross-centered life is the life of true righteousness in the sense of "right living."[1]

There is simply no way these words can be read with clinical detachment if they are read properly. The Apostle Paul's mission and life-desire was enshrined in this eloquent conclusion. As such, it is the favorite text of many Christians. Years ago I memorized it in the Greek, regardless of the fact that a mere technical reading of the text will not help my soul. In fact, though I know these verses well and sometimes pen them beside my signature, I fall far short of Paul's heart—even though I have prayed these lines for years.

To Know Christ (v. 10a)

Paul writes in 3:10, "that I may know him." It had been thirty years since his encounter with Christ on the Damascus Road, where he once and for all came to know Christ. ". . . that I may know him" expresses the longing of a heart that already knows Christ—and in fact has known Christ more intimately than most of us! To know Christ was the overarching and unfolding ambition of Paul's life—a longing for an ever-deepening, ever-widening, personal knowledge of the Son. This passion to know him was what energized Paul's dogged devotion and his epic quest to take the gospel to the ends of the earth—"spires away on the world's end," as John Masefield puts it in his poem "The Seekers." The apostle's intense longing was born of love because love makes us want to know another more and more—just as in a good marriage we come to know another as "a true blood relative even closer . . . than father or mother."[2] The apostle's love-born desire was to know Christ in such a way that his life was so fully identified with that of his Savior that it radiated from him.

Paul's longing has set the example for the church for more than two millennia. If you have anything of the same desire, make this your prayer: "I want to know you, Lord—to really know you."

To Know His Power and Fellowship (v. 10b)

The apostle now unfolded his desire to know Christ in two closely linked expressions that form a single dynamic thought[3]—literally, "the power of his resurrection, and the fellowship of his sufferings." These two principles—power and fellowship—mutually interpret each other.

His Power

First, there is "the power of his resurrection" (v. 10). Two thousand years ago on the first day of the week, Christ's cold body lay on chilled stone in the arms of death. His heart was stilled in the icy grip of the grave, whatever blood remained was congealed in his veins, his eyes were fixed and dilated, and his body was bound tightly with spices and graveclothes. Then, before dawn, his vacant eyes blinked open and coursed with light, focused and glittering life. And with the ease of omnipotence, his body left the wrappings like an empty cocoon.

"[T]he power of his resurrection" is *God's* power, his life-giving power that he deployed in raising Christ from the dead, and the power that God uses to bring about and sustain the new life that the Christian receives from Christ and shares with him.[4] Conversion is, in fact, described in the New Testament as a *resurrection*. As Paul explained to the Ephesians, "And you were dead in the trespasses and sins in which you once walked, following the course of this world, following the prince of the power of the air, the spirit that is now at work in the sons of disobedience" (2:1, 2). We were condemned in our sinfulness. "But God, being rich in mercy, because of the great love with which he loved us, even when we were dead in our trespasses, made us alive together with Christ—by grace you have been saved—and raised us up with him and seated us with him in the heavenly places in Christ Jesus" (Ephesians 2:4–6). It takes nothing less than God's creational power to effect such a change in us. "For God, who said, 'Let light shine out of darkness' [when he created the world], has shone in our hearts to give the light of the knowledge of the glory of God in the face of Jesus Christ" (2 Corinthians 4:6). Conversion is a resurrection effected by the creation power of God himself.

Paul experienced this power when he was transformed from his self-righteous way of life to become a humble follower of Christ. And now he desired to live his present life in the same God-given power—"the immeasurable greatness of his power toward us who believe, according to the working of his great might that he worked in Christ when he raised him from the dead" (Ephesians 1:19, 20). Indeed, this is the way Paul lived—with resurrection power.

> Squeezed but not squashed;
> bewildered but not befuddled;
> pursued but not abandoned;
> knocked down but not knocked out.
>
> 2 Corinthians 4:8, 9
> paraphrased by Merrill Tenney

Again, this was resurrection power, as Paul immediately explains: "always carrying in the body the death of Jesus, so that the life of Jesus may also be manifested in our bodies. For we who live are always being given over to death for Jesus' sake, so that the life of Jesus also may be manifested in our mortal flesh" (2 Corinthians 4:10, 11).

Gordon Fee writes:

> Paul knows nothing of the rather gloomy stoicism that is so often exhibited in historic Christianity, where the lot of the believer is basically that of "slugging it out in the trenches," with little or no sense of Christ's presence and power. On the contrary, the power of Christ's resurrection was the greater reality for him. So certain was Paul that it had happened—after all, he had been accosted and claimed by the Risen Lord on the Damascus Road—and that Christ's resurrection guaranteed his own, that he could throw himself into the present with a kind of holy abandon, full of rejoicing and thanksgiving.[5]

The initial telltale sign of knowing Christ is the power of the resurrection—the joy of new life in Christ, the resiliency and buoyancy that come from spiritual resurrection, holy abandon in serving him. Such was my experience when I came to Christ. I sensed that a great weight had been lifted from my shoulders, and lightness came to my step, as though I were released from earth's gravity. All I wanted was to know more of Christ and to tell others about him. All Christians have experienced this in their own way. And, of course, all of this is capped with the expectation of the future great resurrection—when "the earth and the sea shall give up their dead; and the corruptible bodies of those who sleep in Him shall be changed, and made like unto His own glorious body; according to the mighty working whereby He is able to subdue all things unto Himself."[6]

Do you long to know him and the power of his resurrection? If so, you long rightly. That is an apostolic longing. It is a desire that God is pleased to fulfill. Pause and pray, "I want to know him and the power of his resurrection."

His Fellowship

As we noted earlier, "the fellowship of his sufferings" (literal translation; ESV: "may share his sufferings" [v. 10]) is part and parcel with "the power of his resurrection." They go hand in hand like Good Friday and Easter.[7] In tandem they provide the way to knowing him more.

Here is that word again—"fellowship" (*koinonia*)—and its use is definitely not churchy, as in "Let's have some fellowship" or "That church has good fellowship." Its first usage in 1:5 ("your partnership [fellowship] in the gospel") sounds good enough, and its second occurrence in 1:7 ("partakers [fellowshipers] with me of grace") sounds even better, as does 2:1 ("any participation [fellowship] in the Spirit"). But "the fellowship of his sufferings"—who wants to join that fellowship? "That church has good suffering. Let's join." Actually the Apostle Paul would join because suffering is essential for knowing Christ in the fullness that Paul desired.

The spiritual reality is this: suffering is the lot of every true believer, a fact that Paul referenced frequently. Luke tells us that he and Paul returned to the churches of Asia Minor, "encouraging them to continue in the faith, and saying that through many tribulations we must enter the kingdom of God" (Acts 14:22). Paul told the Thessalonians, "For you yourselves know that we are destined for this. For when we were with you, we kept telling you beforehand that we were to suffer affliction, just as it has come to pass, and just as you know" (1 Thessalonians 3:3, 4). Paul also informed the Romans that suffering is a prerequisite to being glorified with Christ: ". . . and if children, then heirs—heirs of God and fellow heirs with Christ, provided we suffer with him in order that we may also be glorified with him" (Romans 8:17).

Most significantly, the apostle told the Philippians explicitly in 1:29, "For it has been granted [literally, graced] to you that for the sake of Christ you should not only believe in him but also suffer for his sake." Suffering for Christ then is a divine gift. It is a sign of sacred intimacy with Christ. Karl Barth explained of this text, "The grace of being permitted to *believe* in Christ is surpassed by the grace of being permitted to *suffer* for him, of being permitted to walk the way of Christ with Christ himself to the perfection of fellowship with him."[8] The fellowship of Christ's sufferings moves the believer beyond the role of *beneficiary* of Christ's death to a *sharer* in his sufferings (cf. Colossians 1:24). The suffering that comes to a Christian (as a Christian) is not a sign of God's neglect but rather proof that grace is at work in his or her life—sacred intimacy.

There is breathtaking beauty here—namely, that the more a believer becomes like Christ, the more he or she will suffer. Simply put, the fellowship of Christ's sufferings is the fellowship of elevated souls who are growing in their knowledge of Christ. It is a fellowship of continual resurrection and the display of God's power. It is a fellowship of ascent.

We are called with Paul to invite upon ourselves the sufferings of Christ. But who has the courage and temerity to do such a thing? Will it not bring an avalanche of costly sufferings? And who will be able to bear it? The answer is, no one! But we must remember that this desire to fellowship in Christ's sufferings is coupled with the desire to know the power of the resurrection—"that I may know him and the power of his resurrection, and may share the fellowship of his sufferings. (v. 10). Paul's expression "the power of his resurrection" *precedes* "the fellowship of his sufferings." The power of Christ's resurrection first provides the strength and motivation for suffering. No man or woman can embrace the fellowship of Christ's sufferings who does not first know the power of Christ's resurrection. If you have come to Christ and know the power of his resurrection, if you've been raised from the dead, if you are experiencing the ongoing resurrection of new life in Christ, you can do it!

Do you or I want to know Christ? Then we must invoke Paul's longing as our own. *Lord God, I want to know Christ in the power of his resurrection and in the fellowship of his sufferings.* Have you ever prayed this? Do so today.

To Be like Him (v. 10c)

The other sweeping factor in knowing Christ is "becoming like him in his death" (literally, "being conformed to his death"). Paul coined this compound word—this is the only place it is found. It is a present passive participle. So the sense is that Paul is being conformed to Christ's death by the transforming activity of God and that it is an ongoing process.

This process is best understood as a cycle of dying and rising with Christ, and it is found throughout Paul's letters. As Paul experiences the power of the resurrection and is strengthened to participate in Christ's sufferings, he is being conformed to his death.[9] Paul's language indicates a process in which personal crosses produce a series of mini-resurrections that take Paul ever deeper in his personal knowledge of Christ. The bottom line is, Paul wanted to take up his cross and follow Christ; he wanted God to conform him to Christ's death. Jesus was "a man of sorrows, and acquainted with grief" (Isaiah 53:3), and Paul understood that taking up his cross like this is part of knowing the Master.[10]

To Attain Resurrection (v. 11)

Paul concluded his desire to know Christ by expressing enigmatically, "that by any means possible I may attain the resurrection from the dead" (v. 11). Was Paul uncertain about his participation in the resurrection? Not at all. The resurrection was certain, but the intervening events were uncertain as to timing and circumstances. Would he die and later rise from the dead? Or would he remain alive and undergo transformation to his new resurrection body?

What he did know emphatically is that he would experience resurrection "out from among the dead" (literal translation). And what would be his great prize? Certainly a new body and certainly everlasting life. But that is not the prize that he so coveted. The prize he wanted was Christ himself.

When Saul of Tarsus experienced the righteousness that comes through the faithfulness of Christ ("the righteousness from God that depends on faith," v. 9), he cast away all of his accomplishments that had rendered him "blameless" under the Law and threw himself upon Christ. To "know him," then, became the passion of his life. "[T]hat I may know him" (v. 10) describes Paul's day-in, day-out, unremitting, relentless, defining pursuit. Paul set his brilliant mind to learning everything about Jesus that he could, seeking him in all the Old Testament Scriptures. Before he came to Christ, Paul was already an expert in the Torah and the sacred writings. Likely he had them in his head! Thus during his early years in Arabia he sought Christ in all the Scriptures, as we see so deftly illustrated in his epistles. Paul also learned all he could from the apostolic band about Christ. Certainly he and Luke talked incessantly about Christ on the long days and nights of their travels. But it was never knowledge *about* Christ that he sought as an end in itself.

All the apostle's powers were concentrated on knowing Christ personally. The power of the resurrection had dazzled him on the road to Damascus, and he never got over it. Every day was his personal resurrection day, an affirmation that he had been raised with Christ. So Paul kept seeking the power of the resurrection as an avenue for knowing Christ more deeply.

This in turn enabled Paul to share in the fellowship of Christ's sufferings and further increase his intimacy and knowledge of him. Indeed, Paul passionately sought the fellowship of his sufferings as a grace for his soul. Therefore, the apostle was continually being conformed to Christ's death by God himself. His life was stamped with the divine imprint of the cross and a growing knowledge of Christ. This meant that Paul looked with confidence to the indeterminate day of the great resurrection when the full knowledge of Christ would fill his horizon for all eternity.

There is no doubt that if any of us knew today to be the final day of our lives, we would wish that we had made Christ the passion of our existence. But as it is, there is time right now to pray, "that I may know him and the power of his resurrection, and may share his sufferings, becoming like him in his death, that by any means possible I may attain the resurrection from the dead" (v. 10, 11).

Have you ever prayed this? Can you pray this? Will you?

Not that I have already obtained this or am already perfect, but I press on to make it my own, because Christ Jesus has made me his own. Brothers, I do not consider that I have made it my own. But one thing I do: forgetting what lies behind and straining forward to what lies ahead, I press on toward the goal for the prize of the upward call of God in Christ Jesus. Let those of us who are mature think this way, and if in anything you think otherwise, God will reveal that also to you. Only let us hold true to what we have attained.

3:12–16

17

One Thing I Do

PHILIPPIANS 3:12–16

THE APOSTLE PAUL'S famous declaration of his life's desire was stated in the preceding verses: "that I may know him and the power of his resurrection, and may share his sufferings, becoming like him in his death, that by any means possible I may attain the resurrection from the dead" (vv. 10, 11). This passionate declaration meant that every day witnessed the apostle's relentless pursuit of an ever-deepening, ever-widening personal knowledge of the Christ whom he had already known intimately for over thirty years. His growing knowledge of Christ involved his constant pursuit of "the power of his resurrection," and part and parcel with that power was the longing for the fellowship of Christ's sufferings because he knew that suffering for Christ is the sacred path to deeper knowledge of him and the perfection of intimate fellowship with him.

There is nothing in Scripture quite like this explosion of spiritual longing. And Paul's passionate longing is meant to serve as an example for all Christians. We are called to make his passion for Christ our own. Dare we ask for this? Will we pray for it? That remains the great question for every Christian.

Paul's Confession and Resolve (v. 12)

The mere statement of Paul's daunting desire places the apostle in a stratosphere by himself. And we lesser mortals might imagine that Paul attained it over the dynamic years of his epic life.

Confession

But Paul was quick to confess that this was simply not the case because he immediately interjected, "Not that I have already obtained this or am already perfect" (v. 12a). His language here is arresting because he literally said, "Not that I have already received" (without referencing the object), so that the sense is much the same as in English when we say, "Not that I have arrived," stressing the incompleteness of his spiritual journey.[1] Paul had not "received," and neither was he "perfect." This was conscious reality for the apostle. Paul was under no illusions about his attainments and would not promote fictions about his having become "perfect." So we immediately observe that Paul's magnificent quest to know Christ fully was matched by a magnificent humility.

However, while Paul was most humble, he was also very subtle because by raising the subject of perfection, he was co-opting the pious language of his opponents. Paul's enemies claimed to have reached a state of perfection that made them possessors of all the blessings of salvation, in effect the arrival of Heaven itself.[2] Heavenly perfection was theirs now, they argued. If we imagine that "we have Heaven now" is a far-fetched notion, we must understand that certain groups today claim the same thing—namely, that "mature" Christians will stay healthy and enjoy material prosperity and wholly overcome sin. TV preacher Kenneth Copeland, who preaches freedom from sickness and poverty, proclaims, "The world's shortages have no effect on someone who has already gone to heaven. Therefore, they should have no effect on us here who have made Jesus Lord of our lives."[3]

But Paul's confession allowed no such thinking, then or now. Here the Apostle Paul, the most spectacular Christian who ever lived, confessed that he had not arrived or become "perfect." Paul admitted his own need to grow into maturity. His confession stands as a warning against a superspiritual kind of Christianity that imagines that the blessings of the age to come can be had now before the resurrection.

The reality is, the more we come to know Christ, the more we will come to sense our need to grow. And when we imagine that we have arrived, stagnation sets in. We must understand that Paul's prayer—"that I may know him and the power of his resurrection, and may share his sufferings, becoming like him in his death"—is a prayer of humble dissatisfaction that opens us to the blessing of God—and to a sublime cycle of dissatisfaction and satisfaction and dissatisfaction and satisfaction . . . it brings on a life that knows more and more of Christ and then desperately wants to know more and indeed does know more and more and more. Spiritual dissatisfaction is a blessed state. Jesus said, "Blessed are those who hunger and thirst for righteousness, for they shall be satisfied" (Matthew 5:6). Do you long to know Christ better? If so, blessing rains upon your soul.

Resolve

Paul's humble confession—"Not that I have already obtained this or am already perfect"—brings forth something remarkable. It births a mighty resolve in Paul: "but I press on to make it my own, because Christ Jesus has made me his own" (v. 12b). We see how gritty Paul's resolve is in the original Greek, which is tinged with violence: "but I pursue [it] if indeed I may seize [it], because indeed I have been seized by Christ Jesus." Paul's "language comes from the world of war and athletics" (Thielman). In fact, in a battle report the ancient historian Herodotus used the same words Paul used to describe an army's *pursuit* and *seizure* of the retreating columns of the enemy.[4] Paul's rough-and-tumble words explicitly pointed to his conversion on the Damascus Road where the risen, exalted Christ seized him for his own. As Paul trod the road near Damascus, the mighty hand of Christ reached down, seized him by the scruff of his robe, and set him on the path to Ananias's house and then to Arabia and then to the Gentile world as its great apostle. Here Paul expressed his desire to "know" the risen Christ because he was in the grip of Christ's grace! Paul's whole pursuit of Christ was Christ originated, Christ motivated, and Christ propelled.

The present tense Paul used describes an ongoing, grasping, strenuous pursuit. It is a gritty, "I will not be denied," rough-and-tumble pursuit—a sublime violence—which Christ approved and approves of. He said, "From the days of John the Baptist until now the kingdom of heaven has suffered violence, and the violent take it by force" (Matthew 11:12). This is how it was with John the Baptist when he burst from the wilderness clad in his leathers, fiercely heralding the kingdom. So it was with the paralytic's friends when they tore through the roof in Capernaum to get him to Jesus (cf. Mark 2:4). Gracious, loving violence.

Brothers and sisters, if you have been seized by Christ and are in the grip of his grace, you must press on in your own hot, grasping pursuit of an ever-deeper knowledge of him. The gospel allows no room for a bland, middle-class ethic that strives to be neither hot nor cold (cf. Revelation 3:14–16). We are all called (every mother, daughter, father, son) to a single-minded, determined pursuit of Christ.

If you have been grasped by grace, God is speaking to you right now. Do you hear him? Pursue! Seize! Take hold of Christ as he has taken hold of you. This is the only way to live. No fainting hearts permitted.

Paul's Pursuit (vv. 13, 14)

As Paul increased his intensity, he sensed that just one disclaimer was not enough. So he repeated himself in a more personal manner: "Brothers, I do not consider that I have made it my own" (v. 13a). Or literally, "I myself do not consider that I have seized it." "No way have I arrived!"—that is the sense. And Paul knew that to be fact. This was not the subjective confession of an oversensitive, overwrought soul who is blinded to his own progress. Rather, it was grounded in facts that are verifiable. He had not attained to the perfection of the resurrection of the dead.[5]

One Thing!

That is why he was so intense here—"But one thing I do: forgetting what lies behind and straining forward to what lies ahead, I press on toward the goal for the prize of the upward call of God in Christ Jesus" (vv. 13b, 14).

"But one thing I do" introduces a single sentence that draws on the metaphor of a foot race described in the graphic present tense but with clauses that reference the *past* ("forgetting what lies behind"), the *future* ("and straining forward to what lies ahead"), and the *present* ("I press on toward the goal"). It is a picture of absolute focus and intensity.

Past

On August 7, 1954, during the British Empire Games in Vancouver, Canada, the greatest mile-run matchup ever took place. It was touted as the "miracle mile" because Britisher Roger Bannister and Australian John Landy were the only two sub-four-minute milers in the world. Bannister had been the first man ever to run a four-minute mile. Both runners were in peak condition. I remember as a junior high boy carefully turning the pages, examining the photos of the famous runners in *Life* magazine, and absorbing the statistics and predictions. Roger Bannister, M.D., who became Sir Roger Bannister and master of an Oxford college, strategized that he would relax during the third lap and save everything for his finishing drive. But as they began that third lap, the Australian poured it on, stretching his already substantial lead. Immediately Bannister adjusted his strategy, increasing his pace and gaining on Landy.

The lead was quickly cut in half, and at the bell for the final lap they were even. Landy began running even faster, and Bannister followed suit. Both men were flying. Bannister felt he was going to lose if Landy did not slow down. Then came the famous moment (replayed thousands of times in print and flickering black-and-white celluloid) as at the last stride before the homestretch the crowds roared. Landy could not hear Bannister's footfall and looked back, a fatal lapse of concentration. Bannister launched his attack and won the Empire Games that day by five yards.

John Landy's lapse was as old as antiquity. The sports-knowledgeable Apostle Paul would have seen Landy's mistake in a flash because he knew that to be successful a runner must not look back over his shoulder—he must "forget what lies behind"—because when a runner turns even slightly to glance back, there is a momentary loss of focus and rhythm, incurring the critical loss of a fraction of a second or even seconds.

Was the apostle suggesting a blanket of amnesia over the past? No. Paul's extensive writings reveal a remarkable memory of people and events. In one place he reminded the Corinthians of his "anxiety for all the churches," indicating that his heart rose and fell with their ups and downs (2 Corinthians 11:28, 29). The final chapter of Romans reveals a mind and memory that functioned like a mental GPS—Paul lists no less than thirty-three names of people from all over the ancient world whom he knew to be in Rome, though he had not yet been to the Eternal City.

Thus Paul's "forgetting what lies behind" (v. 13) is a special kind of forgetfulness, the kind that does not turn and glance back from the goal to indulge in the complacency of past achievements. That would have been easy for him to do if he yielded to it. He had been *the man*, the heroic apostle amidst beatings and betrayals and shipwrecks and danger upon danger. His epic life is truly without parallel. He was, and remains, *the theologian* of the church. More, he was *the missionary* to the Gentiles, the missionary-general of the early church. The apostle could boast of a trailing ring of established churches, shining as lights across the darkness of Asia and Europe. But Paul chose not to look back on his accomplishments lest they diminish his focus or lull him into complacency or indifference. And we must also understand that he did not allow his failures to turn his head to the fatal backward look. To be sure, there were many sad episodes there for Paul to recollect if he let himself.

But there was none of this. As Paul ran, he shifted into the high gear of forgetfulness—forgetting his achievements and his failures. Paul ran in the liberating freedom of his "one thing" (v. 13). He was flying in his forgetfulness.

There is instruction for everyone here across the spectrum of age and experience. For those who have some miles on them and are battle worn and perhaps have some striking accomplishments, God calls you to selective amnesia so that you will not be lulled from your stride. For all, young and old, do not look back. Lift up your eyes. Look straight ahead. Focus.

Future

As the first clause describes the runner not looking back over his shoulder, the second pictures him "straining forward to what lies ahead" with all that he has. Peter O'Brien observes that this is "a vivid word, drawn from the games, and it pictures a runner with his eyes fixed on the goal, his hand stretching out towards it, and his body bent forward as he enters the last and decisive stages of the race. Again, the present tense of the participle is appropriate, for with this verb it powerfully describes the runner's intense desire and utmost effort to reach his goal."[6] Our imaginations easily flesh out the picture: the runner's breathing has become shallow and fast as he runs flat out for the finish, his legs are drumming like pistons, his feet pound the course with painful thunder—his throat dry, his stomach groaning, he lays himself out for the finish, sweat flying, his outstretched hands flailing the air.

Present

With the final clause, the goal (the finish line)[7] comes in view as Paul concludes, "I press on toward the goal for the prize of the upward call of God in Christ Jesus" (v. 14). "It is the vision of the end of the race that ever directs and speeds his hastening feet" (J. H. Michael).[8] In terms of the modern athlete, he sees the yellow stripe fifty yards ahead, and his adrenaline jolts for the final, last-gasp kick. He runs faster, his arms pumping, pushing off his toes.

He runs for "the prize of the upward call of God in Christ Jesus" (v. 14c). What is the "upward call"? It is the "full and complete gaining of Christ for whose sake everything else has been counted as loss" (O'Brien).[9] For Paul, the greatest reward was to know Christ fully and to experience perfect fellowship with him—"that I may know him and the power of his resurrection, and may share his sufferings, becoming like him in his death, that by any means possible I may attain the resurrection from the dead" (vv. 10, 11). This is the prize that Paul wanted his readers to seize.

The year was 1923, and the competing track teams of Scotland and France were neck and neck. But among the events remaining was the 440. As the runners, clad in traditional 1920s white, came to the first turn, they were bunched tight, shoulder to shoulder, when one of them was pushed to the ground and off the track. For a second he was down—and then up again, running (though twenty meters behind), his knees high, his head back—flying. And as the leaders sprinted to the finish line, he emerged ahead to win! It was a famous win, immortalized in the movie *Chariots of Fire*.

What would most runners have done? Most would have waved a fist, dusted themselves off, and watched the outcome. Perhaps there would have been a few words exchanged after the race. But the athlete in question was beyond the ordinary. It was as if he had been reading this passage—forgetting what is behind and straining forward to what lies ahead, I focus all my energy on the race; and seeing the goal, I fly to the finish.[10]

This is the way everyone who is in the grip of Christ's grace must live. Listen to Paul's explanation to the Corinthians: "But by the grace of God I am what I am, and his grace toward me was not in vain. On the contrary, I worked harder than any of them, though it was not I, but the grace of God that is with me" (1 Corinthians 15:10). Apart from a failing mind or body, we are called to relentlessly press on toward the finish line for the full and complete gaining of Christ, the resurrection, and ultimate perfection. Getting old and tired? Put the pedal to the metal. Young and full of boundless energy? Be a man or woman of "one thing."

Paul's Advice (vv. 15, 16)

Paul concluded with some gentle and wise advice: "Let those of us who are mature think this way, and if in anything you think otherwise, God will reveal that also to you. Only let us hold true to what we have attained" (vv. 15, 16). Mature people don't think they are perfect or have arrived. Those who are mature refuse themselves even a satisfied glance back at spiritual attainments. Instead, forgetting what is behind, they pour their energies into the pursuit of the full knowledge of Christ. They run the race rather than imagine it is over. Paul's confident assertion that if any of them thought otherwise, God would reveal it to them was not a smug assertion that if necessary they would learn the hard way. Rather, he meant that if his brothers and sisters in Philippi had some flaws in their Christian understanding, God himself would graciously correct it. Paul trusted the Spirit of God to bring his people to the knowledge of the truth.[11]

May I say that if you think Paul is a little extreme, if you think that after years of Christian living you will somehow arrive, if you think a time is coming on earth when your knowledge of Christ will be full and satisfying, if you think that a time will come when you can ease up—you're wrong! We are to fly after him in the spring, the summer, the autumn, and the dead of winter.

One final word from Paul: "Only let us hold true to what we have attained" (v. 16). Notice that he included himself with the readers—he said "us" rather than "you." The exact sense is, "Only let us keep in step with what we have attained." Paul wanted them to continue together in accord with the same passion to know Christ. They must not depart from the progress they have made in their pursuit of Christ.[12] This is a fitting word to each of us who love Christ.

Paul's passionate declaration—"that I may know him and the power of his resurrection, and may share his sufferings, becoming like him in his death, that by any means possible I may attain the resurrection from the dead" (vv. 10, 11)—calls us all to a passionate, grasping pursuit of Christ.

Eric Liddell, "the Flying Scotsman," was already famous when he made his phenomenal comeback to win the 440 in the Scotland-France meet. And his fame increased as a runner and a Christian, especially at the Paris Olympics in 1924 where he refused to run in his best events (the 100 meters and the 4 x 100 relay) because they were run on Sunday. *Chariots of Fire* inaccurately portrays this as a last-minute decision in Paris, whereas he actually decided well in advance and began to train for the 200 and 400 meter races.[13] Liddell took a bronze in the 200 and amazed the world by winning the 400 in the world-record time of 47.6 seconds, five meters ahead of the silver medalist— he was truly flying!

Runner he was, but that was only one manifestation of his devotion to Christ. In 1925, having completed his degree in science at Edinburgh and a degree in divinity, he set sail as a missionary to China with the China Inland Mission. In 1932, during his first furlough, he married Florence Mackenzie. In 1941, facing the growing threat of Japanese occupation, he sent his wife and three daughters to Canada to stay with her family while he stayed on to serve among the poor. Liddell suffered many hardships but kept on running hard after Christ. And then in 1943 he was interned in the Weihsien Internment Camp where he again cheerfully served those around him. In 1945, at the age of forty-three, Eric Liddell died of a brain tumor that may have been caused by his malnourishment and overwork. Liddell's grave was marked by a simple wooden cross, with his name written in boot polish.[14] He is interred in the Mausoleum of Martyrs in Shijiazhuang, China.[15]

I do not know what the inscription says. But if I were to imagine one, it would be:

He Died Running

Here was a man whose life was given to one thing. "[F]orgetting what [lay] behind and straining *forward* to what [lay] ahead, [he] press[ed] on toward the goal for the prize of the upward call of God in Christ Jesus" (v. 13).

May we all die running for and with Jesus!

Brothers, join in imitating me, and keep your eyes on those who walk according to the example you have in us. For many, of whom I have often told you and now tell you even with tears, walk as enemies of the cross of Christ. Their end is destruction, their god is their belly, and they glory in their shame, with minds set on earthly things. But our citizenship is in heaven, and from it we await a Savior, the Lord Jesus Christ, who will transform our lowly body to be like his glorious body, by the power that enables him even to subject all things to himself. Therefore, my brothers, whom I love and long for, my joy and crown, stand firm thus in the Lord, my beloved.

3:17—4:1

18

Stand Firm

THE APOSTLE PAUL'S mighty call to a lifelong pursuit of knowing Christ fully peaked with his declaration of relentless determination: "one thing I do: forgetting what lies behind and straining forward to what lies ahead, I press on toward the goal for the prize of the upward call of God in Christ Jesus" (vv. 13, 14). This fervent expression was meant to motivate the Philippians to the same hard-charging pursuit—a life of running after Jesus. Paul wanted his readers to "stand firm," as he had expressed earlier in 1:27 ("so that . . . I may hear of you that you are standing firm in one spirit") and would later command ("stand firm thus in the Lord, my beloved," 4:1). The reason for these admonitions to "stand firm" is that dark forces had already taken their toll on the little church, as Paul would soon explain.

A Call to Imitation (v. 17)

What does Paul commend to the Philippians first in this matter of standing firm? Surprisingly, imitation. "Brothers, join in imitating me, and keep your eyes on those who walk according to the example you have in us." To casual readers, this may not sound like the voice of humility. However, there is no self-promoting ego here calling everyone to focus on his example as the sole model for action, because the call to imitation is larger than Paul himself. Notice that Paul says, "and keep your eyes on those who walk according to the example you have in us"—the "us" includes Timothy and Epaphroditus, whom Paul had held high as spiritual models in chapter 2. Also remember that these excellent men had followed the example of Christ by not seeking their own interests but rather the interests of others (cf. 2:4, 20, 21). They, like Paul, pursued hard after Christ. They were men of "one thing" (3:13).

Thus the apostle is calling the Philippians to join together[1] in imitating both himself and the collective pattern of his fellow soldiers, including the men and women in the Philippian church who walked according to the example of those who indeed pursued Christ.

We all know that we learn by watching others. Young Johann Sebastian Bach was a studied observer of the great organist and composer Dietrich Buxtehude. Bach made repeated long trips on foot to Buxtehude's church to observe and hear the master, even copying the composer's scores by hand—all of which had a marked effect on Bach's style and vitality and the shaping of his brilliance. Bach, surpassing genius that he was, rode on the lesser genius and example of his mentor.[2] So it is in every area from the arts to the trades to business to sports. I remember as a high school boy how my tennis would improve after watching top-flight collegiate or professional players. This is how it works with golf and basketball and art and the professions and the church—especially the church.

Today Paul's passionate longing echoes down to us—"that I may know him and the power of his resurrection, and may share his sufferings, becoming like him in his death, that by any means possible I may attain the resurrection from the dead" (3:10, 11). We also hear his "one thing I do" resolve: "forgetting what lies behind and straining forward to what lies ahead, I press on toward the goal for the prize of the upward call of God in Christ Jesus" (3:13b, 14). Paul's example draws us upward. But along with this we must have the collective example of the church. We need the example of the Eric Liddells, men who died running. We need pastors and missionaries and elders who walk according to the example of Paul and the apostolic band.

It is of greatest importance that those of us in leadership not descend to be professionals—that we constantly desire to know Christ and "the power of his resurrection" (v. 10) and the fellowship of his sufferings—that we "press on toward the goal for the prize of the upward call" (v. 14) with all our being. This is what children and youth and students need to see—living examples to imitate. I say this especially to my fellow ministers, elders, youth workers, and children's workers. Those who pursue Christ will produce those who pursue Christ. And it is only those who continue to run after Christ who will stand firm.

Warning about Apostasy (vv. 18, 19)

Enemies

We immediately see why Paul's call to imitation is so urgent because, tragically, many live as enemies of the cross. "For many, of whom I have often told you and now tell you even with tears, walk as enemies of the cross of Christ" (v. 18). They are the exact opposite of Paul's example. Their walk is the antithesis to Paul's walk—and there are many of them.

Evidently these enemies were at one time professed Christians, perhaps ex-members of the Philippian church, and still around. Philippi was a small place. Likely these men had regular contact with most of the congregation. The intensity of Paul's tearful grief indicates that their apostasy had been a very personal loss to Paul. Literally Paul says, "I speak weeping." There were tears as he dictated or penned this letter. Evidence that these former converts had become "enemies of the cross of Christ" is indicated by the way they now walked. Their lifestyles repudiated all that the cross stands for, specifically the passionate pursuit of Christ and a cross-centered life of suffering. It was all foolishness to them. I've personally known some like this during the forty years of my ministry who are now lethal enemies of the Body of Christ.

Enemies' End

Paul described the destiny and character of these enemies with four brief (verb-less in the original), appalling expressions.[3]

The first was intended to shock because it was the language of perdition[4]—"Their end is destruction" (v. 19; cf. 1:28). These people had faces and names familiar, and even beloved, to the Philippians. Nevertheless, the great judgment would effect their eternal damnation because of their cross-denying behavior.

Paul explained that this was because "their god is their belly" (v. 19). It was not merely the pleasures of the stomach that was their god, but the bodily desires and sensual delights that displaced the divine and became their god. The Philippian apostates were digging their graves with their own teeth as they chewed upon their earthbound impulses and the cud of personal pleasure. The pursuit of creature comforts displaced the pursuit of Christ and the cross. Today the professed Christian whose own physical and personal needs come before the Lord, whose bodily comforts (what and where he eats, how and where he lives, and what he spends to satisfy his own pleasures) displace the cross had better take note because his god has become his belly. Beware of any pleasure that impedes the passionate pursuit of Christ.

Such people, said Paul, also "glory in their shame" (v. 19). This refers to sensual excesses, especially sexual ones, the immoral practices of pagan, pre-Christian lives. This is how many of today's neo-pagans live and glory. As Malcolm Muggeridge wrote:

> Sex is the mysticism of a materialist society, with its own mysteries . . . and its own sacred texts and scripture—the erotica that fall like black atomic rain on the just and unjust alike, drenching us, blinding us, stupefying us. To be carnally minded is life![5]

But Paul said that to be thus-minded is death—desolate, impenetrable night.

Lastly, their "minds [are] set on earthly things" (v. 19). Their whole inner disposition was governed by the earthly sphere of sin.

The effect of these four terse descriptions is to show that the enemies of the cross had come full circle.[6] By abandoning the pursuit of Christ and the cross, their minds once again were set on pre-Christian things rather than on "the upward call of God in Christ Jesus" (v. 14). "They stand diametrically opposed to those whose commonwealth is in heaven."[7]

Paul's message to us is this: the way we live, our walk, our appetites, the things in which we revel, the set of our inner disposition all tell whether we are Christian or post-Christian. We should note that Paul, who had much to say about the nature of authentic faith in other places (cf. Ephesians 2:8–10; Romans 3:21, 22, 28; 10:5–13), did not say a word about faith here. Here lifestyle revealed the authenticity of professed belief. Taking this warning to heart is essential if we are to stand firm.

Assurance about Heaven (vv. 20, 21)

Having warned the Philippians about the enemies around them, Paul switched from the negative to the ultimate positive: "But our citizenship is in heaven, and from it we await a Savior, the Lord Jesus Christ, who will transform our lowly body to be like his glorious body, by the power that enables him even to subject all things to himself" (vv. 20, 21). We have moved from the earthbound focus of the enemies of the cross to the heavenly realities of the followers of the cross, which provide mighty reasons to stand firm.

Our Citizenship

To begin with, the up-front declaration "But our citizenship is in heaven" references a reality already mentioned by Paul in the pivotal text of 1:27: "Only let your manner of life be worthy of the gospel of Christ." "Manner of life" is more exactly "manner of life as citizens" (implicitly, "of heaven"). The same root word that is used there is used here in 3:20 for "citizenship."

You can hear the similarity in the Greek. In 1:27 it is the verb *politeúesthe*, and here in 3:20 it is the noun *políteuma*. Both are built on the noun *polis*, which means "city." All kinds of English words come from this: *police, metropolis, political, politician.*

The reality behind both references is that the Philippians were citizens of the commonwealth of Heaven—they belonged to another *polis*, apart from Philippi. This was particularly poignant for the Philippians because Philippi was a singularly self-conscious little Roman *polis* (legally Italian soil), which kept the locals at a distance while at the same time intruding into their lives.

In fact, the Philippians did not have full citizenship in the Roman-run town. But that was not a problem—they were full citizens of the heavenly commonwealth. That was their present, ongoing reality. And they had to hold on to it as a means of standing firm. This is likewise true for each of us who know and follow Christ. It is a present-tense reality.

Our Eager Expectation

As we look to the next line of Paul's thought, the poignancy deepened for the Philippian church because, in distinction from the imperial cult worship of Caesar as its savior, that church eagerly awaited its "Savior, the Lord Jesus Christ" (v. 20).

This title is the highest of all names, the name already proclaimed in Christ's super-exaltation in 2:9–11: "Therefore God has highly exalted him and bestowed on him the name that is above every name, so that at the name of Jesus every knee should bow, in heaven and on earth and under the earth, and every tongue confess that Jesus Christ is Lord, to the glory of God the Father." The ultimate confession of the universe will be that Jesus, Messiah, is Yahweh, the awesome God who created the heavens and the earth, the one who sets up kings and takes them down (cf. Isaiah 45:5, 6, 14, 18, 22, 23)—the Savior.

Our Transformation

And what will be the outcome when the Savior comes? He "will transform our lowly body to be like his glorious body, by the power that enables him even to subject all things to himself" (v. 21). That which awaits believers is a radical transformation not just of our physical bodies but of our whole person as a totality.[8]

The change will be necessary because our weak, mortal bodies are insufficient to receive and participate in the glorious state. Furthermore, our lowly bodies will be transformed "to be like his glorious body," so that our future bodies will be of the same order as Christ's own resurrected, glorified body. Christ's resurrected body is the prototype of what awaits each of us. As Paul writes in 1 Corinthians 15:49, "Just as we have borne the image of the man of dust, we shall also bear the image of the man of heaven." Murray Harris writes in his classic study *Raised Immortal*:

> Paul is saying, then, that in place of an earthly body that is always characterized by physical decay, indignity, and weakness, the resurrected believer will have a heavenly body that is incapable of deterioration, beautiful in form and appearance, and with limitless energy and perfect health. Once he experiences a resurrection transformation, man will know perennial rejuvenation, since he will have a perfect vehicle for God's deathless Spirit, a body that is invariably responsive to his transformed personality.[9]

What further dazzles us here is that it is Christ who does this (not the Father or the Holy Spirit, as we might expect). As Harris says, "To summarise: just as the event of spiritual resurrection is founded exclusively on the resurrection of Christ, so the ensuing state of spiritual resurrection is totally dependent on the risen life of Christ."[10]

Paul concluded his thoughts here about Christ's power by stating explicitly that Christ does this "by the power that enables him even to subject all things to himself" (v. 21). This is an allusion to Psalm 8:6, which speaks of God's intention to subject all creation to mankind. So here Christ fulfills mankind's destiny, and in doing so he makes the universe subject to himself. Everything is of Christ!

This section heaps encouragement upon encouragement. The Philippians were citizens of the commonwealth of Heaven in the continuing present. This was not a future denouement but ongoing, eternal reality. What an empowering perspective in the midst of the officious Roman unctuousness of the mini-Rome of Philippi. And as citizens of Heaven they didn't await a pale Roman savior, a petty little-caesar, but rather the Savior with a name that is above every other name—Yahweh, Jesus, Messiah—to whom every knee will bow, in Heaven and on earth and under the earth. And this Savior will someday give them bodies like his own glorious body as he subjects everything in the universe to himself. So stand firm.

Exhortations to Stand Firm (4:1)

Now comes the capstone of Paul's thoughts: "Therefore, my brothers, whom I love and long for, my joy and crown, stand firm thus in the Lord, my beloved" (4:1).

This is the most affectionate and endearing language he used anywhere— "brothers"—"beloved"—"long[ed] for." This little church was his favorite. "My joy" (the thirteenth sounding of this merry note) and my "crown"—this is what they were to Paul as he exhorted them, "Stand firm thus in the Lord, my beloved." Paul wanted them to run hard after the full knowledge of Christ (cf. 3:10, 11, 13, 14).

In the light of his call to be imitators of the godly examples in their lives and the fourfold warning about those who had gone full circle to become "enemies of the cross of Christ" (v. 18) and then the stunning *assurance* about their citizenship and its glorious outcome, Paul lovingly exhorted his friends to "stand firm." And that is my prayer for you.

May the Body of Christ provide you with many examples to follow.

May the lives of the enemies of the cross be cause for tears and alarm.

May the wonders of your citizenship and your future dance in your soul.

And may you "stand firm" in your pursuit of "the upward call of God in Christ Jesus" (3:14).

I entreat Euodia and I entreat Syntyche to agree in the Lord. Yes, I ask you also, true companion, help these women, who have labored side by side with me in the gospel together with Clement and the rest of my fellow workers, whose names are in the book of life. Rejoice in the Lord always; again I will say, rejoice. Let your reasonableness be known to everyone. The Lord is at hand; do not be anxious about anything, but in everything by prayer and supplication with thanksgiving let your requests be made known to God. And the peace of God, which surpasses all understanding, will guard your hearts and your minds in Christ Jesus.

4:2–7

19

Garrisoned by Peace

PHILIPPIANS 4:2–7

WOMEN HAD PLAYED A prominent role in the founding of the churches in Macedonia, and especially at the beginning of the church in Philippi where Lydia, a seller of purple, became Paul's first convert on European soil, and a young slave girl became the first to be delivered from an evil spirit (Acts 16:14–18; cf. 17:4–12).

At present the little church in Philippi was graced by two magnificent women, Euodia and Syntyche, whom Paul memorably described here as having "labored side by side with me in the gospel together with Clement and the rest of my fellow workers, whose names are in the book of life" (v. 3). These two were no weak sisters by any means because Paul's description employed a gladiatorial term, better rendered as "fought side by side with me."[1] They had been in "the same conflict" as Paul (1:30) in the battle for the gospel, which placed them amidst the fellowship of the gospel (cf. 1:5)—gospel comradeship in the quest to proclaim the good news to the pagan world. These two women, along with a certain Clement and other fellow workers, all had their names in "the book of life"—the great book that will be opened on the day of judgment, when only those found in its pages will enter the kingdom of Heaven (Revelation 21:27). Euodia and Syntyche were elect warriors. Their certitudes and commitments to the gospel meant that tension was a daily fact of their existence. Those who follow hard after Christ live with tensions and troubles that the uncommitted heart does not know. And the cloying atmosphere of the small Roman colony took its stressful toll on these excellent women.

We do not know what the trouble was. Perhaps it was the rivalry mentioned in 2:3. In any event, they had a falling-out and were not of the same mind. As it was, this magnificent duo's conflict was jeopardizing the witness of the very gospel for which they had fought. Perhaps trite but true,

> To live above with the saints we love,
> Oh, that will be glory.
> But to live below with the saints we know,
> Well, that's another story.

A Plea for Peace (vv. 2, 3)

A Personal Plea

The news of the women's falling-out had reached Paul in his Roman jail cell, and here he interrupted the flow of his thought with a personal plea to each, "as if exhorting them singly, face to face" (Bengel)[2]: "I entreat Euodia and I entreat Syntyche to agree in the Lord" (v. 2). He asks that they literally "think the same thing in the Lord." If anyone was nodding off in the Philippian assembly while the letter was being read, they were awake now! Certainly Paul was gentle, diplomatic, and respectful, but to be named thus in the letter by the great apostle—all eyes were now upon the two women.

Intervention Please

And there was more because Paul asked for intervention by a third party: "Yes, I ask you also, true companion, help these women" (v. 3a). Over the centuries speculations as to who the third party, the "true companion" (literally, "true yokefellow"), was have been endless. But the most responsible guesses have been that he was a leader in the church to whom the letter was sent as the designated reader. Everyone knew who the true yokefellow was, but we do not. Most likely he was a leading elder in the church, or possibly Luke.[3] Luke was with Paul early in his Roman imprisonment, but this letter does not mention him—perhaps because he had returned to Macedonia and was in Philippi.[4]

Whoever this well-known yokefellow was, his duty was most clear: he was to "help" (that is, take hold of together, assist) "these women"—which suggests that the women may have already taken steps toward mending their discord.[5] The apostle didn't lay out a precise remedy for Euodia and Syntyche but handed it over to the church family in Philippi. He gave them tender guidelines and was diplomatic and encouraging. But what is clear is that the church and its leadership were to help Euodia and Syntyche. These women were to be helped by their brothers and sisters, using their prayers and corporate wisdom.

Did the women respond? Very likely, especially if they took Paul's immediately following imperatives to heart, because they are a prescription for the peace and well-being of the whole Body of Christ.[6] This is one of the most memorized texts in the entire Bible. The King James Version with its "careful for nothing" and "passeth" has been with me for fifty years.

> Rejoice in the Lord always: and again I say, Rejoice. Let your moderation be known unto all men. The Lord is at hand. Be careful for nothing; but in every thing by prayer and supplication with thanksgiving let your requests be made known unto God. And the peace of God, which passeth all understanding, shall keep your hearts and minds through Christ Jesus. (4:4–7, KJV)

Imperatives for Peaceful Living (vv. 4–7)

Rejoice

Karl Barth, in a brief survey of the commands to rejoice in the book of Philippians, noted that we meet the command first in 2:18, where Paul tells the Philippians that they "should be glad and rejoice" with him, and then again in 3:1: "Finally, my brothers, rejoice in the Lord," and, lastly, here in 4:4: "Rejoice in the Lord always; again I will say, rejoice."

From the force of these three commands, Barth concludes that "'joy' in Philippians is a defiant 'Nevertheless!'"[7]—nevertheless "Rejoice." Paul's unqualified "Rejoice" certainly does defy the thankless, complaining nature of humanity and human custom through all of history.

Also, remember that Paul wasn't writing while he lounged in a Roman bath or sipped espresso in Café Roma. We must never forget that Paul delivered his defiant command to rejoice whatever the circumstances when it was unsure whether he would live or die and while he was confined to helplessly watching his competitors and enemies make advances among the churches of Rome and Philippi. As if to answer any question from those who might ask incredulously, "Should we really rejoice during afflictions?" he stated twice, "Rejoice in the Lord always; again I will say, rejoice." Get it?

Note also that the apostle's words allow for no loopholes—"always" permits no exceptions regardless of how humiliating or painful things might be. Similarly, the readers are commanded to find their joy "in the Lord" rather than in their circumstances. As such, Christian "joy is a basic and constant orientation of the Christian life, the fruit and evidence of a relationship with the Lord" (Bockmuehl).[8] It comes from what the Lord has done in the past, from what he is doing now, and from the hope of what he will do in the future.

Blaise Pascal, the mathematical genius, physicist, Christian thinker, inventor, and literary stylist—one of the great minds of human history—had an experience that changed the course of his life. The experience was so pivotal that he wrote it down and had it sewn into his jacket. What Pascal wrote was this:

> In the year of Grace, 1654,
>   On Monday, 23rd of November . . .
>   From about half past ten in the evening until about half past twelve
>   FIRE
>   God of Abraham, God of Isaac, God of Jacob, not of the philosophers
> and scholars.
>   Certitude. Certitude. Feeling. Joy. Peace.
>   God of Jesus Christ.
>   "Thy God shall be my God."
>   Forgetfulness of the world and of everything, except God.
>   He is to be found only by the ways taught in the Gospel. . . .
>   Joy, joy, joy, tears of joy. . . .
>   "This is eternal life, that they might know Thee, the only true God, and
> the one whom Thou has sent, Jesus Christ."
>   Jesus Christ.
>   Jesus Christ.
>   I have separated myself from Him: I have fled from Him, denied Him,
> crucified Him.
>   Let me never be separated from Him.
>   We keep hold of Him only by the ways taught in the Gospel.
>   Renunciation, total and sweet.
>   Total submission to Jesus Christ and to my director.
>   Eternally in joy for a day's exercise on earth. . . .[9]

Poignantly, Pascal inscribed this experience on a piece of parchment as a *Mémorial* and had it sewn under the lining of his successive coats until the end of his life.[10] Thus, Pascal always bore close to his heart the memory of the fiery joy of his conversion. Perhaps during needy times he felt for the parchment to steady his fainting soul.

Blaise Pascal's *Mémorial* was rooted in the Biblical reality that "the joy of the LORD is your strength" (Nehemiah 8:10), and here the great apostle calls us to "Rejoice." Those who set their hearts to "Rejoice in the Lord always" will not only "stand firm" (4:1) but will be receptive to "the peace of God" (v. 7) that overcomes the discords that attack the Body of Christ (vv. 2, 3). "When we persistently rejoice, we become open to God and open to what he can do in our lives" (Ogilvie).[11] Rejoicing in the Lord is not a luxury—it is a necessity!

Until the Lord comes back, all of us are going to experience excruciating stresses, interpersonal woes, humiliating sicknesses, our own deaths, and if we live long enough, the wrenching deaths of loved ones and friends. But in every and all circumstances, we are to "Rejoice in the Lord always." How so? At the very foundation we must press close the fiery record of the joy of our salvation. We must take David's words to heart as they were fulfilled by the ultimate Son of David:

> He drew me up from the pit of destruction,
>   out of the miry bog,
> and set my feet upon a rock,
>   making my steps secure.
> He put a new song in my mouth,
>   a song of praise to our God. (Psalm 40:2, 3a)

Because Christ has saved us, we concur with the Apostle Peter, "Though you have not seen him, you love him. Though you do not now see him, you believe in him and rejoice with joy that is inexpressible and filled with glory, obtaining the outcome of your faith, the salvation of your souls" (1 Peter 1:8, 9). Hold the fire close, and you will rejoice.

And, of course, there is more to rejoice in because all of us have a history of sweet providences that both trail in our wake and grace our present lives— deliverances from harm and death, daily provisions for living, loved ones and various people whom God has placed in our way—all these are causes for ongoing rejoicing. And as we look to the hope of his coming, we cannot do anything but rejoice.

So in this world of woe, God's Word commands us to embrace a defiant "Nevertheless!"—"Rejoice in the Lord always; again I will say, rejoice" (v. 4). No exceptions. No muted praise. Because of what Christ has done, "we may rejoice, we will rejoice, we must rejoice, for we rejoice in the Lord . . . always" (Carson).[12]

Be Gentle

The second imperative that Paul commands—"Let your reasonableness be known to everyone" (v. 5a)—introduces the relational quality that rejoicing produces. The word behind "reasonableness" has been translated many ways. William Tyndale's 1525 translation has it, "Let your softness be known to all men," and that idea is very appropriate. The King James Version renders it "moderation." I am convinced that the best rendering is, "Let your gentleness be known to everyone." Paul was enjoining the gentleness that comes from the character of Christ himself, as we see in 2 Corinthians 10:1 where

Paul appeals to the Corinthians "by the meekness and gentleness of Christ." Indeed, Jesus used the same word to describe himself saying, "I am gentle and lowly in heart" (Matthew 11:29).[13] And here in the context of Philippians, the gentleness of Christ is in view—the one who did not "grasp" his own rights (cf. 2:6).

The sequence of Paul's opening commands first to rejoice and second to be gentle tell us that the most immediate outward expression of a rejoicing heart is Christlike gentleness toward all people, which necessarily involves the patient bearing of abuse. Within the church this gentleness or softness or sweet reasonableness will prevent and moderate the kind of rift that occurred between Euodia and Syntyche. Even the surrounding world finds this softness and gentleness winsome and inviting. A rejoicing spirit is a gentle spirit and a healing balm to the church and the world.

When we recite the imperatives (perhaps too quickly)—"Rejoice in the Lord always; again I will say, rejoice. Let your reasonableness [gentleness] be known to everyone"—it is easy to miss the brief assertion that follows—"The Lord is at hand" (vv. 4, 5; literally, "the Lord is near," just two words in the Greek). However, "the Lord is near" radiates with a light that energizes Paul's commands because both the Philippians' joy and their gentleness, as well as the following command ("do not be anxious" [v. 6]), were grounded in the fact that "the Lord is at hand." His nearness causes us to rejoice; his nearness effects gentleness; his nearness allays anxiety.

Does "the Lord is at hand" refer to time—that his return is near—or to his proximity—that he is near to us? Likely the apostle had both time and space in view. The Lord may return at any time, and he is continually near his people.

He is near, in fact ever present. He is never merely spatially here or there because he carries us here and there in his heart.[14]

> Over all, and not ascending,
> Under all, but not depending;
> Over all the world ordaining,
> Under all, the world sustaining.
>
> Hildebert of Tours[15]

Jesus Christ is closer than our breath, and he is returning soon! Think of it and rejoice! Think of it and be gentle!

Don't Worry

Think of this, and don't worry because the next imperative is, "do not be anxious about anything." Again, Paul wasn't lounging under a palm tree on the Isle of Capri sipping a cool drink, dictating, "Don't worry, be happy!" No detachment here. Paul's whole existence was on the bubble; danger was everywhere. Few things were going right for him, humanly speaking. So understand that the apostle's command came with feeling. In fact, he literally declared, "stop worrying about anything!"—which assumes that the Philippians were anxiously wringing their hands. Indeed, as residents of Philippi they had more things to worry about than we do—poverty, hunger, ostracism, interlopers, agents provocateurs, heretics, and a very Roman "city hall." Nevertheless, Paul's absolute prohibition of worry stood and comes down to us with full force.

Paul's command is an echo of Jesus' teaching to his disciples in Matthew 6:25–34. There Jesus identified worry as simply pagan (v. 32) and asked his hearers to consider the birds of the air as examples of God's provision, then asked, "Are you not of more value than they?" (v. 26). Here it may be helpful to imagine how the birds consider us.

Said the robin to the sparrow:
"I should really like to know
Why these anxious human beings
Rush about and worry so."
Said the sparrow to the robin:
"Friend, I think that it must be
That they have no heavenly Father,
Such as cares for you and me."[16]

Three times Jesus forbade worry: "Therefore I tell you, do not be anxious [worry] about your life" (v. 25)—"Therefore do not be anxious [worry]" (v. 31)—"Therefore do not be anxious [worry] about tomorrow" (v. 34). And Paul cuts to the chase: "Stop worrying about anything!"

Pray

The corollary to not worrying is to take up Paul's following command to pray: "but in everything by prayer and supplication with thanksgiving let your requests be made known to God" (v. 6b). Pagan prayers are destitute of thanksgiving (cf. Romans 1:21; 2 Timothy 3:2), whereas truly Christian prayer breathes thanksgiving because thankfulness is the posture of grace. Thus, at the root of our prayers must be thanksgiving for what God has done for us in Christ through the gospel. In fact, every activity is to be freighted with thanksgiving. "And whatever you do, in word or deed, do everything in the name of the Lord Jesus, giving thanks to God the Father through him"

(Colossians 3:17). All our requests are to be made known to God and adorned with lavish praise to God for the innumerable hues and shapes of his grace.

Of course, whatever we make known to God is already known by him. So why are we to do this? Because as we bring our requests, which reflect every possible cause for anxiety, we are casting all our cares on God and are declaring our absolute dependence upon him. This was the way the apostle himself prayed for all the churches—with extravagant, glad remembrances of God's grace.

Peace!

The accrued force of Paul's imperatives produces a sublime result: "And the peace of God, which surpasses all understanding, will guard your hearts and your minds in Christ Jesus" (v. 7). The boon is incredible. It includes "the peace of God." This is the peace that God himself possesses, "the serenity in which he lives," so to speak.[17] In this sense it is the same as the peace that Christ embodies and gives: "Peace I leave with you; my peace I give to you. Not as the world gives do I give to you. Let not your hearts be troubled, neither let them be afraid" (John 14:27). This peace transcends all rationality, which is, to borrow a phrase from Ephesians, far more "than all that we ask or think" (3:20).

Moreover, God's own peace that transcends thought and imagination "will guard [garrison] your hearts and your minds in Christ Jesus." This is an apt metaphor because the Philippians daily saw the Roman garrison and their gleaming military hardware, just as we view today's peacekeeping forces on televised world news.[18] The "hearts and . . . minds" (the whole inner person) of those in union with Christ are garrisoned by the personal, ineffable peace of God. What a powerful peace! And note that this peace is given irrespective of whether the specific requests are granted or not. God's peace will mightily flood over those who with thanksgiving make their requests known to God.[19]

What a marvelous progression Paul's imperatives bring, and what grace they would mean for the Philippian church as they were implemented. How salutary it is to "Rejoice in the Lord always"—to reference the parchments of grace that recall what God did in saving us—the merry fires of salvation—and to learn to rejoice at all times even amidst the worst scenarios (Philippians 4:4). Then, in concert with rejoicing always, we can let our gentleness be known to everyone—the very gentleness of Christ himself. And then more grace flows, enabling us to rejoice and to be gentle in the knowledge that God is near. Thus the command to not be anxious about anything will find fertile ground in our hearts, and we, with glad remembrances of God's grace, will lay out our requests to God who already knows them and so find ourselves garrisoned by the peace of God, that passes all understanding.

The commitment to obey the command to rejoice—to obey the command to be gentle to everyone—to obey the command to not worry about anything—to obey the command to pray with thanksgiving and thus receive the marvelous peace of God—these commitments will elevate the unity and life of the Church and build an inviting haven for a world that needs Christ.

Finally, brothers, whatever is true, whatever is honorable, whatever is just, whatever is pure, whatever is lovely, whatever is commendable, if there is any excellence, if there is anything worthy of praise, think about these things. What you have learned and received and heard and seen in me—practice these things, and the God of peace will be with you.

4:8, 9

20

Good Thoughts

PHILIPPIANS 4:8, 9

THE CAPACITY OF the human brain is the subject of ever-widening scientific wonder. Its twelve to fourteen billion cells are only a shadow of its complexity, because each cell sends out thousands of connecting tendrils so that a single cell may be connected with 10,000 neighboring cells, each of which is constantly exchanging data impulses. These twelve to fourteen billion brain cells times 10,000 connectors make the human mind an unparalleled computer. The mind's activity has been compared to 1,000 switchboards, each big enough to serve New York City, all running at full speed as they receive and send questions and orders. Put another way, there is more electronic equivalent in one human brain than in all the radio and television stations of the entire world put together!

The human brain does not miss a thing. It is capable of giving and receiving the subtlest input—from imagining a universe in which time bends to creating the polyphonic texture of a Bach fugue or transmitting and receiving a message from God himself—feats no computer will ever accomplish.

The dizzying potential of the human mind reaches its apex in the possibility of possessing the mind of Christ through the ministry of the Holy Spirit—a possibility affirmed by Paul when he said, "But we have the mind of Christ"—a mind that is constantly renewed (1 Corinthians 2:16; cf. Romans 12:2). No computer will ever be able to think God's thoughts, nor will any device be able to know the heart of God or do his works. But the mystery that resides between our ears has this capacity. Indeed, it was created for this—to have the mind of Christ.

This God-like potential points us to a great scandal because very often we Christians fall far short of the mind of Christ. Far more often than we will admit, our thinking is not Christian. John Milton wrote, "A mind is its own place, and in itself / Can make a heav'n of hell, a hell of heav'n. . . ."[1] And that is the experience of every Christian.

So it is imperative that we invite Christ to take over our minds. "Keep your heart with all vigilance," says Proverbs, "for from it flow the springs of life" (4:23). When Jesus quoted Israel's great Shema, he said, "And you shall love the Lord your God with all your heart and with all your soul and with all your *mind* . . ." (Mark 12:30). "Mind" is Jesus' addition to the ancient Shema. And as philosopher/theologian Cornelius Plantinga Jr. comments, "Here is a change worth a gasp. What if a four-year-old prayed outright: 'Now I lay me down to sleep, I pray the Lord my brain to keep'? You would notice."[2] But that is what our Lord wants and demands. He wants to keep our minds.

We emphasize this because it has direct bearing on Paul's command about the Philippians' thought lives in 4:8, 9. As we see from the immediately preceding context, in order to counter the discord between Euodia and Syntyche that was threatening the unity of the Philippian church, Paul gave four brief imperatives that, if obeyed, would bring them the peace of God— namely: (1) rejoice, (2) be gentle, (3) do not be anxious, and (4) pray.

If these were implemented, Paul promised, "the peace of God, which surpasses all understanding, will guard your hearts and your minds in Christ Jesus" (v. 7). Now Paul exhorted the Philippians to embrace exalted thought patterns and practices that would enhance God's presence and peace, as he promised in verse 9: "What you have learned and received and heard and seen in me—practice these things, and the God of peace will be with you."

It is important to note that these six rhythmically arranged virtues are qualities that the Greco-Roman culture itself held high. "Paul now offers a cross-cultural Christian exhortation *in the language of Philippi*" (Bockmuehl).[3] Paul took terms that were current in moral philosophy and pressed them into service for Christianity.[4] This was moral language that the surrounding pagan culture could understand. Christian virtues are consonant with the general goodness recognized by non-Christian culture. However, at the same time, as Peter T. O'Brien points out, Paul's "appeal is not to some pagan religious ideal, nor to an acceptance of Stoic presupposition lying behind the ideas, much less to some wholesale acceptance of the norms and values of the world."[5] Paul gives no endorsement of Greco-Roman morality. For example, there is no mention of the four classical virtues of prudence, justice, courage, and self-control. In fact, there is no close parallel to Paul's list anywhere in contemporary literature.[6]

This understood, we see that Paul is calling Euodia and Syntyche and the entire Philippian church to a life that is not only Christian but a life with a broad moral appeal to their contemporary Greco-Roman culture, with the intention that "in the midst of a crooked and twisted generation" the Philippians would "shine as lights in the world" (cf. 2:15). Then, as now, a winsome ethical testimony is a powerful evangelistic force in an unbelieving culture.

Thoughts That Invite the Peace of God (v. 8)

The six parallel clauses are high sounding in the Greek and together evoke a stately impressiveness, which we can sense in the English if we read them slowly: "Finally, brothers, whatever is true, whatever is honorable, whatever is just, whatever is pure, whatever is lovely, whatever is commendable . . ." (v. 8a.). We will briefly touch on each of these six elements and then consider what is required to make them our mental focus.

Six Thought Patterns

First, the Philippians must contemplate "whatever is true," which here means truth in the broadest, most comprehensive sense (v. 8). For followers of Christ, truth begins with his divine person as God the Son, the embodiment of truth. He is all truth, and his gospel is truth—"the word of the truth, the gospel" (Colossians 1:5). God's Word, he says, "is truth" (John 17:17). Everything that is true is from God because all truth is God's truth.

Therefore, a mind that contemplates what is true not only sees Christ, the Word, and the gospel but also rationally engages his creation, rejects irrational thinking, and speaks the truth. This mind seeks "whatever is true" in every avenue of life, from faith to science to relationships to public life to business.

Second, Paul's readers must focus on "whatever is honorable" (v. 8). The Greek word here translated "honorable" is used variously in the Pastoral Epistles to teach what those who are older and in leadership must be like (cf. Titus 2:2 [esv: "dignified"]; 1 Timothy 3:8, 11 [esv: "dignified"]). So the word signifies a personal moral excellence that is dignified and worthy of honor.[7] This is the meaning here in Philippians 4:8—a noble life of spiritual gravitas that evokes honor. It is the opposite of ignoble. The Philippians are to focus on whatever is dignified and noble and honorable and to aspire to such character.

Third, they were to concentrate on "whatever is just" (v. 8). For Paul, that which is "just" or "right" is defined by the character of God. But he also used "just" or "right" in the sense of right thought or action (cf. 1:7), and this broad sense was in view here. The Philippians were to contemplate the things that make for just living—doing the right thing.

Fourth, the readers were to focus on "whatever is pure" (v. 8). This is not limited to sexual purity but extends to all areas of moral purity in thought and speech and actions. They were to focus on that which is not tainted with evil.[8]

Fifth, the Philippians were to contemplate "whatever is lovely" (v. 8). By "lovely" Paul means those things that put themselves forward by their attractiveness.[9] "Lovely" includes not only what is morally lovely but what is aesthetically lovely—"all that is beautiful in creation and in human lives"[10]— from a sunset to a symphony to caring for the poor and powerless—all things beautiful.[11]

Sixth, Paul's readers were to consider "whatever is commendable," which refers to the kind of conduct that is spoken of highly by other people (v. 8).[12]

Summary and Command

These six qualities together form a stunning rhythmic portrait of the mental focus and aspirations that Paul desired for his readers—"whatever is true, whatever is honorable, whatever is just, whatever is pure, whatever is lovely, whatever is commendable" (v. 8a)—a truly stunning portrait of how we must think, which Paul then framed with a comprehensive summary and command: "if there is any excellence, if there is anything worthy of praise, think about these things" (v. 8b). Nothing of moral excellence and nothing that would earn the praise of God or man must be left out of the Philippians' contemplation. And the command is ongoing: "Think [continually] about these things"—let your mind continually dwell on these things (v. 8). Ponder them without ceasing.

No doubt Euodia and Syntyche, while immersed in their conflict, had not been thinking elevated thoughts. However, as they likely took Paul's injunction to heart and began to think thoughts that were "true" and "honorable" and "just" and "pure" and "lovely" and "commendable," they were infused with positive aspirations that facilitated their reconciliation (v. 8). Furthermore, as the beleaguered church embedded in Philippi (that little bastion of Greco-Roman culture) began to think upon and live out these appealing virtues, the light of the gospel further penetrated the pagan culture. And twenty centuries later we who make the decision to continually think only of such things will become more effective agents of grace.

As we apply these truths to ourselves, we must understand that this text has always been relentlessly demanding. The sheer weight of Paul's six positives demands the rejection of negative input. Listen to their inversion: "Finally brothers, whatever is untrue, whatever is dishonorable, whatever is unjust, whatever is impure, whatever is unlovely, whatever is uncommendable, if there is anything not morally excellent, if there is anything unworthy of praise, *do not* think about these things." Paul's command calls for a life of conscious negation. Thinking as we ought to demands the discipline of refusal.

Over the years I have preached and written on this extensively, most recently in two chapters of *Set Apart*, one on "Viewing Sensuality" and the other on "Violence and Voyeurism."[13] Suffice it to say that contemporary media overwhelmingly present the antithesis of Philippians 4:8 as they have become increasingly eroticized, violent, and intolerant of Jesus Christ. And given that there is virtually no distinction between the viewing habits of Christians and non-Christians, the minds of countless Christians have become increasingly eroticized and blasphemous—which is to say, sub-Christian. Today more than ever before we need to heed the psalmist's advice: "I will walk with integrity of heart within my house; I will not set before my eyes anything that is worthless" (Psalm 101:2b, 3a). Perhaps there needs to be the violent refusal voiced by Jesus: "If your right eye causes you to sin, tear it out and throw it away. For it is better that you lose one of your members than that your whole body be thrown into hell" (Matthew 5:29).

Along with the discipline of refusal, there is the ancient, God-given remedy of spending much time reading and meditating on the Scriptures. The greatest danger in our busy, increasingly postliterate world is that we make little or no effort to think God's thoughts after him, to hide his Word in our hearts so that we might not sin against him (cf. Psalm 119:11). We cannot be profoundly influenced by that which we do not know.

We must hide God's Word in our hearts. We must make time for quiet meditation in the early morning or in a private space at noon or in a corner of the house at night. We must read and reread passages, listening to the Spirit, turning the thoughts over in our minds, praying over a word or a phrase. We must acquaint ourselves with all of God's Word by reading and listening to it. Remember, five pages a day will take you through the whole Bible in only a year! It takes this kind of commitment to learning what God says to counter the noisy input that daily assaults our minds "and take every thought captive to obey Christ" (2 Corinthians 10:5).

Here again Paul's charge to think about whatever is "true" and "honorable" and "just" and "pure" and "lovely" and "commendable" is powerfully phrased because "think about these things" uses the word *logizomai*, from which we get the mathematical word *logarithm*. Paul commands the same deliberate, prolonged contemplation of these virtues that it takes to weigh a mathematical problem.[14]

Action That Will Bring the Peace of God (v. 9)

Paul was no armchair coach. He lived out each of the six "whatever" qualities that he was calling his readers to think about so long and so hard. Paul had the mind of Christ. He contemplated whatever was true and then lived it; he thought and lived honorably; he thought and lived justly; he thought and lived purely; he thought of the lovely and lived in accord with it; he thought and lived commendably.

Living Example

Thus he presented his own life as a living example to imitate: "What you have learned and received and heard and seen in me—practice these things, and the God of peace will be with you" (v. 9). The six virtues could have been used as exalted abstractions—materials for deep, esoteric contemplation—but he clothed his call to think about them in the flesh and blood of his own life as he lived it. "What you have learned and received" refers to what he taught his readers through *personal instruction* beginning on the first day of their church's existence. They had received the apostolic faith from Paul.

Along with this, Paul had given them his *personal example*, which they had "heard and seen" in him. Both when Paul was with them and when away, the Philippians heard about Paul's character and conduct—his bravery, how he faced trials, his devotion, his prayer, his patient suffering, his resiliency. And when he was with them, they saw his godly example and his modeling of the "whatevers" he was asking of them. They had before their very eyes the pattern of an excellent and worthy life.

Summary Call

So Paul commanded and promised them unashamedly, "practice these things, and the God of peace will be with you" (v. 9b). In essence he said, "Imitate me, and practice truth, honor, justice, purity, loveliness, and rightness, and the God of peace will be with you." The truth is, we have not learned "these things" until we have lived them out. "Noble thoughts are of little value unless they be translated into deeds. Living surpasses learning; practice outshines priority; living supersedes learning" (Strauss).[15]

The "whatevers" become reality on the basis of the choices we make on the subway, at our work desks, at the gas pump, driving in a car pool, and a thousand other anonymous occasions when we make the choices that shape our lives.[16] Paul called his readers to write these virtues into their own lives by putting them into practice so that in time words like truth and justice and purity would be written large over their (and our) lives.

And the result is that "the God of peace will be with you" (v. 9). In verse 7 Paul promised them "the peace of God"—God's own personal peace—His own serenity. Here the reward is "the God of peace" *himself*.

In verse 7 it is God's salvation that garrisons our hearts; here it is his presence that blesses and saves.[17] God's peace and his presence cannot be separated. They are one as his gift. And when his peace, his *shalom*, firmly reigns in the embedded church—whether in Philippi or Rome or New York or Bombay—it will radiate the light of Christ to the surrounding world.

This matter of our minds, the immensely complex mystery that resides between our temples, is a matter of life and death. On the one hand, there must be a conscious rejection of all that is not consonant with the mind of Christ, and on the other there must also be a conscious taking on of exalted thoughts—and not only the thinking of them but the practice of them day after day so that the mind of Christ shines out to a dark world.

> May the mind of Christ my Savior
> Live in me from day to day,
> By His love and pow'r controlling,
> All I do and say.
>
> Kate B. Wilkinson, 1925

I rejoiced in the Lord greatly that now at length you have revived your concern for me. You were indeed concerned for me, but you had no opportunity. Not that I am speaking of being in need, for I have learned in whatever situation I am to be content. I know how to be brought low, and I know how to abound. In any and every circumstance, I have learned the secret of facing plenty and hunger, abundance and need. I can do all things through him who strengthens me.

4:10–13

21

Content in Christ

PHILIPPIANS 4:10-13

WHEN ZACCHAEUS, the miserly little kingpin of the Jericho tax franchise, strode off to his home for a lengthy conversation with Jesus, no one anticipated the change that would be announced from his own lips for all to hear: "Behold, Lord, the half of my goods I give to the poor. And if I have defrauded anyone of anything, I restore it fourfold" (Luke 19:8). For starters, he gave away 50 percent of everything he had to the poor. And from the remaining half of his fortune, he pledged to make restitution at four times the amount of what he had extorted. In effect, Zacchaeus lived out Jesus' command that had earlier caused the rich young ruler to depart from Jesus: "Sell all that you have and distribute to the poor, and you will have treasure in heaven; and come, follow me" (Luke 18:22).

Tiny Zacchaeus had become huge! The compulsive drive to make money and keep it was gone. He went to Jesus mastered by the passion to get; he left mastered by the passion to give. He went in as the littlest man in Jericho; he left as the biggest man in town. Something wonderful had happened inside that house with Jesus. And Jesus made it forever clear for all to hear: "Today salvation has come to this house, since he also is a son of Abraham" (19:9). Zacchaeus had been regenerated—saved! And the immediate evidence of his new heart was his desire to give. His newfound generosity was prima facie evidence of his salvation.

The Apostle Paul would have known the story well because the teller of this story was Dr. Luke, his apostolic sidekick who later also wrote the book of Acts. So the equation of generosity and salvation was fixed firmly in Paul's mind when he held up the example of the generosity of the Macedonian churches (of which Philippi was the leading congregation) to motivate the Corinthians to give:

> We want you to know, brothers, about the grace of God that has been given among the churches of Macedonia, for in a severe test of affliction, their abundance of joy and their extreme poverty have overflowed in a wealth of generosity on their part. For they gave according to their means, as I can testify, and beyond their means, of their own accord, begging us earnestly for the favor of taking part in the relief of the saints—and this, not as we expected, but they gave themselves first to the Lord and then by the will of God to us. (2 Corinthians 8:1–5)

Using the example of the Philippians, Paul made a penetrating application to the Corinthians: "But as you excel in everything—in faith, in speech, in knowledge, in all earnestness, and in our love for you—see that you excel in this act of grace also. I say this not as a command, but to prove by the earnestness of others that your love also is genuine" (vv. 7, 8; cf. v. 24). So from this we know that Paul had long viewed the Philippian church as the real thing. He was so proud of them and loved them so much!

Paul's Joy (v. 10)

Spontaneous Joy

This background helps us understand Paul's burst of joy when Epaphroditus, very much worse for the wear, showed up at Paul's Roman prison cell with a love offering from the Philippians: "I rejoiced in the Lord greatly that now at length you have revived your concern for me" (v. 10a). The apostle rejoiced in the generosity of the Philippians' monetary gift because prisoners in the Roman system were dependent upon outside support for everything. But Paul's joy went far deeper because the gift was indicative of the distant Philippians' continuing authenticity and spiritual health. Their generosity revealed the same Macedonian health that sprang first from their having given themselves to the Lord.

Paul's choice of words framed his response with bright color. The Greek word translated "revived" is a rare word that means "blossom again" like perennials in the spring. When gift-bearing Epaphroditus appeared in his cell, it was for the apostle like spring flowers suddenly bursting into bloom.

There was no muting of Paul's joy. He rejoiced immensely. And it was "in the Lord." Everyone in earshot knew all about it. Think of the apostle locked up, existing on the most meager provisions, listening to reports about others preaching Christ and intending to afflict him, longing to hear about his churches. And suddenly there was Epaphroditus and thus springtide and great joy.

Sensitive Qualification

The apostle, always a sensitive people person, astutely sensed that his enthusiastic expression of thanks could be misunderstood by some of the Philippians as pointing to their prior lack of care, as if he were saying, "*Finally* you have revived your care for me." So he immediately added, "You were indeed concerned for me, but you had no opportunity" (v. 10b). Paul knew that he was always on their minds, but that there were mitigating reasons for their lapse. Perhaps it was his changing venues, the distance, or recent poverty in Philippi. Whatever, he knew that they really did care.

Paul's Contentment (vv. 11, 12)

Still aware that he could be misunderstood to be saying that his joy came from the Philippians' generous gift and the resulting prospect of a good meal and some warm clothing, Paul stated, "Not that I am speaking of being in need, for I have learned in whatever situation I am to be content" (v. 11). Paul's declaration of contentment was meant to grip the Philippians' attention because the word he used came straight from pagan Stoic philosophy. As Gordon Fee remarks, "On the surface his explanation looks like a meteor fallen from the Stoic sky into his epistle."[1]

The Stoics regarded contentment, *autarkeia*, as the essence of all virtues. For them contentment described the mind-set of the person who had become independent of all things and all people. The Stoic line was, "man should be sufficient unto himself for all things, and able, by the power of his will, to resist the force of circumstances."[2] The Stoic Seneca put it this way: "the happy man is content with his present lot, no matter what it is, and is reconciled to his circumstances."[3] The Stoic ideal was a kind of self-contained superman who could rise above it all in independent self-sufficiency and serenity.[4]

Christ-Centered Contentment

But Paul transformed the term with a "powerfully Christ-centered redefinition of contentment [*autarkeia*]."[5] Paul and all who are in Christ are God sufficient as opposed to self-sufficient. Contentment is rooted in the eternal God rather than in the temporal self. Thus while Paul and Seneca may appear to be close, they are a universe apart! Paul is sufficient and content not because he is independent but because he is totally dependent—upon Christ.[6]

The truth is, over the passage of time and through his epic experiences the Apostle Paul had come to know contentment in every situation. Given the unparalleled miseries and joys he experienced, this affirmation of continual contentment is an astonishing statement—a statement that no honest Stoic could ever make! And as we will see, this contentment is available to any man or woman in Christ.

Dynamic Contentment

In the remainder of the text Paul expounded the dynamics of his contentment in beautifully balanced, rhythmic phrases. Paul said expansively, "I know how to be brought low, and I know how to abound" (v. 12a). To be "brought low" or "humbled" has implicit reference to Christ in the famous statement of 2:8, where we read that Christ "humbled himself by becoming obedient to the point of death." Paul knew how to be humbled and even requested that he share in Christ's humiliation: "that I may know him and the power of his resurrection, and may share his sufferings, becoming like him in his death" (3:10). No Stoic would ever endure such humbling (much less invite it) because humiliation was considered by them to be despicable. Suffering, yes, but it was to be done stoically. But humiliation? Never! Humiliation regularly headed the Stoic's list of things to be avoided.[7]

Paul's balanced sentence, "I know how to be brought low, and I know how to abound" means that Paul knew how to share in Christ's humiliation *and* how to share in his glorious riches (v. 12; cf. 4:19).[8] In this life Paul had been repeatedly beaten to within an inch of his life, but he had also been caught up to the third heaven (cf. 2 Corinthians 11:24, 25; 12:1–6). Paul also came to gladly boast, as he says, "of my weaknesses, so that the power of Christ may rest upon me. For the sake of Christ, then, I am content with weaknesses, insults, hardships, persecutions, and calamities" (2 Corinthians 12:9, 10).

Extreme Contentment

Having stated the larger principle, Paul elaborated on the extremes of his contentment: "In any and every circumstance, I have learned the secret of facing plenty and hunger, abundance and need" (v. 12b.). On the downside "hunger" and "need" echo the extremes of the hardship lists from Paul's letters to the Corinthians.

- "To the present hour we hunger and thirst, we are poorly dressed and buffeted and homeless, and we labor, working with our own hands. . . .

We have become, and are still, like the scum of the world, the refuse of all things." (1 Corinthians 4:11–13)

- "We are afflicted in every way, but not crushed; perplexed, but not driven to despair; persecuted, but not forsaken; struck down, but not destroyed; always carrying in the body the death of Jesus, so that the life of Jesus may also be manifested in our bodies. For we who live are always being given over to death for Jesus' sake, so that the life of Jesus also may be manifested in our mortal flesh. So death is at work in us, but life in you." (2 Corinthians 4:8–12)
- ". . . but as servants of God we commend ourselves in every way: by great endurance, in afflictions, hardships, calamities, beatings, imprisonments, riots, labors, sleepless nights, hunger. . . ." (2 Corinthians 6:4, 5)
- "Five times I received at the hands of the Jews the forty lashes less one. Three times I was beaten with rods. Once I was stoned. Three times I was shipwrecked; a night and a day I was adrift at sea; on frequent journeys, in danger from rivers, danger from robbers, danger from my own people, danger from Gentiles, danger in the city, danger in the wilderness, danger at sea, danger from false brothers; in toil and hardship, through many a sleepless night, in hunger and thirst, often without food, in cold and exposure." (2 Corinthians 11:24–27)

Paul had learned to experience contentment in the extremes of deprivation from hunger to homelessness to being in rags to beatings to labor and exhaustion to intense humiliation.

On the upside "plenty" and "abundance" echo the apostle's experience of those times that were the good times by comparison. While we know much about his deprivations from the hardship lists, we know little about his experiences of abundance, but we can imagine what they were. For example, in Philippi when the church was born, likely there were feasts in the home of his first convert, Lydia, a prosperous seller of purple, and perhaps also in the home of his other notable convert, the Philippian jailer. Certainly there were times in Ephesus and Corinth when the sun shined brightly over the pleasures of friends and feasting amidst the beauty of God's creation and especially the beauty of his people as they honored Paul for bringing them the gospel. And during these times Paul was content.

What is remarkable, of course, is that Paul knew the secret of being content in either extreme—whether hunger or a sumptuous Mediterranean repast. Indeed, it may be more of an accomplishment to be content with plenty. As John Calvin explained:

He who knows how to use present abundance soberly and temperately with thanksgiving, prepared to part with everything whenever it may please the Lord, giving also a share to his brother according to his ability, and is also not puffed up, that man has learned to excel and to abound. This is an excellent and rare virtue, and much greater than the endurance of poverty.[9]

Here Paul's terminology—"I have learned the secret of facing plenty and hunger" (v. 12)—is borrowed from the vocabulary of false religions, where "secret" originally referred to induction into a mystery cult. Though the word *secret* was no longer limited to that usage, the sense of initiation still lingered. So Paul's point is that Christian contentment remains a mystery to those on the outside and can only be learned from the inside by those who are in Christ. In truth, "Contentment is a . . . quiet secret known and cherished only by a few" (Bockmuehl).[10] Paul had come to know the secret of contentment over a period of time. His learning was part of his spiritual growth and sanctification. The question for us is, have we learned the secret?

We can, as we will now observe in the apex of Paul's thought in this section.

Paul's Confidence (v. 13)

"I can do all things through him who strengthens me" is one of the most frequently quoted verses of the Bible. It has been taped on the ceiling over bench presses in weight rooms. Cryptic Philippians 4:13s are affixed on the edges of bathroom mirrors to supply inspiration to face the challenges of the day. This text has been the subject of countless needlepoints and calligraphies.

But, sadly, Philippians 4:13 has been widely misused as it has been removed from its context and employed as an inspirational snippet to say, "I can do *anything* through Christ who strengthens me" or "I can do *everything* (especially extraordinary things) through Christ who strengthens me." It has been especially abused by those who view their Christianity through the lens of triumphalism, who think that through Christ they become superhuman.

As with every other line of Scripture, the assertion "I can do all things" is controlled by the context. Thus what Paul says is that in whatever circumstances I find myself, in whatever extremes—whether experiencing abundance with the wealthy or fellowshiping with the poor or struggling to proclaim the gospel to people who don't want to hear or enduring the wrath of the establishment or bringing peace to the church or languishing in prison— I can be *content* and "can do all things through him who strengthens me" (v. 13). Paul is confident that he will be divinely strengthened to do anything and everything that *God calls* him to do. Not only could Paul be content and confident in every circumstance, he could also be sure that he would be equipped with divine power to deal with it. Paul says much the same thing in

Colossians 1:28, 29 where he reveals that it is Christ who sustains his active ministry: "Him we proclaim, warning everyone and teaching everyone with all wisdom, that we may present everyone mature in Christ. For this I toil, *struggling with all his energy that he powerfully works within me.*" Paul toils and struggles, straining with all his might, but it is the energy and power of Christ that strengthens him!

Here the precise sense of the Greek of Philippians 4:13 will help us because the preposition "through" should be rendered "in," so that the promise reads, "I can do all things *in* him who strengthens me."[11] Whatever comes Paul's way, he has the strength to meet it. If he is brought low, he is a man *in* Christ; if he abounds, he is a man *in* Christ. In any and every circumstance he is a man *in* Christ. As a man *in* Christ he can do all things. As a man *in* Christ he is content regardless of the situation.

Fellow believers, you and I are not one whit behind the Apostle Paul in advantage because we, like Paul, are all *in* Christ. "Therefore, if anyone is in Christ, he is a new creation. The old has passed away; behold, the new has come" (2 Corinthians 5:17). ". . . Christ in you, the hope of glory" (Colossians 1:27). "In Christ" is the most used description of the believer in Paul's letters. This means that you can be confident that you will be divinely strengthened to do whatever God calls you to do.

Of course, this does not mean that you can do everything you want to do. Do you want to fly? Go to flight school. But please do not take the controls of an airplane reciting Philippians 4:13. Are you a nongolfer who wants to shoot 70? Understand that muttering, "I can do all things through him" before you tee off will turn your fellow golfers into atheists! However, if you are following Christ's call and serving him faithfully in the task to which he has called you, Paul's confident words are yours: "I can do all things *in* him who strengthens me."

Wide swings of fortune await us all. At times many of us will experience bounding prosperity. And all of us will know devastating hardships. But because Christ is the center of our life, we can be content.

Both abundance and loss will pass, but Christ remains the same.

Yet it was kind of you to share my trouble. And you Philippians yourselves know that in the beginning of the gospel, when I left Macedonia, no church entered into partnership with me in giving and receiving, except you only. Even in Thessalonica you sent me help for my needs once and again. Not that I seek the gift, but I seek the fruit that increases to your credit. I have received full payment, and more. I am well supplied, having received from Epaphroditus the gifts you sent, a fragrant offering, a sacrifice acceptable and pleasing to God. And my God will supply every need of yours according to his riches in glory in Christ Jesus. To our God and Father be glory forever and ever. Amen.

4:14–20

22

Assurances for
the Generous

PHILIPPIANS 4:14–20

WRITING TOWARD THE END OF HIS LIFE, famed *New Yorker* editor William Maxwell penned this fond remembrance of his aunt:

> When I was a little boy of six I met her on a cinder path at the Chautauqua grounds one day and she opened her purse and took out a dime and gave it to me. "I don't think my father would want me to take it," I said. My father knew a spendthrift when he saw one, and, hoping to teach me the value of money, he had put me on an allowance of ten cents a week, with the understanding that when the ten cents was gone I was not to ask for more. Also, if possible, I was to save part of the ten cents. "It's perfectly all right," Aunt Beth said. "Don't worry. I'll explain it to him." I took off for the place where they sold Cracker Jacks. And she stands forever, on the cinder path at the Chautauqua grounds, smiling at the happiness she has just set free.[1]

Generosity is singularly beautiful and, when remembered, will prompt a genial smile. This is what the latest example of the storied generosity of the Philippian church prompted in the imprisoned Paul in faraway Rome, as we saw in the last study: "I rejoiced in the Lord greatly that now at length you have revived your concern for me" (4:10). And the apostle's smile still lingered as he said, "Yet it was kind of you to share my trouble" (v. 14). In fact, the apostolic smile shines ever-brighter in this paragraph as he assured the Philippians regarding their generosity and the value of their gift and then of God's generous supply to them.

This section overflows with assurance to the generous church, both then and now.

Assurance Regarding Their Generosity (vv. 14–16)

Laudable Partnership

To begin with, Paul viewed the Philippians' generosity as evidence of their partnership or fellowship with him in ministry. Recall that Paul began this letter to the Philippian church celebrating their partnership: "I thank my God in all my remembrance of you, always in every prayer of mine for you all making my prayer with joy, because of your partnership in the gospel from the first day until now" (1:3–5). The word he used for "partnership" is the word *koinonia*, from the *koinon* word group, and means "fellowship" or "partnership" or "active participation." And then he drew from the same word group two verses later in 1:7 where he said, "You are all partakers with me of grace."

Now, notably, here at the end of the letter he dipped into the *koinon* word group again as he declared, "Yet it was kind of you to *share* my trouble" (v. 14) or more exactly, "Yet you did good to become partners in my affliction." Note also that in the following sentence Paul said, "no church entered into partnership [or fellowship] with me in giving and receiving, except you only" (v. 15). Therefore, Paul wanted his readers to understand that giving to support his ministry was taking up fellowship with him as a partner in his present tribulations. Though the Philippians were not in prison with Paul, they participated in his afflictions by their sympathy and monetary sacrifice. And as they thus participated in his afflictions, they were doing so amidst the context of their own sufferings in Philippi (cf. 1:29, 30).

So we see that giving to the mission and ministry of others is established as a Biblical indicator of spiritual health. Why? First, as we saw in the case of Zacchaeus, generosity is a sign of a regenerate heart (cf. Luke 19:8, 9). Second, giving to mission and ministry is substantive evidence of participation in the fellowship of the gospel. In fact, if we're not giving to the gospel ministry, we have no part in it. "'For where your treasure is, there your heart will be also'" (Matthew 6:21). What we do with our resources is a window into our souls. The question is, what does God see when he looks in?

The Philippians had nothing to fear, for the opening line of verse 14 has Paul commending them (in excellent Greek but ungrammatical English)— "You did good."[2] Their partnering with Paul had apostolic and therefore divine approval.

Stellar Generosity

But there is more, because their gospel partnership was marked by extraordinary generosity: "And you Philippians yourselves know that in the beginning of the gospel, when I left Macedonia, no church entered into partnership with me in giving and receiving, except you only. Even in Thessalonica you sent me help for my needs once and again" (vv. 15, 16).

At first glance Paul's declaration that the Philippians were the only church that had fellowship with Paul "in giving and receiving" sounds like the cold language of commerce. And indeed the words are technical accounting terms. However, in the context of Greco-Roman culture they are freighted with friendship—and here a warm and lasting friendship that "recalls the mutual exchange of services and affliction which they had shared in the past"[3] through their "partnership in the gospel from the first day" on (1:5). Thus "giving and receiving" are idioms of deepest affection and friendship.

When Paul left Philippi and traveled ninety-five miles down the Egnatian Way to Thessalonica, the poverty-stricken Philippians repeatedly sent representatives to Thessalonica with gifts to meet his needs. And when Paul left Macedonia, they remained the only church to support him. Even when Paul went to wealthy Corinth (from whose proud people Paul would accept no money), it was the Philippians of Macedonia who helped him, as Paul explained to the Corinthians: "And when I was with you and was in need, I did not burden anyone, for the brothers who came from Macedonia supplied my need" (2 Corinthians 11:9). The Philippians' generosity was stellar! Most certainly they gave from the heart.

But Holy Scripture always has a greater audience in view. And to us the message is unmistakable. First, we are to be a generous people. Further, we are all called to give to enable others to take the gospel to the lost. The example of the Philippians must always challenge us.

> For they gave according to their means, as I can testify, and beyond their means, of their own accord, begging us earnestly for the favor of taking part in the relief of the saints—and this, not as we expected, but they gave themselves first to the Lord and then by the will of God to us. (2 Corinthians 8:3–5)

At the same time, excellent missions stewardship has a downside. If we are part of a missions-focused church, we may imagine we're just fine. But the call to give to reach the world has not gripped our souls unless we ourselves are giving sacrificially to this end. However, if we are generous in our support of evangelism and mission, then there is a boon—becoming full-fledged members of the fellowship of the gospel, those from the apostles on down through the centuries to today who love Christ and the gospel. Lastly, and most importantly, it means that we will sense the same smile of God that rested upon the generous little church in Philippi.

Assurance of Their Gifts' Surpassing Value (vv. 17, 18)

Parenthetical Disclaimer

Paul's kind assurances could have been taken by certain of his hearers in Philippi as an ever-so-subtle manipulation to get them to give more, so he inserted a disclaimer: "Not that I seek the gift, but I seek the fruit that increases to your credit" (v. 17). Again his words were redolent with the language of commerce, but as before they are intensely spiritual in application. The present participle "increases" signifies *continuing* multiplication that creates compound spiritual interest credited to their account.[4]

When people give to a political campaign in the hope that if their candidate is elected they will be remembered, their generosity is questionable. Or when some give to a public service with the proviso that their name be mentioned (for example, in public television—"This program is made possible by a grant from the Kent and Barbara Hughes Foundation"), the motivation may be to advertise themselves as rich people of cultural substance. But most certainly none of the Philippians were seeking to build either their reputation or their heavenly bank accounts by showy displays of generosity.

Nevertheless, Paul's encouragement to generosity was given with an eye to compounding spiritual interest for the Philippians until the return of Christ. And Paul had support for this from Jesus, who told the rich young ruler, "Go, sell what you possess and give to the poor, and you will have treasure in heaven; and come, follow me" (Matthew 19:21). Jesus, in fact, composed a proverb to help his followers remember this: "Do not lay up for yourselves treasures on earth, where moth and rust destroy and where thieves break in and steal, but lay up for yourselves treasures in heaven" (Matthew 6:19, 20).

The truth is, the only money that we will see again is that which we give away. And that money will return with compounded interest!

Immense Value

Having inserted his disclaimer, Paul concluded his use of accounting metaphors, saying, "I have received full payment, and more" (v. 18a), or more exactly, "I have received full payment and am full to overflowing." With this he switched to the exalted Biblical language of sacrifice: "I am well supplied, having received from Epaphroditus the gifts you sent, a fragrant offering, a sacrifice acceptable and pleasing to God" (v. 18b). The picture suggested by a "fragrant offering" is that of the Old Testament's burnt offering in which the offering was consumed, so that a sumptuous, roast-like aroma rose up to God as an acceptable and pleasing sacrifice.[5] Of course, God doesn't really smell the aroma of a burnt offering, and he isn't impressed by the people going through the motions of the sacrifice. What really pleases God is the generous spirit of his people.[6]

Everything here is descriptive of believers' proper response to God, memorialized in the magnificent words of Romans 12:1 (which uses the same Greek terms for "sacrifice" and "acceptable"): "I appeal to you therefore, brothers, by the mercies of God, to present your bodies as a living sacrifice, holy and acceptable to God, which is your spiritual worship." Here in verse 18 "acceptable and pleasing" emphasizes that the Philippians' generosity to Paul was of the highest value to God himself.

This is so clarifying about what is important in life. God's Word lifts the fog.

> My barn burned down
> Last night—now I can
> See the moon.[7]

Assurance of Supply (v. 19)

At last we are at the high point of the text and the conclusion to verses 10–18: "And my God will supply every need of yours according to his riches in glory in Christ Jesus" (v. 19).

Every Need

The first half of this grand promise is closely linked with and echoes the preceding context. Just as the Philippians had kept Paul "well supplied" (v. 18), so now God will most certainly "supply every need" of theirs. Thus we see that this promise of supply is for generous people like the Philippians and cannot be claimed by those who live for themselves.

Paul promised the generous, "And my God will supply every need of yours" (v. 19). This was intensely personal for Paul. His God, who had repeatedly displayed his power in every conceivable circumstance, would supply the Philippians' needs—just as he had done for Paul through them! Moreover, Paul promised that God would meet not their greed but their need; not all they thought they needed, but all they truly needed. "Every need" compasses the breathtaking range of everything that is vital to living for Christ.

Looking to the immediate context, this meant for the Philippians that God would meet any material need created by their great generosity to Paul. Furthermore, in regard to the spiritual concerns laid out in this letter, God would supply the need for joy and for steadfastness and for endurance and for humility and for concord and for peace and for the ability to face all circumstances. The stunning scope of the promise is that there is not one thing that they (and all faithful Christians) truly needed that God would not give.

On the basis of this we can proclaim to every generous believer that God will meet every need he or she has. But to the grudging, there is no such solace. The wholesale application of this great promise does not exist. It is for the generous follower of Christ alone.

His Riches

How does God do this? The answer is equally expansive—"according to his riches in glory in Christ Jesus" (v. 19b). As Gordon Fee explains, "The Philippians' generosity toward Paul, expressed lavishly at the beginning of verse 18, is exceeded beyond all imagination by the lavish 'wealth' of the eternal God, who dwells 'in glory' full of 'riches' made available 'in Christ Jesus.'"[8] God's "riches" are inherent in his being as the Creator and the God of the universe. So his riches include and infinitely exceed the aggregate wealth of the universe. God's incalculable wealth together with the ineffable splendor of his glory form the treasury and the dazzling context from which he lavishes his children "according to his riches."[9]

If I had a million dollars and gave you a hundred dollars I would be giving *out* of my riches. However, if I gave you a blank check I would be giving *according* to my riches. But God does far more because his riches are infinite and cannot be diminished by the endless zeroes of a celestial blank check. The fact that his riches are "in glory" sets up the ultimate locus "in Christ Jesus," which describes in whom and how the riches that come from God's glory are given to His people.[10] Paul began this letter by addressing it "To all the saints in Christ Jesus" (1:1) and concluded "in Christ Jesus" (4:19). For Christians, every need is met in Christ. He is our beginning and our end. All things come to us in him and through him.

What assurance this brings to those who are in Christ, who share in the fellowship of the gospel through their care and generosity—"And my God will supply every need of yours according to his riches in glory in Christ Jesus" (v. 19).

Having reached this height of exaltation, Paul could do nothing but burst into doxology: "To our God and Father be glory forever and ever. Amen" (v. 20). Whereas only a line earlier the apostle used the intensely personal "my God" (v. 19) to assure his readers of God's care, he now used the plural "our God" as he united himself with the Philippians in ascribing glory to God forever and ever, in all ages to come.

Remember that all of this came because of the Philippian church's generosity to the Apostle Paul. Praise to God is the proper response when God's people are generous.

> We give Thee but Thine own,
> Whate'er the gift may be:
> All that we have is Thine alone,
> A trust, O Lord, from Thee.[11]

William W. How, 1858

Greet every saint in Christ Jesus. The brothers who are with me greet you. All the saints greet you, especially those of Caesar's household. The grace of the Lord Jesus Christ be with your spirit.

4:21–23

23

A Fond Farewell

PHILIPPIANS 4:21–23

THE CONCEPT OF FELLOWSHIP in the book of Philippians is, to say the least, robust, as the five occurrences of the fellowship (*koinon*) word group so forcefully demonstrate.[1] The first instance in 1:5, where Paul celebrated the Philippians' "partnership [fellowship] in the gospel from the first day until now," introduces the vigorous fellowship that rose from their mutual commitment to the gospel. The spiritual glue of their fellowship was, of course, the three-way bond between Paul and the Philippians and Christ, which came from their union with Christ. This provided them with cohesion and focus that transcended mere human fellowship. Together they were a community of brothers and sisters in Christ bound together by a great quest that was nothing less than the evangelization of the Gentile world—a quest they had pursued from the very first day.

The second occurrence of the fellowship word group comes almost immediately in 1:7 where Paul told the Philippians, "for you are all partakers [fellowshipers] with me of grace, both in my imprisonment and in the defense and confirmation of the gospel." This was an eye-opening moment in Paul's writings because the "grace" here, in which they shared fellowship, was not just believing (saving) grace. Rather Paul considered suffering and sacrifice and struggle for the gospel all to be grace. This can be seen in 1:29, where the verbal form of *charis* or "grace" was used by Paul to say, "For it has been granted [graced] to you that for the sake of Christ you should not only believe in him but also suffer for his sake." Suffering for the gospel was a grace in Paul's thinking and theology. So when the Philippians fellowshiped in Paul's sufferings, they partook of grace.

The third reference to the fellowship word group is in 2:1, where Paul appealed to the Philippians' experience of fellowship in the Holy Spirit: "So if there is any encouragement in Christ, any comfort from love, any participation [fellowship] in the Spirit . . ." This "fellowship in the Spirit" came about when, as Paul explained to the Corinthians, "in one Spirit we were all baptized into one body—Jews or Greeks, slaves or free—and all were made to drink of one Spirit" (1 Corinthians 12:13). The fellowship of the Holy Spirit is affirmed by the lingering, final word of the Trinitarian benediction: "The grace of the Lord Jesus Christ and the love of God and the fellowship of the Holy Spirit be with you all" (2 Corinthians 13:14). This is not a pious wish. Rather it is the enduring reality of our existence—"fellowship in the Spirit." It is from within this fellowship that we all cry, "Abba! Father!" (Romans 8:15; Galatians 4:6).

The fourth appearance of fellowship comes in 3:10: "That I may know him, and the power of his resurrection, and the fellowship of his sufferings, being made conformable unto his death" (KJV). Paul's longing for such fellowship not only represented his heart's ambition but was presented as the model for every believing heart.

The fifth and final occurrence of fellowship occurs in the epilogue of Philippians: "Yet it was kind of you to share [fellowship in] my trouble. And you Philippians yourselves know that in the beginning of the gospel, when I left Macedonia, no church entered into partnership [fellowship] with me in giving and receiving, except you only" (4:14, 15). Fellowship involves the generous sharing of our material substance for the proclamation of the gospel.

What are we to conclude from the fivefold usages of fellowship-related words in Philippians? For starters, while the Apostle Paul no doubt had at times fellowshipped over a tasty dessert with the Philippians, fellowship for him (apostolic fellowship) was *not* a cup of Starbucks and biscotti! Fellowship involved (1) participation in the great task of getting the gospel out; (2) the grace of participation in others' suffering for the sake of the gospel; (3) participation in the Holy Spirit, through whom we are all baptized into one body; (4) the longing to participate in the sufferings of Christ; and (5) participation in the spread of the gospel through the generous giving of material resources.

Thus we conclude that these five elements must all be included under Paul's opening phrase "partnership [fellowship] in the gospel" (1:5). This fellowship was united in an epic quest that involved sharing in the gospel—in each other's sufferings—in the Spirit—in Christ's sufferings—and sharing from that which they had. The quest here exceeds any novelist's imagination in drama and reality.

I emphasize this because the Philippians' multifaceted participation in the gospel provides the theological and interpersonal background for understanding Paul's letter to the Philippians. Though separated by 800 miles of the Egnatian Way, both Paul and the Philippians had been graced with suffering. The Philippians were poor, despised, and disenfranchised by the provincial Roman government of Philippi, and in Rome Paul was a prisoner of the same system, despised and betrayed. Whenever Paul thought of the Philippians, he lovingly longed for them. He had heard rumblings of division in Philippi amidst their stress. Then unexpectedly Epaphroditus was standing before him with a generous gift from them. And soon Paul was penning a letter to his partners in the fellowship of the gospel, instructing them as to how they were to strive together in unity for the gospel (cf. 1:27; 2:1–4; 4:1).

As we wrap up our studies in Philippians, we will keep this theme in mind while we briefly visit some of the texts that particularly grace our hearts, those that particularly illumine the fellowship of the gospel.

The Prologue (1:3–11)

Scholars are quick to point out that the prologue contains the germ of most of the thoughts that Paul developed throughout his letter. But what gripped me most is his outpouring of affection for the Philippians, who joined with him in the fellowship of the gospel:

> It is right for me to feel this way about you all, because I hold you in my heart, for you are all partakers with me of grace, both in my imprisonment and in the defense and confirmation of the gospel. For God is my witness, how I yearn for you all with the affection of Christ Jesus. (vv. 7, 8)

Notice that Paul bookended his appreciation for their being "partakers" (fellowshipers) with him in the grace of suffering with two poignant expressions of affection (v. 7). First he said, "I hold you in my heart" (v. 7). We can well imagine that while affirming this, the apostle's mind ranged back to the beginning, to Lydia, the mother of the church, the extraordinary seller of purple, and then on through a kaleidoscope of faces, all of whom were lodged in his heart. But unlike so many of us, this was no glib pleasantry because he actually held them at the very center of his being, the center of his consciousness and emotions and will. The geography of their faces and even their souls were embedded at the epicenter of his life.

The other bookend was so profound that he called God as witness to the depth of his affection: "For God is my witness, how I yearn for you all with the affection of Christ Jesus" (v. 8). Such an oath was rare for Paul, but he wanted to drive the truth of his longing and affection for them deep into their understanding. In truth Paul was "so advanced in union with Christ that it is as if Christ were expressing his love through Paul." Indeed, as Alec Motyer explained, "the emotional constitution of Christ himself has taken over possession of his servant."[2]

While I would never claim the depth of Paul's affection, as I look back over forty years of ministry, a collage of names and faces rises pleasantly from the fellowship of the gospel—some near and some very distant. My expectation and prayer for all of us is that the bonds of our affection will become such that we will hold each other in our hearts, remembering with fond affection our fellowship together of grace in gospel ministry and longing for all with the affection of Christ Jesus.

Paul's Confidence In Prison (1:12–26)

Over verses 12–26, in chapter 1, we can write the summary statement "Paul's joyous confidence in prison."

Confidence in the Gospel

Sometimes I have mused, after reading verses 12–18, that when it came time for a change of guard and Paul's manacle was switched to another Roman soldier, he probably murmured a silent prayer—*Thank you, God, for another soul with whom to share Christ*. And then throughout the hours of his guard duty, the soldier watched and listened to a man who was utterly intoxicated with Christ and the gospel. Thus Paul could write, "I want you to know, brothers, that what has happened to me has really served to advance the gospel, so that it has become known throughout the whole imperial guard and to all the rest that my imprisonment is for Christ" (vv. 12, 13). All the elite soldiers of Rome knew that Paul was in prison for Christ! Paul was so utterly confident in his difficult situation that most of the brothers became confident to speak the Word without fear (cf. v. 14). And when rival evangelists preached spitefully to cause him pain, he rejoiced that Christ was proclaimed whether in pretense or in truth (cf. vv. 15–18). Imagine how this played in the beleaguered little fellowship of the gospel back in Philippi! "Can you believe him? What a man! He's still the same. The gospel is going out in Rome. And you know what? The same can happen here in this little Roman *polis*!"

> Two men looked through the bars.
> One saw the mud, the other, the stars.[3]

What do we see?

Confidence in Salvation

The following paragraph (vv. 19–26) contains Paul's declaration of his joyous confidence in salvation. And at the spiritual center of the paragraph is embedded the triumphant aphorism—a proverb and ideal for every believing soul—"For to me to live is Christ, and to die is gain" (1:21). When the Philippians heard this read, the effect must have been stunning because of the parallelism, tonal assonance, and compactness as a verbless Greek sentence: "For to me to live Christ, and to die gain."

Paul could say, "For to me to live Christ" because at the deepest level he was in Christ and Christ was in him. As another of Paul's verbless expressions explosively has it, "If anyone in Christ—new creation!" (2 Corinthians 5:17). But the overarching point here that Paul made with his declaration "For to me to live is Christ" was that he had willingly taken up the sufferings of Christ, joyously embracing the burdens of the cross. Thus "For to me to live is Christ" was not a pious declaration of spiritual achievement but a confident declaration of life commitment.

Beautifully, Paul's confidence in this life even extended into death—"and to die is gain" (v. 21). Death for Paul would bring an expansion of his life, which was Christ himself. He would be like Christ. He would repose in perfect righteousness. The pleasures of Christ would be everywhere. What an aphorism for the beleaguered fellowship of the gospel in Philippi: "For to me to live Christ, and to die gain."

As long as I live, I will never forget former church elder Andrew Chong taking a pen in hand shortly before his death and with intense deliberation writing these twelve words in a single column for his children: *For to me to live is Christ and to die is gain*—to which he added *Hallelujah*. He then said softly, "Nothing has changed. Nothing has changed." Andrew's *Hallelujah* was the deliberate signature of his soul's confidence and submission to the will of God. Now, from the grave, Andrew's appropriation of Paul's aphorism calls us to do the same.

Paul's Call for Unity in the Gospel (1:27–30)

It is commonly understood that the section that begins in the middle of chapter 1 at verse 27 and continues to the end of chapter 2 is a cohesive unit and that verse 27 best articulates the theme of Paul's letter: "Only let your manner of life be worthy of the gospel of Christ, so that whether I come and see you or am absent, I may hear of you that you are standing firm in one spirit, with one mind striving side by side for the faith of the gospel."

This sentence is notable for two reasons. First, it is the first of nineteen commands in this short letter. Remarkably, Paul's brilliant and passionate writing featured no imperative until now, so we should take note. Secondly, the language of the command is uniquely rich and evocative because the verb shares its root with the cognate noun *polis* or "city," as does a noun in 3:20 that means "citizenship." So the command should read, "Only let your manner of life as citizens [implicitly of Heaven] be worthy of the gospel of Christ." Paul in effect called the fellowship of the gospel to live out a counter-citizenship whose capital and seat of power was not earthly but heavenly. And the evidence of this counter-citizenship would be that they would work together in unity—"standing firm in one spirit, with one mind striving side by side for the faith of the gospel" (v. 27b). The enemies to unity that Paul had in mind were both external and internal. Paul briefly gave advice for standing against the external foes of unity in 1:28–30 and then addressed the greater problem of divisions from within in the opening sentences of chapter 2.

> So if there is any encouragement in Christ, any comfort from love, any participation in the Spirit, any affection and sympathy, complete my joy by being of the same mind, having the same love, being in full accord and of one mind. Do nothing from selfish ambition or conceit, but in humility count others more significant than yourselves. Let each of you look not only to his own interests, but also to the interests of others. (2:1–4)

This call to humbly put others first brings us to one of the high points of the New Testament as Paul held up Christ, the ultimate citizen of Heaven, as one who did not seek his own interests but those of others.

Christ's Humiliation and Exaltation (2:5–11)

One commentator, Markus Bockmuehl, has likened this section to "the soaring, unanswerable language of a Bach cantata which is best understood by being heard out to the end—and then heard again." And certainly it does function this way because when read and reread it takes us down in Christ's humiliation and then up in soaring exaltation.

His Humiliation

Here Paul commanded the Philippians to have the mind of Christ and then immediately articulated the three downward movements of Christ's self-humiliation. The downward movement began in Heaven where Christ "did not count equality with God a thing to be grasped" (v. 6). Next his self-humiliation moved further downward in the incarnation as he "emptied himself, by taking the form of a servant, being born in the likeness of men" (v. 7). And finally Christ's self-humiliation reached the lowest point possible when he became "obedient to the point of death, even death on a cross" (v. 8). Nothing could be lower! This was the crowning ignominy.

And it was all his own doing. No one humbled him. Herod did not humble him. Neither did Pilate or Caiaphas. The mighty Romans did not humble him. There was no power in Heaven or on earth or in the abyss that could do it.

His Exaltation

But the downward trajectory of Christ's humiliation was followed by his soaring exaltation. A divine catapult, so to speak, had been effected as each movement downward had ratcheted the gears tighter and tighter, so that the final click created an explosive tension. Then the gear was tripped, launching his super-exaltation,

> Therefore God has highly exalted him and bestowed on him the name that is above every name, so that at the name of Jesus every knee should bow, in heaven and on earth and under the earth, and every tongue confess that Jesus Christ is Lord, to the glory of God the Father. (vv. 9–11)

There is reference here to Isaiah 45. The name given to Jesus was Yahweh, the name that trumps all other titles—the awesome covenant name of the God of Israel—"the name that is above every name" (Philippians 2:9). And one day every knee will bow and every tongue will confess that Jesus Messiah is Yahweh to the glory of God the Father!

It was important to Paul that these trajectories of Christ's humiliation and exaltation recycle through the Philippians' minds so they would have a fuller understanding of Christ. What we understand of him will determine the way we live.

But there was a more prosaic reason to recall these ravishing trajectories—so the Philippians would walk worthy of the gospel, pursuing unity with one another in humility. Paul was calling them to follow Christ's humble example and live out Paul's words: "Do nothing from selfish ambition or conceit, but in humility count others more significant than yourselves. Let each of you look not only to his own interests, but also to the interests of others" (vv. 3, 4). Furthermore, in this humble, others-first attitude they were to work out their own salvation in the church "with fear and trembling" (v. 12), following the others-directed examples of Timothy and Epaphroditus (cf. vv. 19–30).

Christ Alone (3:1–11)

This paragraph pulses with passion from beginning to end. It begins in verse 2 with a trio of alliterated warnings that effectively slapped Paul's legalistic detractors with their own conceits. Then in the body of the paragraph (verses 3–9) Paul listed his seven righteous superiorities that left him "blameless" (v. 6) under the Law, only to reject them with an emotional and indelicate expletive. Paul wanted no doubt left that when he, as Saul of Tarsus, experienced the righteousness that comes through the faithfulness of Christ (the righteousness of God that depends on faith), he cast away all his accomplishments and threw himself on Christ alone.

That is why in verses 10, 11 he breathed out his matchless longing: "that I may know him and the power of his resurrection, and may share his sufferings, becoming like him in his death, that by any means possible I may attain the resurrection from the dead." For me this is the most inspiring and intimidating prayer in Scripture. Who has the temerity to pray for the fellowship of Christ's sufferings as Paul did? Only those who (1) know and believe that suffering with and for Christ is the path to deepest intimacy with him, (2) know and believe with Paul that such sufferings are a grace (cf. 1:29), and (3) see also that such sufferings are linked with the joyous power of the resurrection, which provides the strength to endure the sufferings.

This is my greatest personal takeaway from this book and my greatest challenge—to pray daily with all my heart, "that I may know him and the power of his resurrection, and may share his sufferings, becoming like him in his death, that by any means possible I may attain the resurrection from the dead" (3:10, 11). This was certainly a key longing for those bound together in the fellowship of the gospel.

More Gems from Philippians

The wonders of this tiny letter continue: for example, the call to press on— "But one thing I do: forgetting what lies behind and straining forward to what lies ahead, I press on toward the goal for the prize of the upward call of God in Christ Jesus" (3:13, 14)—to die running like Eric Liddell.

The double command to "Rejoice in the Lord always; again I will say, rejoice" (4:4) are joy notes fourteen and fifteen on the apostle's sixteen-note carillon. As the Philippians participated in the fellowship of the gospel and in others' sufferings and in the Holy Spirit and in Christ's sufferings and in giving, it was entirely a fellowship of joy.

And by virtue of the Philippians' commitments, the great promises of

4:13, 19 were theirs: "I can do all things through him who strengthens me. . . . And my God will supply every need of yours according to his riches in glory in Christ Jesus" (v. 19). As the Philippians looked to God, he met their every need with his provision and strength.

Final Greetings

Even Paul's final greetings, brief as they are, would have brought a smile to the fellowship of the gospel: "Greet every saint in Christ Jesus. The brothers who are with me greet you. All the saints greet you, especially those of Caesar's household" (vv. 21, 22). Remember the soldiers guarding Paul? They were handpicked soldiers who received double pay for their services in Rome. And though Paul would have been guarded by only a few of them, the soldiers who were assigned to Paul got the word out. And most certainly these elite troops had access to the household of Caesar.

So it was that some soldiers and cooks and housecleaners and civil servants in Caesar's house had come to Christ. Here John Calvin cuts to the chase: "it is evidence of divine mercy that the Gospel had penetrated that sink [pit] of all crimes and iniquities."[4] Yes! Though both the Philippians and Paul were under Roman oppression, there were brothers and sisters within Caesar's walls who were on their side and praying for them.

Thus this innocuous final greeting trumpets the grand reality that one day the very seat of imperial power will bow its knee and "confess that Jesus Christ [Messiah]) is Lord [Yahweh], to the glory of God the Father" (2:11).

Everything is of God's grace. "The grace of the Lord Jesus Christ be with your spirit" (4:23).

Amen.[5]

COLOSSIANS

The Supremacy of Christ

Paul, an apostle of Christ Jesus by the will of God, and Timothy our brother, To the saints and faithful brothers in Christ at Colossae: Grace to you and peace from God our Father. We always thank God, the Father of our Lord Jesus Christ, when we pray for you, since we heard of your faith in Christ Jesus and of the love that you have for all the saints, because of the hope laid up for you in heaven. Of this you have heard before in the word of the truth, the gospel, which has come to you, as indeed in the whole world it is bearing fruit and increasing—as it also does among you, since the day you heard it and understood the grace of God in truth, just as you learned it from Epaphras our beloved fellow servant. He is a faithful minister of Christ on your behalf and has made known to us your love in the Spirit.

1:1–8

24

The Celebration
of the Church

COLOSSIANS 1:1–8

WHEN WE STUDY Paul's epistles we see that each has a dominant theme. In Romans, it is justification by faith. In Ephesians, it is the mystery of Christ and his Church. In Philippians, it is the joy that Christ brings. In Colossians, it is the absolute supremacy and sufficiency of Jesus Christ as the Head of all creation and of the Church. There is no book in the New Testament, including John's Gospel, that presents such a comprehensive picture of the fullness of Christ. Accordingly, there is no writing better equipped to draw us upward than the book of Colossians.

> If then you have been raised with Christ, seek the things that are above, where Christ is, seated at the right hand of God. (3:1)

> Therefore, as you received Christ Jesus the Lord, so walk in him. (2:6)

As we study Paul's letter to the Colossians, may our view of Christ be so expanded and permanently impressed on us that we will as a habit seek those things that are above.

Background of the Epistle

The town of Colossae was located about eighty miles inland from the city of Ephesus, in the Lycus River Valley, in what is today the western part of Turkey. At one time it was one of the prominent towns of the valley, but by the New Testament era it was a small town well in the shadow of its nearby neighbors, Laodicea and Hierapolis. Biblical scholarship believes that the

Colossian church came into being during Paul's two-year ministry in Ephesus, because Acts 19:10 says that during that time "all the residents of Asia [which included Colossae] heard the word of the Lord."

The Scriptures reveal that as Paul was preaching in Ephesus, two visitors from Colossae came to believe—namely, Epaphras (4:12) and Philemon (Philemon 19). Philemon later hosted the Colossian church in his home (Philemon 1, 2), and Epaphras served as Paul's lieutenant in evangelizing the Lycus Valley. Thus a new, thriving church sprouted in Colossae though Paul had never been there himself. Paul, of course, had a deep interest in the church and prayerfully advised Epaphras and Philemon as necessary. So it was quite natural that when a major problem arose in Colossae, Epaphras came to him for help.

The problem came from false teachers who were propagating what is called Gnosticism. Gnostics considered themselves to be people of superior knowledge who could help "lesser" Christians attain deeper spirituality. The very word for Gnosticism comes from the Greek word *gnosis*, which means "to know." The Gnostics, "people in the know," the spiritual elite with all the answers, held as their basic doctrine that matter (anything physical or created) was evil and that only the spirit was good. They reasoned, therefore, that God could not be involved in creation, because being perfect he could not touch matter, which was intrinsically evil. Therefore, the world came into being through a complicated surrogate process as God put forth thousands of emanations (or lesser gods), each of which was a little more distant from him, so that finally there was an emanation (a little god) so distant from God that it could touch matter—and it created the world. Of course, this lesser god of creation was so far removed from the ultimate God that it was evil.

This reasoning led to the belief that Jesus Christ, if he really was the Son of God, could not have taken on a human body because matter is evil. This delusion spawned the Gnostic romances about Jesus being only a ghost-like phantom. To the Gnostics, Christ was not Creator, the incarnation was not real, and Christ was not enough!

So the Gnostics built a system by which one could begin with Christ and work one's way up the series of emanations to God. In Colossae, this system (*gnosis*) consisted of ascetic disciplines (many of which were borrowed from Jewish legalism, see 2:20–23), secret passwords (borrowed from Eastern mysticism), the esoterica of astrology, and elements of Christianity.[1] It was all very complex and proudly intellectual. The Gnostics, those "in the know," looked down upon the simple Colossian believers, browbeat them, and led some astray.

This is the alarming message that Epaphras brought Paul as he waited in prison. Paul's brilliant response was the letter to the Colossians, which presented Christ as the Creator and all-sufficient Redeemer in the sublimest terms found anywhere in Scripture. Paul's masterful answer has served the Church well through the centuries as it has repeatedly faced similar heresies and is in fact today assaulted by false teachers and cultists who see Christ as only part of the answer.

As we take up Paul's letter, we immediately see that the apostle did not directly attack the Colossian problem, but rather began with an exuberant introduction that celebrated the Colossian church. This was typical of Paul, who characteristically praised the churches before dealing with them pastorally. Paul's heartfelt commendation rose from the miracle that had taken place in Colossae: a poor, pagan people without God and without hope in this world had found Christ. Their lives had been changed, and some remarkable things had happened, which Paul will duly note. His celebration was honest and beautiful, and the celebration is ours as well—for we are the Church.

Celebration of Joy (vv. 1, 2)

> Paul, an apostle of Christ Jesus by the will of God, and Timothy our brother,
> To the saints and faithful brothers in Christ at Colossae: Grace to you and peace from God our Father.

Though Paul had never met the Colossians, he called them "saints and faithful brothers in Christ," which was purposely exalted language. They were God's holy ones, set apart for him. They with Paul shared the same paternity, and they both addressed God intimately as "Abba" (see Galatians 4:6). They shared a mutual domesticity of soul. They were "family," and they naturally called each other brother and sister.

But best of all, they were "in Christ," which is one of the deepest and most joyous of mysteries. In barest terms it means that the Colossians, and indeed all authentic believers, partook of all that Christ had done, all that he was (and is), and all that he ever would be. This is also the essence of the great paragraph with which Paul opened the book of Ephesians. There Paul also defined the Church as being "in Christ" (v. 1), believers whom "God . . . has blessed . . . in Christ with every spiritual blessing" (v. 3), having chosen them "in him before the foundation of the world" (v. 4), which resulted in redemption and forgiveness of sins "[i]n him" (v. 7), which in turn eventuated in the hope of glorification "in Christ" and their marking "in him" with the seal of the Holy Spirit. The first fourteen verses of Ephesians use "in Christ" or "in him" no less than ten times to describe the profundity of regeneration in Christ.

As believers, they were "in Christ," and the old had gone, the new had come (2 Corinthians 5:17). Archaeologists tell us that many of the nameless slabs in the catacombs of Rome carried the inscription "*in Christo*" (in Christ) and significantly also bore on the same slab its spiritual corollary "*In pace*" (In peace), testifying to the radical newness and joy that came in Christ.[2] Being in Christ has always been ample reason to celebrate as Paul and the ancient Christians did, and it is the same for us today. This is a wonder of wonders!

We must note that by sealing the above with "Grace and peace to you from God our Father," Paul created a Christian blend of Hebrew and Greek greetings. The customary greeting in the ancient Greek world was *chairen*, which was a form of "grace" and meant "greetings" (see James 1:1; Acts 15:23; 23:26). But in Paul's hands, it became the freshly minted Christian salutation *charis*, "grace."[3] Greeting fellow-believers with this word celebrated the work of grace in their lives. "You are a recipient of God's unmerited favor. Praise God for his grace! This is indeed wonderful!" It was also a commissioning to live under grace.[4] "May you be a great taker. May you have the disposition, the dependency, the humility that makes you a ready receptor of God's grace."

The other half of the greeting, "peace," came originally from the Hebrew *shalom*, which meant more than simply the absence of trouble, but well-being that springs from a sense of the presence of God.[5] Paul's wish for the Colossians was that they would comprehend more fully their peace and enjoy it in all its depth.

It is the same for all people: there must be grace before we experience the *shalom* of God. Grace (God's work) comes before peace (our new relationship).[6] Among the tragedies of our time is humanity's pursuit of personal peace apart from God's enabling grace. That pursuit takes many forms: material, intellectual, social, even religious; but they all end in futility. When sinners find peace through God's grace, that is beautiful, that is cause for rejoicing! "Grace . . . and peace" is the proper Christian greeting and celebration (v. 2).

A Celebration of Thanksgiving (vv. 3–5a)

As Paul continued his greeting, he gratefully made reference to the familiar Christian trio of faith, hope, and love, but placed hope last.

We always thank God, the Father of our Lord Jesus Christ, when we pray for you, since we heard of your *faith* in Christ Jesus and of the *love* that you have for all the saints, because of the *hope* laid up for you in heaven. (vv. 3-5a)

Faith, hope, and love are mentioned numerous times in Scripture[7] as a sort of "apostolic shorthand" for genuine Christianity.[8] None of these qualities can be manufactured by man; they all come from God.

Paul first celebrated their "faith in Christ Jesus" (v. 4). Faith is always mentioned first in the trio because apart from faith there is no Christian experience. Here Paul was very specific about the object of their faith. It was "Christ Jesus." "Everybody needs faith. You gotta have faith," we hear people say. It is considered to be a component of a balanced life—another charm on the bracelet of one's well-being. Having faith means you're okay. But the truth is, faith has no intrinsic value in itself. It must derive its value from its object. When someone says that he or she has faith, the question that must be asked is: "Faith in what? In reincarnation? That God is good? Faith in faith?"

Salvation does not come by believing in belief, or even in a set of doctrines or a creed. Salvation comes by believing in Christ. When John G. Paton was translating the Bible in the Outer Hebrides, he searched for the exact word to translate *believe*. Finally he found it: the word meant "lean your whole weight upon."[9] That is what the Colossians, despite their Gnostic detractors, had done. That was something to celebrate!

Paul then continued to laud the Colossians for "the love" they had "for all the saints" (v. 4). For Paul, faith proved its reality by "working through love" (Galatians 5:6). Loving God is seen in how one loves his neighbor, and particularly another believer (John 13:34, 35). We have all met people who claimed to be good Christians, who were upstanding, honest, and orthodox— but unloving. They had a loveless goodness, an orthodoxy without charity, a questionable faith. They were the kind of people Mark Twain had in mind when he said, "He is a good man—in the worst sort of way." Love for the brethren is a sign of true faith.

When Chuck Colson was serving his prison sentence after the Watergate scandal, his newfound faith was severely tested. His wife did not understand the "born again" business, his son was picked up on drug charges, and Colson himself was despondent. But God met him in his misery. A group of Christians in Washington, including Senators Hatfield, Hughes, and Quie, were praying for him. Senator Quie discovered an old law that allowed an innocent man to serve a prison term for another, and Quie volunteered to serve the remainder of Colson's term.[10] Colson turned him down, but he had experienced "love . . . for all the saints" (v. 4), and Charles Colson was again refreshed in the reality of his faith.

It is a beautiful thing when you see in the Church love for all the saints—not just for some, not just for the lovable, but for all. This is what made the early church so amazing and so enticing to the ancient world. Barbarian, Scythian, slave and free, male and female, Jew and Greek, learned and ignorant joined hands and sat down at one table. They knew themselves to be all one in Christ Jesus. There never had been anything like it. The world began to babble about sorcery and conspiracies and complicity in unnameable vices. But Christians were only living out their "love . . . for all the saints" (v. 4). A new thing had come into the world—a community held together by love and not by geographical accidents or common language or by the iron chains of the conqueror. The world wondered, and not a few were drawn to Christ. Genuine love for all was cause for Paul's joyous celebration of the apostolic Church, and it is cause for celebration today, for the results are the same.

Finally, Paul celebrated their hope: "the hope laid up for you in heaven" (v. 5). Hope is placed last because, in this instance, Paul saw faith and love as springing from it.[11] How does hope of Heaven cause faith and love to come forth? As pagans, the Colossians had been without God and without hope in this world. Then came the gospel from Epaphras and Philemon and the wonderful, surprising joy of salvation and hope of Heaven. This joy naturally enlarged their love and faith. This new hope thrust them together as it earned them the natural enmity of the prevailing religious system. In addition, by partaking of the same hope (1 Timothy 1:1), sharing the same secret, they were bound more closely in their love, and thus encouraged greater faith in one another.

How important the hope of glory is! Paul tells us that the hope of the return of Christ and heavenly reward makes a difference in how we live:

> For the grace of God has appeared, bringing salvation for all people, training us to renounce ungodliness and worldly passions, and to live self-controlled, upright, and godly lives in the present age, waiting for our blessed hope, the appearing of the glory of our great God and Savior Jesus Christ. (Titus 2:11–13)

John says the same thing:

Beloved, we are God's children now, and what we will be has not yet appeared; but we know that when he appears we shall be like him, because we shall see him as he is. And everyone who thus hopes in him purifies himself as he is pure. (1 John 3:2, 3)

We ought to cultivate our hope. Remember C. S. Lewis's great exhortation?

Indeed, if we consider the unblushing promises of reward and the staggering nature of the rewards promised in the Gospels, it would seem that Our Lord finds our desires, not too strong, but too weak.[12]

A Celebration of the Gospel (vv. 5b–8)

The apostle celebrated the gospel's success:

Of this you have heard before in the word of the truth, the gospel, which has come to you, as indeed in the whole world it is bearing fruit and increasing—as it also does among you, since the day you heard it and understood the grace of God in truth, just as you learned it from Epaphras our beloved fellow servant. He is a faithful minister of Christ on your behalf and has made known to us your love in the Spirit. (vv. 5b–8)

Here Paul engaged in a little justified hyperbole, for though the gospel had not spread through "the whole world," it was well on its way. What he was celebrating was its dynamic power and its universality. Unlike the Gnostic elitist foolishness, Christ's good news was for everybody and was daily reaching new people.

The miracle of the little church in the Lycus Valley was cause for celebration. It is our celebration too, for:

- We are God's holy and faithful ones, saints.
- We are brothers and sisters with a common Father.
- We are "in Christ" and are part of the joyous mystery of his Body.
- The grace of God has been freely poured on us, "grace upon grace" (John 1:16).
- We have peace, *shalom*, the well-being that results from divine grace and the presence of God.
- God has given us faith, love, and hope: ". . . faith in Christ . . . love . . . for all the saints . . . hope laid up . . . in heaven" (vv. 4, 5).

Let us, in joyful continuity with the Colossian church, daily celebrate the good news of abundance of life in Jesus Christ!

And so, from the day we heard, we have not ceased to pray for you, asking that you may be filled with the knowledge of his will in all spiritual wisdom and understanding, so as to walk in a manner worthy of the Lord, fully pleasing to him, bearing fruit in every good work and increasing in the knowledge of God. May you be strengthened with all power, according to his glorious might, for all endurance and patience with joy, giving thanks to the Father, who has qualified you to share in the inheritance of the saints in light. He has delivered us from the domain of darkness and transferred us to the kingdom of his beloved Son, in whom we have redemption, the forgiveness of sins.

1:9–14

25

The Prayer for the Church

COLOSSIANS 1:9–14

ALMOST SIXTY YEARS AGO a young missionary named Raymond Edman staggered in from an Ecuadorian jungle, desperately ill. "He'll be dead by morning," the doctor predicted. Edman's wife dyed her wedding dress black, so it would be ready for the funeral. (In the tropics funerals must be held immediately.) However, thousands of miles away in Boston, Edman's friend, Dr. Joseph Evans, interrupted a prayer meeting, saying, "I feel we must pray for Ray Edman in Ecuador." The group prayed earnestly, until finally Evans called out, "Praise the Lord! The victory is won!" The rest is oft-repeated history: Raymond Edman recovered, his wife's dress did not, and Dr. Edman went on to become president of Wheaton College and to minister for forty years![1] This beautiful story unforgettably affirms the power of intercessory prayer.

Motivated by stories like this, we naturally ask, how are we to pray for the Church, the members of Christ's Body? A classic answer is provided by Paul in the introductory lines of his letter to the Colossians, because they contain his intercession for that distant little church.

In the opening lines of the letter, recorded in verses 1–8, Paul celebrated the miracle of this little church's existence in the Lycus Valley. Predictably, this overflowed in prayer, which began in verse 9. His prayer was a beautifully constructed tapestry that makes a perfect model for the fabric of our own prayers. His example tells us how to pray for the knowledge, and then for the conduct, of the Church.

A Prayer for Knowledge (v. 9)

And so, from the day we heard, we have not ceased to pray for you, asking that you may be filled with the knowledge of his will in all spiritual wisdom and understanding.

It is significant that Paul prayed for the Colossians' knowledge, because they were under siege by people who were telling them they needed a better knowledge, a *gnosis*. The Gnostics were teaching that Christ was a good place to begin, but that there was so much more they could know and experience if only they would incorporate the Gnostic system of passwords, rites, and initiations. Their superior, know-it-all air was intimidating, and some of the Colossians were made to feel they were lacking. What is more, the system, by promising a special understanding, appealed to the people's natural, elitist instinct. And some had fallen. So Paul's prayer that the Colossians "be filled with the knowledge of his will in all spiritual wisdom and understanding" hit the problem head-on.

This knowledge for which Paul prayed was set in bold contrast with that of the Gnostics because Paul used a word for knowledge that "is almost a technical term for the decisive knowledge of God which is involved in conversion to the Christian faith."[2] The Gnostics' characteristic word for knowledge was *gnosis*. But Paul used the word *epignosis* as a reference to full knowledge for the Colossians. Knowing that they have this personal knowledge of Christ and his will, Paul prayed for an *epignosis* that would fill them in such a way that it would instill a wisdom and understanding that was singularly "spiritual" (the word "spiritual" is emphatic in the Greek).

From the apostle's perspective, a deep, growing knowledge of Christ and his will is of the greatest importance to the spiritual life of all Christians.

And it is my prayer that your love may abound more and more, with knowledge and all discernment. (Philippians 1:9)

I pray that the sharing of your faith may become effective for the full knowledge of every good thing that is in us for the sake of Christ. (Philemon 6)

I do not cease to give thanks for you, remembering you in my prayers, that the God of our Lord Jesus Christ, the Father of glory, may give you the Spirit of wisdom and of revelation in the knowledge of him. (Ephesians 1:16, 17)

Here in Paul's Colossian prayer, when he said, "we have not ceased to pray for you, asking that you may be filled with the knowledge of his will"

(v. 9), he was using language of great intensity, for he knew that spiritual knowledge is foundational to a sound, fruitful Christian life.[3] God puts no premium on ignorance.

Warren Wiersbe says that he once heard a preacher say, "I didn't never go to school. I'm just a igerant Christian, and I'm glad I is!" To which Wiersbe comments, "A man does not have to go to school to gain spiritual intelligence; but neither should he magnify his 'igerance.'"[4] Spiritual knowledge comes, as we all know, through the work of the Holy Spirit (John 16:8–11). He reveals Jesus Christ and gives us the special saving knowledge of him (John 17:3). But the Holy Spirit does not work alone. The Scriptures become the primary source of "knowledge" for the believer as they are studied in the power of the Holy Spirit. This produces a Christian mind, which in fact is what Paul is praying for—a mind, as Harry Blamires says, that is trained to handle life within a framework constructed of Christian presuppositions.[5] It is this mind, this *epignosis*, that God blesses.

> Blessed is the man
> . . . [whose] delight is in the law of the LORD,
>   and on his law he meditates day and night. (Psalm 1:1, 2)

> This Book of the Law shall not depart from your mouth, but you shall meditate on it day and night, so that you may be careful to do according to all that is written in it. For then you will make your way prosperous, and then you will have good success. (Joshua 1:8)

Typically when we pray for ourselves or for others, we pray for physical health, well-being, social relationships, and spiritual growth. But part of our intercessory prayers ought to be for "the knowledge of his will in all spiritual wisdom and understanding." Have you prayed like this for others? It is an important prayer for your pastor, for new believers, for your family members.

And we ought to be part of the answer to our own prayers! Every believer should be reading and meditating on God's Word. The very blood they bleed ought, in Spurgeon's words, to be "bibline." Every Christian should be concentrating when he or she hears the preaching of God's Word. Every believer should be able to filter his culture's seductive *gnosis* through the grid of God's *epignosis*.

A Prayer about Conduct (vv. 10–14)

Paul's prayer for the Colossians is that they might "walk in a manner worthy of the Lord, fully pleasing to him" (v. 10).

In Hebrew vocabulary throughout the Old Testament Scriptures, the word "walk" symbolically referred to one's conduct, and this carried over into the Greek of the New Testament. For example, in Colossians it is used that way several times:

> . . . so as to walk in a manner worthy of the Lord. (1:10)

> . . . as you received Christ Jesus the Lord, so walk in him. (Colossians 2:6)

> In these you too once walked, when you were living in them. (Colossians 3:7)

In the Hebrew mind, knowledge and conduct were bound together. But in Gnostic culture, teaching was highly speculative and theoretical, not related to life. There was even one school of Gnosticism that reasoned that since the body was evil and the spirit was good, it did not make any difference what one did in the body. So they did anything and everything!

A Worthy Walk

The Hebrews saw an absolute connection between knowledge and conduct. From their perspective, a person did not know something unless he or she did it. From this Paul and indeed all authentic Christianity springs. True spiritual knowledge means action! This strikes at the very heart of the unhealthy dichotomy that is so prevalent today. I am speaking of the tendency of people of knowledge not to be activists, and the reverse tendency of people of action to neglect the pursuit of knowledge—thus producing unbalanced extremes.

Let me mention two examples: on the one hand you have the ignorant "soul-winner" who knows only a rabbit track through Scripture and has no thought-through answers of his own, and on the other hand you have the contemplative scholar filled with knowledge who has never led a soul to Christ. Neither situation was ever meant to be! Paul was the ultimate contemplative mind, but also an incredible man of action. John Calvin, utilizing his transcending intellectual powers, would lie upon his bed and dictate commentaries, but he was also actively involved with people and politics and life. That was also part of the genius of John Wesley, and of Francis Schaeffer in our own day. We need balance.

A profound knowledge should profoundly affect one's walk. It must be understood that any doctrine that isolates the believer from the needs of the world is not a spiritual doctrine. Or put another way, if our doctrine lifts us so high that our feet cannot reach the ground, it is false. Paul prayed that the

Colossians would walk their talk, that their knowledge of Christ would grow, and that this in turn would produce a conduct that was worthy of the Lord, pleasing him in all respects. This is how we should pray.

What is to be the result of this worthy walk? ". . . bearing fruit in every good work" (v. 10). Good works are the outworking of Christ's life in his people. Paul thus prayed that they would act out Christ's kind of life in every situation. Thus the reality of the Colossians' faith would be seen by the surrounding community, and Christ would be glorified and souls drawn to him. The participle "bearing fruit" is present and continuous. Paul prayed that this fruit-bearing would be a constant, ongoing reality.

A Knowlegeable Walk

The next thought in Paul's intercession for the Colossians' walk completes verse 10: "increasing in the knowledge of God." This is what Paul so powerfully asked for in the beginning of this prayer. Why does he mention it again as he prays for their conduct? Simply because Paul saw the dynamic connection between action and knowledge. He knew that as they continued "bearing fruit in every good work," they would naturally open themselves to "increasing in the knowledge of God." One begets the other in a delectable upward spiral: the more one truly serves him, the more one opens to knowledge of him—the more one knows of him, the more one wants to serve. So it goes onward and upward! Jesus himself made it clear that doing the Father's will makes possible the reception of knowledge of the Son (cf. John 7:17). This mutual cause-and-effect relationship between knowing and doing is one of the fundamental laws of spiritual growth. It was one of the secrets of the Wesleyan movement, for John Wesley and his followers did not just find the truth and sit on it—they did the truth! And the doing of it opened them to an increase in the knowledge of God.

A Powerful Walk

The next clause that describes Paul's prayer for the Colossians' walk occupies the whole of verse 11:

> May you be strengthened with all power, according to his glorious might, for all endurance and patience with joy. . . .

The power that Paul prayed upon the church is immense, for "strengthened" was continuous, denoting a steady supply. And the strengthening is on God's own scale: "according to his glorious might." Colossal power!

The focus of the power is, first, for "endurance." The kind of steadfastness Paul meant is that which "enables one to hold one's position in battle."[6] He had in mind the evil forces in the Lycus Valley that were trying to destroy the Colossian church. Paul was praying that they would stand . . . endure . . . persevere . . . remain steadfast . . . stay at it. Sir Winston Churchill was invited back to his alma mater, Harrow, to address the students near the end of his storied life of public service, which included guiding Britain through her darkest and finest hours. When the five-foot, five-inch bulldog of a man took the platform, everyone waited breathlessly upon his words—and they would never forget what they heard: "Young gentlemen, never give up. Never give up. Never give up! Never! Never! Never!" With that he sat down. Paul would have liked that, especially in regard to the gospel.

To "endurance" Paul added "patience," or as the Greek more literally says, "long-suffering." "Endurance" is in reference to adverse circumstances, whereas "patience" is in reference to difficult people.[7] Paul was praying that the Colossians would have a long-suffering, patient spirit as they related to one another and to those outside the church. Possessing "endurance" does not mean one will succeed in "patience." Moses endured in his titanic struggle with Pharaoh in Egypt, but his patience with the people failed at Kadesh, and he lost his right to enter the promised land (Numbers 20).

> A man without self-control
>   is like a city broken into and left without walls. (Proverbs 25:28)

How beautiful "endurance" and "patience" are when they are wedded in our life. In 2 Corinthians 6:4–6 Paul listed them as marks of a true minister of Jesus Christ. They perfectly existed in the Lord Jesus himself, who remained steadfast to the end and was long-suffering with all. Paul knew that such qualities could only come by being "strengthened with all power, according to his glorious might" (v. 11). This is the way we must pray for our brothers and sisters. "Lord, give them perseverance in difficulties and patience with people. Do it by constantly strengthening them with your power." When King David controlled himself as he was maligned by Shimei, it was a greater victory than his killing Goliath (2 Samuel 16:5–13).

> Whoever is slow to anger is better than the mighty,
>   and he who rules his spirit than he who takes a city. (Proverbs 16:32)

The church with "endurance and patience" is a great church (v. 11). It is a church that walks "in a manner worthy of the Lord" (v. 10).

A Thankful Walk

How else do we walk worthy? By giving thanks, as verses 11, 12 say: "with joy, giving thanks to the Father." This is the summit of the prayer, and thanksgiving is diffused through all of it. We cannot walk worthy of God without constantly giving joyous thanks, as the Greek participle here emphasizes.

Many years ago Northwestern University had a lifesaving team that assisted passengers on Lake Michigan boats. On September 8, 1860, the *Lady Elgin* foundered near the campus, and a ministerial student named Edward Spencer personally rescued seventeen people. The exposure from that episode permanently damaged his health, and he was unable to continue preparation for the ministry. Some years later when he died, it was noted that not one of the seventeen people he had saved ever came to thank him.[8]

Believers who walk worthy of Christ constantly give thanks to God for their salvation. Why? Paul lists three specific reasons in verses 12–14. First, in verse 12 we are to be joyously giving thanks to the Father because he "has qualified you to share in the inheritance of the saints in light." This is a *present* reality (note the aorist tenses). *We are now in the realm of light!*

> For God, who said, "Let light shine out of darkness," has shone in our hearts to give the light of the knowledge of the glory of God in the face of Jesus Christ. (2 Corinthians 4:6)

> For you are all children of light, children of the day. (1 Thessalonians 5:5)

> But you are a chosen race, a royal priesthood, a holy nation, a people for his own possession, that you may proclaim the excellencies of him who called you out of darkness into his marvelous light. (1 Peter 2:9)

We are presently in the light, but it is also a *future* reality! It has not yet been manifested in all its infinite brightness, but we are being made ready for the ultimate inheritance in light. One day we shall pass beyond the stars, and when they have burned themselves out, we will shine even brighter. As C. S. Lewis so memorably put it:

> Nature. Nature is mortal; we shall outlive her. When all the suns and nebulae have passed away, each one of you will still be alive. Nature is only the image, the symbol; but it is the symbol Scripture invites me to use. We are summoned to pass in through Nature, beyond her, into that splendor which she fitfully reflects.[9]

This is because God the Father "qualified" us for it! It was not due to anything we have done. It is all of him. Thus, we give joyous thanks constantly!

The next reason to give thanks is closely associated with the first. Verse 13 says:

He has delivered us from the domain of darkness and transferred us to the kingdom of his beloved Son.

The word for "transferred" is used in other places to describe a mighty king picking up a whole population and deporting it to another realm.[10] That has already been accomplished. All believers have been sublimely deported into "the kingdom of his beloved Son" (v. 13) which, at the Consummation, will be the eternal kingdom of God (1 Corinthians 15:24).[11] We are in the "kingdom of his *beloved* Son," a kingdom enveloped in love. For this reason we give joyous thanksgiving.

The final reason for thanksgiving is, as verse 14 says: "in whom we have redemption, the forgiveness of sins." We have been purchased from the slave market, and our sins have been sent away. Why? Because we are in him. That is the *present* reality, right now! And we bow in thanksgiving.

Interceding for other Christians is of greatest importance. Joseph Evans in faraway Boston experienced the urging of the Holy Spirit to lead his congregation to pray for Dr. Edman in Ecuador, and it is my own belief that if he had not followed that urging, Ray Edman would not have lived to minister for the next forty years. When God calls his people to pray and they obey, things happen! When they refuse to follow his urgings, they shorten his sovereign hand.

Why not covenant to pray for both the knowledge and conduct of your fellow believers? A church that is growing in the knowledge of Christ and his will, and is walking worthy of him, will do great things. Let us commit ourselves to sensitive, fervent intercession for our brothers and sisters.

He is the image of the invisible God, the firstborn of all creation. For by him all things were created, in heaven and on earth, visible and invisible, whether thrones or dominions or rulers or authorities—all things were created through him and for him. And he is before all things, and in him all things hold together. And he is the head of the body, the church. He is the beginning, the firstborn from the dead, that in everything he might be preeminent.

1:15–18

26

The Preeminent Christ

COLOSSIANS 1:15–18

ALMOST A HUNDRED YEARS AGO (in 1893), the famous World's Columbian Exposition was held in Chicago, and an astronomical number of people, especially in those pre-automobile days, some twenty-one million, visited the exhibits. America, and particularly Chicago, which had risen phoenixlike from the great fire of 1873, was showing off to the rest of the world. And the show was good. Among the features of the Columbian Exposition was the "World Parliament of Religions," in which representatives of the world's religions met to share their best points and perhaps come up with a new world religion.

D. L. Moody saw this as a great chance for evangelism. Moody commissioned evangelists and assigned them to "preaching posts" throughout the city. He used churches and rented theaters. He even rented a circus tent to preach the Word. Moody's friends wanted him to attack the "Parliament of Religions," but he refused, saying, "I am going to make Jesus Christ so attractive that men will turn to him." D. L. Moody knew that preaching Christ preeminent—the peerless, supreme, all-sufficient Christ, clearly presented—would do the job. And indeed it did. The "Chicago Campaign" of 1893 is considered to be the greatest evangelistic work of Moody's celebrated life, and thousands came to Christ.[1]

Moody's approach was actually nothing new, but rather a time-honored approach that goes all the way back to the apostolic Church and is especially evident in the section of Colossians considered in this chapter. It presented Christ as the One who has first place in creation and in the Church. The Gnostics had their own version of the "Parliament of Religions" because they considered Jesus to be only one of thousands of emanations from the great unseen God. According to them, Christ was not the way, the truth, and the life (John 14:6), but only the beginning rung in the ladder to the true God.

The apostolic Church believed otherwise. They believed, to use a cliché, that he is Lord of all or he is not Lord at all! This is what Paul taught so positively and beautifully here. Verses 15–20 are the most closely reasoned presentation of the supremacy of Christ anywhere in the Bible.

Christ: Supreme in Eternity (v. 15a)

The opening line of verse 15 describes Christ as "the image of the invisible God." That God is invisible is a given in both the Old and New Testaments (1 Timothy 1:17; Hebrews 11:27). However, John 1:18, which begins by affirming this, saying, "No one has ever seen God," goes on to say, "the only God, who is at the Father's side, he [Jesus] has made him known." Jesus is literally the *exegesis* of God. How does he do this? Much of the answer is found in our text as we understand how Christ is the image of God.

The Greek word translated "image" is *eikon*, from which we derive our English word *icon*. This means "an image or representation." Sometimes the Greek word itself meant picture, as when an ancient soldier sent a portrait to his father with the note, "I sent you a little portrait (*eikonion*) of myself painted by Euctemon."[2] From this kind of usage we can say that Jesus is the portrait of God. However, the meaning goes even beyond this because being the *eikon*, the image, of God also carries the idea of revealing the personal character of God. We see this in some of the texts in the Wisdom Literature, such as Proverbs 8:22–31 or the extra-Biblical Wisdom of Solomon 7:24–26, where wisdom was described as the *eikon*, the image or revelation, of God's goodness.[3] Thus, Christ as the "the image of the invisible God" is not just a plaster representation of him, but the revelation of what God is really like.[4] The writer of Hebrews expressed the same thought in very powerful language: "He is the radiance of the glory of God and the exact imprint of his nature" (1:3). The Greek word translated "exact imprint" here meant the impress left by a die on a coin or a seal on wax. He is the exact impress of the essence of God.[5]

Christ's supremacy in eternity is boldly proclaimed as Paul says he is the *eikon* of the invisible God. *He is supreme!* Jesus is no second-rate emanation from the true God, a Gnostic step in the ladder to the true God. He is God. This not only tells us about Christ—it also tells us about ourselves, because as Jesus is the image of God, he is what we were meant to be in terms of character: we were created in his image (Genesis 1:26, 27). Jesus is supreme in eternity, and we ought to give him first place in our lives.

As "image" emphasizes Christ's relationship to the Father, "the firstborn of all creation" introduces his relationship to creation (v. 15). Here also he is supreme.

Christ: Supreme in Creation (vv. 15b–17)

Paul describes Christ's supremacy in creation in four ways in verses 15–17. In verse 15b Christ is firstborn; in verse 16 he is Creator; in verse 16b he is the goal; and in verse 17 he is sustainer.

Verse 15b calls Christ "the firstborn of all creation," which at first sight might be taken as teaching that Jesus was the first person created. Indeed the Jehovah's Witnesses, and the heretic Arius long before them, take it this way. But they do so by ignoring the context, which makes him Creator of everything, as well as the rest of New Testament revelation, which makes him eternal (cf. John 1:1). Most of all, they ignore the indisputable fact that while "firstborn" can mean first child, it very often is simply a term that means "first in rank or honor." Sometimes the Torah was called firstborn to indicate its elevated rank. "Firstborn" was a code word for the coming Messiah, as in Psalm 89:27—"And I will make him the firstborn, the highest of the kings of the earth." The people of Israel as a whole were sometimes called "firstborn" to indicate their high position as recipients of the Father's love (Exodus 4:22). So when Paul called Christ "the firstborn of all creation," he meant that highest honor belongs to him. Christ is completely supreme in creation!

Why? Because Christ is Creator. "For by him all things were created, in heaven and on earth, visible and invisible, whether thrones or dominions or rulers or authorities—all things were created through him and for him" (v. 16). Jesus is the agent of creation ex nihilo, from nothing.[6] The extent of his creation is dazzling. It includes even the things in the heavens and the invisible. In fact, it even includes the angels. The Scriptures and Jewish literature reveal that the four descriptions "thrones . . . dominions . . . rulers . . . authorities" refer to four classes of angelic powers, with the last two referring to the highest orders of the angelic realm.[7]

The Gnostics taught that Christ was a spiritual emanation from the true God, but here Paul boldly said that he is the true God who created everything, even the invisible spirit-world. *This is an astounding, combative proclamation!*

Christ is Creator of all! We are well aware of what this implies when we think of a universe that is millions of light-years across, but here on our earth it is astounding too. He created even the tiniest creatures. There are 800,000 catalogued insects, with billions in some of the species—all created by Christ.

Christ is not only the Creator of creation, but he is also the end, the goal: "all things were created through him and for him" (v. 16b). This is an astounding statement. Peter O'Brien says, "Paul's teaching about Christ as the goal of all creation . . . finds no parallel in the Jewish wisdom literature or in the rest of the extant Jewish materials for that matter."[8] Some translate the word "for" as *toward*, which makes the sense even more dramatic: "All things were created by him and *toward* him."[9] Everything began with him and will end with him. All things sprang forth at his command, and all things will return to him at his command. He is the beginning and he is the end—the Alpha and Omega. One day everything will give him glory (cf. Philippians 2:11)!

Since this is true, we should live completely for him. Any other course is completely irrational for the believer. Paul used similar logic in Romans 11:36 where he said, "For from him and through him and to him are all things. To him be glory forever. Amen." Then he called us to total commitment, which he concluded is "your reasonable [*logikos*, logical, rational] service" (Romans 12:1, KJV). As a believer, is your life rational or irrational? Are you living totally for God, or are you living outside rationality?

In verse 17, Paul reached the apex of his argument: Christ is superior in creation because he is the sustainer: "And he is before all things, and in him all things hold together." The perfect tense here tells us that he continues now to hold all things together, and that apart from his continuous activity, all would disintegrate. The writer of Hebrews puts it this way: "He is the radiance of the glory of God and the exact imprint of his nature, and he upholds the universe by the word of his power" (1:3).

Physicists tell us that among the atom's whirling protons and electrons there is vast space, not unlike our solar system. Though some have theories as to why the atom holds together, none know for sure. Christ is not contained in matter, but he holds it together by his word!

There is a medieval painting that shows Christ in the clouds, and below him is the world of humans and nature. From Christ to every object is painted a thin gold thread. The artist was saying that Christ is responsible for sustaining the existence of every created thing.

> I see His blood upon the rose
> And in the stars the glory of His eyes,
> His body gleams amid eternal snows,
> His tears fall from the skies.
>
> I see His face in every flower;
> The thunder and the singing of the birds
> Are but His voice—and carven by His power
> Rocks are His written words.

All pathways by His feet are worn,
His strong heart stirs the ever-beating sea,
His crown of thorns is twined with every thorn,
His cross is every tree.[10]

Seeing Christ as he is will keep us from heresy, for it will steel us against a scaled-down Christ that has captured so many lost hearts. And it will cause us to begin to love him with a real love.

Paul's hymn sings of the supremacy of Christ in creation: he is *firstborn* and thus has the highest place. He is *Creator* of everything, every cosmic speck, every spirit. He is the *goal*, and all creation is moving toward him and for him. He is the *sustainer*. He is holding the very breath that falls on these pages. What a stunning revelation this is! It is meant to stretch our puny minds and dominate our thinking and change us. When we truly understand what is being said here, it is amazing that we should ever look anywhere else for meaning and purpose in life. Since he is the Creator who holds all things together, he knows how to best fix and order our lives.

Some years ago a South American company purchased a fine printing press from a firm in the United States. After it had been shipped and completely assembled, the workmen could not get it to operate properly. The most knowledgeable personnel tried to remedy the difficulty and bring it into proper adjustment, but to no avail. Finally the company wired a message to the manufacturer, asking that the company send a representative immediately to fix it. Sensing the urgency of the request, the US firm chose the person who had designed the press. When he arrived on the scene, the South American officials were skeptical—the young man was obviously wet behind the ears. After some discussion, they sent this cable to the manufacturer: "Your man is too young; send a more experienced person." The reply came back: "He made the machine. He can fix it!"

Christ not only created us—he sustains us, and we are made for him. We need to submit our personal problems to him, for he knows how to solve them.

Christ: Supreme in the Church (v. 18)

"And he is the head of the body, the church." Christ is sovereign over the Church, just as he is sovereign over creation. When we became believers, we became part of Christ's Body through the baptizing work of the Holy Spirit (1 Corinthians 12:13). "[S]o we, though many, are one body in Christ" (Romans 12:5). As members of his Body we are totally dependent upon the Head, Christ, for direction. He is to control us.

The reason for Christ's exalted position in the Church is that "He is the beginning, the firstborn from the dead" (v. 18). We saw this word "firstborn" in verse 15, where it meant first in rank, and here it means the same thing. Paul was not saying that Jesus was the first person to be raised from the dead, for he was not. However, he was the most important of all who have been raised from the dead, because without his resurrection there could be no resurrection for others (cf. 1 Corinthians 15:20ff.).

Christ chose to enter his own creation, take on a body created and sustained by his power, die, and then undergo resurrection and so be "the firstborn from the dead"—*and first in rank in salvation*. What a wonder! The Gnostics in all their arcane speculations could never have dreamed up something as stupendous as this. Such a plan, such a dream could only come from the mind of God.

What should this mean to us? Simply this: "that in everything he might be preeminent" (v. 18). "Everything" extends his "firstness" to as wide a scope as is conceivable and beyond. There is no room for a "Parliament of Religions" here—only Christ preeminent. He must have first place in everything.

- First place in our families
- First place in our marriages
- First place in our professions
- First place in our mission and ministry
- First place in matters of the intellect
- First place in time
- First place in love
- First place in conversation
- First place in pleasures
- First place in eating
- First place in play
- First place in athletics
- First place in what we watch
- First place in art
- First place in music
- First place in worship

Let us give him first place!

For in him all the fullness of God was pleased to dwell, and through him to reconcile to himself all things, whether on earth or in heaven, making peace by the blood of his cross. And you, who once were alienated and hostile in mind, doing evil deeds, he has now reconciled in his body of flesh by his death, in order to present you holy and blameless and above reproach before him, if indeed you continue in the faith, stable and steadfast, not shifting from the hope of the gospel that you heard, which has been proclaimed in all creation under heaven, and of which I, Paul, became a minister.

1:19–23

27

The Supreme Reconciliation

COLOSSIANS 1:19–23

ON APRIL 15, 1912, the White Star Liner *Titanic* raised her stern high above the frigid waters of the North Atlantic and began a slow, seemingly calibrated descent as her lighted portholes and towering stern slid silently toward the ocean floor. That famous night saw the extremes of human behavior—from abysmal cowardice to the terrible beauties of sacrificial love. But with the *Titanic* gone and her lifeboats spread upon the icy waters among the crying, drowning swimmers, the story was almost totally devoted to self-serving cowardice, for of the 1,600 people who were not able to get into the lifeboats, only thirteen were picked up by the eighteen half-empty boats that hovered nearby.

In Boat No. 5, when Third Officer Pitman heard the anguished cries, he turned the boat around and shouted, "Now, men, we will pull toward the wreck!" But the passengers protested, "Why should we lose all our lives in a useless attempt to save others from the ship?" Pitman gave in. And for the next hour No. 5, with forty people on board and a capacity of sixty-five, heaved gently on the calm Atlantic, while the forty listened to the fading cries of swimmers 300 yards away. The story was much the same on the other boats. In No. 2, Fourth Officer Boxhall asked the ladies, "Shall we go back?" They said no, so Boat No. 2, about 60 percent full, likewise drifted while her people callously listened. On Boat No. 6, the situation was reversed as the women begged Quartermaster Hitchens to return, but he refused, painting a vivid picture of the drowning overturning the boat. The women pleaded as the cries grew fewer. Of the eighteen boats, only one boat, No. 14, returned to help—and this was an hour after the *Titanic's* sinking, when the thrashing crowd had "thinned out."[1]

To me, the personal drama of the sinking of the *Titanic* is a parable of a world gone wrong. Fallen humanity is adrift on the unfriendly sea, alienated, unable to help one another despite some furtive individual attempts. The wrongness of everything points to the fundamental problem of people's estrangement from each other and from creation by sin. It is a picture of a world desperately in need of reconciliation and the harmony and rightness that brings.

Even apart from the terrible story of the *Titanic*, there is no doubt that the world is in need of reconciliation. The inscription on Louis XIV's cannons—*ultima ratio regem* ("the final argument of kings")—is equally descriptive of the mentality of today's rocket-studded world. Man is as profoundly alienated from God now as he has always been since the fall (see Romans 3:9–18). Indeed, the whole of creation is in desperate need of reconciliation. It is toward this profound need that Paul has been moving us in our study of his letter to the Colossians and that he now takes up.

The Father's Reconciling Pleasure (vv. 19, 20a)

> For in him [Christ] all the fullness of God was pleased to dwell, and through him to reconcile to himself all things, whether on earth or in heaven. (vv. 19, 20a)

Paul tells us that God the Father found pleasure in having "all [his] fullness" dwell in Christ (v. 19). Paul's use of the word "fullness" here was an intentional slap at the Gnostics, who used the same word, *pleroma*, to denote the totality of all the thousands of divine emanations or lesser gods.[2] But Paul said, "No way! Jesus is not one of the lesser gods of the fullness. He is *the* Fullness!" Colossians 2:9 says it even more explicitly: "For in him the whole fullness of deity dwells bodily." "Fullness" means that the totality of divine power and attributes is in Christ. "The whole fullness—the full fullness"—Jesus Christ is the "exhaustion of God."[3] Moreover, the fullness is said to "dwell . . . in him" (v. 19). It is not temporary. It was, and is, there to stay.

This means that we need look to no one except Jesus for the full revelation of God's character. If God could only be perceived in closely-reasoned theological language, only the most brilliant could understand him. But the fullness was in Christ, and all we have to do is look at him. As we see him in the Gospels and hear him preached, we can know what God is like.

Secondly, it was God's pleasure "to reconcile to himself all things, whether on earth or in heaven" (v. 20a). God means to reconcile creation to himself. Creation suffered a curse because of the fall (Genesis 3:17, 18). Romans 8:19–22 tells us in sweeping terms that man's sin has subjected the creation to futility:

> For the creation waits with eager longing for the revealing of the sons of God. For the creation was subjected to futility, not willingly, but because of him who subjected it, in hope that the creation itself will be set free from its bondage to corruption and obtain the freedom of the glory of the children of God. For we know that the whole creation has been groaning together in the pains of childbirth until now.

This is more than poetry. Creation actually does moan, but it will be brought back to its primal obedience—like it was before the fall. That is why we sing at Christmas:

> No more let sins and sorrow grow,
> Nor thorns infest the ground;
> He comes to make his blessings flow
> Far as the curse is found.

The land and seas will lose their hostility! Everything in the universe will be reconciled except that which rejects him—which brings up the main focus of this verse: the reconciliation of sinners to himself. In every reference to reconciliation between God and man in the New Testament, it is God who takes the initiative (see Ephesians 2:16, which uses the same word as here; also the verbs in Romans 5:10 and 2 Corinthians 5:18–20 and the nouns in Romans 5:11 and 11:15 and 2 Corinthians 5:18, 19). Reconciliation to God is an explicitly one-sided process! He does virtually everything. All we have to do is respond.

What we should note here is that "God was pleased" (v. 19) to have the fullness dwell in Jesus and through him to reconcile us. Salvation is God's joyous work. What an inviting revelation to a lost world!

The Father's Reconciling Method (vv. 20b, 22a)

The Father's method of reconciliation is seen in two parallel clauses from verses 20 and 22: "making peace by the blood of his cross"; "[H]e has now reconciled [you] in his body of flesh by his death." God's method is the death of Christ.

It is said that years ago in a western city a husband and wife became estranged and chose to separate. They moved away and lived in different parts of the country. The husband happened to return to the city on a matter of business and went out to the cemetery to the grave of their only son. He was standing by the grave in fond reminiscence when he heard a step behind him. Turning, he saw his estranged wife. The initial impulse of both was to turn away. But they had a common-hearted interest in that grave, and instead of turning away they clasped hands over the grave of their son and were reconciled. They were reconciled by death![4]

Our personal reconciliation took nothing less than the death of God's Son; but his death and its effects went far beyond any human death.

> [I]n Christ God was reconciling the world to himself, not counting their trespasses against them, and entrusting to us the message of reconciliation. . . . For our sake he made him to be sin who knew no sin, so that in him we might become the righteousness of God. (2 Corinthians 5:19, 21)

Jesus bore the separation of sin so reconciliation could take place. He made "peace by the blood of his cross" (v. 20). "[H]e himself is our peace" (Ephesians 2:14). As Dorothy Sayers put it, "Whatever the answer to the problem of evil, this much is true: God took His own medicine." The cross is the ultimate evidence that there is no length the love of God will refuse to go in effecting reconciliation.

> He who did not spare his own Son but gave him up for us all, how will he not also with him graciously give us all things? (Romans 8:32)

It is God's *pleasure* to give you all things. Have you responded to him?

The Father's Reconciling Purpose (vv. 21, 22)

> And you, who once were alienated and hostile in mind, doing evil deeds, he has now reconciled in his body of flesh by his death, in order to present you holy and blameless and above reproach before him. (vv. 21, 22)

God's purpose rises from mankind's miserable condition. In the original, "alienated" was an unusually powerful word that indicated a persistent and permanent condition.[5] This continuous alienation from God expressed itself in a mind that was "hostile" to him and eventuated in "evil deeds." This is the way all people are without Christ, but humanity doesn't like to hear it.

When a great seventeenth-century Christian woman and encourager of God's servants, Lady Huntingdon, invited one of her friends, the Duchess of Buckingham, to hear George Whitefield preach, she received this reply:

> It is monstrous to be told, that you have a heart as sinful as the common wretches that crawl on the earth. This is highly offensive and insulting; and I cannot but wonder that your ladyship should relish any sentiments so much at variance with high rank and good breeding.[6]

Paul's pronouncement that we are "alienated . . . hostile . . . doing evil deeds" may sound a bit harsh to us too, but it is terribly true (v. 21). All it takes is a telling difficulty, like floating on the cold Atlantic, to find out what is really there.

Humanity's condition is terrible, but God's reconciling purpose is "to present you holy and blameless and above reproach before him" (v. 22). While the Scriptures paint the darkest possibilities for man apart from Christ, they also give us the highest, noblest vision of man known to any religious conception anywhere! When one is reconciled to Christ, he or she will be presented before him as holy, without blame, and beyond reproach. This person is a "fellow heir" of Christ's promises (Romans 8:17) and will remain eternally glorious and holy. If we have been reconciled, this is our position before God right now, and it will be increasingly true in our life as we grow into his image. R. C. Sproul tells us:

> Luther used a simple analogy to explain it. He described the condition of a patient who was mortally ill. The doctor proclaimed that he had medicine that would surely cure the man. The instant the medicine was administered, the doctor declared that the patient was well. At that instant the patient was still sick, but as soon as the medicine passed his lips and entered his body the patient began to get well. So it is with our reconciliation and justification. As soon as we truly believe, that very instant we start to get better; the process of becoming pure and holy is underway and its future completion is certain.[7]

Fellow believers, in light of our reconciliation we ought to do everything in our power to be practically blameless and holy in this life. We must become what we are in the Lord. We must submit ourselves ever more completely to "God who works in you" (Philippians 2:13). Practical holiness should be our life's business.

The Father's Reconciling Condition (v. 23)

> . . . if indeed you continue in the faith, stable and steadfast, not shifting from the hope of the gospel that you heard, which has been proclaimed in all creation under heaven, and of which I, Paul, became a minister. (v. 23)

Paul is not expressing doubt as to whether they will continue on; that is not what the Greek construction means. The scholar Peter O'Brien paraphrases the idea: "At any rate if you stand firm in the faith—and I am sure you will."[8] The positive application of Paul's words are this: the gospel does not work like magic. The mind, the heart, and the will must be involved. Our minds must feed on Christ and his Word. Our hearts are to focus on him in love. Our wills are to take their practice and pattern from him. Present faith leads to present results; present drinking is for present thirst. We must fill our lives every day from him.

It is imperative that all of us be reconciled to Christ. Without reconciliation we will remain adrift on the cold seas—alienated from God, from creation, and from others, though we may wish otherwise. God wants to reconcile us. He enjoys reconciling. His Son "for the joy that was set before him endured the cross " (Hebrews 12:2). What God has in mind for us is the greatest vision ever conceived for any mortal. There is only one thing to do, and that is to say yes.

D. L. Moody related this incident between his sister and her son:

My sister, I remember, told me her boy said something naughty one morning, when his father said to him, "Sammy, go and ask your mother's forgiveness." "I won't," replied the child. "If you don't ask your mother's forgiveness I'll put you to bed." It was early in the morning—before he went to business and the boy didn't think he would do it. He said "I won't" again. They undressed him and put him to bed. The father came home at noon expecting to find his boy playing about the house. He didn't see him about, and asked his wife where he was. "In bed still." So he went up to the room, and sat down by the bed, and said: "Sammy, I want you to ask your mother's forgiveness." But the answer was "No." The father coaxed and begged, but could not induce the child to ask forgiveness. The father went away, expecting certainly that when he came home at night the child would have got all over it. At night, however, when he got home he found the little fellow still in bed. He had lain there all day. He went to him and tried to get him to go to his mother, but it was no use. His mother went and was equally unsuccessful. That father and mother could not sleep any that night. They expected every moment to hear the knock at their door by their little son. How they wanted to forgive the boy. My sister told me it was just as if death had come into their home. She never passed through such a night. In the morning she went in to him and said: "Now, Sammy, you are going to ask my forgiveness." But the boy turned his face to the wall and wouldn't speak. The father came home at noon and the boy was as stubborn as ever. It looked as though the child was going to conquer. It was for the good of the boy that they didn't want to give him his own way. It is a great deal better for us to submit to God than have our own way. Our own way will lead us to ruin; God's way leads to life everlasting. The father went off to his office, and that afternoon my sister went in to her son about four o'clock and began to reason with him, and, after talking for some time, she said, "Now, Sammy, say 'mother.'" "Mother," said the boy. "Now say 'for.'" "For." "Now just say 'give.'" And the boy repeated "give." "Me," said the mother. "Me," and the little fellow fairly leaped out of bed. "I have said it," he cried; "take me down to papa, so that I can say it to him."[9]

What a picture of how we are! Just those words, "Father, forgive me," said from the heart, bring us to God.

Now I rejoice in my sufferings for your sake, and in my flesh I am filling up what is lacking in Christ's afflictions for the sake of his body, that is, the church, of which I became a minister according to the stewardship from God that was given to me for you, to make the word of God fully known, the mystery hidden for ages and generations but now revealed to his saints. To them God chose to make known how great among the Gentiles are the riches of the glory of this mystery, which is Christ in you, the hope of glory. Him we proclaim, warning everyone and teaching everyone with all wisdom, that we may present everyone mature in Christ. For this I toil, struggling with all his energy that he powerfully works within me.

1:24–29

28

The Supreme Ministry

COLOSSIANS 1:24–29

R. C. SPROUL, president of Ligonier Study Center, a popular theologian and a gifted and colorful communicator, tells of having the following exchange with one of his students:

> I remember a starry-eyed college student who looked at me and said in wonderment, "What was it like for you when you were just a minister?" I lost it. I exploded in a paroxysm of indignation. "What do you mean *just* a minister? Don't you realize that the parish ministry is the highest calling on earth? God had only one Son and He made Him a preacher!"[1]

In my mind's eye I see Dr. Sproul at his theatrical best, standing over his student like a latter-day Luther, while the student is trying to find somewhere to hide. Actually Sproul was just having fun, but he was serious about his point, which is that the Christian ministry is the highest calling. Of course, Sproul is not the first to think this way. John Wycliffe, the English "Morning Star" of the Reformation, wrote:

> The highest service that men may attain to on earth is to preach the Word of God. This service falls peculiarly to priests and therefore God more straightly demands it of them. . . . And for this cause, Jesus Christ left other works and occupied himself mostly in preaching, and thus did his apostles, and for this God loved them.[2]

In the last century, Alexander Whyte of Edinburgh wrote to a discouraged pastor, "The angels around the throne envy your great work. . . . Go on and grow in grace and power as a gospel preacher."[3] In our own day, W. E. Sangster of the Westminster Central Hall in London said:

> Called to preach! . . . commissioned of God to teach the word! A herald of the great King! A witness of the Eternal Gospel! Could any work be more high and holy! To this supreme task God sent his only begotten Son. In all the frustration and confusion of the times, is it possible to imagine a work comparable in importance with that of proclaiming the will of God to wayward men?[4]

And indeed, notwithstanding the fact that we are called to many different occupations and all of them holy if they are God's will, the gospel ministry in its various forms is the highest call possible.

Having introduced us in succession to the supremacy of Christ in creation (vv. 15–17), in the Church (v. 18), and in reconciliation (vv. 19–23), Paul now gives us a supremely magnificent perspective on his resulting ministry. It is a remarkably balanced view that delineates four aspects of his own ministry: his ministerial *attitude*, his ministerial *charge*, his ministerial *purpose*, and his ministerial *devotion*. It will be especially profitable for those who are in the professional ministry, but it ought to prove equally helpful for every serious believer, because we are all called to the "ministry," whatever our stated vocation.

Paul's Ministerial Attitude (v. 24)

> Now I rejoice in my sufferings for your sake, and in my flesh I am filling up what is lacking in Christ's afflictions for the sake of his body, that is, the church. (v. 24)

Paul explicitly said he rejoiced in his sufferings. From a secularist perspective, what he says is incomprehensible—"baptized masochism." But Romans 5:3 speaks of exulting in tribulation; 1 Peter 4:13 says to suffer and rejoice; Acts 5:41 tells of the apostles rejoicing that they had been counted "worthy" to suffer. Paul too rejoiced. But why?

First, because his suffering brought good to the Church. "Now I rejoice in my sufferings for your sake, and in my flesh I am filling up what is lacking . . . for the sake of his body, that is, the church" (v. 24). Without his willingness to suffer (described in 2 Corinthians 11, where he listed an amazing catalogue of miseries he had undergone to bring the gospel to Asia), there would have been no church in Asia. The gospel has always spread through missionary hardship. But there is something more here, and it is far more subtle: believers grow through their personal suffering, and the good they receive flows to others—thus edifying the Church.

John Newton, the author of "Amazing Grace," said:

> God appoints his ministers to be sorely exercised, both from without and
> within; that they may sympathize with their flock, and know in their own
> hearts the deceitfulness of sin, the infirmities of the flesh, and the way in
> which the Lord supports and bears all who trust in Him.

God's servants benefit, and everyone benefits. For Paul, this is cause for
rejoicing. This is why very often the suffering of a brother or sister in Christ
is a great source of blessing to the Church, for their elevated character is
transferred to fellow believers.

Secondly, Paul described his suffering as "filling up what is lacking in
Christ's afflictions" (v. 24). This is one of the most debated verses in all of
Scripture! Whole books have been written on its interpretation over the last
2,000 years.[5] We know it does *not* mean that Paul made up that which was
lacking in the atoning sufferings of Christ, for the whole of Colossians as
well as the rest of the New Testament teaches the sufficiency of Christ in
atonement (cf. 2:13, 14; 1:12–14, 19–22). Paul did not help with the atonement; that was Christ's solo work. But one thing that the phrase does teach
for sure (and everyone agrees on this) is that a close identification develops
between Christ and the Church through suffering. Before Saul's Damascus
Road encounter, Saul had been making Christ suffer in the people he was
persecuting. Christ's first words to Saul made this clear: "Saul, Saul, why are
you persecuting me?" (Acts 9:4). Jesus was being persecuted in the bodies
of his followers. However, immediately after Paul's conversion Jesus said,
"I will show him how much he must suffer for the sake of my name" (9:16).
Now Paul would suffer, and Christ would suffer in him—a stupendous truth!

Dr. Helen Roseveare, a British medical doctor, served more than twenty
years in Zaire, Africa. For twelve and a half years she had a frenetic but generally wonderful time serving as the only doctor to an area containing more
than half a million people (today about one and a half million). But in 1964
revolution overwhelmed the country, and she and her coworkers were thrown
into five and a half months of almost unbelievable brutality and torture. On
one occasion when Dr. Roseveare was on the verge of being executed, a
seventeen-year-old student came to her defense and was savagely beaten as
a result. He was kicked about like a football and left for dead. Dr. Roseveare
was sick. For a moment she thought that God had forsaken her, even though
she did not doubt his reality. But God stepped in, overwhelmed her with the
sense of his own presence, and said something like this: "Twenty years ago
you asked me for the privilege of being a missionary, the privilege of being
identified with me. These are not your sufferings; they are my sufferings."

As the force of that hit home, the doctor said she was overcome with a great sense of privilege. Helen Roseveare's sense of identification with Christ, of union with him, was elevated by her suffering, and she rejoiced. Paul likewise rejoiced in the sublime oneness he sensed as Christ participated with him in his sufferings.

How then did Paul fill up "what is lacking in Christ's afflictions" (v. 24)? No one knows for sure. Many top scholars today, such as Ralph Martin and Peter O'Brien, believe that Paul's words have reference to the common Jewish understanding that the Messianic Age was to be preceded by a definite amount of suffering (1 Enoch 47:14; 2 Baruch 30:2). Thus the sufferings are the sufferings of God's people, but they are ultimately Christ's sufferings because of his identity with his people. So Paul in his sufferings helped fulfill Christ's and thus hastened the Messianic Age.[6] If this is the correct interpretation, Paul was rejoicing because his sufferings (which are Christ's sufferings) were bringing the total nearer the ultimate goal and hastening the day of the kingdom.

However that may be, one thing is clear: Paul knew his sufferings were good for the Church and that they brought to him a special closeness with Christ. Every blow that fell on him fell on his Master and thus bound them even closer together in mutual suffering. Paul's experience was like that of Shadrach, Meshach, and Abednego, who in the fiery furnace were joined by a fourth person: the Lord (Daniel 3:25). That is why Paul could pray from a Roman jail:

> [I want to] know him and the power of his resurrection, and . . . share his sufferings, becoming like him in his death. (Philippians 3:10)

Paul knew sufferings are miserable, but the resulting sense of union with Christ is wonderful.

Paul's Ministerial Charge (vv. 25–27)

> I became a minister [of the church] according to the stewardship from God that was given to me for you, to make the word of God fully known. (v. 25)

This charge has preaching as its main function, and specifically Biblical exposition. The phrase "to make the word of God fully known" (v. 25) literally reads, "that I might complete the Word of God." The idea is to lay out the Word of God fully. People cannot know Christ better without knowing the Scriptures. Preaching (exposition) was the heart of God's call to Paul.

Preaching must open the Word of God. Paul affirms here that such preaching is primary to an authentic ministry. There is no shortcut—it takes work. Joseph Parker put it this way:

> If I had talked all the week, I could not have preached on Sunday. That is all. Mystery there is none. I have made my preaching work my delight, the very festival of my soul. That is all. Young brother, go thou and do likewise, and God bless thee![7]

The specifics of this preaching are given in verses 26, 27:

> . . . the mystery hidden for ages and generations but now revealed to his saints. To them God chose to make known how great among the Gentiles are the riches of the glory of this mystery, which is Christ in you, the hope of glory.

Paul's preaching set forth a "mystery"—namely, that in some way God's saving purpose was going to be extended to the Gentiles (cf. Isaiah 49:6; Romans 15:9–12). From the ancient Jewish perspective, this seemed impossible because of the mutual disdain that Gentiles and especially Jews had for one another. It was a mystery indeed!

Bishop John Green of Sydney tells about working with a group of boys, some of aboriginal blood and some of English descent, and how the racial tensions were such that they would not sit peaceably with each other on the bus. One day when things were out of hand, he stopped the bus, ordered them all out, and told them they were no longer black and white but green. He lined them up in alternate order and made each one say, "I'm green" as he got back on the bus. They drove along quietly "integrated," until he heard a voice from the back of the bus say, "OK, light green on one side and dark green on the other!"

The ancient Jews and Gentiles were like that, but with distinctly less humor, and their animosities went far beyond skin. The prophesied reconciliation of Jews and Gentiles was truly a mystery. Then Christ came, and the middle wall was broken down, and Jews and Gentiles became together a new man establishing *shalom*, peace (Ephesians 2:13–18).

> . . . the mystery of Christ, which was not made known to the sons of men in other generations as it has now been revealed to his holy apostles and prophets by the Spirit. This mystery is that the Gentiles are fellow heirs, members of the same body, and partakers of the promise in Christ Jesus through the gospel. (Ephesians 3:4–6)

Jews and Gentiles all sat down at one table and counted themselves one in Christ. It was a miracle! This had come about only because of "Christ in you, the hope of glory" (v. 27b). The indwelling of the Lord Jesus Christ is what made the miracle possible.

This happened in Colossae, and it can happen today. One of the greatest glories of the gospel is that it brings people who are different from each other together.

Paul's Ministerial Purpose (v. 28)

Him we proclaim, warning everyone and teaching everyone with all wisdom, that we may present everyone mature in Christ. (v. 28)

Paul's goal is nothing short of presenting to Christ complete, mature, full-grown Christians. He was not into the "I'll save 'em, you raise 'em!" type of thinking. Rather, his great joy was to present to Christ believers who have reached their maximum earthly potential.

For what is our hope or joy or crown of boasting before our Lord Jesus at his coming? Is it not you? For you are our glory and joy. (1 Thessalonians 2:19, 20)

Listen to Paul's benediction in 1 Thessalonians 5:23:

Now may the God of peace himself sanctify you completely, and may your whole spirit and soul and body be kept blameless at the coming of our Lord Jesus Christ.

Paul's means of bringing believers to maturity, according to verse 28, was threefold: proclamation, warning, and teaching.

He *proclaimed* Christ. Christ was the beginning and the end of his message. As George Whitefield said, "Other men may preach the gospel better than I, but no man can preach a better gospel."

When the preaching of Christ brought converts, Paul spent time "*warning* everyone," which means that he corrected and admonished them (v. 28). Paul did not shrink from this unpleasant task of admonishment, because he cared. I understand that when Henrietta Mears, one of the most effective Christians of our time, entered a room, people often had the feeling that she was saying to each person, "Where have you been? I've been looking all over for you."[8] This was certainly the way it was with Paul.

He also spent his time "*teaching* everyone." The Greek text of verse 28 is emphatic, mentioning "everyone" three times.[9] Paul proclaimed Christ and warned and taught everyone because he truly believed Christ was for everyone, and he saw great potential in every soul he touched. What a way to look at life!

Paul's Ministerial Energy (v. 29)

> For this I toil, struggling with all his energy that he powerfully works within me. (v. 29)

The truth is, no one can hope to have a Biblically authentic ministry without hard work. Paul's language in this verse is brutally compelling. The Greek word translated "toil" was used for work that left one so weary it was as if the person had taken a beating. It denotes labor to exhaustion.[10] "Struggling," a stronger term than "toil," was the Greek word from which we derive the English word *agony* and was used for agonizing in an athletic event or in a fight.[11] The words together describe the tremendous energy of Paul's apostolic ministry. He strained every physical and moral sinew to present every man complete in Christ. First Thessalonians 2:9 pictures this:

> For you remember, brothers, our labor and toil: we worked night and day, that we might not be a burden to any of you, while we proclaimed to you the gospel of God.

It is often said, "When all is said and done, there is more said than done." It ought not to be that way! Luther worked so hard that many days, according to his biographers, he fell into bed. Moody's bedtime prayer on one occasion, as he rolled his bulk into bed, was, "Lord, I'm tired! Amen." John Wesley rode sixty to seventy miles many days of his life and preached an average of three sermons a day, whether he was riding or not. Alexander Maclaren would get to his office when the workmen went to work so he could hear their boots outside and would put on workmen's boots to remind him why he was in his study. G. Campbell Morgan kept a newspaper clipping for twenty years entitled "Sheer Hard Work" and said:

> What is true of the minister is true of every man who bears the name of Christ. We have not begun to touch the great business of salvation when we have sung, "Rescue the perishing, care for the dying." We have not entered into the business of evangelizing the city or the world until we have put our own lives into the business, our own immediate physical endeavor, inspired by spiritual devotion.[12]

Paul's ministerial drive is a model for us all. We will never have an authentic, apostolic ministry unless we are willing to work to the point of exhaustion.

R. C. Sproul is right: the ministry of the gospel is a glorious thing. But we do not have to be an apostle or a reformer or a preacher to do it. Some years ago a woman in Africa became a Christian. Being filled with gratitude, she decided to do something for Christ. She was blind, uneducated, and seventy years of age. She came to her missionary with her French Bible and asked her to underline John 3:16 in red ink. Mystified, the missionary watched her as she took her Bible and sat in front of a boys' school in the afternoon. When school dismissed, she would call a boy or two and ask them if they knew French. When they proudly responded that they did, she would say, "Please read the passage underlined in red." When they did, she would ask, "Do you know what this means?" And she would tell them about Christ. The missionary says that over the years twenty-four young men became pastors due to her work.[13] She had it all:

- a ministerial attitude
- a ministerial charge
- a ministerial purpose
- a ministerial energy

This call is for all of us!

For I want you to know how great a struggle I have for you and for those at Laodicea and for all who have not seen me face to face, that their hearts may be encouraged, being knit together in love, to reach all the riches of full assurance of understanding and the knowledge of God's mystery, which is Christ, in whom are hidden all the treasures of wisdom and knowledge. I say this in order that no one may delude you with plausible arguments. For though I am absent in body, yet I am with you in spirit, rejoicing to see your good order and the firmness of your faith in Christ.

2:1–5

29

The Supreme Concern

COLOSSIANS 2:1–5

W. E. SANGSTER was once interviewing applicants for the Methodist ministry when an interesting young man presented himself before the committee. When it came his time to speak, the would-be preacher said he felt that he ought to explain that he was rather shy and not the sort of person who would set the Thames River on fire—that is, stir up the city. Dr. Sangster responded with consummate wisdom:

> My dear young brother, I'm not interested to know if you could set the Thames on fire. What I want to know is this: if I picked you up by the scruff of your neck and dropped you into the Thames, would it sizzle?[1]

Dr. Sangster was looking for something apostolic, something passionate, something Pauline in the young candidate. The Apostle Paul was indeed a passionate man. It is said that when George Whitefield's preaching was getting people out of their beds in Edinburgh, a man on the way to the great tabernacle met David Hume, the Scottish philosopher and skeptic. Surprised at meeting him on his way to hear Whitefield preach, the man said, "I thought you did not believe in the gospel." To which Hume replied, "I don't, but he does."[2] Paul was like Whitefield; or better, Whitefield was like Paul.

In Colossians 2:1–5 Paul states his specific concerns for the Colossian church. Up to this point, this is by far the most personal part of the letter. In expressing his concern, he models for us what and how our hearts ought to feel for the Church.

The Intensity of Paul's Concern (v. 1)

> For I want you to know how great a struggle I have for you and for those at
> Laodicea and for all who have not seen me face to face. (v. 1)

In mentioning his struggle, Paul again uses the noun *agon*, from which
we get *agony*. The word originally was derived from the place where the
Greeks assembled for their Olympic games, a place where they agonized in
wrestling and footraces, where they fought to win.[3] Paul had been agonizing,
fighting for the Colossians with everything he had.

What makes this truly remarkable is that he had never once personally
visited them or their neighboring churches. Aside from Epaphras, Philemon,
and perhaps a few others he had met in Ephesus, he had never seen the Colossians. He had no idea what the people looked like, he knew nothing of their
personalities; yet he agonized for them. Why this strain for people he had
never seen? Because he was God's "chosen instrument" to bring the gospel to
the Gentiles (Acts 9:15). His old stony heart had been replaced with an apostolic heart that beat with love for the despised Gentiles. It was like the heart
of the shoemaker William Carey, some eighteen centuries later, who made
a leather globe so he could pray for a world still unseen to him. Ultimately
Carey's "world-class" heart propelled him to India as he became the founder
of modern missions.

But there was even more, for Paul and the Colossians shared the same
relationship with Christ. He was also their spiritual father because he had won
them through Epaphras. All of these elements contributed to his dynamic,
agonizing struggle, and perhaps his persecution as well. (He was in prison
when writing this letter.) Wherever Paul went, there was conflict: riots in
Ephesus, beatings in Philippi, stoning in Lystra, shipwreck at sea, dangers
everywhere. Paul bared his heart in 2 Corinthians 1:8.

> For we do not want you to be unaware, brothers, of the affliction we expe-
> rienced in Asia. For we were so utterly burdened beyond our strength that
> we despaired of life itself.

The words he used here described a beast of burden that had fallen and
could not get up because the load was so heavy. This was how Paul felt in
Asia—he thought he was going to die.

There was also the *agon* of labor. It was a struggle to work night and day
so as not to be a burden to anyone, just to present the gospel (1 Thessalonians
2:9). In addition, there was the *agon* that came from caring so much how his
converts were doing that he said, "Who is weak, and I am not weak? Who is

made to fall, and I am not indignant?" (2 Corinthians 11:29). It hurts to care, and there were nights when Paul tossed and turned as he thought about his converts and empathized with their ups and downs.

But most of all, he wrestled in prayer for them. That is where the real fight was (and is)! In Colossians 4:12 he told how faithful Epaphras was "always struggling on your behalf in his prayers" (the same word as in 2:1). In Ephesians 6, where he described how to put on the full armor of God so as to do battle, he concluded by telling the fully armed warrior to be

> . . . praying at all times in the Spirit, with all prayer and supplication. To that end keep alert with all perseverance, making supplication for all the saints. (v. 18)

This is where the greatness of his struggle for the Colossian believers lay! Paul agonized in prayer for people he had never met.

What a great heart was Paul's! Enlarged hearts always know the *agon*. They have sleepless nights; they empathize; they struggle in prayer. But these big hearts also know the most joy. It is this kind of heart to which all of us are called, whether we are missionaries or merchants: a heart that is willing to agonize not only over our own little circle but the Church Universal.

There is a pastor in Chicago who likes to say: "When the tide is in, all the ships are riding high. When the Holy Spirit is working, then we'll all be riding high; none of us will be scraping bottom." His concern is not just for his church, but for the greater Church. If we have a heart like Paul's, we won't just pray for our little fellowship group or for the church we attend—we'll pray for other churches in our city, we'll pray for the world.

The Heart of Paul's Concern (vv. 2, 3)

> [I struggle so] that their hearts may be encouraged, being knit together in love, to reach all the riches of full assurance of understanding and the knowledge of God's mystery, which is Christ, in whom are hidden all the treasures of wisdom and knowledge. (vv. 2, 3)

Perceptive Christians have always known that the key to spiritual well-being is an increased knowledge and focus upon Christ. Less than one month before C. S. Lewis died, he wrote this letter to a little girl:

> Dear Ruth . . . Many thanks for your kind letter, and it was very good of you to write and tell me that you like my books; and what a very good letter you write for your age! If you continue to love Jesus, nothing much can go wrong with you, and I hope you may always do so.[4]

What you think of Christ, your conception of him, is *everything*. If you believe in Jesus Christ, that he is eternal, without beginning and without end, that he always was continuing; if you believe that he is Creator of everything, every cosmic speck across trillions of light-years of trackless space, the Creator of the textures and shapes and colors that daily dazzle your eyes; if you believe that he is the sustainer of all creation, the force that is presently holding the atoms of your body, your town, this universe together, and that without him all would dissolve; if you believe that he is the mystery, the incarnate reconciler who will one day reconcile the universe and redeem humanity to himself; if you believe that he is the lover of your soul, who loves you with a love bounded only by his infinitude; then, despite the fact that life will be full of trouble, nothing much will go wrong. Your vision of Christ will quicken and shape your life. What you believe about Christ makes all the difference in the world now and in eternity.

How does this knowledge of Christ come? Through brotherly love in the Church.

> . . . that their hearts may be encouraged, being knit together in love, to reach all the riches of full assurance of understanding. (v. 2)

In other words, depth of understanding is facilitated when believers' hearts are bound together in love.

F. F. Bruce comments: "Paul emphasizes that the revelation of God cannot be properly known apart from the cultivation of brotherly love within the Christian community."[5]

This means that mere intellectual comprehension of the mystery of Christ will not bring full understanding of the mystery, for understanding also comes through the love of Christians one for another. How is this so? When we are loved by other believers, we experience Christ through them, and thus our knowledge of Christ is enhanced. The complementary side of this is that when we allow the Holy Spirit through us to live the life of Christ (and we experience this when we do acts of love toward members of the Body of Christ), then too we have our knowledge of him enhanced. If we love, there are "riches of full assurance of understanding."

This is an important message for an alive Christianity. No intellectual process will lead to a full grasp of the mystery of Christ unless it is accompanied by a love for him and for Christians that knits us, the Church, together in love. We cannot pursue knowledge of God in willful, unloving isolation, rejecting fellowship with others. Historically, some have tried and have suffered incomplete or even distorted understanding. A complete understanding of the mystery comes in loving community.

This was so for both Luther and Calvin. Their lives were filled with people, for they were great lovers of the Body of Christ. The same was true of the great John Wesley. The deepest knowledge of the mystery of Christ comes from both the head and the heart. We must study the Scriptures about him intensely, with all our heart, and we must love him and his people with all our heart—and then we will know as we ought.

So when brotherly love is present and continuing, it facilitates a profound knowledge of Christ, which in turn results in wisdom and knowledge. This connection was underscored by Paul in verses 2, 3 where he states his desire:

> . . . that their hearts may be encouraged, being knit together in love, to reach all the riches of full assurance of understanding and the knowledge of God's mystery, which is Christ, in whom are hidden all the treasures of wisdom and knowledge.

This was a swing at the Gnostic heretics who claimed to have the way to wisdom and knowledge. Paul said there was (and is) no other treasury of knowledge, for "all the treasures of wisdom and knowledge" are in Christ. Of this truth Alexander Maclaren remarked:

> In Christ, as in a great storehouse, lie all the riches of spiritual wisdom, the massive ingots of solid gold which when coined into creeds and doctrines are the wealth of the Church. All which we can know concerning God and man, concerning sin and righteousness and duty, concerning another life, is in Him Who is the home and deep mine where truth is stored. . . . The central fact of the universe and the perfect encyclopaedia of all moral and spiritual truth is Christ, the Incarnate Word, the Lamb slain, the ascended King.[6]

Here's the point: when we love him and love the Scriptures and love the Church so that we are united in love with each other, the mystery unfolds and we are in touch with "all the treasures of wisdom and knowledge." It can be so now, if we know Christ. It ought to be so. The fact is, this treasure is meant to grow in this life and in eternity. There is really nothing beyond the truth that "God so loved the world, that he gave his only Son" (John 3:16). Grasped even imperfectly, this brings life. But as it is loved and lived, it brings undreamed light and warmth with each million miles until it fills the entire sky. As Christians we grow toward Christ and he fills more and more of our horizon until there is no sky—only him and his riches.

The heart of Paul's concern was that the Colossians would grow ever more toward Christ. He was concerned for their minds, and that is why the bulk of the first chapter presents such a heady picture of Christ. But he was also concerned for their hearts, because the journey involved a heart's love for Christ and fellow believers. Can you say:

> I love Thy Kingdom, Lord,
> The House of Thine abode,
> The Church our blest Redeemer saved
> With His own precious blood.
>
> For her my tears shall fall;
> For her my prayers ascend,
> For her my cares and toils be giv'n,
> Till toils and cares shall end.[7]

If you can say these words to God, you are on your way to a deeper knowledge of Christ.

The Motivation behind Paul's Concern (vv. 4, 5)

Paul was motivated to say all of the above because he was concerned that the Colossians were being led astray. In verse 4 we read, "I say this in order that no one may delude you with plausible arguments." The Gnostics' clever arguments could easily lead astray those who were not knit together in brotherly love and thus fully enjoying the treasures of Christ's wisdom and knowledge. It was an important warning in Paul's day, and it is equally apropos today when the means of persuasion are so highly developed. We are subject to space-age subtleties that the apostle could never have imagined. For our souls' sake, there must be a deep, growing knowledge of Christ and a love among us!

That was part of Paul's motivation. The other part, the positive part, is seen in verse 5, and here we come full circle:

> For though I am absent in body, yet I am with you in spirit, rejoicing to see your good order and the firmness of your faith in Christ.

The Spirit of God had united both Paul and the Colossians to Christ. Because they all lived in Christ, Paul was present in spirit with them, going through a "struggle" on their behalf. Paul's great heart sizzled!

Paul's passion was that the Church might be "knit together in love" (v. 2) so that it would attain the mystery of God—namely, Christ. This ought to be our passion.

Thou, O Christ, art all I want;
More than all in Thee I find.

Let us journey toward the Son until he fills the whole sky.

Therefore, as you received Christ Jesus the Lord, so walk in him, rooted and built up in him and established in the faith, just as you were taught, abounding in thanksgiving.

2:6, 7

30

The Supreme Charge

COLOSSIANS 2:6, 7

TWENTY-FIVE YEARS AGO I was beginning the final stretch of my fresh-man year in college on the West Coast. I was pleased and impressed with everything, but nothing impressed me more than one of my friends in Greek class. He was a senior and the "complete" collegian: student body president; captain and star halfback on the football team; big, handsome, with a ready smile; and quite intelligent. His family seemed to know all the Christian leaders in the world. To top it off, he was a nice person. I was impressed—really impressed!

Due to circumstances, it was necessary for me to continue my education elsewhere after my freshman year, and I lost track of my acquaintance until a few years later when a mutual acquaintance handed me a copy of the student newspaper of a major California university, featuring a front-page photograph of a professor posing nude in his classroom with some of his students, males and females alike. The professor was my old acquaintance. Subsequent articles in the *Los Angeles Times* revealed that he was the leader of a group of campus radicals and that he now expounded a crude nihilism that had led him to write a book intentionally using bad grammar and filthy language. The university, noted for its tolerance of viewpoints, was trying to kick him out (and later succeeded). How I sorrowed at the news!

Apostasy can come to those who appear to be the best of Christians. I have even seen colleagues in the ministry fall to the lure of what they con-sidered "deeper things." I remember one in particular who would no longer discuss the meaning of Scripture with me or others because he had a "higher hermeneutic," by which he meant that because he meditated on Scripture so much, he could see truths that transcended grammatical and traditional theological interpretation. With self-proclaimed "superior knowledge," he fathered a terrible legalism and led many into a false cult.

Paul was aware that the Gnostics were offering "deeper knowledge" to the Colossians. He knew well their tactics: coming as wiser, more mature brethren who claimed that "love" had compelled them to help lift the Colossian Christians from their baby-faith up to the real thing. In verses 6 and following he went on the offense against these false teachers.

> Therefore, as you received Christ Jesus the Lord, so walk in him, rooted and built up in him and established in the faith, just as you were taught, abounding in thanksgiving. (vv. 6, 7)

Here we have Paul's protective charge to the Colossians. What is the walk that protects us like?

A Birth Walk (v. 6)

"Therefore, as you received Christ Jesus the Lord, so walk in him." This means our experience of first coming to Christ ought to mirror how we walk in him all the days of our lives. What was our spiritual genesis like?

When we were born again, we "received Christ Jesus the Lord." Receiving him means more than simply accepting him. The Colossians received the teaching and tradition handed down about Christ. They did not receive him just as Jesus or just as Christ, but in his fullness. They received him as the "Christ," the Anointed One or the Messiah. They received him as the One who fulfilled all the messianic prophesies of the Old Testament. He was their divine Prophet, Priest, and King.

They also received him as "Jesus," a historical person rooted in humanity through the incarnation. *Jesus* is Greek for the Hebrew name *Joshua*, which means, "the Lord is salvation." So they received him as the captain of salvation, and so rejected salvation in any other name (Acts 4:12).

And they received him as "Lord." "Lord" gathers up all that Paul had previously said about Christ in Colossians.[1] It is a dynamic, comprehensive title. When the Colossians received him, they received him in full knowledge of this teaching, and they bowed before him as their Sovereign, their Lord!

Billy Graham says in *The Annals of America*:

> No man can be said to be truly converted to Christ who has not bent his will to Christ. He may give intellectual assent to the claims of Christ and may have had emotional religious experiences; however, he is not truly converted until he has surrendered his will to Christ as Lord, Savior and Master.[2]

Spurgeon comments on this, saying:

It is interesting to notice that the Apostles preached the Lordship of Christ. The word Savior occurs only twice in the Acts of the Apostles (Acts 5:31, 13:23). On the other hand it is amazing to notice the title "Lord" is mentioned 92 times; "Lord Jesus" 13 times; and "The Lord Jesus Christ" 6 times in the same book. The Gospel is: "Believe on the Lord Jesus Christ, and thou shalt be saved."[3]

Paul's point is that the Colossians had "received Christ Jesus the Lord" (v. 6) and that they would remain safe from spiritual seduction (apostasy) if they continued to walk in submission to him.

We too will be resistant to the gnosticizing influences around us if we walk in the reality of Christ Jesus as our Lord. The reason the major cults are cults is because they have defective doctrines of Christ. The Mormons, Jehovah's Witnesses, Christian Science, etc., say, like the Gnostics, that they believe in Christ—*but what kind of Christ?* It is certainly not the Christ of the Scriptures. This is also true of virulent forms of legalism and some of the extreme forms of the "prosperity gospel" that eat away at the fringes of evangelicalism. The safeguard against this is a perpetual bowing before Christ Jesus, the Lord, in line with our initial awareness that we are Christ's and our sins are forgiven.

Recall how it was then? Remember the submission? Remember the joy? Recently I read the conversion account of Charles Simeon of Cambridge, the founder of the evangelical movement in the Church of England. He came to Christ on an Easter morning after a great inner struggle. He said:

I awoke early with those words upon my heart and lips, "Jesus Christ is risen today! Hallelujah! Hallelujah!" From that hour peace flowed in rich abundance into my soul, and at the Lord's Table in our Chapel I had the sweetest access to God through my blessed Saviour.[4]

Remember the humility? Remember the gratitude? We are to walk in the new-birth realities. Paul makes this a present, active imperative: "walk in him." There must be ongoing progress in this genesis way.

A Walk in Him (vv. 6b, 7a)

". . . so walk in him, rooted and built up in him." When I was in grade school, our family home sat across the street from twenty-five acres. Each year thousands of huge tumbleweeds would grow, turn brown, and await the first strong wind. When that happened, there were tumbleweeds all over the place, which we gathered and burned. Tumbleweeds have a single, rather narrow root that turns brittle with age. Their limited root structure results in a short life, death, and subjection to the will of the winds.

The Colossian Christians, in contrast, were "rooted" in Christ. Paul probably had the imagery of Psalm 1 in mind, picturing them as trees that send their roots wide and deep into the soil of Christ, thus drawing from his very life. Believers are in Christ as trees are rooted in the earth. There is absolute dependence on the believer's part. In other passages we read of the vine metaphor (for example, John 15:1–4), and there the image is similar: the life of the vine flows into the branches. With trees, a general rule is that the visible spread of the branches is roughly equal to the invisible spread of the roots. The deeper and more widespread our roots in Christ, the greater shade, fruit, and beauty we provide.

The next metaphor is that of a building: "built up in him" (v. 7). As believers, our foundation rests on Christ and in Christ, and we are to be about the business of enhancing this relationship. We are to dig deep into the soil of Christ, there plant our lives, and spend our remaining days becoming a building worthy of the foundation. Such a life in and upon Christ will not succumb to the sweet gnosticizing of the false teachers. Center down on Christ.

A Walk in Faith (v. 7b)

". . . established in the faith, just as you were taught." They were to continue to be established in the faith that they believed and were taught in the beginning. Growth does not discard the early truths of Jesus Christ for newer truth, as the Gnostics were teaching. Jesus is not a beginning, to be left behind by the "mature." R. C. Lucas, Rector of St. Helen's Church in London, has said:

> This has something uncomfortably trenchant to say to Christian leaders. Did not many owe their first knowledge of Christ to evangelical truth? Yet how many now say that they have "grown out" of such simplicities. But to grow beyond the saving truths as we were faithfully taught them is not to grow up in a way that can please God or profit the church. Such fancied superiority in knowledge calls for honest self-examination to see if true loyalty to Christ remains.[5]

To outgrow the basic truth of Christianity is to become post-Christian and pagan, despite objections to the contrary. Moreover, the vast doctrines of God (the incarnation, reconciliation, adoption) would defy exhaustive exposition if we studied them for a thousand years.

Seeing the greatness of the essentials, we need to pray, like the saintly

Rutherford, for hearts and minds that are bigger, that we might hold more of Christ. I think Paul's prayer for the Ephesian church applies well here:

> [I pray] that you, being rooted and grounded in love, may have strength to comprehend with all the saints what is the breadth and length and height and depth, and to know the love of Christ that surpasses knowledge, that you may be filled with all the fullness of God. (Ephesians 3:17–19)

As we love him, we learn more; as we learn more, we love him more. We are not arguing for some sort of cliché-ridden Christianity, but for a profound head-and-heart study of God's Word, with an eye on the magnificent essentials.

A Walk in Thankfulness (v. 7c)

". . . abounding in thanksgiving." A healthy Christian walk spills over with gratitude and praise. We are not talking about the mindless mouthing of clichés. Two men were walking through a field when suddenly an angry bull chased them. They headed for the fence as fast as they could move. "Say a prayer," cried the one to the other. "I don't know any," answered his huffing and puffing companion. "You've got to," said the first, "that bull is getting closer." "O.K.," shouted his friend, "I'll pray the only one I know." As the horns of the bull came within striking range, the running man offered, "For what we are about to receive, the Lord make us truly grateful!" Paul is not talking about mindless piety, but praise deep in the soul.

Thankfulness is a good test of our spiritual state. A thankless spirit betrays a life that is no longer focusing on the greatness of Christ. It is looking down, not up. Thankful hearts herald spiritual health. Alexander Maclaren wrote insightfully:

> The life which is all influenced by thanksgiving will be pure, strong, happy, in its continual counting of its gifts, and in its thought of the Giver, and not least happy and beautiful in its glad surrender of itself to Him who has given Himself for and to it. The noblest offering that we can bring, the only recompense which Christ asks, is that our hearts and our lives should say, We thank thee, O Lord. "By Him, therefore, let us offer the sacrifice of praise to God continually." And the continual thanksgiving will ensure continuous growth in our Christian character, and a constant increase in the strength and depth of our faith.[6]

The Gnostics had little success around thankful people, and it is the same today. In fact, the thankful often draw others away from false teaching and to Christ.

It is our duty to give thanks:

> . . . give thanks in all circumstances; for this is the will of God in Christ Jesus for you. (1 Thessalonians 5:18)

> . . . giving thanks always and for everything to God the Father in the name of our Lord Jesus Christ. (Ephesians 5:20)

> Through him then let us continually offer up a sacrifice of praise to God, that is, the fruit of lips that acknowledge his name. (Hebrews 13:15)

> And let the peace of Christ rule in your hearts, to which indeed you were called in one body. And be thankful. Let the word of Christ dwell in you richly, teaching and admonishing one another in all wisdom, singing psalms and hymns and spiritual songs, with thankfulness in your hearts to God. (Colossians 3:15, 16)

There are enticing voices all around, and, as with the Gnostics, what they say sounds logical. If you are making a counterfeit dollar, you do not use yellow construction paper, cut it in the shape of a triangle, and put Batman's picture in the middle with a big "3" on the corners. Deception looks authentic. It is supported by intelligence, credentials, popularity, even a touch of class. Elsewhere Paul said:

> For such men are false apostles, deceitful workmen, disguising themselves as apostles of Christ. And no wonder, for even Satan disguises himself as an angel of light. So it is no surprise if his servants, also, disguise themselves as servants of righteousness. Their end will correspond to their deeds. (2 Corinthians 11:13–15)

The Devil knows what he is doing. As Screwtape said to Wormwood: "Old error in new dress, is ever error nonetheless."

Memorize the verses we have studied. Keep them close to heart. Understand that the dangers are real and deceptive. Walk the walk that insures.

> Thou, O Christ, art all I want,
> More than all in Thee I find.

See to it that no one takes you captive by philosophy and empty deceit, according to human tradition, according to the elemental spirits of the world, and not according to Christ. For in him the whole fullness of deity dwells bodily, and you have been filled in him, who is the head of all rule and authority.

2:8–10

31

The Safeguard
against Seduction

COLOSSIANS 2:8–10

WE DO NOT HAVE TO LIVE very long to know that it is easy to fool people, and that it is very easy to be fooled ourselves. Dr. Donald Grey Barnhouse, the great preacher and writer, used to illustrate this by telling of a practical joke that he and his teenaged friends played on some unsuspecting passersby in a large city. His group stood on a busy street corner and stared intently into the air. One of them pointed, while another said (loudly enough to be overheard), "It is not." A third friend argued, "It is so!" At this, one or two people stopped and began to look up in the same direction as Barnhouse and his friends. As the argument grew more heated, others stopped to gaze fixedly at the point his group discussed. Then, one by one, Barnhouse and his friends quietly slipped out of the crowd and gathered a few yards away to watch the results. By this time, some fifteen people were looking into the air. The crowd changed as new passersby came along and joined the group and those who had been staring longest left. Twenty minutes later several people were still looking upward. Several others had gone off to the side and were leaning against a building, looking up for something that was not there and never had been. About his childhood trick, Barnhouse observed:

> That little incident is a good illustration of all the earth-born religions. People talk about having faith; they tell you to look in a direction where there is absolutely nothing. Some people are so desperately in need of seeing something that they will look till they are almost blind, yet they never catch a glimpse of anything real.[1]

His point is so true. Over my years of ministry, I have seen those who were once perfectly healthy Christians set their sight on and their faith in something that was absolutely nothing! I have seen vibrant Christian young women don floor-length dresses and wear bonnets, all because a "leader" said this was the path to true godliness. I have seen intelligent, college-age men refuse to wear shirts or trousers made of mixed fibers because the Old Testament forbade Israelites to wear clothing that was part wool and part linen (Deuteronomy 22:11). Eventually some of these were led off into a cult.

It is amazingly easy for intelligent people to rest their lives on what will ultimately prove to be nothing. We see them standing on street corners selling their literature. We read of them following their guru to another land, giving him all they have, and dying there. We see them attending religious pep rallies, where they are told that health and wealth are theirs if they will only believe in themselves. We see vast religious empires held together by an enslaving sociology that is almost impossible to escape.

It is possible for seemingly healthy believers to be led astray. It happens every day!

Paul found this to be eminently true of the Colossian church and issued a warning that described the danger and then prescribed the safeguard against spiritual seduction. His charge is delivered in verse 8.

Charged to Resist (v. 8)

See to it that no one takes you captive by philosophy and empty deceit, according to human tradition, according to the elemental spirits of the world, and not according to Christ. (v. 8)

We must first understand that Paul was not putting down philosophy. *Philosophy* simply means "love of wisdom." Everything that had to do with theories about God, the world, and the meaning of human life was called philosophy, both in the pagan and Jewish schools of the day.[2] Both Judaism and Christianity are philosophical because they make holistic claims about the nature of reality and set values to guide life.

What Paul was warning against was a dangerous philosophy made up of both elements of Judaism and Greek Gnosticism. Greek Gnosticism taught that a person must work his or her way up a long series of lesser gods, called emanations, before reaching the ultimate god. Here false Jewish teachers combined Hebrew rites and ascetic regulations with their philosophy as a better way to move up the spiritual ladder. It was all very mysterious, complicated, astrological, and snooty. But worst of all, it was very deadly because it mixed some of the truth of Hebrew religion with the delectably enticing mysteries of Eastern mysticism and Greek philosophy. This was presented as "something more" that would elevate the ignorant Colossian Christians from their crude baby-faith to the truly deep things of God. Evidently some succumbed.

Paul's warning here noted four characteristics of this dangerously seductive philosophy.

First, it was deceptive. It sounded great, but it was "empty deceit" (v. 8). We have all heard such talk in politics, academics, religion, and science. It sounds so learned, but it says nothing and sometimes is even inane. Edwin Newman, in his classic *Strictly Speaking*, subtitled "Will America Be the Death of English?" cites an unintentionally humorous example of this, found in a "working paper" of Hampshire College, South Amherst, Massachusetts. Newman says the language of this paper, outlining the plans for the college, has never been equaled.

> . . . that social structure should optimally be the consonant patterned expression of culture; that higher education is enmeshed in a congeries of social and political change; that the field of the humanities suffers from a surfeit of leeching, its blood drawn out by verbalism, explication of text, Alexandrian scholasticism, and the exquisite preciosities and pretentiousness of contemporary literary criticism; that a formal curriculum of academic substance and sequence should not be expected to contain mirabilia which will bring all the educative ends of the college to pass, and that any formal curriculum should contain a high frangibility factor; that the College hopes that the Hampshire student will have kept within him news of Hampshire's belief that individual man's honorable choice is not between immolation in a self but instead trusts that his studies and experience in the College will confirm for him the choice that only education allows: detachment and skill enough to feel, and concern enough to act, with self and society in productive interplay, separate and together; that an overzealous independence reduces linguistics to a kind of cryptographic taxonomy of linguistic forms and that the conjoining of other disciplines and traditional linguistics becomes most crucial as problems of meaning are faced in natural language; and that the College expects its students to wrestle most with questions of the human condition, which are, What does it mean to be human? How can men become more human? What are human beings for?[3]

The Gnostics could talk like that (in their religious realm) and impress and intimidate those who knew no better. Yet, if Gnosticism's basic idea was accepted, then everything became supremely rational, even the most absurd rites and mumbo jumbo. It is the same way with the modern cults. One of the great, flourishing cults of our day has as its credo this theological couplet:

> As God was, man is.
> As God is, man can become.

This cult's belief is that God was once a man, but because he lived a virtuous life, he was reincarnated to successively higher lives, until finally he became a god of his own planet, and then the god of Heaven. Today thousands are setting out to become gods!

A classic example is Gordon Hall, the Nautilus sports equipment tycoon, of whom *The Arizona Republic* reports:

> He is worth more than $100 million, he says, because it was his goal to be worth more than $100 million before the age of 33. (Others say it is closer to $60 million.) There are other goals. By the time he is 38, he will be a billionaire. By the time his earthly body expires—and he is convinced he can live to be 120 years old—he will assume what he believes to be his just heavenly reward: Gordon Hall will be a god. "We have always existed as intelligences, as spirits," he says. "We are down here to gain a body. As man is now God once was. And as God is now, man can become. If you believe it, then your genetic makeup is to be a god. And I believe it. That is why I believe I can do anything. My genetic makeup is to be a god. My God in heaven creates worlds and universes. I believe I can do anything, too."[4]

Gordon Hall is a highly intelligent man, yet deceived.

The brand of Gnosticism that Paul attacked was perversely rational, yet moral. F. F. Bruce says of the Gnostic philosophies:

> The spiritual confidence-tricksters against whom they are put on their guard did not inculcate a godless or immoral way of life; the error of such teaching would have been immediately obvious. Their teaching was rather a blend of the highest elements of natural religion known to Judaism and paganism.[5]

Those trying to lead the Colossians astray were not "bad people" in respect to conventional morals. They may even have exceeded many of the Christians in their lifestyle. Moreover, they were sincere. Their sophisticated language, their stringent rationality within the system, and their self-conscious morality made a huge, religious Venus flytrap. These are the hallmarks of the great cults today: seductive, deadly deceit, and as vacuous as a hot air balloon. One day Gordon Hall, like the Gnostics of old, will awake to the reality that he was deceived.

Second, the Gnostic philosophy was purported to come from ancient and primal "human tradition" (v. 8). What this means is that the false teachers presented their philosophy as having "antiquity, dignity and revelational character."[6] Every cult today, even those that claim new revelation, hawk their deceptions as ancient in origin, but now brought to light by historical exigencies, or their own holiness, or the position of the stars, or . . .

Third, this false teaching was demon controlled, depending on "the elemental spirits of the world, and not according to Christ" (v. 8b). The overwhelming majority of recent commentators agree that "elemental spirits" is the correct translation.[7] These demonic spirits were thought to control the planetary spheres and thus men's lives—the world order.[8] Paul here argued that these evil forces were in control of this false doctrine and desired to bring the Colossians back into the bondage they knew before Christ.

Certainly this is true of the non-Christian cults in our present day. Read the history of their founders and you will regularly see evidences of supernatural, occult intervention and direction. These "elemental spirits" are just as active today, and their hallmark is that they are not based on Christ. They may use the name of "Christ," even worship a "Christ." However, they do not mean the Christ who is taught in Scripture, but a Christ of their imaginations, a Christ of the "elemental spirits." Again, the result is bondage.

Last, this false Gnostic philosophy is enslaving. Paul warned, "See to it that no one takes you captive by philosophy and empty deceit" (v. 8). The phrase "take you captive" means to carry off, as prisoners were led away by victorious armies. Cultic teaching asserts a death-like grip on its followers, and few come out of it. Paul is saying, stay away from false teaching if you value your life. "See to it that no one takes you captive" (v. 8). How is it possible for one not to be sucked in by a philosophy that is subtly deceitful in its language, logically compelling within its system of reason, and enticingly moral? The only answer is the fullness of Christ.

Reasons to Resist (vv. 9, 10)

"For in him the whole fullness of deity dwells bodily" (v. 9). Christ is more than merely Godlike. He is more than simply overflowing with the character of God. Rather:

> The *essence* of God, undivided and in its whole fullness, dwells in Christ in His exalted state, so that He is the essential and adequate image of God.[9]

This statement that "in him the whole fullness of deity dwells bodily"

(v. 9) forever blasts the Gnostics' idea that the fullness came through the emanations and angelic mediators. We can see the fullness of God in his work in the heavens and creation around us. But in Christ we see the face of God. Christ is the sole Temple of Deity in whom the divine glories are stored. How can we go anywhere else but to him?

This truth is great in itself. It ought to steel us against being taken captive by deceitful, empty philosophies. But there is something else that is utterly breathtaking: Christ, full of Deity, fills us. "[A]nd you have been filled in him" (v. 10). Christ can hold all the fullness of Deity; we cannot. But we are full of his fullness.

My wife and I once stood on the shore of the vast Pacific Ocean—two finite dots alongside a seemingly infinite expanse. As we stood there, we reflected that if I were to take a pint jar and allow the ocean to rush into it, in an instant my jar would be filled with the fullness of the Pacific. But I could never put the fullness of the Pacific Ocean into my jar! Thinking of Christ, we realize that because he is infinite, he can hold all the fullness of Deity. And whenever one of us finite creatures dips the tiny vessel of our life into him, we instantly become full of his fullness.

From the perspective of our humanity, the capacity of our containers is of greatest importance. Our souls are elastic, so to speak, and there are no limits to possible capacity. We can always open to hold more and more of his fullness. The walls can always stretch further; the roof can always rise higher; the floor can always hold more. The more we receive of his fullness, the more we can receive.

We must also understand that his fullness meets our individual needs. He gives us what the moment requires: wisdom, strength, courage. We must remember, too, that as we continue in him, we experience the satisfaction of his fullness, a continual stream filling and overflowing our lives.

> He is a path, if any be misled;
> He is a robe, if any naked be;
> If any chance to hunger, he is bread;
> If any be a bondman, he is free;
> If any be but weak, how strong is he!
> To dead men, life he is, to sick men health,
> To blind men sight, and to the needy, wealth.[10]

If you are full of Christ, and growing in that fullness, if you are over-flowing with Christ, the Gnostic appeals of the empty philosophies of our age will bear little appeal to you. If you are full of him, how can you want anything else?

Alexander Maclaren put it this way:

> Though all the earth were covered with helpers and lovers of my soul, "as the sand by the sea shore innumerable," and all the heavens were sown with faces of angels who cared for me and succoured me, thick as the stars in the milky way—all could not do for me what I need. Yea, though all these were gathered into one mighty and loving creature, even he were no sufficient stay for one soul of man. We want more than creature help. We need the whole fulness of the Godhead to draw from. It is all there in Christ, for each of us. Whosoever will, let him draw freely. Why should we leave the fountain of living waters to hew out for ourselves, with infinite pains, broken cisterns that can hold no water? All we need is in Christ. Let us lift our eyes from the low earth and all creatures, and behold "no man any more," as Lord and Helper, "save Jesus only," "that we may be filled with all the fullness of God."[11]

Let us covenant with God to invite more of his fullness.

In him also you were circumcised with a circumcision made without hands, by putting off the body of the flesh, by the circumcision of Christ, having been buried with him in baptism, in which you were also raised with him through faith in the powerful working of God, who raised him from the dead. And you, who were dead in your trespasses and the uncircumcision of your flesh, God made alive together with him, having forgiven us all our trespasses, by canceling the record of debt that stood against us with its legal demands. This he set aside, nailing it to the cross. He disarmed the rulers and authorities and put them to open shame, by triumphing over them in him.

2:11–15

32

The Fullness in Christ

COLOSSIANS 2:11–15

AS WE TAKE UP PAUL'S WORDS in verses 11–15, we find him further elaborating upon how the Colossians' fullness, and by implication our fullness, was accomplished in Christ. He began by explaining that the Colossians were full because being "in him [Christ]," they participated in the events of the cross—namely, Christ's death, burial, and resurrection. This was foundational to their fullness—and ours.

"In Christ": His Death, Burial, and Resurrection (vv. 11, 12)

Paul describes their participation in Christ's death in verse 11:

> In him also you were circumcised with a circumcision made without hands, by putting off the body of the flesh, by the circumcision of Christ.

Death

Normally circumcision does not refer to death, but rather to the common rite of circumcising males on the eighth day by cutting away a small portion of flesh. But here it provides a gruesome metaphor for the crucifixion.[1] His circumcision on the cross involved not the stripping away of a small piece of flesh, but the violent removal of his entire body in death. The Colossians, now "in him" as believers, *spiritually* shared in this circumcision, this death. Their "body of . . . flesh" was cut away; they died to their former way of life.

Burial

Paul's emphasis here was that the Colossians really did spiritually participate in Christ's death. He reinforced his point by alluding to their baptism—i.e.,

their burial with Christ: "having been buried with him in baptism" (v.12a).
Peter O'Brien says:

> As the burial of Christ (1 Corinthians 15:4) set the seal upon his death,
> so the Colossians' burial with him in baptism shows that they were truly
> involved in his death and laid in his grave. It is not as though they simply
> died *like* Jesus died, or were buried as he was laid in the tomb. . . . The
> burial proves that a real death has occurred and the old life is now a thing
> of the past.[2]

The practical implications are immense. When Christ's body was circumcised from him in his death on the cross, we were circumcised, we died.[3] Paul said in Galatians 2:20 that he was "crucified with Christ." Since we died with him, we do not have to serve sin. Romans 6:6, 7 gives the rationale:

> . . . our old self was crucified with him in order that the body of sin might
> be brought to nothing, so that we would no longer be enslaved to sin. For
> one who has died has been set free from sin.

The "old self," the person we were before conversion, was crucified with Christ. The "body of sin," formerly a vehicle for sin, has been rendered inoperative. Here is the fullness that Christ has given us. We are free to live life to its fullest—free from the domination of sin. In a world that is always seeking the full life, believers are the only ones for whom it is truly possible.

Resurrection

But there is even more. This fullness reaches full blossom by virtue of the believer's participation in Christ's resurrection:

> . . . in which [or, in him][4] you were also raised with him through faith in the
> powerful working of God, who raised him from the dead. (v. 12)

This resurrection is not future, but *now*. When we became part of the Body of Christ by the baptizing and identifying work of the Holy Spirit, we were baptized into the ascension of our Lord Jesus Christ. Thus we have resurrection life now. In fact, we are even seated with Christ in the heavenly places (Ephesians 2:6). As Phillips Brooks said:

> The great Easter truth is not that we are to live newly after death—that is
> not the great thing—but that we are to be new here—not so much that we
> are to live forever, as that we are to, and may, live nobly now.

We are resurrected now! We need to allow this truth to saturate our beings, so it will empower us to live honorably today.

> Now if we have died with Christ, we believe that we will also live with him. We know that Christ, being raised from the dead, will never die again; death no longer has dominion over him. For the death he died he died to sin, once for all, but the life he lives he lives to God. So you also must *consider yourselves dead to sin and alive to God in Christ Jesus.* (Romans 6:8–11)

The word "consider" means "to set to our account, to compute." We are to reflect on our position in Christ and then to set two things to our account: we are "dead to sin," and we are "alive to God in Christ Jesus" (v. 11). The Colossians possessed a fullness that was created and maintained by the fact that they actually participated in the death, burial, and resurrection of Christ. The practical application for us is this: we are to daily reckon to our account that we died with Christ, that we were buried with him, and that we were resurrected with him. This ought to come into our minds again and again, so that it dominates our being.

"In Christ": Delivered from Bondage (vv. 13–15)

> And you, who were dead in your trespasses and the uncircumcision of your flesh, God made alive together with him. (v. 13)

"Dead" is the description of the spiritual state of every human being who is apart from Christ. It is not a flattering term, but we cannot escape it.

> . . . you were dead in the trespasses and sins in which you once walked, following the course of this world . . . (Ephesians 2:1–2a)

Outside of Christ, humanity cannot perceive the truth of divine revelation.

> The natural person does not accept the things of the Spirit of God, for they are folly to him, and he is not able to understand them because they are spiritually discerned. (1 Corinthians 2:14)

Without Christ, we can do nothing to get life. There must be a sovereign communication of life from God. When Elijah stretched himself upon the dead boy, his heart beat against the stillness of the boy's chest until it kindled life. Even so, Christ must lay his full life on our deadness—and then comes life!

All of us who are believers today were once dead. But through Christ, divine surgery was performed. We were empty, but now we are full. If you have not experienced this, let me assure you that it is real. We were dead, blind, empty. Our new relationship requires the most positive of expressions: *life, light, fullness!*

We were not only delivered from the bondage of death, but from the guilt of sin:

> God made [you] alive together with him, having forgiven us all our tres-
> passes, by canceling the record of debt that stood against us with its legal
> demands. This he set aside, nailing it to the cross. (vv. 13b, 14)

The apostle says our guilt was like a "record of debt" (v. 14)—an IOU signed by our own hand, promising to obey God. This, by our lack of obedi-ence, announced our guilt. The Jews had contracted to obey the Law of Moses (see Deuteronomy 27:14–26; 30:15–20). The Gentiles had countersigned through their consciences to keep the moral Law as they understood it (see Romans 2:14, 15). The burden of guilt was immense. The more they and we sinned, the more the record "stood against us" (v. 14). Christ took the IOUs and nailed them to the cross above his head (just as the charges were nailed over him by Pilate), and then completely forgave us all. J. B. Phillips's trans-lation catches the idea:

> He has forgiven you all your sins: Christ has utterly wiped out the damning
> evidence of broken laws and commandments which always hung over our
> heads, and has completely annulled it by nailing it over his own head on
> the cross.

Martin Luther experienced the reality of this truth in a dream in which he was visited at night by Satan, who brought to him a record of his own life, written with his own hand. The Tempter said to him, "Is that true, did you write it?" The poor terrified Luther had to confess it was all true. Scroll after scroll was unrolled, and the same confession was wrung from him again and again. At length the Evil One prepared to take his departure, having brought Luther down to the lowest depths of abject misery. Suddenly the Reformer turned to the Tempter and said: "It is true, every word of it, but write across it all: 'The blood of Jesus Christ, God's Son, cleanses us from all sin.'"

The Colossians were complete, whole, because they had been released from the bondage of guilt. There is no tyranny like that of guilt, and having it lifted is wonderful. It is like escaping the pull of gravity—you feel so light and buoyant. This is why the Colossians were full. This is why they needed nothing else!

Paul concluded his exposition of the fullness that comes from being in Christ by stating that it involves deliverance from the bondage of evil powers. "He disarmed the rulers and authorities and put them to open shame, by triumphing over them in him" (v. 15). The "rulers and authorities" are the demonic powers arrayed against Christ and his Church. This is a picture of a triumphal procession through the streets in celebration of a military victory, with the conquered rulers and authorities put on display. The image that Paul had in mind can be seen in Plutarch's description of the three-day Triumph given the Roman General Aemilius Paulus upon his return from capturing Macedonia. Great scaffolds were erected in the forum and along the boulevards of Rome for spectator seating, and all of Rome turned out, dressed in festive white. On the first day, 259 chariots displayed in procession the statues, pictures, and colossal images taken from the enemy. On the second day, innumerable wagons bore the armor of the Macedonians. As Plutarch tells it:

> . . . all newly polished and glittering; the pieces of which were piled up and arranged purposely with the greatest art, so as to seem to be tumbled in heaps carelessly and by chance: helmets were thrown upon shields, coats of mail upon graves; Cretan targets, and Thracian bucklers and quivers of arrows, lay huddled amongst horses' bits, and through these there appeared the points of naked swords, intermixed with long Macedonian sarissas. All these arms were fastened together with just so much looseness that they struck against one another as they were drawn along, and made a harsh and alarming noise, so that, even as spoils of a conquered enemy they would not be held without dread.[5]

Following the wagons came 3,000 carrying the enemies' silver in 750 vessels, followed by more treasure. On the third day came the captives, preceded by 120 sacrificial oxen with their horns gilded and their heads adorned with ribbons and garlands, next Macedonian gold, then the captured king's chariot, crown, and armor. Then came the king's servants, weeping, with hands outstretched, begging the crowds for mercy. Next came his children. Then King Perseus himself, clad entirely in black, followed by endless prisoners. Finally came the victorious general,

> . . . seated on the chariot magnificently adorned, dressed in a robe of purple, interwoven with gold, and holding a laurel branch in his right hand. All the army, in like manner, with boughs of laurel in their hands, divided into their bands and companies, followed the chariot of their commander; some singing verses, according to the usual custom songs of triumph and the praise of Aemilius's deeds.[6]

In the death, burial, and resurrection of Christ, God the Father achieved a great victory over the evil powers of this world; he "put them to open shame" (v. 15). He wants us to see that though they still exist, they are defeated. Satan's demons have been sentenced to be in the train of God's victory parade. Thus, we need no longer fear the outcome of our battle with evil. Christ has conquered! We have conquered! And we *will* conquer!

In view of all this, why look to anyone but Christ for fullness? Cultivate human relationships, but do not look for ultimate fulfillment in them because they will disappoint you. Energetically pursue your career, but do not imagine that you will find transcending fulfillment in it. In Christ we have everything. May our prayer be to:

> . . . know him and the power of his resurrection, and . . . share his sufferings, becoming like him in his death. (Philippians 3:10)

If you are spiritually dead—without resurrection life—under sin—under guilt—empty, Christ invites you to come to him:

> Come, everyone who thirsts,
>   come to the waters;
> and he who has no money,
>   come, buy and eat!
> Come, buy wine and milk
>   without money and without price.
> Why do you spend your money for that which is not bread,
>   and your labor for that which does not satisfy?
> Listen diligently to me, and eat what is good,
>   and delight yourselves in rich food. (Isaiah 55:1, 2)

> The Spirit and the Bride say, "Come." And let the one who hears say, "Come." And let the one who is thirsty come; let the one who desires take the water of life without price. (Revelation 22:17)

If you are empty, call out to Christ. Do not let yourself go through another day without coming to him. Be born again, receive life, be filled, be delivered, join the victory parade!

Therefore let no one pass judgment on you in questions of food and drink, or with regard to a festival or a new moon or a Sabbath. These are a shadow of the things to come, but the substance belongs to Christ. Let no one disqualify you, insisting on asceticism and worship of angels, going on in detail about visions, puffed up without reason by his sensuous mind, and not holding fast to the Head, from whom the whole body, nourished and knit together through its joints and ligaments, grows with a growth that is from God. If with Christ you died to the elemental spirits of the world, why, as if you were still alive in the world, do you submit to regulations— "Do not handle, Do not taste, Do not touch" (referring to things that all perish as they are used)—according to human precepts and teachings? These have indeed an appearance of wisdom in promoting self-made religion and asceticism and severity to the body, but they are of no value in stopping the indulgence of the flesh.

2:16–23

33

The Guarding of
Your Treasure

COLOSSIANS 2:16–23

SEVERAL YEARS AGO my wife and I, along with our friends Peter and Anita Deyneka, visited the ancient city of Krakow, Poland. Krakow's magnificent square is bordered on one side by the massive spires of St. Mary's Church. From the great steeple of St. Mary's, a bugle has been sounded every day for the last 700 years. The last note on the bugle is always muted and broken, as if some disaster had befallen the bugler. This 700-year commemoration is in memory of a heroic trumpeter who one night summoned the people to defend their city against the hordes of the invading Tartars. As he was sounding the last blast on his trumpet, an arrow from one of the Tartars struck and killed him. So there is always the muffled note at the end. The Krakovians have never forgotten this heroic warning.

The text under consideration also carries an ancient warning, as the Apostle Paul sounded a note that has brought deliverance to all those through the years who would hear it. Originally a warning for the Colossian church that was being besieged by its cultured enemies, it still pertains today in a world where the Church is beset by equally sophisticated and deadly foes. Here is a powerful bulwark against the very subtle attacks that would rob the believer of his or her fullness.

"Do Not Let Anyone Judge You":
A Warning against Legalism (vv. 16, 17)

> Therefore let no one pass judgment on you in questions of food and drink, or with regard to a festival or a new moon or a Sabbath. These are a shadow of the things to come, but the substance belongs to Christ. (vv. 16,17)

The warning included two areas: diet and days.

Regarding their being judged about diet, there were evidently those who were saying that the way to God and spiritual fullness would be enhanced if the Colossian believers returned to the dietary laws of the Old Testament. As you know, the Old Testament categorized certain foods as clean and unclean (see Leviticus 11:2–20). Unknown to the Jew, there were excellent physical reasons for the Old Testament laws, which Dr. S. I. Macmillen has catalogued in his interesting book, *None of These Diseases*. There were also spiritual reasons, for the distinctions between foods were meant to familiarize God's people with the fact of purity and impurity, and thus to stimulate the conscience in everyday life. But when Jesus came, those dietary laws were abolished.

Jesus said to the Pharisees, who were offended by his liberated eating habits: "'Then are you also without understanding? Do you not see that whatever goes into a person from outside cannot defile him, since it enters not his heart but his stomach, and is expelled?' (Thus he declared all foods clean.)" (Mark 7:18–20; cf. Matthew 15:1–20). Peter's vision settled it for him, as he saw a sheet lowered from Heaven, crawling with clean and forbidden animals. Peter was scandalized! "And there came a voice to him: 'Rise, Peter; kill and eat.' But Peter said, 'By no means, Lord; for I have never eaten anything that is common or unclean.' And the voice came to him again a second time, 'What God has made clean, do not call common.' This happened three times, and the thing was taken up at once to heaven" (Acts 10:13–16).

Paul made this conclusion in 1 Corinthians 8:8—"Food will not commend us to God. We are no worse off if we do not eat, and no better off if we do." So the New Testament Scriptures are unified in telling us that all food and drink are lawful. Of course, dietary principles are a good idea. Eat too many Twinkies and you will no longer be "twinkletoes"; too many Snickers are no laughing matter. But dietary discipline is not a sign of spirituality. We are not to judge others, or allow anyone to pass a religious judgment on us, in regard to food and drink.

The same applies to days. The Jews had their special feast days (Leviticus 25) and their "New moon" celebrations (Isaiah 1:13) and their Sabbaths

(Exodus 20:9–11). When Christ came, he fulfilled them all! We no longer celebrate the Sabbath because we now worship on "the Lord's day" (Revelation 1:10), the first day of the week (1 Corinthians 16:2; Acts 20:7), the day that commemorates the resurrection (John 20). Verse 17 says that these things are "a shadow of the things to come, but the substance belongs to Christ." The dietary rules sensitized God's people to purity, the great feasts taught various aspects of God's work, and the Sabbath displayed something of the rest into which he leads his people. But they were just "a shadow." The real thing has come in Christ (cf. Luke 24:27).

The idea that spirituality can be quantified provides an unfortunate basis for pride and judgmentalism. The flesh finds doing truly spiritual things difficult, as "[t]he spirit indeed is willing, but the flesh is weak" (Matthew 26:41). But the flesh has no trouble with religious rules and regulations. There is an authentic lure to legalism.

However, legalism also has its downside. It spawns judgmentalism. Judgmentalism is miserable for the judged and the judging, because it shrivels their souls.

Legalism is intrinsically *joyless*, as the savage tribesman observed when a missionary was trying to convert him. The tribesman was very old, and the missionary was very Old Testament, with a version of Christianity that leaned very heavily on the "thou shalt nots." After listening to what the missionary said, the tribesman replied, "To be old and to be Christian, they are the same thing!"[1]

Legalism also demands *uniformity*. Whenever you find legalism dominant, you will find people who dress the same way and use the same speech, posture, and manners—even the same facial expressions! "Do nots" produce a grotesque uniformity.

Lastly, such legalism produces a *surface faith*, because its adherents emphasize the things that are not really important. Their "do nots" ignore deadly sins such as covetousness, gossip, slander, bitterness, and hatred. Legalism limits one to shallow self-righteousness, and thus damns him.

Interestingly, Paul does not say, "Forbid the faithful to keep special days and special diets." Rather he says, "Therefore let no one pass judgment on you" in these things. (v. 16) There is great liberty in what we Christians can do: we can keep days and diets, or forget them. But he rejects the right of anyone to judge and/or compel another to comply with his own preferences. We are not to judge others by these things, and we are not to allow others to judge us. This is a warning to take to heart, because time and time again as legalism has come into the Church, the Church has become judgmental, joyless, uniform, and shallow in faith. As bad as legalism is, there is another danger equally harmful—the sister error of mysticism.

"Let No One Disqualify You": A Warning against Mysticism (vv. 18, 19)

Before we explore this idea, we must say that Christian mysticism per se is not evil, for its goal is a deeper knowledge of God. What we are talking about here is a deceptive mysticism that is not rooted in Christ. In the context here, it is a mysticism derived from the pretense and imagination of the Gnostics. It bears some similarity to the pretense that Coach Johnny Kerr tried to get his Chicago Bulls to practice. As Kerr tells it:

> We had lost seven in a row, and I decided to give a psychological pep talk before the game with the Celtics. I told Bob Boozer to go out and pretend he was the best scorer in basketball. I told Jerry Sloan to pretend he was the best defensive guard. I told Guy Rodgers to pretend he could run an offense better than any other guard, and I told Eric Mueller to pretend he was the best rebounding, shot-blocking, scoring center in the game. We lost the game by 17. I was pacing around the locker room afterward trying to figure out what to say when Mueller walked up, put his arm around me and said, "Don't worry about it, coach. Just pretend we won."[2]

The Gnostics were great pretenders and fooled not only themselves, but the Colossians. Paul says that the Colossians were in danger of being deprived of their reward and future glory by the pretense of their cultured Gnostic friends.

> Let no one disqualify you, insisting on asceticism and worship of angels, going on in detail about visions, puffed up without reason by his sensuous mind, and not holding fast to the Head, from whom the whole body, nourished and knit together through its joints and ligaments, grows with a growth that is from God. (vv. 18, 19)

The Gnostics' power to fool people came from their deceptive approach, which is delineated in the clauses of verse 18.

They used bogus humility by "insisting on asceticism and [the] worship of angels." They loved to act humble and say, "We are not good enough to go directly to God, so we begin humbly with one of the angels, which, if we are in correct spirit, will elevate our requests through the hierarchy to God."

Next the Gnostics claimed to have special revelations, "going on in detail about visions" (v. 18). This was a technical phrase used in that day to describe "someone being admitted to a higher grade in one of the mystery religions."[3] Through this, they claimed to be on the inside. The Gnostics were actually proud. They were "puffed up without reason by [their] sensuous mind," says Paul. Advertising humility, they were filled with huge conceit.

It was all vanity and sham, but learning the secrets of the spirit world can be enticing. Tarot cards, for example, are inviting. Their aesthetic design is meant to exude mystery, and millions have fallen into their lie. Likewise, the mystic signs of the zodiac have claimed many. An exceptional display of piety is also attractive to many. Some people are drawn to those who say they are the "humblest" people in town. And the thought of being excluded from the "inner circle" is so devastating for some, they will do anything to get in.

C. S. Lewis, giving a guest lecture in 1944 to King's College (at the University of London), said that the desire to be in the inner circle (whatever it may be) is one of the "great permanent mainsprings of human action. Of all passions, the passion for the Inner Ring is most skillful in making a man who is not yet a very bad man do very bad things."[4] Applied to the realm of religion, this is especially true! Like the ancient dog of fable who while carrying his bone paused at seeing its own reflection in the water and grabbing at the mirrored prize lost the one he had, multitudes have lost *all* to deception.[5]

The root of the problem is laid bare in verse 19: "[He is] not holding fast to the Head, from whom the whole body, nourished and knit together through its joints and ligaments, grows with a growth that is from God." The false teachers had (and have) no part in the true Body of Christ. Conversely, this was (and is) the answer for those who want to steel themselves against their delusive teaching. We must hold fast to Christ, the Head.

> We drink of Thee, the Fountainhead,
> And thirst our souls from Thee to fill.
>
> Bernard of Clairvaux

"Let No One Enslave You": A Warning against Asceticism (vv. 20–23)

Spiritual discipline is good. But here Paul warns against extreme asceticism:

> If with Christ you died to the elemental spirits of the world, why, as if you were still alive in the world, do you submit to regulations—"Do not handle, Do not taste, Do not touch" (referring to things that all perish as they are used)—according to human precepts and teachings? These have indeed an appearance of wisdom in promoting self-made religion and asceticism and severity to the body, but they are of no value in stopping the indulgence of the flesh. (vv. 20–23)

Sadly, church history is replete with stories of ascetic excess in the rejection of beautiful and good things in the pursuit of God: rejection of marriage, sex, parenthood, the beauty of God's creation, even rejection of self. But this "self-made" religion does not do any good. In fact, it can heighten fleshly temptation and along with it produce a joyless, defensive approach to life.

Yet, surprisingly asceticism has its own seductiveness. Today, in its Eastern form, it attracts the indulgent, cultured elite. Thousands today have their gurus through whom they make their ascetic "nod-to-God." Seen for what it really is, this is an expression of independence from God that says, "I'm going to get to God on my own terms, by my own might." Asceticism feeds the flesh by starving it.[6]

The answer to such delusion is in the beginning of this section on asceticism, in verse 20: we have "with Christ . . . died to the elemental spirits of the world." Our death in Christ has freed us from the demonic powers of this world that promote and thrive on human asceticism. Because we died with Christ, they have no actual power over us. We need to reckon this to our account (Romans 6:11, 12) and live in the full joy of God's creation, enjoying him and his people.

Paul has sounded a clear warning, calling us to look at things as they really are. Several years ago Royal Robbins, a professional mountain climber, wrote an article for *Sports Illustrated* (March 6, 1978) that demonstrates the importance of seeing ourselves and life as we really are. He wrote:

> If we are keenly alert and aware of the rock and what we are doing on it, if we are honest with ourselves and our capabilities and weaknesses, if we avoid committing ourselves beyond what we know is safe, then we will climb safely. For climbing is an exercise in reality. He who sees it clearly is on safe ground, regardless of his experience or skill. But he who sees reality as he would like it to be, may have his illusions rudely stripped from his eyes when the ground comes up fast.

The reality is this: "in him [Christ] the whole fullness of deity dwells bodily," and in him we have been made full (2:9, 10). But we can lose the benefits of that fullness very easily. We can fall to *legalism* and its attendant self-righteousness, joylessness, and judgmentalism. We can succumb to *mysticism* and develop a proud, elitist spirit that contributes nothing to true worship. We can get into *asceticism*, thinking it will make us more holy, when actually it will feed our flesh.

The answer to legalism is the continual realization of the grace of Christ. The answer to mysticism is an understanding of how profoundly we are related to Christ. The answer to asceticism is the reckoning that we have died, been buried, and are resurrected with Christ. The answer is where it all began: at the foot of the cross.

I have seen in my own life and the lives of those I have counseled that there is a tendency to move away from where we had our beginning: the cross. All of our theology, all of our preaching, all of our singing hymns together, the disciplines of life experienced in family and relationships are meant to keep us right at the foot of the cross—simply drinking long and deep from the Fountainhead, Jesus Christ.

If then you have been raised with Christ, seek the things that are above, where Christ is, seated at the right hand of God. Set your minds on things that are above, not on things that are on earth. For you have died, and your life is hidden with Christ in God. When Christ who is your life appears, then you also will appear with him in glory.

3:1–4

34

The Seeking of Things Above

COLOSSIANS 3:1–4

PAUL HAS TRUMPETED his ancient warnings against evil teachings that would have robbed the Colossians of their wholeness in Christ. Now we see him provide a positive counterpart as he gives some coaching that will enhance the Colossians' fullness in Christ if it is taken to heart. His coaching will do the same for us, if we allow it, for although we are separated by 2,000 years, the human predicament is still the same, and the same advice still works.

When I was a boy growing up in the tennis-playing culture of Southern California, I learned that coaching can make all the difference. Those with the best mentors played best; those with good basic ability and the very best mentors could even become great. Coaching made the difference. Those who have heeded Paul's teaching have gone a long way, because it is instruction from God.

Instructions Regarding Our Fullness (vv. 1, 2)

"If then you have been raised with Christ, seek the things that are above, where Christ is, seated at the right hand of God" (v. 1). What are "the things that are above"? Certainly they are not the physical things of Heaven, such as Christ's literal throne at the Father's right hand. Paul and the other apostles knew they were using figurative language. Luther railed at the erring artists of the Middle Ages, "Oh, that heaven of the charlatans, with its golden chair and Christ seated at the Father's side vested in a choir cope and a golden robe, as the painters love to portray Him!"[1] "The things that are above" (v. 1) are not material, but rather have to do with Christ's sovereign reign over the universe as he fills the universe with his power. They include his character, his presence, his heavenly joys. We are not to be seeking heavenly geography, but the One who dwells there.

Furthermore, the verb "seek" is in the present imperative, which means a continuous, ongoing effort is required. We are to persistently seek and keep on seeking. Life abounds with examples of the persistence to which we are called. Albert Einstein was dismissed from school in Munich because he was thought to lack interest in his studies. He next failed to pass an examination to enter a polytechnic school in Zurich. He became a tutor for the boys in a Zurich boarding house but was soon fired. But he persisted over and over again, and you know how that story ended.[2]

Or consider the folklore about Lou Gehrig who, as an awkward rookie, was observed by Ty Cobb, who said, "Look at those piano legs—he'll never last." But with all his shortcomings, he set an all-time record of 2,130 consecutive games, the "Iron Man" of baseball.[3] Or there is the fabled record of archaeologist Howard Carter's monumental persistence through tons of rubble and discouragement and ridicule that eventuated in his finding the priceless tomb and treasure of Tutankhamen, King Tut. Such persistence is focused on rewards that, great as they are, cannot hold a candle to "the things that are above" (v. 1). This heavenly seeking is to be foremost through prayer, as we ask, seek, and knock for the things above (Matthew 7:7; cf. Luke 18:1–5). This seeking ought to pervade our conversations, friendships, studies, work—even our play. And when it does, it will enhance our fullness in Christ.

The *act* of seeking depends upon the *set* of the mind: "Set your minds on things that are above, not on things that are on earth" (v. 2). As the story goes, penny-pinching Jack Benny was walking along when suddenly an armed robber approached and said, "Your money or your life!" There was a long pause as Benny did nothing. The robber impatiently cried, "Well?" Jack Benny replied, "Don't rush me! I'm thinking about it." Millions of people today think their things are their life. I once saw a poster that pictured a coffin with pallbearers and the deceased's possessions: a mansion, a helicopter, nine cars, including a Ferrari, a Rolls, an MG, a Porsche, etc., with the caption: "He who dies with the most toys wins!" For many, this is the philosophy of life. Sadly, many in the Church are not far behind:

> Theologies compete brazenly to rationalize wealth, success and material blessing. Prosperity doctrines gush forth from rallies, radio and television. ("God's got it, I can have it, and by faith I'm going to get it.") Even Psalm 23 has been revised ("The Lord is my banker, my credit is good. He giveth

me the key to his strongbox. He restoreth my faith in riches. He guideth me in the paths of prosperity for his name's sake").[4]

People today spend not because they need, but for identity.

Paul says in response that we are *not* to set our minds "on things that are on earth." This includes not only material possessions, but the immaterial things of this world: earthly honors, position, advancement. We must note that Paul is not suggesting that the Christian withdraw from commerce and any possibility of prominence or achievement. Taken to absurdity, there would never be a Christian surgeon or chef; there would be no excellence. The difference is that the Christian is no longer to see these things as if they are all that matter. Moreover, his mind-set is to be dominated by "the things that are above" (v. 1). Paul is precise in his command: "Set your minds on things that are above" (v. 2) and keep it that way. Implicit here is the idea of concentration.

I recently played catch with a little dog named Bozie. After spending forty-five minutes tossing the ball for Bozie, I concluded that when she dies an autopsy will reveal she has a tennis ball for a brain! Bozie sleeps with her tennis ball, carries it to her water dish, and can find it wherever it is thrown. Her mind is constantly set on the tennis ball. So it should be with us regarding "the things that are above" (v. 1).

We see in these verses the "Great Divide" in the Christian life. What we set our minds on determines our seeking and thus the direction of our Christian lives. What do you think about when you have nothing else to do? Some common-sense qualifications are in order here, because we all variously daydream about our favorite team or a coming vacation or our yard. Sometimes we are under such pressures at home or work that we can scarcely think of anything else. But these things aside, do our minds regularly go up to Christ and "the things that are above" (v. 1)? If they do not, we are in trouble. The Bible says, "For where your treasure is, there will your heart be also" (Luke 12:34; cf. Matthew 6:21). What will the divine postmortem reveal to be our highest priority? A dress? A fishing pole? Christ?

This mind-set begins with prayer: "Lord, set my mind on things above." Jesus said, "If you abide in me, and my words abide in you, ask whatever you wish, and it will be done for you" (John 15:7).

We must also remember that our mind-set is a deliberate act of the will. We set our minds on taking a vacation. We set our minds on buying an object. We set our minds on finishing a project. We can set our minds on "the things that are above" (v. 1).

In addition, we need to hold loosely to the things below, our possessions. Remember the parable of the rich, young ruler who came to Jesus asking what he must do to inherit eternal life. Jesus told him to sell all he had, and the man went away sorrowing. The truth is, every one of us is that rich, young ruler. Every one of us has incredible wealth—more things than we know what to do with. Because of our possessions, it is difficult to set our minds on things above. There are two ways to hold something: with a clenched fist or with an open hand. A good exercise for each of us is to learn to regularly give something away that we value very much.

Finally, it is immensely helpful to memorize Scriptures that have to do with a heavenly mind-set, such as Colossians 3:1–4, Ephesians 1–2, or 2 Corinthians 12:1–4. Follow the advice above, and the fullness of Christ will be perpetual and growing—and no one will be able to rob you of it.

The Reasoning behind Paul's Instructions (vv. 3, 4)

Paul's reasoning is based on the *past* and *future* history of all true believers. Our *past* is given in verse 3: "For you have died, and your life is hidden with Christ in God." We actually died when we were baptized into the Body of Christ by the Holy Spirit (1 Corinthians 12:13; Romans 6:1–5). Thus, our life was "hidden with Christ in God." The tense here is imperfect, which stresses ongoing effects. Our lives have been hidden with Christ's, and they remain that way. Because we are in Christ and Christ is in God, we are inseparable and secure. Our lives are a part of the "above." The world without Christ does not understand the source of our life in him. There is something genuine about the believer that will tax the brightest intelligence to explain. In him there is fullness. His fullness has passed into our emptiness, his righteousness into our sinfulness, his life into our death.

Our *future* is described in verse 4: "When Christ who is your life appears, then you also will appear with him in glory." Right now our lives are hidden in Christ, but when he is revealed at his coming in his glorious body, we will also be revealed because we will have bodies like his. Paul describes this in Philippians 3:20, 21: "But our citizenship is in heaven, and from it we await a Savior, the Lord Jesus Christ, who will transform our lowly body to be like his glorious body, by the power that enables him even to subject all things to himself." Then we will be revealed! Those without Christ cannot now understand this, but then it will be perfectly clear. So sure is this that Paul speaks in Romans 8:29–31 as if it has already happened:

For those whom he foreknew he also predestined to be conformed to the image of his Son, in order that he might be the firstborn among many brothers. And those whom he predestined he also called, and those whom he called he also justified, and those whom he justified he also glorified. What then shall we say to these things? If God is for us, who can be against us?

What a spectacular future awaits us!

Let us covenant to not fix our thoughts on the material and immaterial things of this world, but to pray for minds set on things above, to hold the Scriptures close to our hearts, to reflect on our past history, and to rejoice in anticipation of our future in him.

Put to death therefore what is earthly in you: sexual immorality, impurity, passion, evil desire, and covetousness, which is idolatry. On account of these the wrath of God is coming. In these you too once walked, when you were living in them. But now you must put them all away: anger, wrath, malice, slander, and obscene talk from your mouth. Do not lie to one another, seeing that you have put off the old self with its practices and have put on the new self, which is being renewed in knowledge after the image of its creator. Here there is not Greek and Jew, circumcised and uncircumcised, barbarian, Scythian, slave, free; but Christ is all, and in all.

3:5–11

35

The Putting Off,
Putting On, I

COLOSSIANS 3:5–11

IN PAUL'S WRITING, theology is always followed by a call to live it out. For example, in the book of Ephesians, the first three chapters are given to highest theology, only to be followed with this practical call in 4:1: "I therefore, a prisoner for the Lord, urge you to walk in a manner worthy of the calling to which you have been called." This call introduces the remainder of the book. Similarly, the magisterial theology of Romans 1–11 culminates in this great doxology: "For from him and through him and to him are all things. To him be glory forever. Amen" (11:36). This is followed by a most practical call: "I appeal to you therefore, brothers, by the mercies of God, to present your bodies as a living sacrifice" (12:1).

We have the same thing here in Colossians, where the sublimely esoteric theology of Chapters 1, 2 spawns the challenge in 3:5—"Put to death therefore what is earthly in you." For Paul, doctrine demands duty; creed determines conduct; facts demand acts.

We will now begin to study the practical application of the vast theology we have already studied.

Laying Aside the Old Life: The Challenge (vv. 5–9a)

Put to death therefore what is earthly in you: sexual immorality, impurity, passion, evil desire, and covetousness, which is idolatry. On account of these the wrath of God is coming. In these you too once walked, when you were living in them. (vv. 5–7)

Jesus spoke of this same idea when he said: "If your right eye causes you to sin, tear it out and throw it away" (Matthew 5:29). Obviously neither Paul nor Jesus was recommending literal surgery, for sin does not come from the eye (or the hand), but from the heart—the evil within. In past centuries in England, if a pickpocket was caught and convicted, his right hand was cut off. If he was caught again, his left hand suffered the same fate. One pick-pocket lost both hands and continued his occupation with his teeth![1] Physical dismemberment cannot change the heart. "Put to death" (v. 5), as Paul uses it, means to discard evil practices and, here in Colossians, to get rid of the twin evils of sexual sin and covetousness.

Specifically, there are four elements of sinful sensuality that must be executed. The first is "sexual immorality" (v. 5), *porneian*, from which we get the word *pornographic*. It means every kind of immoral sexual relation. Chastity was the one completely new virtue that Christianity brought to the world.[2] Paul's call was radical to the pagan culture in its day, and it is almost as radical today. As you voice Biblical morality, you often will be labeled a moral brontosaurus! The second element of sensuality that we are to kill is "impurity" (v. 5), moral uncleanness. This is wider and subtler than physical immorality, for it embraces the lurid imagination, speech, and deed of a sensual heart or filthy mind. The third element is "passion" (v. 5), the shameful emotion that leads to sexual excesses. Paul used the same word to describe the passionate lust of the Gentiles who do not know God (1 Thessalonians 4:5) and the "dishonorable passions" of homosexuality (Romans 1:26). The fourth element of sensuality to be discarded is "evil desire" (v. 5)—wicked, self-serving, rapacious lust. What a deadly quartet we have here, and Paul said it must be slain outright—executed!

Personally I can think of no other array of sins more prominent in our society—and more in need of being put away. Daily living subjects the average American to a sea of sensuality. It is conceivable that on a given evening of TV watching, one may see more sensual sights than one's grandparents did in their lifetimes. The magazine ads for certain brands of blue jeans defy adequate description in polite company, and the Fellini-inspired TV ads for perfume promote a mystical eroticism. The January 1984 issue of *Psychology Today*, a magazine not known for promoting Biblical concern, stated that a pervasive cultural desensitization has taken place through films that feature sexual violence and suggested that such films be packaged with warning labels (as are cigarettes)!

What makes the situation even worse is the amazing human capacity for self-delusion in respect to sensuality. I have known professing, Bible-carrying "Christians" who talked sensitively about theology and serious issues, yet were adulterous and even incestuous. I have known Christian workers who were fundamentalists at work (mouthing all the shibboleths) and cable TV voyeurs at home. Even more tragic, the delusion is so deep that they see no inconsistency in their behavior.

Regardless of man's delusion, God's Word still speaks: "Put to death therefore what is earthly in you: sexual immorality, impurity, passion, evil desire" (v. 5). This is a violent metaphor that expresses pain and effort. Killing naturally means tears and blood, but here it means even more. As Alexander Maclaren said: "It is far easier to cut off the hand, which after all is not me, than to sacrifice passions and desires which, though they be my worst self, are myself."[3]

This metaphor teaches us that we must execute sensuality whatever the cost! Proverbs 6:27 says, "Can a man carry fire next to his chest and his clothes not be burned?" Many Christians are daily heaping fire onto themselves and are being profoundly scarred. We need to be like Job, who said, "I have made a covenant with my eyes; how then could I gaze at a virgin?" (Job 31:1). We need to apply this across the board. There are books and magazines we must discard. Some of us need to toss out TVs. I am not endorsing any type of legalism, but God's Word speaks today, and we are to kill the members of our body that lead us into sensuality or promote greed, which our text calls "covetousness, which is idolatry" (v. 5).

The word "covetousness" that Paul used here denotes not merely the desire to possess more than one has, but more than one ought to have, particularly that which belongs to someone else.[4] The mention of this at the end of a list of sexual sins is highly significant, for it is intimately associated with them. It is really another form of the same evil desire, except that it is fixed on material things. Often when sensuality loses its hold, materialism takes its place. In my opinion, this is why many middle-aged men who were once devoted to sensuality are now equally given to money. These sins have the same source. Such greed is really the lowest form of idolatry, for nothing could be lower than putting our trust in a material thing and making that our god.

Whatever I put my trust in, I worship. Materialism is the true religion of thousands of confessing Christians today. There is a sense in which covetousness is even more dangerous than sensuality, because it has so many respectable forms. So often it is the successful covetous person whom we honor. As the proverb goes: If a man is drunk with wine, we kick him out of the church; if he is drunk with money, we make him a deacon!

This is serious business, because both these sins provoke the wrath of God: "On account of these the wrath of God is coming. In these you too once walked, when you were living in them" (vv. 6, 7). Paul's message is clear: since we have died and have been buried, resurrected, and ascended with Christ, since we have been made full of his fullness, there are some things we must put off: namely, sensuality and materialism. We are to slay them, regardless of the blood and the pain!

We are also to put off evil attitudes and speech: "But now you must put them all away: anger, wrath, malice, slander, and obscene talk from your mouth. Do not lie to one another" (vv. 8, 9a). It is said that Jonathan Edwards, third president of Princeton and America's greatest thinker, had a daughter with an ungovernable temper. As is often the case, the problem was not known to the outside world. A young man fell in love with this daughter and sought her hand in marriage.

> "You can't have her," was the abrupt answer of Jonathan Edwards.
> "But I love her," the young man replied.
> "You can't have her," said Edwards.
> "But she loves me," replied the young man.
> Again Edwards said, "You can't have her."
> "Why?" asked the young man.
> "Because she is not worthy of you."
> "But," he asked, "she is a Christian, is she not?"
> "Yes, she is a Christian, but the grace of God can live with some people with whom no one else could ever live."[5]

So it is with the believer filled with "anger, wrath, malice" (v. 8). The "anger" described here is growing, inner anger, like sap in a tree on a hot day that swells the trunk and branches until they are in danger of bursting. "Wrath" is that anger boiling over. We see it in a quick temper. "Malice" bespeaks a viciousness of mind. It is the malignant attitude that plans evil and rejoices when misery falls on the one it hates, like Haman's glee in building the gallows for Mordecai (Esther 5:14). These evil attitudes must be put away. If they are not, "the heated metal of anger will be forged into poisoned arrows of the tongue."[6] Further, "slander" (v. 8) will follow—that is, hurtful speech that defames another's character. This, unchecked, will turn into "obscene talk from your mouth" (v. 8)—foul, abusive speech. Do not naively suppose that such things do not exist among professing believers. They do! "The grace of God can live with some people with whom no one else could ever live."

Paul continued, "Do not lie to one another" (v. 9a). Lying is a great sin against God, against the Church, and against love. That is why God struck down Ananias and Sapphira in the first church. He wanted truth, not deception, not hypocrisy. "Therefore, having put away falsehood, let each one of you speak the truth with his neighbor, for we are members one of another" (Ephesians 4:25). A great church demands great honesty.

Laying Aside the Old Life: The Rationale (vv. 9b–11)

Paul's reason for living a godly life was this: ". . . seeing that you have put off the old self with its practices and have put on the new self, which is being renewed in knowledge after the image of its creator" (vv. 9b, 10). We must put off the evil practices of our former life because when we came to Christ, being baptized into his Body (1 Corinthians 12:13) and born again (John 3:5–7), we spiritually "put off the old self" (v. 9) and "put on the new self" (v. 10). "Therefore, if anyone is in Christ, he is a new creation. The old has passed away; behold, the new has come" (2 Corinthians 5:17). All authentic believers have a new self, with new spiritual sensitivities and abilities, and thus wonderfully new possibilities in this life.

This "new self . . . is being renewed in knowledge after the image of its creator" (v. 10). There is constant renewal taking place in the believer's life as he keeps increasing in true knowledge of what God is like. This knowledge leads to progressively being conformed to the image of the Creator, and thus building a life like his. What a thought! Paul says similarly in 2 Corinthians 4:16, "So we do not lose heart. Though our outer self is wasting away, our inner self is being renewed day by day." And again, in 2 Corinthians 3:18, "And we all, with unveiled face, beholding the glory of the Lord, are being transformed into the same image from one degree of glory to another. For this comes from the Lord who is the Spirit." The more we put off the old nature, the greater freedom we have for the renewal of our new self according to the image of God.

The final reason for putting off the evils of the old self is that the new self brings a renewal that is so radical, it changes all human relationships. Paul says in verse 11: "Here there is not Greek and Jew, circumcised and uncircumcised, barbarian, Scythian, slave, free; but Christ is all, and in all." If we make a practice of putting to death our sensuality and covetousness, laying aside evil attitudes and malignant speech, we will fully experience this astounding removal of barriers in human relationships. The "new self" (v. 10), lived out, brings the destruction of *racial* barriers ("Greek and Jew"), *religious* barriers ("circumcised and uncircumcised"), *cultural* barriers ("barbarian, Scythian"), and *social* barriers ("slave, free"). This will bring a resounding affirmation of Tertullian's exclamation: "See how these Christians love one another!"[7] An amazed world will acknowledge that Christians have the "real thing": "By this all people will know that you are my disciples, if you have love for one another" (John 13:35).

As in Paul's letters to the Romans and the Ephesians, the high theology of Colossians 1, 2 demands immense application. We must put off:

- *Sensuality*—"sexual immorality, impurity, passion, evil desire, and covetousness" (Colossians 3:5)
- *Evil attitudes*—"anger, wrath, malice" (v. 8)
- *Evil speech*—"slander, and obscene talk" (v. 8)
- *Deception*—"Do not lie to one another" (v. 9)

Why must we put these things off? Because we have:

- *A new self*—"which is being renewed in knowledge after the image of its creator" (v. 10)
- *New relationships*—"Here there is not Greek and Jew . . . but Christ is all, and in all" (v. 11)

What motivation to put off the old and put on the new!

Put on then, as God's chosen ones, holy and beloved, compassionate hearts, kindness, humility, meekness, and patience, bearing with one another and, if one has a complaint against another, forgiving each other; as the Lord has forgiven you, so you also must forgive. And above all these put on love, which binds everything together in perfect harmony.

3:12–14

36

The Putting Off, Putting On, II

COLOSSIANS 3:12–14

THE APOSTLE BEGAN a new section with a welcome and a soothing description of believers: "God's chosen ones, holy and beloved" (v. 12). What is remarkable is that each of these three titles was an honored Old Testament appellation for Israel, "God's chosen ones." "It was not because you were more in number than any other people that the LORD set his love on you and chose you, for you were the fewest of all peoples, but it is because the LORD *loves* you" (Deuteronomy 7:7, 8a). The Colossians were now chosen by God and thus were secure. "Who shall bring any charge against God's elect? It is God who justifies" (Romans 8:33). Israel also had been designated "holy"— that is, set apart for God himself. These Colossians were now given that august title. And, most beautifully, Israel was called "beloved." These Colossian believers now wore this title with all its privileges and rights.

What a rich array of titles! These opulent appellations were meant to soothe the Colossian believers' Gentile Christian hearts and prepare them for the great putting on that was immediately commanded. In these verses the Colossians were commanded to put on virtues that stood in brilliant contrast to the vices that the Colossians were previously commanded to put off. Here we have the wardrobe of the saints, and what beautiful garments they are!

Putting on Saints' Clothing (v. 12)

"Put on then, as God's chosen ones, holy and beloved, compassionate hearts, kindness, humility, meekness, and patience." The first article of clothing is "compassionate hearts." The old King James Version renders this more literally, "bowels of mercies" because the word literally refers to the stomach or entrails, where so much of our emotion is felt. Peter O'Brien says that this term forcefully expressed personality at the deepest level, especially in the matter of living.[1] A good translation might be "tenderness of heart" or "tender mercies."

The ancient world, apart from Biblical revelation, was merciless. The maimed and sickly and aged were discarded; the mentally ill were subjected to inhumanities. But Christianity brought compassion, and it still does. "It is not too much," says William Barclay, "to say that everything that has been done for the aged, the sick, the weak in body and in mind, the animal, the child, the woman has been done under the inspiration of Christianity."[2] The gospel brings with it sympathy and tenderness of heart. That is one of its great glories!

Paul is telling us here that if we are new creatures in Christ, we must be compassionate people. John Perkins, in his book *Let Justice Roll Down*, tells about a time of dark, extended discouragement in his life when he was ill and seriously thinking of giving up the struggle. Then he met a Dr. Roberts. In Perkins's words: "Dr. Roberts was one of the few white persons I had contact with at that time, and she—well, she met me on the level of my humanity and not just on the theological level preferred by so many church folks."[3] Dr. Roberts saw him through his great crisis with her merciful compassion. This is something of what we are called to—every one of us! All of us must be tenderly merciful. This is the first garment.

The second item of clothing is simply "kindness" (v. 12). Kindness does not happen naturally in human relationships. George Bernard Shaw once wrote a letter to Churchill: "Enclosed are two tickets to the opening night of my first play . . . bring a friend (if you have one)." Churchill replied, "Dear Mr. Shaw, unfortunately I'll be unable to attend the opening night of your play due to a prior engagement. Please send me tickets for a second night (if you have one)." We should probably understand that there is considerable playfulness by these words. But the human personality naturally descends to harshness in word and deed.

The great Archbishop Trench, the prime mover behind the *Oxford English Dictionary*, says that the Greek word here translated "kindness" is a lovely word for a lovely quality. It was used to describe wine that has grown mellow with age and has lost its harshness.[4] It was used by Jesus to describe his yoke: "my yoke is easy" (Matthew 11:30). It is listed in Galatians 5:22 as a fruit of the Spirit, and thus is a result of the fullness of God in human life. It is a quality of God himself, for Romans 2:4 tells us that God's "kindness" leads us to repentance. Kindness is an altogether lovely article of clothing.

The third garment we are to don is that of "humility," a word the Greeks never applied to themselves (v. 12). William Gladstone, the learned prime minister of England, once remarked to his scholarly peer John Morley: "It is a pathetic reflection that while humility is the sovereign grace of Christianity, the Greeks had no symbol in their language to denote it. Every word akin to it has in it some element of meanness, feebleness, or contempt."[5] But the gospel took this word of contempt and made it one of its chief graces. It was used to describe Christ's humbling himself by becoming obedient to death (Philippians 2:8). Christians are called to serve God (Acts 20:19) and one another (Ephesians 4:2) with all humility and lowliness. Jesus himself invited his followers to learn from him, as he was lowly in heart (Matthew 11:29).

Jesus was *not* suggesting a cringing, groveling servility; nor was he teaching his followers to think poorly of themselves. Rather, he was teaching the necessity of the absence of self-exaltation. He wanted us to have nothing of the arrogant pride that Churchill evidently saw in his antagonist Sir Stafford Cripps when he remarked as Cripps walked by: "There, but for the grace of God, goes God." The person who wears the garment of humility knows who God is, what man is, and who he or she is. Those who walk with awareness through a wheat field will notice that it is the drooping ears that are heavy with grain. Humility is a proper garment for every believer.

The fourth item with which we are to clothe ourselves is "meekness" (v. 12).[6] Some time ago humorist J. Upton Dickson said he was writing a book titled *Cower Power* and that he had also founded a group for submissive people called DOORMATS, which stands for: "Dependent Organization Of Really Meek And Timid Souls—if there are no objections." Their motto is, "The meek shall inherit the earth—if that's okay with everybody." Their symbol is the yellow traffic light.[7] Mr. Dickson has a clever sense of humor, but the misconception he exploits is no laughing matter, for most people think that meekness/gentleness is weakness. Nothing could be farther from the truth.

There is gentleness and self-effacement in this word, but behind the gentleness is a steel-like strength, for the supreme characteristic of the meek man or woman is that he or she is under perfect control. Gentleness/meekness is strength under control. Numbers 12:3 tells us that Moses was the most "meek" (KJV) man on earth, but at the same time Moses was a man who could act decisively, be as hard as nails, and rise in anger at the proper time.[8] Those wearing the true garment of gentleness/meekness are immensely powerful people, for they are controlled by God.

The final garment from the celestial closet is "patience," long-suffering in the face of insult or injury (v. 12). This is one of the fruits of the Spirit (Galatians 5:22), and it means more than just enduring difficulties or passive resignation to the circumstances. It is based on a lively, outgoing faith in God and is to be exercised toward "all," as Paul instructs us in 1 Thessalonians 5:14. It is an excellent garment, to be sure.

So we have Heaven's wardrobe from the hand of the Ultimate Tailor. It is revealing to note, as many have before, that all of these garments were perfectly worn by Christ. Therefore, when we put on these five graces, we are putting on a family resemblance to Christ.

> I want the adorning divine
> Thou only, my God, can bestow,
> I want in those beautiful garments to shine
> Which distinguish Thy household below.[9]

One other fact about this wardrobe: all these garments can be worn only in community with others, in relationships. How tempting to think that these garments would be so much easier to wear if we did not have to wear them among people. How much easier to *think* about compassion than to *do* it. How much easier to be kind when we are away from mean people. It would be far easier to put on "humility" and "meekness" if we were not being jostled by the proud and assertive. How much easier "patience" is in isolation. But that is not the way it works! Christians become better Christians in community, in their families, among their associates, in their dorms, in their churches, where there is sweat and breath. The truth is: the very things we may think are keeping us from putting on these garments are the things that make possible their wearing. "Put on" is a present imperative: "Put them on and keep putting them on."

Wearing Saints' Clothing (v. 13)

What will happen when we don this marvelous attire? ". . . bearing with one another, and forgiving each other, whoever has a complaint against anyone; just as the Lord forgave you, so also should you" (NASB). Wearing saintly attire promotes the capacity to bear with one another. That is no small accomplishment! In the days before smoking sections on planes, a passenger started to light a cigar when the stewardess informed him that cigar smoking was not allowed unless it was all right with the other person in the immediate area. "Do you object to his smoking?" she asked the woman seated next to the man. "I absolutely detest cigars," was the stony reply. The stewardess then spoke to a young man near the front of the cabin and came back to report that he would not mind sitting next to a cigar smoker. As the cigar-smoking man walked forward to his new seat, his former seatmate, the boisterous woman, turned to the stewardess and confided, "I've been married to that man for thirty years, and I still can't stand his awful cigars." This is a humorous example of how closely related people—family—often relate (or fail to relate) to each other. Further, it is a parable of what all too frequently happens in God's family.

> To live above with the saints we love,
> Oh, that will be glory.
> But to live below with the saints we know,
> Well, that's another story.

The church is the place where people must bear with one another in love. Paul tells us in Ephesians 2:10 that we are Christ's "workmanship," or more literally, "his masterwork." We are in process, and ultimately we will be masterpieces, though it may be difficult to perceive it now. We are not yet what we are going to be; and we need to bear with one another as the process goes on.

Inevitably this mutual forbearing must extend to mutual forgiving: "forgiving each other; as the Lord has forgiven you, so you also must forgive" (v. 13). Forgiveness has never been in vogue. Primitive Lamech strutted before his wives and gave this chest-thumping speech: "[Y]ou wives of Lamech, listen to what I say: I have killed a man for wounding me, a young man for striking me. If Cain's revenge is sevenfold, then Lamech's is seventy-sevenfold" (Genesis 4:23, 24). "If God avenges himself only seven times, I will do it seventy-seven times!" Similarly, the colonial General Oglethorpe is reported to have raged at John Wesley, "I never forgive." Though many people retain the poison of hatred in their lives, forgiveness is commanded and is possible through Christ.

John Perkins tells how he was beaten in a Mississippi jail, being repeatedly kicked and stomped on as he lay in a fetal position for protection. The beating went on and on as he writhed in a pool of his own blood while inebriated officers took turns, using their feet and blackjacks. At one point an officer took an unloaded pistol, put it to Perkins's head, and pulled the trigger. Then another bigger man beat him until he was unconscious. As the night wore on, it got worse. During a conscious period, one officer pushed a fork down his throat.[10] It was barbarous torture, a great, substantive reason to hate. But this is what happened, as John Perkins tells it:

The Spirit of God worked on me as I lay in that bed. An image formed in my mind. The image of the cross—Christ on the cross. It blotted out everything else in my mind. This Jesus knew what I had suffered. He understood. And He cared. Because He had experienced it all Himself. This Jesus, this One who had brought good news directly from God in heaven, had lived what He preached. Yet He was arrested and falsely accused. Like me, He went through an unjust trial. He also faced a lynch mob and got beaten. But even more than that, He was nailed to rough wooden planks and killed. Killed like a common criminal. At the crucial moment, it seemed to Jesus that even God Himself had deserted Him. The suffering was so great, He cried out in agony. He was dying. But when He looked at that mob who had lynched Him, He didn't hate them. He loved them. He forgave them. And He prayed God to forgive them. "Father, forgive these people, for they don't know what they are doing." His enemies hated. But Jesus forgave. I couldn't get away from that. . . . It's a profound, mysterious truth—Jesus' concept of love overpowering hate. I may not see its victory in my lifetime. But I know it's true. I know it's true, because it happened to me. On that bed, full of bruises and stitches—God made it true in me. He washed my hatred away and replaced it with a love for the white man in rural Mississippi. I felt strong again. Stronger than ever. What doesn't destroy me makes me stronger. I know it's true. Because it happened to me.[11]

"[A]s the Lord has forgiven you, so you also must forgive" (v. 13). It is not enough to put up with each other, to refuse retaliation—we must truly forgive. And if we struggle with this, we must, as did John Perkins, recall the immense forgiveness of Christ.

The Ultimate Saintly Garment (v. 14)

"And above all these put on love, which binds everything together in perfect harmony." The apostle envisions a man dressing his body with the flowing garments of the day; and then it occurs to the man that as beautiful and fine as his garments are, they can never be worn with comfort or grace until they are held in place by a belt. So he adds the belt: "love." It is possible to have some of the five recommended garments and not have love, but it is impossible to have love and not have all of the five garments. Bruce calls love "the grace that binds all these other graces together."[12] And that it is. The imperative thrust is continuous: keep putting on love over and over and over again.

May we never neglect "love, which binds everything together in perfect harmony" (v. 14).

And let the peace of Christ rule in your hearts, to which indeed you were called in one body. And be thankful. Let the word of Christ dwell in you richly, teaching and admonishing one another in all wisdom, singing psalms and hymns and spiritual songs, with thankfulness in your hearts to God. And whatever you do, in word or deed, do everything in the name of the Lord Jesus, giving thanks to God the Father through him.

3:15–17

37

The Fullness of His Peace, Word, and Name

COLOSSIANS 3:15–17

THIS CHAPTER'S TEXT deals with the pleasurable commands that come to the child of God who has put off the old self and put on the new. Specifically, these commands touch on the fullness of Christ's *peace* (v. 15), the fullness of his *Word* (v. 16), and the fullness of his *name* (v. 17).

R. E. O. White, the British preacher, observed regarding the fullness that these verses command: "The surest sign that you are carrying a full bucket is wet feet." That is true to our experience, is it not? Whenever we attempt to carry a full bucket to clean the floor or wash the car, we *always* get wet feet! And when our lives are full, they *will* overflow.

The Fullness of His Peace (v. 15)

"And let the peace of Christ rule in your hearts, to which indeed you were called in one body. And be thankful." What is this peace like?

I can still remember my first experience of this peace. Though I was not quite a teenager, I knew my sins were separating me from God. I had been under deep conviction for several months, for I had been attending a church where the gospel was clearly preached. I knew that I was on the outside of the mysteries of spiritual life, and I wanted in. Finally one night, in a rustic chapel high in the Sierra-Nevada Mountains, I met Christ. I yet remember the aroma of that room, the cedar and the redwood, the expression of the man who talked with me, and the initial fullness of Christ's peace. It saturated my whole being!

That night after "lights out," I scooted down in my sleeping bag and switched on my flashlight. There I opened the tiny India-paper Bible that my grandmother had given me when I was seven years old and reread the verses that I had underlined in the chapel that night. The peace of God surged over me again and again. I was at peace with God and the world!

"The peace of Christ" (v. 15) is different from any other kind. In the brief hours before he died, Jesus said to his disciples, "Peace I leave with you; my peace I give to you. Not as the world gives do I give to you" (John 14:27). He gives us a special peace that he calls "my peace." He gives us his own *personal* peace. It is not just the peace we experience when there is no conflict. It is a sense of wholeness and well-being, completeness and totality. But it is even more—it is the *presence* of Christ. His peace and his presence are marvelously associated in both the Old and New Testament Scriptures (see, for example, Numbers 6:24–26). It was his presence that was with me in the chapel and in my grubby sleeping bag! It is this experience of peace—the cessation of hostility with God, the sense of well-being, and the sense of his presence—that has marked my life.

What are we to do with this peace? "Let the peace of Christ rule in your hearts." What does that mean? F. F. Bruce, the New Testament scholar to whom we owe so much, says "rule" carried the idea of "arbitrate."[1] In many extra-Biblical sources, the Greek word used here referred to the function of one who took it on himself to decide what is right in a contest. The sense here is, "Let the peace of Christ be umpire in your heart amidst the conflicts of life. Let it decide what is right. Let it be your counselor."

An old story that comes from the Salvation Army in the last century tells of a strong-willed woman who had been nicknamed "Warrior Brown" because of her fiery temper. She was often belligerent and became enraged whenever she got drunk. Then one day she was converted. Her entire life was wonderfully changed by the indwelling presence of the Holy Spirit. At an open-air meeting a week later, she told everyone what Jesus had done for her. Suddenly a scoffer threw a potato at her, causing a stinging bruise. Had she not been converted, she would have lashed out at the man furiously. God's grace, however, had made such a profound change in her conduct that she quietly picked up the potato and put it into her pocket without saying a word. No more was heard of the incident until the time of the "harvest festival" months later. Then the dear lady who had been known as "Warrior Brown" brought as her offering a little sack of potatoes. She explained that after the open-air meeting she had cut up and planted the "insulting potato," and what she was now presenting to the Lord was "the increase." Warrior Brown had allowed "the peace of Christ" to be umpire of her life.

How much misery we would avoid if we permitted "the peace of Christ" to umpire in our hearts (v. 15). How many words we would hold back if he were the arbitrator in our lives. How many sleepless nights we would forgo if we did that. How the Church needs this too, since we "were called [to peace] in one body" (v. 15).

Paul concludes his exhortation in verse 15 by saying, "And be thankful," a command repeated at the end of verses 16 and 17. When the buckets we carry are full of Christ, our lives are bathed with the peace of God in thanksgiving.

The Fullness of His Word (v. 16)

> Let the word of Christ dwell in you richly, teaching and admonishing one another in all wisdom, singing psalms and hymns and spiritual songs, with thankfulness in your hearts to God. (v. 16)

How can we allow the Word of God to dwell richly among us? We must begin by reading it. The Bible is not all that hard to understand, though there are admittedly some very difficult passages. Mark Twain put it in perspective when he said, "Most people are bothered by those passages of Scripture which they cannot understand; but as for me, I have always noticed that the passages in Scripture which trouble me most are those which I do understand." The Bible is understandable, and we need to read it. We need to be both comforted and troubled by it, as is appropriate to each of our lives.

We must also realize that reading does not guarantee that the Word of Christ will "dwell" in us "richly." The parallel quotation in Ephesians 5:18, 19, which lists the *same* results from the filling of the Spirit, teaches us that God's Word must be read and meditated on under the influence of the Holy Spirit if it is to dwell richly in us. Richness comes when, as we are yielded to the Holy Spirit, we meditate upon short passages, memorize others, and then do what they say. It is not just a question of disciplined study. It is a matter of the heart. It is Spirit-filled participation in Christ and his Word. And is it ever rich!

That night when I was deep in my sleeping bag, with flashlight on, turning the pages of my Bible with my grimy fingers, reading verse after verse, the Word of God was dwelling richly within me. There was music in my unmusical soul.

My experience of this richness perfectly accords with how Paul says it manifests itself—". . . teaching and admonishing one another in all wisdom, singing psalms and hymns and spiritual songs, with thankfulness in your hearts to God" (v. 16). This also accounts for Tertullian's second-century description of a Christian love feast at which "after water for the hands and lights have been brought in, each is invited to sing to God in the presence of the others from his own heart."[2] It is the telltale sign of the richly indwelling Word.

Imagine the early church. One got up and sang perhaps from a psalm, and another answered antiphonally. Hymns broke forth in hearty chorus. Others sang spontaneously about what God had done. There was music in their hearts. That is what this verse is talking about. You can find this repeated in church history. The record of Christian awakenings during the last 2,000 years shows that whenever the Word of God is recovered, it is received with great joy that is inevitably expressed in song. The medieval Latin hymns cluster around the fresh days of the monastic movements. The Protestant Reformation brought a rebirth of music to the Church. When we think of the Wesleyan Revival, we not only think of John Wesley, but his brother Charles, who has given us so many great hymns. The great harvest of souls here in our own country in the late 1960s and 1970s brought a revival of Scripture singing. When the Word of God dwells richly within you, you want to sing "with thankfulness in your hearts to God" (v. 16).

As a new Christian, I sang those old gospel hymns with all I had. And so it has been whenever my heart is right with God. When the buckets of our lives are full to the brim with God's Word, we cannot move without spilling forth in song. Music is the window of the soul. How is it in our souls?

The Fullness of His Name (v. 17)

> And whatever you do, in word or deed, do everything in the name of the Lord Jesus, giving thanks to God the Father through him. (v. 17)

Few exhortations in Scripture are more comprehensive than this one. "Word or deed" takes in everything in life. "Deeds" can be preaching, teaching, eating, exercising, driving, cleaning house, shopping, visiting, working, playing (basketball, soccer, tennis, fishing, even watching)—everything! Our words are everything that passes our lips, even in unguarded moments. *Everything* we say or do is to be done "in the name of the Lord Jesus."

Our actions must say that Jesus is and does exactly what he claims! Just a few seconds of sin can disgrace the greatest of names. The Hebrew name *Judah* means "praise"; the New Testament equivalent is *Judas*. When our lives are full of Christ, praise to his name in word and deed floods our paths, bringing refreshment to all. What a responsibility is ours!

The fullness of Christ comes from an overflow of his *peace* and his *Word* and his *name*. It is also seen in our thankfulness. Verse 15 ends with, "And be thankful." Verse 16 concludes with, "thankfulness in your hearts to God." Verse 17 says, "giving thanks to God the Father through him."

The most direct of these exhortations to thankfulness is in verse 15, "And be thankful." Literally it says, "become thankful," because we are to keep on striving for a deeper gratitude than we have yet attained. The word for "thankful" is the word *eucharesteo*, from which we get the English word *Eucharist*, another word for the Lord's Supper—a time for giving thanks.

Full pails cannot help but overflow. May each day result in deep thanksgiving.

Wives, submit to your husbands, as is fitting in the Lord. Husbands, love your wives, and do not be harsh with them.

3:18, 19

38

The Christian Family, I

COLOSSIANS 3:18, 19

WE HAVE CONSIDERED the cosmic fullness of Christ, who created and presently sustains the universe by his power. We have also examined the implications of his fullness for every area of life. Now we will look at the *domestic fullness* of Christ. In the earlier studies we saw the cosmic, supra-mundane; here all is domestic and totally mundane. We move from the religion of the universe to the religion of the kitchen and bedroom. Since Christ is the fullness of the universe, he must also be the source of fullness in the home.

Colossians 3:18—4:1 could well be titled, "How to Have a Full, Rich Family Life." The text contains three sets of exhortations: verses 18, 19 to wives and husbands, verses 20, 21 to children and parents, 3:22—4:1 to servants and masters.

Colossians 3:18, 19 is patently domestic. It has to do with home, specifically a Christian home. Moreover, it has to do with the relationship between a *Christian* husband and a *Christian* wife. As such, it has nothing to say about men's and women's roles in society, such as the marketplace or politics. There are other texts that give us some guidance in these areas, but we do Scripture a great disservice by applying it where it was never intended. The teaching here is for Christians who want to live as Christians within the home and experience all the fullness God intended for them. It is teaching that is much needed today when marriage has fallen into disrepute, as with the seven-year-old girl who had just seen the movie *Cinderella* and was testing her neighbor lady's knowledge of the story. The neighbor, anxious to impress the little girl, said, "I know what happens at the end." "What?" asked the girl. "Cinderella and the prince live happily ever after." To which the little girl answered, "Oh no, they didn't. They got married!" It was totally innocent, unwitting cynicism. But others are more calculated, like the famous literary figure William Congreve, who wrote, "Every man plays the fool once in his life, but to marry is playing the fool all of one's life."[1]

Fullness in Marriage (vv. 18, 19)

These Scriptures are *radically elevating*. "Wives, submit to your husbands, as is fitting in the Lord. Husbands, love your wives, and do not be harsh with them." This contrasts with the plight of women in the ancient world. William Barclay writes:

> Under Jewish law a woman was a thing; she was the possession of her husband, just as much as his house or his flocks or his material goods were. She had no legal right whatever. For instance, under Jewish law, a husband could divorce his wife for any cause, while a wife had no rights whatever in the initiation of divorce. In Greek society a respectable woman lived a life of entire seclusion. She never appeared on the streets alone, not even to go marketing. She lived in the women's apartments and did not join her menfolk even for meals. From her there was demanded a complete servitude and chastity; but her husband could go out as much as he chose, and could enter into as many relationships outside marriage as he liked and incur no stigma. Both under Jewish and under Greek laws and custom, all the privileges belonged to the husband, and all the duties to the wife.[2]

The domestic rules given here in Colossians were vastly different from those of the day. Wives here were addressed *equally* with their husbands, something radically new. Also, both husbands and wives had duties—not just the wives.[3] They were both admonished "in the Lord" (v. 18). The context of this phrase begins in verse 17, which makes it clear that the totality of their lives was to be regulated by it. This brought a vast dignity to both men and women.[4] They were both under the lordship of Christ as equals. All of this was immensely elevating to women and would raise their positions greatly in the ancient and modern world.

At the same time, within the marital relationship these words established a definite *hierarchy*. As F. F. Bruce says, Paul "does hold that there is a divine instituted hierarchy in the order of creation, and in this order the place of the wife comes next after her husband."[5] However, this does not suggest (here or anywhere else in Scripture) that the wife is naturally or spiritually inferior to the husband, or vice versa. There is a hierarchy in the Holy Trinity, and yet equality. Orthodoxy teaches that the Son is simultaneously *equal* to the Father and *submissive* to him. Likewise, *equality* and *submissiveness* can coexist in human relationships, including the marriage relationship.

Fullness through the Wife (v. 18)

Christ's word to the woman in the Christian home is: "Wives, submit to your husbands, as is fitting in the Lord" (v. 18). I know of few statements that will rouse the ire of our modern assertive, rights-seeking, power-seeking culture than this. But it is God's Word, and we must resist those who would explain it away. It is God's design for fullness. Are there qualifications? Of course. "Submit" is not a synonym for servile, menial bondage. The appeal is to free, responsible people and can only be heeded voluntarily. Moreover, none are called to follow it into sin or irrationality or harm of any kind. "We must obey God rather than men" (Acts 5:29). This is a charge for *Christians* who are living as *Christians.*

Fullness through the Husband (v. 19)

Verse 19 gives us the counterpart injunction: "Husbands, love your wives, and do not be harsh with them." Here the commandment to men is just as radical as that to women. As Eduard Lohse has shown, such a command does not appear in any of the extra-Biblical household rules of the day.[6] The novelty of such a religious command must have struck the Colossian Christians with great power. Husbands were commanded to love their wives! What a novel thought! The command was not to *erotic* love (as some would expect) or to *friendship* love, but to *agape* love, which involves unceasing care and loving service for the wife's entire well-being. The Christian ethic for a husband's love for his wife was light-years beyond the formal domestic ethics of the day.

A parallel passage (Ephesians 5:25–33) gives the archetype of the love that is called for here, especially verse 25: "Husbands, love your wives, as Christ loved the church and gave himself up for her." Thus, this radical command to love is only fulfilled when a husband loves his wife in imitation of Christ's love.

A husband's love must first, then, be *incarnational.* Genesis 2:24 anticipated this high call when it said, "a man shall leave his father and his mother and hold fast to his wife, and they shall become one flesh." The idea is something of a *mutual* incarnation. With this ancient truth in mind Paul wrote in Ephesians 5:28, 29, "In the same way husbands should love their wives as their own bodies. He who loves his wife loves himself. For no one ever hated his own flesh, but nourishes and cherishes it." This is a high call and may seem impossible. But it is possible to incarnate ourselves into our wives' *emotions* and *mental processes*. It is possible to have *spiritual* incarnation with her. It is possible to love our wives as we love our own bodies.

Dr. Robert Seizer, in his book *Mortal Lessons: Notes in the Art of Surgery*, tells of performing surgery to remove a tumor in which it was necessary to sever a facial nerve, leaving a young woman's mouth permanently twisted in palsy. In Dr. Seizer's own words:

> Her young husband is in the room. He stands on the opposite side of the bed, and together they seem to dwell in the evening lamp light, isolated from me, private. Who are they, I ask myself, he and this wry-mouth I have made, who gaze at and touch each other so generously, greedily? The young woman speaks. "Will my mouth always be like this?" she asks. "Yes," I say, "it will. It is because the nerve was cut." She nods, and is silent. But the young man smiles. "I like it," he says. "It is kind of cute." All at once I know who he is. I understand, and I lower my gaze. One is not bold in an encounter with a god. Unmindful, he bends to kiss her crooked mouth, and I, so close, can see how he twists his own lips to accommodate to hers, to show her that their kiss still works.[7]

It is possible to love your spouse as your own body. Practically, this means that the husband must do all he can to understand her world.

When my wife visited her sister in Connecticut, I was in charge of our four small children for a week. I fixed all the meals, changed thousands of diapers, fixed hurts, settled quarrels, gave baths, cleaned up catastrophes, and cleaned them up again. I was at work *before* I got up and *after* I went to bed. The experience so marked me that I invented a new kitchen, modeled on a car wash. The walls are tiles, and the floors slope to a large drain in the middle of the room. A hose hangs on the wall, nozzle ready to spray things down after the meal!

Loving incarnationally means we must work at spending time together. The June 1986 issue of *Psychology Today* carried an article entitled "Marriages Made to Last" in which they surveyed several hundred happily married couples. The interviews were conducted privately with each spouse alone. The top two things they said kept a marriage going were:

> My spouse is my best friend.

and

> I like my spouse as a person.

The researchers said good marriages develop among those who purposely spend a lot of time together.

Along with this, loving incarnationally means *listening*. As Howard Hendricks says, "Marriage is sometimes the dialogue of the deaf." *The Harvard Business Review* says 65 percent of an executive's time should be spent listening. So much more so in our most intimate relationships. "If one gives an answer before he hears, it is his folly and shame" (Proverbs 18:13). Incarnational love spends time, listens, gives itself. Such is Christ's love.

Christ's archetypal love was not only *incarnational*—it was *sacrificial*, for he died for us. If we are to have a love like Christ's, we will be willing to die for our wives. This also calls us to a daily dying, and that is far more difficult. The rubber meets the road when we have to make a decision between free tickets to the baseball game and fixing the leaky faucets we promised to fix.

The positive side of dying is that we learn to live not only for Christ, but for our wives. When Anne Morrow married Charles Lindbergh, she was a timid, young woman, and he, having been the first to cross the Atlantic solo by air, was one of the most famous men in all the world. He *was* the American Eagle—a bona fide national hero. She could easily have been swept aside in all the adulation that came his way. But, loved by him, she grew to become one of our country's most popular writers. Here is how she puts it:

> To be deeply in love is, of course, a great liberating force and the most common experience that frees. . . . Ideally, both members of a couple in love free each other to new and different worlds. I was no exception to the general rule. The sheer fact of finding myself loved was unbelievable and changed my world, my feelings about life and myself. I was given confidence, strength, and almost a new character. The man I was to marry believed in me and what I could do, and consequently I found I could do more than I realized.[8]

The Eagle's soaring love caused shy, delicate Anne Morrow Lindbergh to fly too. This is what sacrificial love can do. Sacrificial love mutually elevates both partners in the marital relationship.

Loving our wives as Christ loved the Church also involves *intercessory prayer*. Christ so perfectly participates in our lives that he perfectly prays for us. We husbands should strive to pray with the deepest "incarnational" knowledge possible. But we will be weak intercessors if we have failed to love our wives with incarnational sympathy. Peter says, "Likewise, husbands, live with your wives in an understanding way, showing honor to the woman as the weaker vessel, since they are heirs with you of the grace of life, so that your prayers may not be hindered" (1 Peter 3:7). A foundering prayer life may be due to a failing in our most fundamental personal relationship. We must pray for our spouses in intimate detail, not just with a blanket beatitude. We must praise God for her strengths and lay her needs before him. She needs detailed prayer for what she faces each day, for how she relates with the children, for her interaction with the neighbors, for her many duties, for her insecurities, for her challenges.

We have seen two radical calls. One call is to wives: *submission*. The other is to husbands: to *love* as Christ loves. These cannot be read in isolation; they go together. It is unthinkably absurd for a Christian husband to demand submission of his wife if he is not radically loving her; likewise, it is errant logic for a wife who is not submissive to demand such love.

These brief words give us the pattern for fullness in Christian marriage—full love, full commitment, full exchange, full blessing. Whether we are beginning or far along, let us have no other goal than having the best marriages possible!

Children, obey your parents in everything, for this pleases the Lord. Fathers, do not provoke your children, lest they become discouraged.

3:20, 21

39

The Christian Family, II

COLOSSIANS 3:20, 21

He began his life with all the classic handicaps and disadvantages. His mother was a powerfully built, dominating woman who found it difficult to love anyone. She had been married three times, and her second husband divorced her because she beat him up regularly. The father of the child I'm describing [the writer is Dr. James Dobson] was her third husband; he died of a heart attack a few months before the child's birth. As a consequence the mother had to work long hours from his earliest childhood.

She gave him no affection, no love, no discipline, and no training during those early years. She even forbade him to call her at work. Other children had little to do with him, so he was alone most of the time. He was absolutely rejected from his earliest childhood. When he was thirteen years old a school psychologist commented that he probably didn't even know the meaning of the word *love*. During adolescence, the girls would have nothing to do with him and he fought with the boys.

Despite a high IQ, he failed academically, and finally dropped out during his third year of high school. He thought he might find acceptance in the Marine Corps; they reportedly built men, and he wanted to be one. But his problems went with him. The other Marines laughed at him and ridiculed him. He fought back, resisted authority, and was court-martialed and thrown out of the Marines with an undesirable discharge. So there he was—a young man in his early twenties, absolutely friendless. He was small and scrawny in stature. He had an adolescent squeak in his voice. He was balding. He had no talent, no skill, no sense of worthiness.

Once again he thought he could run from his problems, so he went to live in a foreign country. But he was rejected there also. While there he married a girl who had been an illegitimate child and brought her back to America with him. Soon she began to develop the same contempt for him that everyone else displayed. She bore him two children, but he never enjoyed the status and respect a father should have. His marriage continued to crumble. His wife demanded more and more things that he could not provide. Instead of being his ally against the bitter world, as he hoped, she

331

became his most vicious opponent. She could outfight him, and she learned to bully him. On one occasion she locked him in the bathroom as punishment. Finally she forced him to leave.

He tried to make it on his own, but he was terribly lonely. After days of solitude, he went home and literally begged her to take him back. He surrendered all pride. Despite his meager salary, he brought her $78.00 as a gift, asking her to take it and spend it any way she wished. But she belittled his feeble attempts to supply the family's needs. She ridiculed his failure. At one point he fell on his knees and wept bitterly as the darkness of his private nightmare enveloped him.

Finally, in silence he pleaded no more. No one wanted him. No one had ever wanted him.

The next day he was a strangely different man. He arose, went to the garage, and took down a rifle he had hidden there. He carried it with him to his newly acquired job at a book storage building. And from a window on the third floor of that building, shortly after noon, November 22, 1963, he sent two shells crashing into the head of President John Fitzgerald Kennedy.

Lee Harvey Oswald, the rejected, unlovable failure, killed the man who, more than any other man on earth, embodied all the success, beauty, wealth, and family affection which he lacked. In firing that rifle, he utilized the one skill he had learned in his entire, miserable lifetime.[1]

Lee Harvey Oswald's story stands out from that of others because of the incredibly documented public infamy of the final days of his life. His miserable life experience is paralleled today by thousands upon thousands who have known the same or even greater lack of affection, discipline, and training because much of the American family experience is a relational desert.

This chapter's short text contains the bare outline of what brings fullness to parent/child relationships. Again, as we observed with wives, this teaching beautifully elevated the position of children in the culture of that day. Under a section of Roman law entitled *Patria Potestes*, "The Power of the Father," the father could do anything he wanted with his children. He could sell them, turn them into slaves, even take their lives. But here, as with husbands and wives, both children and parents were presented as under God. The dominating example was the loving fatherhood of God.

The instructions were given to children first: "Children, obey your parents in everything, for this pleases the Lord" (v. 20), and second to parents: "Fathers, do not provoke your children, lest they become discouraged" (v. 21).

Instructions to Children (v. 20)

The first thing we should realize here is that discipline is indispensable if we are to have Christ's fullness in the home. Unfortunately, this is not true of

American households in general. In the recently published letters between Karl Barth, the famous German theologian, and his friend Carl Zuckmayer, the celebrated German writer, Zuckmayer wrote:

> If one has lived in America and seen in countless cases what injustice is done to children, one has enough of it. One sees too much that someone, hidden behind misunderstood psychoanalytical maxims, allows them to become little tyrants and ill-humored despots, despots whom adults crawl in front of for pure convenience, only to get peace; and one sees how this takes effect in the unfortunate adolescents when they, brought up without authority are confronted with the difficulties of life.[2]

These foreign observers see the situation as an injustice, not so much to adults, but to children!

In this, their views are in perfect accord with the Bible, especially the writer of Hebrews: "For what son is there whom his father does not discipline? If you are left without discipline, in which all have participated, then you are illegitimate children and not sons" (12:7, 8). An evidence of being a child of God is God's discipline. So it is with human fathers. The absence of discipline means fatherhood is not being practiced, and weak, inconsistent discipline shows a lack of love. Discipline is therefore a key to child-parent fullness!

It is interesting to note that many psychologists are finding more evidence that discipline is, indeed, the great ingredient for domestic fullness. Dr. Stanley Coopersmith, associate professor of psychology at the University of California, surveyed 1,738 normal middle-class boys and their families, beginning in the preadolescent period and following them through to young manhood. After determining the boys with the best self-esteem, he then compared their homes and childhood influences with those of the boys having a lower sense of self-esteem. He found three important characteristics that distinguished them:

1. The high-esteem children were clearly more loved and appreciated at home than were the low-esteem boys. The parental love was deep and genuine, not just an empty display of words. The boys knew they were the object of pride and interest, increasing their own sense of self-worth.

2. The high-esteem group came from homes where parents had been significantly more strict in their approach to discipline. By contrast, the parents of the low-esteem group had created insecurity and dependence by their permissiveness. Furthermore, the most successful and independent young men during the latter period of the study were found to have come from homes that demanded the strictest accountability and responsibility. And

as could have been predicted, the family ties remained the strongest—not in the wishy-washy homes—but in the homes where discipline and self-control had been a way of life.

3. The homes of the high-esteem group were also characterized by democracy and openness. Once the boundaries for behavior were established, there was freedom for individual personalities to grow and develop. The boys could express themselves without fear of ridicule, and the overall atmosphere was marked by acceptance and emotional safety.[3]

Discipline and obedience are indispensable if we are to experience the fullness that God wants for us in our homes.

The command "obey" is significant for two reasons. First, it is a different word than that used in verse 18, where wives are told to "submit" to their husbands. The word there suggests a voluntary submission, a choice; here the command is more absolute. The other reason this word is significant is that it really consists of two words ("listen" and "under") and can be read literally, "listen under your parents," or "really listen to your parents and do it!" Common phrases in America today are: "Are you listening to me?" "Did you hear what I said?" "Do you ever listen?" "Now, listen to me!" Obedience begins with listening.

Implicit in this also is not just hearing and doing, but doing it with the right attitude. Children are all too often like the proverbial little boy who was told by his teacher to sit in the corner. As he sat there he was thinking, "I'm sitting down on the outside, but I'm standing up on the inside." The Scriptures call for a heart obedience to parents.

You will note too that it says, "in everything" (v. 20). Are there any exceptions? Of course. "We must obey God rather than men" (Acts 5:29). We are never to go against our conscience or Scripture to obey anyone. Nor must we sin or do anything irrational or harmful to us or anyone else in carrying out parental obedience. The command is not a carte blanche for a cruel parent! But these cases aside, the Scripture before us says that obedience "pleases the Lord" (v. 20). The parallel passage in Ephesians 6:1–3 similarly says, "this is right," and then goes on to say, "'Honor your father and mother' (this is the first commandment with a promise), 'that it may go well with you and that you may live long in the land.'" The terrible relationships of Lee Harvey Oswald's early life so marked his psyche that he was bound for trouble—and in fact a shortened life. I believe there are millions who suffer less dramatic workings of this syndrome.

The point is, we have here a simple and powerful command to *all* children to truly, from the heart, obey their parents. Neglect of this command brings great sorrow, if not now, then surely later in life. But if obeyed, it brings fullness.

Instructions to Parents (v. 21)

The other half of the commandment is: "Fathers, do not provoke your children, lest they become discouraged."

During much of my college years, I worked for a store that had a large part of the trade of the rodeo cowboys in southern California. I learned there are at least two ways to break a horse. One is with the progressive use of a halter, bit, blanket, and saddle. Done correctly, this can produce a full-spirited, obedient horse. Another way is sometimes used with especially difficult horses. The method is simple. The wrangler simply takes a 2 x 4 and knocks the recalcitrant horse to its knees. A horse, it is said, can be tamed this way, but with great cost. You will have a spiritless animal, an animal that though "obedient" will never be what it could have been. There are children who are like this. Their spirits have been broken, they are "obedient," but something is missing. They have, to use Paul's words in verse 21, "[lost] heart" (NASB). They withdraw and keep it all inside. Or they rebel when they get big enough. The results are painful either way.

Paul's advice to parents who want to avoid this trap is: "Fathers, do not provoke your children" (v. 21). Notice that the advice is primarily to "fathers," the reason being that this would be more typically a father's sin.[4] The husband is naturally away from the children more than the mother and is thus less in touch with their feelings and more prone to false judgments and unwise direction. The specific sense of the Greek word is to irritate one's children either by nagging or deriding them—putting them down.[5] The parallel in Ephesians 6:4 says, "Fathers, do not provoke your children to anger" and has the same idea of irritating them through perpetual faultfinding.

Millions of children, even in Christian homes, experience a constant rain of criticism. John Newton, the great preacher and hymn writer, who experienced such a wretched life before turning to Christ, said, "I know that my father loved me—but he did not seem to wish me to see it."[6] Parents, fathers, discipline is to be given, but so is encouragement. Obedience is to be nurtured by love and praise. We must never cause our children to lose heart.

Another kind of father who exasperates a child is the one given to irritability or grouchiness. Most people maintain a placid veneer at work because they *have* to do so. But at home . . . Only the Lord knows how many children lose heart because their fathers have hard days. This reminds me of a cartoon in which the boss is grouchy to his employee, who in turn comes home and is irritable with the children. His son, in turn, kicks the dog. The dog runs down the street and bites the first person he sees—the boss! We parents must never let our pressures drive us into this unhappy cycle. The costs are too high!

Others exasperate their children with their harsh and overstrict rules. Contemporary culture is especially filled with deadly traps. The tragic deaths of the Celtics' Larry Bias and Cleveland's defensive back Don Rogers seem to point out the extremes. Because of this, the zealous Christian parent can be tempted to say no to virtually everything his child asks. Rather, the parent should be looking for opportunities to say yes to as many things as he or she can conscionably say yes to. Our reasons for saying no must be valid, such as safety, morality, or health. Overstrictness (not strictness!) sometimes clothes a lazy approach to raising children.

Another way this can happen is through a father's capricious inconsistency. The poor horse who has a rider who is constantly digging his heels into its side and pulling the reins at the same time learns that nothing is ever right. So it is with the child who receives conflicting messages. As parents we must work at consistency. Of course, this does not mean we never change our minds, but wise parents will prompt each other *privately*, inviting all the criticism and help possible in being consistent parents.

Finally, perhaps one of the most exasperating things parents can do is keep their children at a distance. An oft-quoted survey says that fathers spend an average of thirty-seven seconds a day with their children. Few things could be more disheartening and resentment building than to hear your life directed, as it were, from a shadowy figure from Mount Olympus who leaves before you go to school, returns after dinner, and hands down edicts of conduct after church at Sunday dinner. Perhaps the character is a bit overdrawn, but there is no substitute for spending time with your children—and when you are with them, really be with them.

Parents, especially fathers, if we want to have all the fullness in our primary family relationships that God would have for us, we must discipline our children. To refrain from discipline is an act of hatred toward our own— unloving indifference—cruel permissiveness. But at the same time, our discipline must be given with encouragement. We must be patient, not irritable. While strict, we must not be overstrict. We must look for ways to say yes as well as no. We must be consistent and stable in our direction. We must spend time with our own, listening and loving.

Bondservants, obey in everything those who are your earthly masters, not by way of eye-service, as people-pleasers, but with sincerity of heart, fearing the Lord. Whatever you do, work heartily, as for the Lord and not for men, knowing that from the Lord you will receive the inheritance as your reward. You are serving the Lord Christ. For the wrongdoer will be paid back for the wrong he has done, and there is no partiality. Masters, treat your bondservants justly and fairly, knowing that you also have a Master in heaven.

3:22—4:1

40

The Christian Family, III

COLOSSIANS 3:22—4:1

AS WE HAVE EXPLORED the theme of domestic fullness, we have seen how Christ brings this fullness to the relationship of husband and wife (vv. 18, 19) and to fathers and children (vv. 20, 21). Now we see how Christ extends his fullness to masters and slaves.

Paul's teaching here was accompanied by a great amount of tension, for several reasons. Primary was the amazingly vast extent of slavery and its dehumanizing nature. Ancient historians estimate that there were some 60,000,000 slaves in the Roman Empire, or about half the population. Because of this, work was considered below the dignity of the slave-owning Roman free man. Practically everything was done by slaves, even doctoring and teaching. Though there were some felicitous relationships between masters and slaves,[1] basically the lot of a slave was not very happy. Ancient tradition, dating back to Aristotle, classified slaves as things, living tools. The Roman Varro classified farm implements into three classes: the articulate, the inarticulate, and the mute—the articulate being slaves. A later Roman writer recommended a grim utilitarianism in buying a farm: toss out the old slaves to die, because they were broken tools. Some did just that.

Gaius, the Roman lawyer, said, "We may note that it is universally accepted that the master possesses the power of life and death over a slave." If a slave ran away, he was branded on the forehead with the letter *F* for *Fugitivus* and sometimes even put to death, with no trial.[2] The situation of slaves in general was not good, and for some it was terrible. Thus a melancholy blanketed the lives of millions in the ancient world. Christianity's preaching of the gospel with its explicit doctrine of equality raised the tension. Consider, for example, Paul's teaching in Galatians 3:28—"There is neither Jew nor Greek, there is neither slave nor free, there is no male and female, for you are all one in Christ Jesus."

We can be sure that Paul's teaching in Colossians 3:22—4:1 was attended eagerly by both slaves and masters in Colossae. That, no doubt, is why it was far more extensive than the previous domestic instruction to husbands/wives and children/fathers.

The advice Paul gives here was ultimately revolutionary, because in time it brought the downfall of slavery as an institution. But it was also immediately revolutionary in that it brought fullness to the Christian's life, whether slave or master. In the ancient world this was a *domestic* fullness, because slavery was an intensely personal family matter. Today the application is largely *professional* as we are either masters or serve our masters.

Today the average worker still divides five or six days of his week into more or less equal periods of eight hours work, eight hours sleep, and eight hours "free time." Work is so important that our society normally defines people by *what* they do. In order for Christ to bring fullness to life, he must bring it to what we do for a living, whether slave or master, employer or employee.

A Full Life for Servants/Employees (vv. 22–25)

Bondservants, obey in everything those who are your earthly masters, not by way of eye-service, as people-pleasers, but with sincerity of heart, fearing the Lord. Whatever you do, work heartily, as for the Lord and not for men. (vv. 22, 23)

Hearing these words without explanation, one could easily say, "Paul, whose side are you on?" Think of how these words must have sounded to the exploited servant! "Bondservants, obey in everything those who are your earthly masters" (v. 22). Of course, the apostle was not encouraging submission to immoral or hurtful commands, and yet "everything" is so encompassing. Slaves were very often asked to do unpleasant things. This was a tough command, especially when linked with the next phrase: "not by way of eye-service, as people-pleasers" (v. 22). The phrase "eye-service" refers to work that is only done when the boss is looking. We all know what that is like. In gym class, when the coach is watching there are perfect push-ups. But when he looks away . . . Eye-service results in half-done jobs. The room is swept, but the dirt is brushed under the carpet. Work breaks extend until the boss returns.

This is not the way it is supposed to be. Rather, our service is to be "with sincerity of heart" (v. 22). This high call makes no distinction between pleasant or unpleasant tasks, dull or challenging, menial or interesting. It simply states that everything must be done energetically, from the heart, whether the boss is present or not. I have known some who have gotten themselves in trouble with fellow workers because, in respect to this principle, they worked hard and were honest about their hours. Some hardworking Christians have even lost their jobs due to the lies said about them by their peers. Yet we must obey the Lord.

If this high call stood alone, it would be supremely impossible. But it is accompanied by an enabling rationale: it is for the Lord. "Whatever you do, work heartily, as *for the Lord* and not for men, knowing that *from the Lord* you will receive the inheritance as your reward. *You are serving the Lord Christ*" (vv. 23, 24). It is this reality that inspired the great work of Mother Teresa in Calcutta. Taking Matthew 25 seriously, she believed that when she and her Sisters of Charity were cleansing sores and touching the ill for Christ, they were doing it to Christ. The most menial tasks—washing floors, scrubbing pots and pans—were *for* the Lord. Mother Teresa believed and did the truth! However, Mother Theresa's example must not promote an over-romanticizing of this truth. Most of us in our daily work are not dressing the sores of lepers or tending the dying. Some of us work "nothing" jobs. Some shuffle meaning-less mounds of paper. Some dig holes and fill them up. Some can see nothing noble in the tasks they perform. They are nevertheless serving God as they work. This truth transformed the lot of the Christian slave in the ancient world. His "nothing" tasks were actually noble when done for Christ. Because of this, Christian slaves invariably brought higher prices in the slave market.[3]

At the end of verse 22, the apostle adds that our work is to be done "fearing the Lord." The pagan slave served his master because he was bound by fear; the Christian slave served his master *better* because he feared God. Working hard at our tasks from the heart brings glory to God.

In verses 24, 25 the writer further enlarged the rationale for the believers' work ethic by adding that the God we serve will reward us: ". . . knowing that from the Lord you will receive the inheritance as your reward. You are serving the Lord Christ. For the wrongdoer will be paid back for the wrong he has done, and there is no partiality." The "reward" will be good or bad, depend-ing upon performance. All believers, though under the ultimate forgiveness of Christ, will have their works judged. "For we must all appear before the judgment seat of Christ, so that each one may receive what is due for what he has done in the body, whether good or evil" (2 Corinthians 5:10). This can, of course, be good or bad news, depending upon how we live our Christian lives. But to the first-century Christian slave this was largely good news, because under Roman law a slave could inherit nothing.[4] Yet here he learned that he could receive an "inheritance as [his] reward" (v. 24). God rewards faithful workers. This ought to be an encouragement to us, whatever our lot in life. God pays us so well that when we get to Heaven we will wish we had served him even more.

In verses 22–25 we have Paul's teaching regarding the work of slaves (employees) in the Colossian church. How does this impact our work ethic?

First, we must not suppose that if we try to live up to the Biblical teaching regarding work, all will go well on the job. I learned this early in life (on my very first job). I was fourteen years old and got an after-school job working at a nursery watering plants, stocking, and waiting on customers. I was anxious to do my very best, and I did. I was always on time, I never stood around, I looked for extra things to do. But I just could not please my boss, though he was a good man. Finally there came a payday when he took me aside and said, "You are terminated." That can, of course, happen at any age, and even when you are doing your very best as unto the Lord.

Second, the apostle's teaching here is not a call to overwork or workaholism. Correct as the Biblical ethic is, capitalism was and is easily perverted to the worship of work in the nineteenth, twentieth, and twenty-first centuries, providing theological guise for addiction to wealth, power, and the exploitation of workers. This has happened in self-consciously Christian societies such as England where children were abused and exploited to an unbelievable degree. Today the exploitation is more subtle, but just as deadly. The ironic evils of *self*-exploitation in obsessive work habits touch virtually every family.

A third aspect of our work ethic is that Christians ought to be the *best* workers. I once had an employer tell me that he had become skeptical about Christian employees because of his experience with two theological students who seemed to be always standing around talking about God during work hours. But what really did it was when the boss observed one go into the bathroom for twenty minutes. When the employee emerged, he said to his fellow student, "I just had the most wonderful time. I read three chapters of John in the john!"

Christians ought to be the best in attitude, the best in dependability, and the best in integrity. All of us who are employed must be faithful, hard workers or we are sinning.

Last, we must realize that there is intrinsic nobility in work offered to God. Gerard Manley Hopkins put it this way:

Smiting on an anvil, sawing a beam, white-washing a wall, driving horses, sweeping, scouring, everything gives God some glory if being in His grace you do it as your duty. To go to Communion worthily gives God great glory, but to take food in thankfulness and temperance gives Him glory too. He is so great that all things give Him glory if you mean they should. So then, my brethren, live.[5]

Our lives will be full when we do our very best, "not by way of eye-service, as people-pleasers, but with sincerity of heart, fearing the Lord" (v. 22).

A Full Life for Masters/Employers (4:1)

Masters, treat your bondservants justly and fairly, knowing that you also have a Master in heaven. (Colossians 4:1)

Remember, under Roman law the slaves had no rights at all. So these words had a strange ring to non-Christians and to the newly believing master. Also, given the social conditions of the times, this command may have been more difficult to carry out than what was asked of the slaves. The master who attempted to treat his slaves "justly and fairly" (v. 1) ran a deep risk of ostracism from his fellow slave owners, much like Christians today, such as Michael Cassidy in South Africa, who are living a Biblical ethic amidst the persecution of right and left.

The guiding reality for the master/employer is that both he and his servant have the same Lord: "[you know] that you also have a Master in heaven" (v. 1). Some have thought that this was too general. But as Alexander Maclaren said, "If we try to live that commandment for twenty-four hours, it will probably not be its vagueness of which we complain."[6] Employers, if you truly realize that you must answer to God for the way you conduct yourself with your employees, you will care about what happens to them. You will be concerned that they are paid properly. You will be concerned about their illnesses, their spouses, their children, their education. Along with this, you may have more problems. In fact, this kind of caring attitude assures that you will. But you will also have the fullness of Christ.

Masters/slaves—employers/employees, one thing is for sure: disregard the apostle's advice and you will never know fullness in your domestic/professional life, no matter how well you succeed. Disregard his advice and something will always be missing.

Jesus, who is the fullness of the universe, wants us to be full in our marital relationships, our family relationships, and our professional relationships.

Moreover, he desires that this fullness overflow to the world. Justin Martyr wrote in the second century:

> Our Lord urged us by patience and meekness to lead all from shame and the lusts of evil, and this we have to show in the case of many who have come in contact with us, who were overcome and changed from violent and tyrannical characters, either from having watched the constancy of their Christian neighbors, or from having observed the wonderful patience of Christian travelers when overcharged, or from doing business with Christians.[7]

As people "do business" with us, may our fullness become their fullness!

Continue steadfastly in prayer, being watchful in it with thanksgiving. At the same time, pray also for us, that God may open to us a door for the word, to declare the mystery of Christ, on account of which I am in prison— that I may make it clear, which is how I ought to speak. Walk in wisdom toward outsiders, making the best use of the time. Let your speech always be gracious, seasoned with salt, so that you may know how you ought to answer each person.

4:2–6

41

The Fullness in Communication

COLOSSIANS 4:2-6

FOR ME, one of the most beautiful phrases in all of Scripture is the Apostle John's identification of Jesus as "the Word": "In the beginning was the Word" (John 1:1). Before the creation of all things, Christ was eternally continuing as the Word. As "the Word," Jesus is the ultimate communication of God. Before there was time or earth or water or fire, before we were, God had determined to communicate with us. "In the beginning was the Communication." John further writes, "And the Word [the Communication] became flesh and dwelt among us" (John 1:14a). When Christ did this, he became to us the ABC of God, the alphabet of Deity. "[W]e have seen his glory, glory as of the only Son from the Father, full of grace and truth" (John 1:14b). Because he is the Word, we understand something of how much we have always been loved. He spelled out God's love for us (John 3:16)!

This chapter's text calls us to fullness in communication with God and to fullness in communicating with the world. Since Christ is the fullness of the universe and we have been made partakers of his fullness, our fullness should flow back up to him and out to the world.

Fullness in Communication with God (v. 2)

Continue steadfastly in prayer, being watchful in it with thanksgiving.

At the very heart of our communication must be full devotion to prayer. The idea here is persistence in prayer—continual prayer. Elsewhere the Lord himself encouraged this by telling the story of a widow who got her way with a godless, uncaring judge because she nagged him. It was "a parable," Luke says, "to the effect that they ought always to pray and not lose heart" (Luke 18:1). Such continual prayer was the abiding experience of the apostolic church (Acts 1:14; 2:42). The apostles were constantly encouraging this, as did Paul when he challenged the Thessalonians to "pray without ceasing" (1 Thessalonians 5:17)—full, continual communication with God.

How is this possible? Are we always to be carrying on a constant verbal dialogue, whatever we are doing? They have places for people who do this, and the doors lock from the outside! There cannot be unbroken verbal communication with God, otherwise we would never be really "there" for anything we did. But in another sense prayer is not so much the speaking of words as the posture of the heart.

The Quaker Thomas Kelly said in his *Testament of Devotion*:

> There is a way of ordering our mental life on more than one level at once. On one level we can be thinking, discussing, seeing, calculating, meeting all the demands of external affairs. But deep within, behind the scenes, at a profounder level, we may also be in prayer and adoration, song and worship, and a gentle receptiveness to divine breathings.[1]

The delightful medieval monk Brother Lawrence wrote in the classic *The Practice of the Presence of God*:

> The time of business does not differ with me from the time of prayer; and in the noise and clatter of my kitchen, while several persons are at the same time calling for different things, I possess God in as great tranquility as if I were on my knees.[2]

Full devotion to prayer is possible in a busy life. "Continue steadfastly in prayer" (v. 2).

Paul continued, "being watchful in it with thanksgiving" (v. 2). Being devoted to prayer does not mean the mind goes into a devotional neutral while an easy "stream of consciousness" flows between us and God. Rather, a habit of prayer demands mental alertness to the dangers of life and the needs of those around us, an awareness that can at any moment launch us into fervent prayer. Paul's parallel challenge in Ephesians 6:18 presents the attitude in no uncertain terms: "praying at all times in the Spirit, with all prayer and supplication. To that end keep alert with all perseverance, making supplication for all the saints."

All of this is part of full communication with God. This devotion is vigilant and is also wonderfully positive because it is thankful. It remembers

God's goodness. Joshua returned to Gilgal to gaze on the stones of remembrance (the stones taken from the Jordan when God held back the waters so Israel could cross). Thus he was refreshed, and his heart rejoiced in thanksgiving (Joshua 4). Likewise, we are to recall our stones of remembrance and give thanks in our communication with God.

Is your communication with God full? If not, it is because you are not appropriating his fullness (see 2:9, 10). If your life falls short, dip your cup in now. When your heart is overflowing, it will flow up to God in communication—alert and with an attitude of thanksgiving.

Fullness in Communcation with the World (vv. 3–6)

Paul asked first for fullness in his own communication with the world: "At the same time, pray also for us, that God may open to us a door for the word, to declare the mystery of Christ, on account of which I am in prison—that I may make it clear, which is how I ought to speak" (vv. 3, 4). Paul did not seem to care whether he was in prison or not—he just wanted more opportunity to communicate the good news. It was preaching that got him into prison and would keep him in prison, and that was okay if he could preach more—and we know that he did! Paul burned to communicate the gospel. In 1 Corinthians 16:8, 9 we see him saying of his Ephesian ministry, "But I will stay in Ephesus until Pentecost, for a wide door for effective work has opened to me, and there are many adversaries." When he left the Ephesian church, he told its elders that night and day for three years he had continuously admonished each one with tears (Acts 20:31). Paul's desire for opportunities to preach the mystery of Christ is a model for us.

In addition, Paul wanted to proclaim Christ's gospel in a "clear" way (v. 4). Unfortunately, this is not always the concern of preachers, as we often hear of "a mist in the pulpit and a fog in the pew." R. C. Sproul says, "I use big words to disguise my ignorance. Big words are great for that. If I can use a word that nobody understands, chances are people will think that at least I understand what I am talking about even if they don't."[3]

C. S. Lewis agrees: "Any fool can write *learned* language. The vernacular is the real test. If you can't turn your faith into it, then you either don't understand it or you don't believe it."[4]

Spurgeon once commented, "Christ said, 'Feed my sheep. . . . Feed My lambs.' Some preachers, however, put the food so high that neither sheep nor lambs can reach it. They seem to have read the text, 'Feed my giraffes.'"[5]

Joe Bayly, in his book *I Love to Tell the Story*, commented:

Someone passed the following quotation on to me, from a graffiti wall at St. John's University in Minnesota: "Jesus said to them, 'Who do you say that I am?' And they replied, 'You are the eschatological manifestation of the ground of our being, the kerygma in which we find the ultimate meaning of our interpersonal relationships.' And Jesus said, 'What?'" I like that. I like it because it sets the simplicity of our Lord's words and teaching over against the complexity of some technical expressions of truth. Not that theology is wrong. We need deep thinkers who can explain the ramifications of our faith. But such complexity of ideas belongs in a seminary classroom, not on the hillside where Jesus taught multitudes, or in the room where I teach my Sunday school class. Jesus was profound, but simple in expression. To use an old but true way of expressing it, He put the cookies—or the bread of life—on the lowest shelf, where anyone could reach it. And so must I. I cannot show off my knowledge (the little that I have) or my vocabulary and still teach as Jesus taught. Nor get through to people as He got through to them.[6]

In saying to the Colossians, "[Pray] . . . that I may make it clear, which is how I ought to speak" (v. 4), Paul acknowledged that prayer makes all the difference in communicating the gospel. There is a great story that comes from the life of Hudson Taylor. There was a mission station that was particularly blessed in the China Inland Mission, far above the others. There seemed to be no accounting for this, because others were equal in devotion and in ability. Hudson Taylor was traveling and speaking in England, and after a meeting a man came up and began to ask him about that particular station. Then he began to ask many personal questions. It turned out that the man had been the college roommate of the missionary at that station many years earlier, and he had committed himself to daily praying for the work there. Hudson Taylor said, "Then I knew the answer."

In verses 5, 6 Paul expressed his concern for the Colossians' witness: "Walk in wisdom toward outsiders, making the best use of the time. Let your speech always be gracious, seasoned with salt, so that you may know how you ought to answer each person." "Gracious" speech presupposed grace in their hearts, "[f]or out of the abundance of the heart the mouth speaks" (Matthew 12:34). As grace flows through the heart, it flows outward in kindness. This conversation is never insipid or boring. In fact, it is "seasoned with salt" (v. 6)—salty, savory, scintillating—not the dull, sanctimonious vocabulary that seems to be demanded in some church circles. It is thoughtful speech, words with content. It is joyful, even witty, for this is what salty speech meant in classical Greek.

Spurgeon, one of the greatest gospel communicators who ever lived, was once criticized by a woman who thought he was too witty. Spurgeon replied, "Madam, if you knew what I *didn't* say, you wouldn't say that!"

Believers and their gospel are to be interesting. Their remarks are to be contextualized; that is, they are to speak to the people where they are, according to their interests and needs. Becky Pippert, whose husband served as UPI Bureau Chief in the Middle East, wrote:

> Recently at a party I was introduced by a very staid diplomat with: "This is Becky and she really believes. She's really devout and she's so interesting!" Wes and I have laughed many times over how people have introduced us here with great enthusiasm, fascination and respect. This comes out of the context of our efforts to genuinely get to know these people and their interests. We go to concerts together, see films together and out of scores of conversations, our Christian beliefs have emerged. We don't do this as a gimmick to slip in the gospel. We do it because we are genuinely interested in relating to non-believers and their world views.[7]

This is full communication—speech filled with grace and salt, meeting the other person where he or she is. Let us make "the best use of the time" (v. 5).

Jesus Christ was and still is the Word. As such he is the ultimate communication to us. Our best response is to allow our hearts to overflow in communication.

Our hearts must flow back to God in continual, prayerful devotion, vigilance, and thanksgiving. They must flood the world with the gospel in clarity, grace, and salt.

This is proper communication for hearts filled with the fullness of God.

Tychicus will tell you all about my activities. He is a beloved brother and faithful minister and fellow servant in the Lord. I have sent him to you for this very purpose, that you may know how we are and that he may encourage your hearts, and with him Onesimus, our faithful and beloved brother, who is one of you. They will tell you of everything that has taken place here.

4:7–9

42

The Fullness in Fellowship, I

COLOSSIANS 4:7–9

MYRA BROOKS WELCH tells the story of a battered, scarred violin held up for bid by an auctioneer who hardly thought it worth his time. And it apparently wasn't, for the final bid was a grudging three dollars. But as he was calling, "Three dollars once, three dollars twice, going for three," a gray-haired man came forward and picked up the bow, wiped the dust from the old instrument, tightened the strings, and played the most beautiful melody—"as sweet as an angel sings." When the music ceased, the auctioneer, holding it up with the bow, said in a different tone, "What am I bid for the old violin?" Instead of three dollars, it went for three thousand!

> The people cheered, but some of them cried,
> "We do not quite understand—
> What changed its worth?" The man replied,
> "THE TOUCH OF THE MASTER'S HAND."
> And many a man with a life out of tune,
> And battered and torn with sin,
> Is auctioned cheap to the thoughtless crowd.
> Much like the old violin.
> A "mess of pottage," a glass of wine,
> A game and he travels on.
> He's going once and going twice,
> He's going—and almost gone.
> But the MASTER comes, and the foolish crowd
> Never can quite understand
> The worth of a soul, and the change that's wrought
> By the TOUCH OF THE MASTER'S HAND.

Such change is incomprehensible for those outside. But all who have experienced that touch *perfectly* understand.

Some who have experienced the Master's touch are mentioned by name in the closing paragraphs of Paul's letter. The study of these ancient lives can bring a transforming touch to our modern lives and thus fullness in everyday service.

Tychicus: Full Service (vv. 7, 8)

The first name Paul mentioned was Tychicus, in verses 7, 8: "Tychicus will tell you all about my activities. He is a beloved brother and faithful minister and fellow servant in the Lord. I have sent him to you for this very purpose, that you may know how we are and that he may encourage your hearts."

The Scriptures mention Tychicus only five times (here, Acts 20:4, Ephesians 6:21, 2 Timothy 4:12, and Titus 3:12), but we can draw some distinct conclusions about his experience and place in life. Tychicus popped up at the end of Paul's missionary work in Ephesus, and since he was a native of the province of Asia (Acts 20:4), of which Ephesus was the major city, we think he was probably a convert of Paul's long ministry in Ephesus. Very likely he had been born in that city, lived there, and found new life under Paul's ministry. Thus, he probably witnessed the great Ephesian silversmiths' riot against Paul, which prompted the apostle to leave Ephesus for Macedonia (Acts 19:35—20:1). As such Tychicus experienced danger himself and shared Paul's immense bravery. A short time later when Paul decided to return to Jerusalem, where he would ultimately be arrested, Tychicus was one of the seven who accompanied him as a traveling companion (Acts 20:4). Very likely he carried with him the Ephesians' offering for the poor in Jerusalem.

When Paul was arrested, Tychicus, along with Dr. Luke and others, stayed with Paul through the thick and thin of his arrest and imprisonment in Caesarea, his dramatic appearances before kings and governors, his miserable voyage and shipwreck en route to Rome, and his residence in Rome awaiting trial. Thus we see that Tychicus was a man of intense devotion to God and Paul. Paul said,

> I was shipwrecked; a night and a day I was adrift at sea; on frequent journeys, in danger from rivers, danger from robbers, danger from my own people, danger from Gentiles, danger in the city, danger in the wilderness, danger at sea, danger from false brothers; in toil and hardship, through many a sleepless night, in hunger and thirst, often without food, in cold and exposure. (2 Corinthians 11:25–27)

Tychicus could have written this about himself as well, due to his remarkable loyalty to the apostle.

Because of this, Paul chose him to travel as his messenger back to the churches of provincial Asia. As such, Tychicus was charged with two duties. First, to deliver Paul's letters: one to the Colossians, another to a slave owner in Colossae named Philemon, another to the Ephesians (see Ephesians 6:21), and quite probably a last letter to the Laodiceans (see Colossians 4:16). His second duty was simply to tell the churches in Asia about Paul's situation. Tychicus was Paul's errand boy! Later references in Titus 3:12 and 2 Timothy 4:12 confirm that he performed this humble function throughout Paul's life and ministry. Tychicus left no writings that survived. He did no feats that were thought worth preserving by Dr. Luke in Acts. He was a very common violin. However, God used him as a part of his divine symphony, and the music was beautiful.

Notice what our verses reveal about his character. In verse 7 Paul called him "a beloved brother." He was greatly loved by Paul and the church in Rome, which is no small thing. Many kings and presidents and senators never accomplish this in life.

He was also called a "faithful minister [or servant]" (v. 7). There is no hint of his being a great thinker or orator, but only a servant, a title assumed by the Lord himself. Someone has said, "The greatest ability in the world is dependability," and in this Tychicus was an immensely gifted man.

Paul rounded off his description with "fellow servant in the Lord" (v. 7). This term expressed an equality between Paul and Tychicus. It is almost as if Paul said, "Don't think because I wrote the letter and Tychicus is delivering it that I am better than he. We are both servants of the same Lord, who has given us separate tasks. I'm not Tychicus's master, though he is serving me."

From the beautiful teamwork of Paul and Tychicus we learn some great truths about fullness in service. *There is greatness in the smallest things done for Christ.* What would be the use of Paul's writing a letter if it did not get delivered? What would be the use of his towering thought in the opening chapters of Colossians and its compelling application if no one ever read it? "For the loss of a nail, lose a horseshoe; for the loss of a horseshoe, lose a horse; for the loss of a horse, lose a soldier; for the loss of a soldier, lose a battle; for the loss of a battle, lose a kingdom." What was the name of Charles Lindbergh's mechanic? Who blocked for Barry Sanders when he won the Heisman Trophy? So it is with the seemingly small, unromantic things we do for Christ. Some of them are absolutely indispensable to God's work, and we will never know how much so until we get to Heaven.

When Tychicus was doing the smallest thing, he was serving Christ. We moderns run the danger of dichotomizing our lives into religious/non-religious, sacred/secular, great/small. But our Lord said and did otherwise: "I always do the things that are pleasing to him" (John 8:29). Jesus, living in a human body for thirty-three years, never once performed a nonsacred act. God is in all our little deeds, and we ought to ask him to keep reminding us that it is so. We need to pray for this in our regular prayer times as well as in a thousand brief sighs.[1] How liberated our lives will then be.

We must realize that momentary things done for Christ are eternal. The letters that Tychicus bore to Asia would outlast the Roman Empire! Tychicus's name would be known until the end of time. The world may not see our part (rarely does it), but God does, and God says, "I will never forget their works."

The Colossian church now seems a failure. Today if you travel to the Lycus Valley, you will find only a few stones and some poor farmers. But in that day the church flourished, and its life spread contagiously around the world with the blessed truths of the supremacy of Christ. The Church now is far richer because of Colossae and Paul and his fellow servant Tychicus.

The life of this common, not remarkably gifted man who loyally served Christ and Paul graces all of our lives today. We know of Tychicus, but there are thousands who have equally blessed us whom we will only know in glory—common violins with whom the Master has made eternal music.

Oneimus: Full Transformation (v. 9)

Paul described another of the Master's servants in verse 9 as "Onesimus, our faithful and beloved brother, who is one of you."

We know from Paul's letter to Philemon that Onesimus was Philemon's errant slave. From it we understand that Onesimus must have been a very difficult person, for Philemon had become a Christian and thus was not the overbearing, insensitive master that some were. His Christian theology taught that he and Onesimus were equal before God and would have to answer to God for their actions. Moreover, Onesimus as an unbelieving slave was, to quote his own self-evaluation, "useless" (Philemon 11). Miserable, ungrateful Onesimus had stolen from Philemon and fled to Ephesus and then on to Rome to become lost in the anonymity of the huge, faceless populace—where instead of losing himself, he was found by his master's Lord, Jesus Christ.

An amazing transformation had taken place. Once restless and insolent, Onesimus was now clear eyed and straightforward. Once ungrateful and unloving, Onesimus now abounded with love. Once dishonest, he was willing to make restitution. Once morose, he now entered joyfully into the psalms and hymns and spiritual songs of the persecuted church in Rome. Onesimus had been revolutionized by God's grace! Anytime a man or a woman voluntarily takes steps toward restitution, we can be sure something radical has happened. Some time ago I saw a newspaper clipping that had appeared in *The East African Standard* in Nairobi:

> ALL DEBTS TO BE PAID
> I ALLAN HARANGUI ALIAS WANIEK HARANGUI, of P.O. Box 40380, Nairobi, have dedicated services to the Lord Jesus Christ. I must put right all my wrongs. If I owe you any debt or damage personally or any of the companies I have been director or partner i.e.
> GUARANTEED SERVICES LTD.
> WATERPUMPS ELECTRICAL
> AND GENERAL CO. SALES AND SERVICE LTD.
> Please contact me or my advocates J. K. Kibicho and Company, Advocates, P.O. Box 73137, Nairobi, for a settlement. No amount will be disputed.
> GOD AND HIS SON JESUS CHRIST BE GLORIFIED

Here is a man with the spirit of Onesimus—so converted that it even touched his wallet. Christ does that! Recently in Nevada a man won $130,000 in a preliminary round of the poker world championship. Then he came to Christ and gave back $127,000 to get out of the final tournament. God's transforming grace is the same, whether in Rome or Las Vegas.[2]

God is still in the life-changing business today. I have seen him take a clever, filthy-mouthed young man and turn him into a masterful Christian executive who lives for Christ, his wife, and his family. I have seen a young woman who went for everything the self-worshiping culture of the seventies offered find Christ. Overnight she was elevated beyond her egoism, becoming a bright advertisement for Jesus. I have seen Christ take a young man lost in a middle-class desert of materialism and success—empty and rich—and fill him to overflowing. How does this occur? "For in him [Christ] the whole fullness of deity dwells bodily, and you have been filled in him" (2:9, 10). Their emptiness became an opportunity for his fullness, their weakness for his strength, their thirst for his filling, their misery for his joy, their meaninglessness for his purpose.

> A man with a life out of tune
> And battered and torn with sin,
> Is auctioned cheap to the thoughtless crowd,
> Much like the old violin.
> But the MASTER comes, and the foolish crowd

Never can quite understand
The worth of a soul, and the change that's wrought
By the TOUCH OF THE MASTER'S HAND.

Some may feel like their lives are "going once, going twice, going almost gone." If so, what is needed is the touch of the Master's hand.

Edith Schaeffer tells the story of how the girl doing the cooking for L'Abri was supposed to be making the cakes, but made some errors until all she had left was an amorphous mess of goo. The logical thing was to throw it out. But the Schaeffers did not have extra money and had learned to be very economical in the kitchen. So Mrs. Schaeffer sat down with the girl, figured out what was in the gooey mess, and by adding an extra ingredient was able to make what her husband described as "the most marvelous noodles you have tasted in your life." If we place ourselves in the Lord's hands, he can shape us into something that has both usefulness and beauty.[3]

Full transformation awaits those who invite the Master's touch. Full, overflowing service is the characteristic of life in Christ.

Aristarchus my fellow prisoner greets you, and Mark the cousin of Barnabas (concerning whom you have received instructions—if he comes to you, welcome him), and Jesus who is called Justus. These are the only men of the circumcision among my fellow workers for the kingdom of God, and they have been a comfort to me. Epaphras, who is one of you, a servant of Christ Jesus, greets you, always struggling on your behalf in his prayers, that you may stand mature and fully assured in all the will of God. For I bear him witness that he has worked hard for you and for those in Laodicea and in Hierapolis. Luke the beloved physician greets you, as does Demas.

4:10–14

43

The Fullness in Fellowship, II

COLOSSIANS 4:10–14

WHEN I CAME TO CHRIST, I discovered an amazing new kinship with other believers, who were now my brothers and sisters by Biblical definition. My heart not only was drawn freely up to God, but ineluctably out to them. They loved the same things I loved. They wanted to talk about the same things I wanted to talk about. They understood. I was experiencing, of course, the fellowship, the Biblical *koinonia*, that every believer experiences as an outgrowth of knowing Christ.

My new life in Christ became the basis for lasting peer friendships. The shared mystery of Christ has been the basis for my relationship with my wife, Barbara, as well. In him our hearts beat together. She is not only my wife, but my best friend, my confidante, my counselor and joy.

In Christ we have developed mutual soul friendships with others that are among our dearest treasures. Indeed our regular prayers focus on them. Christian fellowship, and as a result friendship, is one of the principal boons of knowing Christ.

The dynamics of the Christian fellowship and friendship were beautifully explained by the Apostle John in 1 John 1:3—"that which we have seen and heard we proclaim also to you, so that you too may have fellowship with us; and indeed our fellowship is with the Father and with his Son Jesus Christ." A primary motivation behind John's proclaiming of the gospel was that his hearers be brought into fellowship with the Father and Son, *and thus into fellowship with John and the Church*! Fellowship with the Godhead spawns fellowship with other believers.

The key to the quality of our earthly fellowship is the quality of our fellowship with God. Those with the richest fellowship with God have the richest fellowship with each other. They share the same view of *reality* as they regard the world around them. They share the same view of *self* and understand the reality of sin as it affects the human personality. They share the same *values and ethical standards*. They share the same *love* for Christ, his Church, and his Word. They share the same *hopes* and the same *cause*—all of which makes for an exhilarating, satisfying mutuality.

That is why a businessman, Allan Emery, amidst the rush of the Thirtieth Street Station in Philadelphia, could hear the conductor whistling a refrain from a hymn, greet him in the Lord, and have an exchange of soul in a few brief moments that he will remember the rest of his life.[1] We have all experienced the same thing. Sometimes hardly a word is spoken, but there is an immediate sense of oneness and the ability to communicate on the deepest level. You sense that you both belong—that you are family.

In Colossian terminology, the fullness of Christ floods our souls and overflows to others. If the others are believers, their lives also overflow. There is mutual recognition and mutual refreshment in fellowship with believers. In the book of Acts there are more than 100 different Christians associated with Paul. He named sixteen different friends in Romans 16 alone![2] Here in Colossians he was true to form as he named ten people in closing. This, along with what we can cull from their backgrounds and from the nature of their greetings, suggests an overflowing fullness of fellowship in Christ.

Fellowship Crossing Racial and Religious Barriers

In this passage six individuals sent greetings (through Paul) from Rome to Colossae. Three were Jews and three Gentiles. The three Jews (vv. 10, 11) were Aristarchus, Mark, and Jesus called Justus. Paul said of them, "These are the only men of the circumcision among my fellow workers for the kingdom of God, and they have been a comfort to me" (v. 11). Then he went on to name the Gentiles: Epaphras, Luke, and Demas (vv. 12–14). Language, national animosities, and differences in religion and culture had divided the world of that day into hostile camps that could only be held together by the sword. Here under Paul's aegis both camps were meeting together willingly and lovingly—an amazing unity!

From the very beginning Jesus had demonstrated that this was the intent of the gospel. When he crossed forbidden barriers in reaching out to the Samaritan woman, as recorded in John 4, the woman was amazed, and the Jews who heard of it even more so. Hatred between Judea and Samaria had lasted over 400 years. While the Jews had kept their racial purity during the Babylonian captivity, the Samaritans had lost theirs by intermarrying with the Assyrian invaders. To Jewish eyes this was unforgivable. Also, the Samaritans had built a rival temple on Mt. Gerizim—only to have it destroyed by the Jews in Maccabean times. In Christ's time bitter hatred reigned supreme. A Jewish prayer even included, ". . . and, Lord, do not remember the Samaritans in the Resurrection."

Added to this was the fact that the Samaritan was a "woman." (Strict rabbis forbade other rabbis to greet women in public. Some Pharisees were called "the bruised and bleeding Pharisees" because they shut their eyes whenever they saw a woman and so stumbled into the street, incurring pious bruises.) But Jesus not only spoke to the woman, he used the woman's drinking utensil, thereby becoming ceremonially defiled—a scandalous act. Jesus leapt far beyond the conventional barriers of his day! And in doing so, he modeled one of the supreme glories of the Church. Jesus not only reaches people like me, he does not just reach people like you, he does not reach just rich people, he does not only reach poor people, but all of us, and he brings us together.

This is what had happened in Rome (and elsewhere), but it had not been easy. The Gentiles in Rome were ready to mix, but it was not so with the Jewish believers who legalistically demanded that the Gentiles be circumcised and follow Jewish ceremonial law. When Paul came to Rome, these legalistic-minded Jewish believers gave him a cool reception, even rejecting the authenticity of his missionary charge. Only the three Jews named here helped him. They were receptive and loving; they understood grace; and so here they sent their greetings to the Colossian church. These three had the "Colossian fullness." It is impossible to hold racial prejudices in the heart and be Spirit filled; such goes against everything Christ taught and teaches. When a Christian refuses fellowship with other healthy, Spirit-filled believers, there can only be one conclusion: something is wrong in his or her relationship to God. When we are having fullness of fellowship with the Father and with his Son, Jesus Christ, we have fellowship (and friendship!) with one another regardless of background. Three Jewish believers in Rome were experiencing fullness in fellowship, and it was overflowing to the church in Colossae.

Fellowship Transcending Grievances

Believers at their worst are capable of holding on to grievances. Two congregations, located only a few blocks from each other in a small community, thought it might be better if they would become one united body, and thus larger and more effective, rather than two struggling churches. But they were not able to pull it off. They could not agree on how to recite "the Lord's

Prayer." One group wanted, "forgive us our trespasses," while the other demanded, "forgive us our debts." So one church went back to its *trespasses*, while the other returned to its *debts*! Believers can be stubborn, unchanging, and unforgiving. But others, like Paul and Mark, are able to forgive and forget.

Earlier young Mark (John Mark) had accompanied Paul and Barnabas on Paul's first great missionary journey when they set out from Antioch. After ministering in Cypress, John Mark abandoned Paul when they reached the shores of Pamphylia, returning to Jerusalem. We do not know why. We can guess from Paul's writings that the hardships were incredible, with stress very much like that experienced by combat soldiers. Later, when Paul was planning another journey, Barnabas insisted that John Mark come along, and Paul refused. The result was the famous separation as Barnabas took John Mark with him and Paul recruited Silas. Paul was not running "Holy Land Tours," and he did not want anyone who had been fainthearted on his team. But now, twelve years later, John Mark was with Paul in Rome, ministering to him in his imprisonment. As Paul sent Mark's greeting to Colossae, he even commended him saying, "if he comes to you, welcome him" (v. 10). In the accompanying letter to Philemon Paul numbered him among his "fellow workers" (Philemon 24). And later, at the sunset of his ministry, he said to Timothy, "Luke alone is with me. Get Mark and bring him with you, for he is very useful to me for ministry" (2 Timothy 4:11).

There was no way that two men who both loved God and were walking in fellowship with him would not have fellowship with one another. This is what true fellowship brings! If two believers cannot be reconciled, then either both or one is not in fellowship with God. Is there someone whom you will not forgive—whom you have no desire to forgive though this person has humbly sought your forgiveness? If so, you need the fullness of Christ. If you are full of him, you will be like him—forgiving.

Fellowship That Is Large-Hearted

The expansiveness of Christian fellowship is seen in the desire of the six to send greetings to those in Colossae. Most of the six had never been to Colossae, but they loved the believers there anyway. They understood that they were all part of each other.

What Paul said about Epaphras suggests something of what they were like: "Epaphras, who is one of you, a servant of Christ Jesus, greets you, always struggling on your behalf in his prayers, that you may stand mature and fully assured in all the will of God. For I bear him witness that he has worked hard for you and for those in Laodicea and in Hierapolis" (vv. 12, 13).

Epaphras was from Colossae. He had come all the way to Rome because he was concerned about the Gnostic heresy that threatened to rob the Colossians of their fullness. Epaphras had a profound concern for his fellow believers. Paul represented him as "always struggling on your behalf in his prayers" (v. 12). From the Greek word used here we get our English word *agonize*. Paul had watched Epaphras pray for Colossae, and this was the one word that best described his prayer. The same root word was used to describe Jesus' fervent prayer in Gethsemane (Luke 22:44).

Epaphras cared! He prayed that they would "stand mature and fully assured in all the will of God" (v. 12). His prayer was specifically directed against the heretics who falsely offered perfection and fullness through their system. The Colossians already had divine perfection in Christ. "God, help them to stay there!" prayed Epaphras. This was selfless, giving, big-hearted prayer.

Paul concluded his brief portrait of Epaphras by saying, "For I testify for him that he has a deep concern [literally, pain or distress] for you and for those who are in Laodicea and Hierapolis" (v. 13 NASB). When you are in full fellowship with Christ, you naturally take on something of his heart for others, and this overflows in "deep concern." Phillips Brooks, the peerless preacher of Boston, put it this way:

> To be a true minister to men is always to accept new happiness and new distress. The man who gives himself to other men can never be a wholly sad man; but no more can he be a man of unclouded gladness. To him shall come with every deeper consecration a before untasted joy, but in the same cup shall be mixed a sorrow that it was beyond his power to feel before.[3]

That is the way it was with Epaphras and his coworkers. His enlarged heart made him vulnerable to the burdens of others.

Also, fullness in fellowship encompasses "marginal" people. Paul concluded the greetings with, "Luke the beloved physician greets you, as does Demas" (v. 14). Luke was the only Gentile writer of any book in the New Testament. He was a much-loved Christian, physician, devoted friend, careful historian—all in one! But Demas is another story. Later Paul would write of him, "Demas, in love with this present world, has deserted me" (2 Timothy 4:10). Perhaps Paul was already aware of Demas's spiritual slide because he was the only one of the six about whom there was no comment in the greeting. Christian fellowship is not meant to be perfect. It must always be stretching.

Some draw a circle that shuts men out;
Race and position are what they flout;
But Christ in love seeks them all to win,
He draws a circle that takes them in!

Edwin Markham, altered

Our Lord even takes in those who disappoint and hurt. Christian fellowship makes us bigger people who have a greater capacity for sorrow—and for joy.

We have something wonderful to offer to the world: "that which we have seen and heard we proclaim also to you, so that you too may have fellowship with us; and indeed our fellowship is with the Father and with his Son Jesus Christ" (1 John 1:3). We offer first fellowship with God—not just knowledge of God, but a relationship with him. The gospel also offers a fullness of fellowship with his children. This dynamic fellowship:

- overcomes barriers
- transcends grievances
- produces largeness of heart

Through believing in Christ, all can have this fullness of fellowship, for he offers it to everyone.

Give my greetings to the brothers at Laodicea, and to Nympha and the church in her house. And when this letter has been read among you, have it also read in the church of the Laodiceans; and see that you also read the letter from Laodicea. And say to Archippus, "See that you fulfill the ministry that you have received in the Lord." I, Paul, write this greeting with my own hand. Remember my chains. Grace be with you.

4:15–18

44

The Fullness of
Paul's Heart

COLOSSIANS 4:15–18

FOR THOSE OF US who claim the name of Christ, there are two distinct courses of life available. One is to cultivate a small heart. It is by far the safest way to go because it minimizes the sorrows of life. If our ambition is to avoid the troubles of life, the formula is simple: minimize entangling relationships, do not give yourself to people, carefully avoid elevated and noble ideals. If we will do this, we will escape a host of afflictions. Many people, even some who profess to be Christians, get through life with a minimum of tribulation by having small hearts.

The other path is to cultivate a ministering heart like that of the Apostle Paul. Open yourself to others and you will become susceptible to an index of sorrows scarcely imaginable to a shriveled heart. Enlarge your heart and you will enlarge your potential for pain.

The effects of these two kinds of hearts upon those around them are drastically different. Little hearts, though safe and protected, never contribute anything. No one benefits from their restricted sympathies and vision. On the other hand, large hearts, though vulnerable, also know the most joy and leave the greatest imprint on other hearts. Cultivate deafness and we will never hear discord, but neither will we hear the glorious strains of a great symphony. Cultivate blindness and we will be spared the ugly, but we will never see the beauty of a sunset or a bird on wing. Cultivate a small heart and life may be smooth sailing, but we will never know the heady wind of the Holy Spirit in our sails, the power and exhilaration of being borne along by the Spirit in accomplishing great eternal things for God. Cultivate a small heart, and we certainly will never have a great heart like the Apostle Paul's.

As we come to the final paragraph of the book of Colossians, we need to remind ourselves of the background of the book. Paul was under house arrest in Rome, chained to a Praetorian guard night and day. His feet, which had trod the length of the Roman Empire, now could scarcely find room to pace. His eyes, which were always on the Gentile world, were now restricted to four walls. But his great heart, though caged in prison, would continue to mark the world as Paul wrote some of his most powerful letters, part of the Holy Scriptures.

Far away, over 1,000 miles distant, beat a similar heart in a man by the name of Epaphras, a leader in a tiny house church in Colossae. Epaphras had probably come to know Christ when Paul was ministering in Ephesus and had gone back to the Lycus Valley where God used him to bring the good news to its towns. People were coming to Christ regularly; the fruits of the Spirit were everywhere evident among the people.

It seemed to some that it would not be long until everyone in Colossae believed. But there were dark forces at work. Men and women began to attend their fellowship who brought with them an intimidating air of superiority. They explained that they liked what they saw in the church, for it was a promising beginning to a deeper, more fulfilling knowledge of God. So with conscious patience (the kind people use with inferiors) they explained that Christ could not be the Creator, and his incarnation at best was an illusion because God could not touch physical matter. The way to a true knowledge of God's fullness was by using ascetic disciplines and secret passwords to work one's way up a long series of emanations until they finally reached God. It was so intellectual and appealing, and some of the Colossians were led away from their fullness to the desolation of Gnosticism. Epaphras did his best against this heresy, but he needed help. And so, perhaps after some restless nights, he decided to seek Paul out in Rome.

No one knows by what port he entered Italy or how he found Paul in Rome, but we can surmise that their meeting was emotional and intense as Epaphras poured out his concern to the chained apostle. The effect on Paul was completely predictable, as it always is with enlarged hearts. Epaphras's concern became Paul's. A wonderful apostolic anxiety engulfed Paul's heart, as was common with him: "And, apart from other things, there is the daily pressure on me of my anxiety for all the churches. Who is weak, and I am not weak? Who is made to fall, and I am not indignant?" said Paul to the Corinthian church (2 Corinthians 11:28, 29). To the Galatians he said, "I am afraid I may have labored over you in vain" (Galatians 4:11). Out of the same concern, Paul once sent a friend to the Thessalonians to find out about their faith, for fear that the Tempter might have tempted them and his labor be in vain (1 Thessalonians 3:5). Epaphras now had a soul brother in his concern!

Immediately Paul's brilliant, original intellect set itself to analyzing the Colossian problem: here is a little church overflowing with the joy of new faith, and now comes a desolating philosophy that, ironically, is beguiling the people away from their fullness by promising a bogus fullness! Paul prayed and meditated much, and when his heart and mind were full, he called for his secretary and began to dictate. During the next hour, under the inspiration of the Holy Spirit, Paul gave the world the beautiful letter to the Colossians, a letter written to perpetuate the Colossians' fullness and ours.

We will review Paul's argument and then cap it off with his overflowing conclusions.

Paul's Full-Hearted Argument

Paul began, in the opening verses, with a celebration of the miracle of the tiny Colossian church in the Lycus Valley, a church that he had never seen. He especially celebrated the gospel, which had produced the remarkable faith, hope, and love of the new church.

Paul followed with a prayer for the Colossians' knowledge (1:9–14). The Gnostics had promoted their knowledge (*gnosis*) as the way to fullness. So Paul prays for the *epignosis* of Christ for the Colossians. Specifically, he prays "that [they] may be filled with the knowledge of his will in all spiritual wisdom and understanding, so as to walk in a manner worthy of the Lord" (vv. 9, 10).

Having finished his prayer, he went on in verses 15–18 to give the most stupendously full revelation of Christ to be found in any of the epistles. It was a sublime poem/hymn of Christ's supremacy that speaks for itself:

> He is the image of the invisible God, the firstborn of all creation. For by him all things were created, in heaven and on earth, visible and invisible, whether thrones or dominions or rulers or authorities—all things were created through him and for him. And he is before all things, and in him all things hold together. And he is the head of the body, the church. He is the beginning, the firstborn from the dead, that in everything he might be preeminent.

According to this, Christ is preeminent in four ways:

First, because he is "the firstborn of all creation" (v. 15), which in Hebrew thought means *first in rank or honor*. He is completely supreme in creation.

There is none higher; there is no Gnostic god above him. One day every knee will bow to the name of Jesus, and every tongue will confess that Jesus Christ is Lord (Philippians 2:10, 11).

Second, he is supreme because he is Creator: "For by him all things were created, in heaven and on earth, visible and invisible, whether thrones or dominions or rulers or authorities—all things were created through him and for him" (v. 16). He created the invisible spirit world. He created the vast physical world. Einstein estimated that there are ten octillion stars in the universe. How many is that? Well, one thousand thousands make one million; 1,000 millions make one billion; 1,000 billions make one trillion; 1,000 trillions make one quadrillion; 1,000 quadrillions make one quintillion; 1,000 quintillions make one sextillion; 1,000 sextillions make one septillion; 1,000 septillions make one octillion. Ten octillion!—10,000,000,000,000,000,000,000,000,000,000. Jesus created them all. He created the unseen microcosms, the incredible rainbow, the beauty of the cell, and he did it all ex nihilo, out of nothing. He did it by the word of his power!

Third, he is the sustainer of creation: "He is before all things, and in him all things hold together" (v. 17). The perfect tense here tells us that he continues to hold all things together, and that apart from his continuous activity all would disintegrate. He holds every speck of matter and every incorporeal spirit together. He is not contained in matter, but simply holds it together by his word! The Gnostics never dreamed of a God like this!

Fourth, he is the goal of creation: "all things were created through him and for [toward] him" (v. 16). All creation is moving toward its goal in him. All things sprang forth at his command, and all things will return to him at his command. He is the beginning and he is the end.

What we think of Christ is everything! If you believe that Christ is eternal, without beginning and without end, that he always was continuing; if you believe that he is Creator of everything, every cosmic speck across trillions of years of trackless space, the Creator of textures and shapes and colors that dazzle our eyes; if you believe that he is the sustainer of all creation, the force that is presently holding the universe together, and that without him all would dissolve; if you believe that he is the goal of everything, that all creation is moving toward him; if you believe this, nothing much can go wrong with you! We cannot think too highly of Christ.

This is the heart of the book of Colossians. Everything else flows from it, for this Christ is the One who "fills all in all" (Ephesians 1:23). Christ's fullness makes full reconciliation possible, "For in him all the fullness of God was pleased to dwell, and through him to reconcile to himself all things

. . . making peace by the blood of his cross" (Colossians 1:19, 20). Christ's fullness makes it possible for his blood to reconcile all who trust him and to effect the redemption of creation. His fullness makes the ministry of the gospel supreme (1:24–29). His fullness motivates Paul's supreme concern for the Colossians (2:1–5) and elicits a supreme charge to walk in Christ (2:6, 7).

Now Paul warned them not to fall captive to Gnostic foolishness, and then gave a rationale based on Jesus' fullness: "For in him the whole fullness of deity dwells bodily, and you have been filled in him" (2:9, 10). Christ is full with all the fullness of Deity, and we, as Christians, are full of his fullness. It is incumbent upon us to have our lives open up more and more so we can receive this fullness—to cultivate an elasticity of soul. That is an antidote to dull, insipid Christianity.

In the remainder of chapter 2, Paul explained more of the dynamics of this fullness (vv. 11–15) and successively warned them against Gnostic legalism, mysticism, and asceticism.

Colossians 3:1–4 bears the high point of exhortation in the letter:

> If then you have been raised with Christ, seek the things that are above, where Christ is, seated at the right hand of God. Set your minds on things that are above, not on things that are on earth. For you have died, and your life is hidden with Christ in God. When Christ who is your life appears, then you also will appear with him in glory.

Our minds and hearts must consistently be focused upward. We cannot be too heavenly minded! Sometimes we hear people say, "He is so heavenly minded, he's no earthly good." But they are wrong. He may be so self-righteous, so pious, so "goody-goody," but never too heavenly minded. This is, I believe, what made Paul stand above even the other apostles. He wrote, "I know a man in Christ who fourteen years ago was caught up to the third heaven—whether in the body or out of the body I do not know, God knows. And I know that this man was caught up into paradise—whether in the body or out of the body I do not know, God knows—and he heard things that cannot be told, which man may not utter" (2 Corinthians 12:2–4). Paul was the man in this vision, but he humbly used the third person. This experience marked his life with the eternal, and it made him different.

As Joe Bayly expressed it, "Lord, burn eternity into my eyeballs." Only when it is thus can we really live! "If then you have been raised with Christ, seek the things that are above, where Christ is, seated at the right hand of God. Set your minds on things that are above, not on things that are on earth. For you have died, and your life is hidden with Christ in God."

Paul followed this with marvelous practical exhortations regarding putting off the old man and putting on the new (3:5–14). In 3:15—4:1 he issued a series of challenges for church and family. His rationale was sublime: since Christ is the *cosmic* fullness, he is also the One who brings relational, *domestic* fullness to our lives. We ought to live in the fullness of his peace, his Word, and his name (vv. 15–17). This cosmic fullness must bring domestic fullness to husband and wife (vv. 18, 19), parents and children (vv. 20, 21), and employers and employees (3:22—4:1). When we are all tuned to him, we are automatically tuned to each other. Because we receive direction from the same conductor, the music we play is in harmony.

Finally, this fullness brings fullness of communication with God in prayer and fullness of communication with the world (4:2–6).

Paul ended his letter by elaborating the fullness of fellowship with believers in a final greeting. Now we will take a brief look at those final greetings, Paul's personal salutation.

Paul's Full-Hearted Conclusion

Paul's final greeting was a three-part encouragement. First, in 4:15: "Give my greetings to the brothers at Laodicea, and to Nympha and the church in her house." Paul had never been to Laodicea either, but his large-heartedness compelled him to greet the church there and the woman, Nympha, who so graciously hosted it.

Second, in verse 16: "And when this letter has been read among you, have it also read in the church of the Laodiceans; and see that you also read the letter from Laodicea." Paul encouraged an exchange of the letters he was sending to Laodicea and Colossae. He wanted them read aloud *as Scripture*.[1] We know that in the future Laodicea would need all the help it could get, as it became a church that was neither hot nor cold and was rejected by Christ (Revelation 3:14–22).

Third, in verse 17 he encouraged a young leader in the Colossian church: "And say to Archippus, 'See that you fulfill the ministry that you have received in the Lord.'" From Philemon 2 many deduce that Archippus was the son of Philemon and Apphia. Perhaps Epaphras told the apostle of Archippus's budding spiritual life and potential. At any rate, Paul reminded him that his ministry originated "in the Lord." It was divinely given and must be treated as such. Paul told him that he must "fulfill" it, calling to mind for the final time the grand theme of fullness.

For perhaps an hour now Paul had been caught up in the sublime themes of Colossians. But now he stretched out his hand for the stylus to write his last words, and as he did so, the chain that fastened him to the Praetorian guard at his side hindered him. He reawoke to the consciousness of his prison. The exhaustion after such an hour of high communion made him consciously dependent, and all his profound teaching, all his thunderings and lightnings, ended in the simple cry that goes straight to the heart: "I, Paul, write this greeting with my own hand. Remember my chains. Grace be with you" (v. 18).[2] Paul was in jail, but no power on earth could cage his soaring heart. He had made himself vulnerable and thus knew deep miseries. But he also knew the winds of the Holy Spirit in his sails, and he had been flying!

Paul closed with the apostolic benediction, "Grace be with you." A closing word of grace was the trademark of Paul in all his letters. "May God's unmerited, freely given favor rest on you." The communication of God's grace to a needy, sinful world is the end of God's deeds, and it is the end of this letter. John put it this way: "And the Word became flesh and dwelt among us, and we have seen his glory, glory as of the only Son from the Father, full of grace and truth. . . . For from his fullness we have all received, grace upon grace" (John 1:14, 16).

Have you received Christ's fullness? Say, "Here's my cup, Lord; fill it up, Lord." May we hold the miracle of being filled with the fullness of God high before us. May we seek those things that are above where Christ is seated at the right hand of God. There is more fullness for our lives as we open our lives more fully to him. May we experience that, and may the theme of this great epistle burn into our lives. May we be filled to overflowing with Jesus Christ!

PHILEMON

Paul, a prisoner for Christ Jesus, and Timothy our brother, To Philemon our beloved fellow worker and Apphia our sister and Archippus our fellow soldier, and the church in your house: Grace to you and peace from God our Father and the Lord Jesus Christ. I thank my God always when I remember you in my prayers, because I hear of your love and of the faith that you have toward the Lord Jesus and for all the saints, and I pray that the sharing of your faith may become effective for the full knowledge of every good thing that is in us for the sake of Christ. For I have derived much joy and comfort from your love, my brother, because the hearts of the saints have been refreshed through you. Accordingly, though I am bold enough in Christ to command you to do what is required, yet for love's sake I prefer to appeal to you—I, Paul, an old man and now a prisoner also for Christ Jesus—I appeal to you for my child, Onesimus, whose father I became in my imprisonment. (Formerly he was useless to you, but now he is indeed useful to you and to me.) I am sending him back to you, sending my very heart. I would have been glad to keep him with me, in order that he might serve me on your behalf during my imprisonment for the gospel, but I preferred to do nothing without your consent in order that your goodness might not be by compulsion but of your own accord. For this perhaps is why he was parted from you for a while, that you might have him back forever, no longer as a bondservant but more than a bondservant, as a beloved brother— especially to me, but how much more to you, both in the flesh and in the Lord. So if you consider me your partner, receive him as you would receive me. If he has wronged you at all, or owes you anything, charge that to my account. I, Paul, write this with my own hand: I will repay it—to say nothing of your owing me even your own self. Yes, brother, I want some benefit from you in the Lord. Refresh my heart in Christ. Confident of your obedience, I write to you, knowing that you will do even more than I say. At the same time, prepare a guest room for me, for I am hoping that through your prayers I will be graciously given to you. Epaphras, my fellow prisoner in Christ Jesus, sends greetings to you, and so do Mark, Aristarchus, Demas, and Luke, my fellow workers. The grace of the Lord Jesus Christ be with your spirit.

PHILEMON

45

The Reconciling Wisdom

PHILEMON

IT IS DIFFICULT TO SAY why Onesimus ran away from his master, Philemon. Some say it was because Philemon was a harsh taskmaster. But that hardly seems likely from what the Scriptures reveal of that master's character. Far more probable is the supposition that Onesimus was a lazy, ungrateful servant with a dishonest streak who saw his chance to make off with a big chunk of his master's savings and did it, leaving Philemon deeply hurt and in financial straits. Though we do not know how Onesimus made his getaway, whether under the cover of darkness or in the guise of a business trip, the direction of flight was predictable—Rome. Maybe he fled to Ephesus where he purchased some handsome clothing that would identify him as a well-to-do man of the road; then he hopped a ship bound for Rome, disembarked at the Italian port of Puteoli, and made his way to Rome where, the historian Tacitus said, "all things horrible and disgraceful find their way."[1] There he melded into the dark, sordid world of alias names, lawlessness, and immorality, and there he and his money were soon parted.

Onesimus was in big trouble, for he was guilty of two capital crimes: running away and theft. They were capital because they were sins against the existing social order. If allowed to spread, they would mean the demise of slavery and the Roman Empire, for the Empire was built on slavery. Rebellious slaves, if not eliminated, were at least branded on the forehead with F for *Fugitivus* (Fugitive) or CF for *Cave Furem* (Beware of thief!). Onesimus theoretically could have gotten both, if his master was in a *good* mood.

Almost contemporary to this letter to Philemon, Pedanius Secundus, a wealthy Roman, was murdered by one of his 400 slaves. During the trial, Tacitus reports, the prosecution argued for the execution of all 400 slaves.

The prosecution won, and the 400 were publicly executed as an example.[2] In the hands of a cruel master, Onesimus could have been subjected to a cruel death. Onesimus was in immense trouble. Slave hunters, with descriptions and warrants in hand, often mixed among the transient population of Rome.[3] It is very probable that Onesimus used a pseudonym and at times even disguised himself.

We do not know how he happened upon Paul. Perhaps he was down and out, heard Paul's name discussed, remembered his contact with Philemon, and sought him out for help. Whatever the case, he returned again and again and was truly converted! And his life was changed.

Mickey Cohen was one of the most infamous gangsters of the fifties, and something of a publicity hound. On one occasion he visited an evangelistic meeting and there showed an interest in Christ. Christian leaders, realizing that Cohen's conversion could have a great influence upon others, visited him regularly. One night after a lengthy conversation on Revelation 3:20, he "opened the door of his life." There were great expectations, but as the months passed there was no substantive change in the gangster's life. Finally his Christian friends confronted him. Cohen responded that "no one had told him he would have to give up his work or his friends. After all, there were Christian football players, Christian cowboys, Christian politicians; why not a Christian gangster?"[4]

Onesimus was not like that. Christ was everything to him, and he was totally transformed. Soon he became one of Paul's devoted disciples, doing whatever he could to ease his imprisonment—running errands, doing manual labor to help with expenses, counseling others. As Onesimus grew, the conviction that he must return to Philemon also grew. Perhaps he had heard of the Lord's words from the Sermon on the Mount: "So if you are offering your gift at the altar and there remember that your brother has something against you, leave your gift there before the altar and go. First be reconciled to your brother, and then come and offer your gift" (Matthew 5:23, 24). Onesimus determined to make things right.

A perfect opportunity presented itself, for Tychicus, another of Paul's disciples, was planning to depart for Asia as bearer of the letters Paul was writing to the churches in Colossae and Laodicea. When Onesimus indicated an interest in returning, Paul included a brief letter to Philemon on his behalf, which a no less hostile critic than Ernest Renan called "a true little masterpiece of letter writing." The letter to Philemon was the most brilliantly nuanced, compelling letter of reconciliation in ancient history. It is a model of grace and charm. As such, it can be a great help to us all if we care to enhance our human relationships—especially those in the Body of Christ, where we have special stake in each other's lives.

Paul's Approach to Reconciliation: Strategy

In light of the magnitude of Paul's apostolic office, he could have assumed a Jimmy Cagney stance: "See here, Phil, this is Paul writing, the Boss Apostle. I've got this guy here, Onesimus, and he's converted and he's swell. So don't give him any trouble, see. If you do, I'll be over to see you. We have a little Latin saying here in Rome for people who don't go along with the program. It begins with *Jerkus*. You can fill in the rest. Now you wouldn't want that said about you, would you? So get with the program. So long, pal. Paulus Maximus." That was not Paul's way, nor is it ever the Christian way!

Notice Paul's tact. First, in verses 1–3 he cheerfully greeted Philemon and family by name, calling him "brother" (NASB) and his wife "sister" and their son a "fellow soldier."

Second, he *sincerely* complimented Philemon in verses 4–7.

I thank my God always when I remember you in my prayers. (v. 4)

. . . because I hear of your love and of the faith that you have toward the Lord Jesus and for all the saints. (v. 5)

For I have derived much joy and comfort from your love, my brother, because the hearts of the saints have been refreshed through you. (v. 7)

Next, in verses 8, 9, Paul affirmed that his attitude was not dictatorial. He appealed to Philemon "for love's sake" (v. 9), and love cannot be compelled. In addition, he mentioned that he was both aged and in jail, thus further appealing to Philemon's sympathy.

Lastly, as he got to his point in verses 10, 11, Paul used some unexpected humor by making a pun on Onesimus's name, which meant "*useful*": "I appeal to you for my child, Onesimus, whose father I became in my imprisonment. (Formerly he was useless to you, but now he is indeed useful to you and to me.)." There was undoubtedly a twinkle in Paul's eye, some playfulness. Paul was 179 words into his letter of 460 words, and this was the first mention of Onesimus, the main subject, and it was with a gracious lightness.

Paul's masterful approach to Philemon provides us with needed wisdom in dealing with our own relational problems. His example teaches us that fundamental to human reconciliation is taking the time to reflect on where people are: how they are feeling, how they perceive the problem, how they think we perceive them. We, above all people, ought to understand the secrets of human personality. Christian sensitivity is fundamental to reconciliation in human relationships.

Also, we must learn to choose our words carefully. Some people never give a compliment without a negative barb—"backhanded compliments." But Solomon says, "Like apples of gold in settings of silver is a word spoken in right circumstances" (Proverbs 25:11, NASB). Human reconciliation runs on loving tact, something every Christian should master regardless of personality or position.

Next, in his attempt to effect reconciliation, Paul described to Philemon his own *intimate* relationship with Onesimus. We see this in several key words prudently sprinkled throughout the letter. They are powerful, emotive nouns: "*child*," "*heart*," and "*brother*" (vv. 10, 12, 16). In verse 10 he said, "I appeal to you for my child, Onesimus, whose father I became in my imprisonment." Paul describes Onesimus as his *child*, thus calling to mind one of the most precious and intimate of human relationships. Paul was bonded to Onesimus.

Paul reached for an equally strong expression in verse 12 when he said, "I am sending him back to you, sending my very heart." The Greek word for "heart" is not the normal *kardia*, from which we get such words as *cardiac*, but an entirely different word that includes the idea of the feelings and compassion. Paul says, "I am sending you part of myself. That is how I feel about Onesimus."

Lastly, in verse 16 Paul used another emotive term in describing him as "a beloved brother." The apostle could hardly be more forceful. *Onesimus was his child, his heart, his brother!* From this we learn an indispensable canon for building relationships: reconciliation and its cousins—intimacy, closeness, and fellowship—thrive when believers are able to express their true feelings. We think that others know how we feel when, in fact, they have not the slightest idea. If Paul had said he loved Onesimus, it would have indicated *something* of how he felt. But his choice of language left no doubt in Philemon's mind. This was a great step toward reconciliation.

Next, we observe briefly that Paul's approach was *positive*, as we see in verse 21 where he said to Philemon, "Confident of your obedience, I write to you, knowing that you will do even more than I say." Paul believed in Philemon, and thus he expected good things to happen. I once heard George Sweeting say that optimism is when an eighty-five-year-old man marries a thirty-five-year-old woman and they move into a five-bedroom house next to a grade school! Here Paul was optimistic, and he expected good things to happen.

Paul let Philemon know that he believed in him. And Paul's positive faith did more for Philemon than a thousand queries and doubts could ever do. Faced with a tough relational situation? Pray and believe God for the best. You will be pleasantly surprised with the result.

In the same positive vein, in verses 15, 16 Paul tantalized Philemon with the potential soul-satisfying relationship that awaited him and Onesimus: "For this perhaps is why he was parted from you for a while, that you might have him back forever, no longer as a bondservant but more than a bondservant, as a beloved brother—especially to me, but how much more to you, both in the flesh and in the Lord."

Onesimus was a double brother to Philemon "in the flesh and in the Lord." This is something of what Abraham Lincoln had in mind when he answered Thaddeus Stevens, who was demanding destruction of the enemy at the end of the Civil War. "Mr. Stevens," said Lincoln, "do I not destroy my enemy when I make him my friend?" Reconciliation makes our enemy our friend, perhaps even our intimate friend.

Finally note Paul's promise to pay all expenses for Onesimus, coupled with the assertion that Philemon "owed" him. "If he has wronged you at all, or owes you anything, charge that to my account. I, Paul, write this with my own hand: I will repay it—to say nothing of your owing me even your own self. Yes, brother, I want some benefit from you in the Lord. Refresh my heart in Christ" (vv. 18–20). At this point Paul actually took the pen from his secretary and wrote the equivalent of a first-century IOU with his own hand. He "put his money where his mouth was." Indeed, according to Roman law he was liable to Philemon for the loss of work suffered[5]—not that he thought Philemon would really try to collect. Here again Paul's humor sparkled with another pun, for in verse 20 the word translated "benefit" had the same root as "Onesimus." He is saying, "Onesimus is your benefit or profit. So now, Philemon, you be my Onesimus, my benefit."

Paul's Approach to Reconciliation: Success

Putting it all together, consider Paul's gentle, artful tact with its cheerful greeting, his sincere compliments to Philemon, his loving attitude, his playful puns, and then Paul's description of his bond with his *child*, his *heart*, his *brother*. He really let Philemon know how he felt about Onesimus. Next came his positive expectation regarding Philemon's actions.

> High Heaven rejects the lore,
> Of nicely calculated less and more.[6]

Then came his tantalizing presentation of what would happen if they were reconciled, and finally his absurd offer to pay if necessary, along with the humorous reminder that Philemon "owed" him. Who could resist this, especially when it was read to the whole church (v. 2) while Philemon and Onesimus stood before them?

Surely forgiveness flowed! There were undoubtedly repeated embraces and kisses, Onesimus's repeated confessions, and Philemon's constant response, "That is enough, my dear brother!" As the church watched, there was constant praising of God.

Was this the end of the story? Surely not. Onesimus and Philemon went on to lead even more productive lives for Christ. Many believe that Philemon, in deference to Paul's expressed desire to have Onesimus back (vv. 13, 14, 20), returned him to Paul in Rome, where he further developed into a great man of God. The historical evidence is most suggestive of this. Fifty years later when Ignatius, one of the great Christian martyrs, was being transported from Antioch to Rome to be executed, he wrote letters to certain churches. In writing to Ephesus he praised their Bishop Onesimus, even making the *same* Pauline pun on his name! It appears likely that Onesimus, the runaway slave, had become, with the passing of years, the great Bishop of Ephesus.[7] This is one of the great stories of the gospel and of the Church—a jewel in her crown.

Think of what God did to secure Onesimus's reconciliation. Paul alluded to it in verse 15: "For this perhaps is why he was parted from you for a while, that you might have him back forever." Paul recognized that Philemon's whole story was ultimately woven by God's hand. Onesimus's crime and flight were made to become, by God's grace, part of the plan for bringing Onesimus to himself—much as Joseph's being sold into Egypt by his brothers eventually brought their salvation. The more we study the story, the more we see that it transcends "chance." Onesimus fled the length of the world to escape his master and lose himself in the bowels of Rome, only to meet the very man to whom his master owed his spiritual life—and thus found spiritual life himself! How he must have marveled at God's tapestry.

The most confused, twisted life can ultimately come to be seen as a marvelous tapestry of God's grace. The evil that you did, or has been done to you, can be turned into the very thing that brings you to Christ. Onesimus is indeed "profitable," for from his life we learn the anatomy of reconciliation.

Soli Deo gloria.

Notes

PHILIPPIANS

Chapter One: A Particular Joy

1. Frank Thielman, *Philippians*, The NIV Application Commentary (Grand Rapids, MI: Zondervan, 1995), p. 24.

2. Markus Bockmuehl, *The Epistle to the Philippians*, Black's New Testament Commentary (London: A & C Black Limited, 1998), p. 3.

3. Peter T. O'Brien, *Commentary on Philippians*, New International Greek Testament Commentary (Grand Rapids, MI: Eerdmans, 1991), p. 4.

4. Bockmuehl, *The Epistle to the Philippians*, p. 4.

5. Ibid., pp. 9, 10.

6. Ibid., p. 15.

7. Thielman, *Philippians*, p. 18.

8. Bockmuehl, *The Epistle to the Philippians*, p. 32.

9. O'Brien, *Commentary on Philippians*, p. 38.

10. Moisés Silva, *Philippians*, 2nd ed., Baker Exegetical Commentary on the New Testament (Grand Rapids, MI: Baker Academic, 1992, 2005), p. 39.

11. Karl Barth, *Epistle to the Philippians*, trans. James W. Leitch (Louisville: Westminster/John Knox, 2002), p. 9.

12. Bockmuehl, *The Epistle to the Philippians*, p. 50.

13. Ibid., p. 41.

Chapter Two: Paul's Joyous Thanksgiving

1. Tony Payne, ed., *D. Broughton Knox, Selected Works*, vol. 1 (New South Wales, Australia: Matthias Media, 2000), p. 58.

2. Ibid.

3. Gordon D. Fee, *Paul's Letter to the Philippians*, The New International Commentary on the New Testament (Grand Rapids, MI: Eerdmans, 1995), p. 80.

4. Moisés Silva, *Philippians*, 2nd ed., Baker Exegetical Commentary on the New Testament (Grand Rapids, MI: Baker Academic, 1992, 2005), p. 42, writes:

> It is the intensity of Paul's emotion that accounts for the syntax; it also accounts for the fourfold recurrence of *pas* (in the forms *pase* [two times], *pantote*, and *panton*), for the apparent emphasis on joy (*meta charas*), and for the forcefulness of subsequent expressions (from the first day; being persuaded).

5. Markus Bockmuehl, *The Epistle to the Philippians*, Black's New Testament Commentary (London: A & C Black Limited, 1998), p. 59.

6. Ibid.

7. Frank Thielman, *Philippians*, The NIV Application Commentary (Grand Rapids, MI: Zondervan, 1995), p. 38.

8. Silva, *Philippians*, p. 43, writes:

Meyer perceptively emphasizes that the constancy of the Philippians' commitment to the gospel "is the very thing which not only supplies the motive for the apostle's thankfulness, but forms also the ground of his just confidence for the future."

9. Fee, *Paul's Letter to the Philippians*, p. 13.

10. Payne, ed., *D. Broughton Knox, Selected Works*, pp. 60, 61.

11. Fee, *Paul's Letter to the Philippians*, p. 85.

12. Bockmuehl, *The Epistle to the Philippians*, p. 62.

13. Silva, *Philippians*, p. 45.

Chapter Three: Paul's Joyful Affection

1. Fred B. Craddock, *Philippians: INTERPRETATION*, A Bible Commentary for Teaching and Preaching (Atlanta: John Knox Press, 1985), p. 18 mentions the passionate affection of Paul for his people in Romans 9:1–5 as a possible exception. But that is about his passion for his people, the Jews, not a church.

2. Peter T. O'Brien, *Commentary on Philippians*, New International Greek Testament Commentary (Grand Rapids, MI: Eerdmans, 1991), p. 68, explains:

Καπδια is employed in its customary OT sense of the whole person to describe the seat of the physical, spiritual, and mental life. It denotes the center and source of both physical life (Pss. 101:5; 103:15; Acts 14:17) and the whole inner life with its thinking (2 Cor. 4:6; Eph. 1:18), feelings or emotions (Rom. 1:24; 9:2; 2 Cor. 2:4, etc.), and volition (2 Cor. 9:7).

3. Gordon D. Fee, *Paul's Letter to the Philippians*, The New International Commentary on the New Testament (Grand Rapids, MI: Eerdmans, 1995), p. 91.

4. Markus Bockmuehl, *The Epistle to the Philippians*, Black's New Testament Commentary (London: A & C Black Limited, 1998), p. 64.

5. Fee, *Paul's Letter to the Philippians*, p. 92, explains:

There can be little question that the first phrase, "in my chains," refers to Paul's present imprisonment. Here is the first mention of the "suffering" motif, which surfaces throughout this letter, and probably carries more significance than many interpreters are ready to allow. Although "chains" could possibly be a metonymy for imprisonment as such, most likely Paul was literally chained to his guards. The way this similar idea is expressed in 2 Tim 2:9 makes it difficult to imagine anything other than literal chains in that case. Probably the same is true here, since in Roman prisons "imprisonment without chains was a concession to high status." In any case, the repetition of the phrase, "my chains," in vv. 13, 14, and 17 indicates that he is smarting under the imprisonment, in part perhaps because he is not free to roam about.

6. O'Brien, *Commentary on Philippians*, p. 69.

7. J. A. Motyer, *Philippian Studies: The Richness of Christ* (Downers Grove, IL: InterVarsity Press, 1966), p. 26.

Chapter Four: Paul's Prayer

1. D. A. Carson, *Basics for Believers: An Exposition of Philippians* (Grand Rapids, MI: Baker, 1996), p. 20.

2. *Bengel's New Testament Commentary, Vol. 2: Romans—Revelation*, trans. Charlton T. Lewis and Marvin R. Vincent (Grand Rapids, MI: Kregel, 1981), p. 426.

3. F. J. Sheed, *Theology and Sanity* (New York: Sheed & Ward, 1946), pp. 9, 10.

4. Peter T. O'Brien, *Commentary on Philippians*, New International Greek Testament Commentary (Grand Rapids, MI: Eerdmans, 1991), p. 76.

5. Markus Bockmuehl, *The Epistle to the Philippians*, Black's New Testament Commentary (London: A & C Black Limited, 1998), p. 67.

6. O'Brien, *Commentary on Philippians*, pp. 76, 77.

7. Earl F. Palmer, *Integrity: A Commentary on the Book of Philippians* (Vancouver: Regent, 1992), p. 53.

8. Bockmuehl, *The Epistle to the Philippians*, p. 68.

9. Ibid.

10. Marvin R. Vincent, *A Critical and Exegetical Commentary on the Epistles to the Philippians and to Philemon*, The International Critical Commentary (Edinburgh: T. & T. Clark, 1897), p. 14, explains:

εἰς, not 'till,' as A.V., but 'for,' 'against,' as those who are preparing for it. For this sense of εἰς, comp. ii. 16; Eph. iv. 30; 2 Tim. i. 12.

11. Bockmuehl, *The Epistle to the Philippians*, p. 68.

12. See 1 Corinthians 1:7, 8; Colossians 1:12; 1 Thessalonians 3:13; 2 Thessalonians 1:10–12.

13. Bockmuehl, *The Epistle to the Philippians*, p. 68.

14. O'Brien, *Commentary on Philippians*, p. 78. See also Moisés Silva, *Philippians*, 2nd ed., Baker Exegetical Commentary on the New Testament (Grand Rapids, MI: Baker Academic, 1992, 2005), p. 51.

15. Ibid., p. 80.

16. John Piper, *Desiring God* (Portland: Multnomah, 1986), p. 42.

Chapter Five: The Gospel First!

1. Peter T. O'Brien and David G. Peterson, eds., *God Who Is Rich in Mercy: Essays Presented to Dr. D. B. Knox* (NSW, Australia: Lancer Books, 1986), p. 229.

2. Peter T. O'Brien, *Commentary on Philippians*, New International Greek Testament Commentary (Grand Rapids, MI: Eerdmans, 1991), p. 94.

3. D. A. Carson, *Basics for Believers: An Exposition of Philippians* (Grand Rapids, MI: Baker, 1996), p. 23. Carson's pertinent reference to the "Auca five" inspired me to share my personal account.

4. O'Brien, *Commentary on Philippians*, p. 99, n. 4.

5. Ibid.

6. Henry Fairlie, *The Seven Deadly Sins* (Notre Dame, IN: Notre Dame Press, 1979), p. 79.

7. O'Brien, *Commentary on Philippians*, p. 101, explains:

They recognize that he has been 'set' for that defence by God. χειμαι, originally a military term, here indicates that Paul is under orders, issued by God. There is therefore no sense of divine disfavour in his captivity. Quite the reverse. Because he has been divinely appointed for the defence of the gospel, his captivity is entirely understandable. They are not embarrassed or put off by his bonds.

8. Markus Bockmuehl, *The Epistle to the Philippians*, Black's New Testament Commentary (London: A & C Black Limited, 1998), p. 80.

9. John R. Claypool, *The Preaching Event* (Waco, TX: Word, 1980), p. 68.

10. O'Brien, *Commentary on Philippians*, p. 102.

11. Carson, *Basics for Believers*, pp. 25, 26.

12. Ibid., pp. 26, 27. Note: Here I have taken Carson's more specific observation based on the experience of Dr. Paul Hiebert and given it general application.

13. Charles Colson, *Kingdoms in Conflict: An Insider's Challenging View of Politics, Power, and the Pulpit* (New York: William Morrow and Grand Rapids, MI: Zondervan, 1987); Marvin Olasky, *Abortion Rites: A Social History of Abortion in America* (Wheaton, IL: Crossway Books, 1992); Marvin Olasky, *The Tragedy of American Compassion* (Wheaton, IL: Crossway Books, 1992).

Chapter Six: Paul's Joyous Confidence

1. Peter T. O'Brien, *Commentary on Philippians*, New International Greek Testament Commentary (Grand Rapids, MI: Eerdmans, 1991), p. 110.

2. Frank Thielman, *Philippians*, The NIV Application Commentary (Grand Rapids, MI: Zondervan, 1995), p. 76, explains:

The word "help" (*epichoregia*) in the NIV rendering of verse 19 can also mean "supply" and is closely related to a Greek verb that means to "furnish, provide, give, grant," and less frequently, "support." Paul used this verb in Galatians 3:5 to speak of God as the one who has "given" his Spirit to the Galatians. It seems likely, then, that here in Philippians 1:19 the word does not mean the help that the Spirit gives to Paul but the Spirit himself, whom God supplies to Paul. This supply of the Spirit, moreover, is more closely tied to the prayers of the Philippians than the NIV implies. In the Greek text, one definite article stands in front of both "prayers" and "supply" so that the phrase runs, literally, "through the prayer [the term is singular in Greek] of you and supply of the Spirit of Jesus Christ." Paul is suggesting that the presence of the Spirit will be supplied to Paul through the prayers of the Philippians. In some mysterious way, those prayers are linked with God's furnishing of the Spirit to him, and together they provide the help he needs to face the Roman tribunal with courage.

3. Ibid., p. 82.

4. Markus Bockmuehl, *The Epistle to the Philippians*, Black's New Testament Commentary (London: A & C Black Limited, 1998), p. 83.

5. Ibid., p. 84.

6. Thielman, *Philippians*, pp. 76, 77.

7. William Barclay, *The Letters to the Philippians, Colossians, and Thessalonians*, The Daily Study Bible (Philadelphia: The Westminster Press, 1957), p. 32.

8. D. D. Hastings, ed., *The Speaker's Bible*, vol. 16 (Grand Rapids, MI: Baker, 1971), p. 37.

9. *Hymns for the Living Church* (Carol Stream, IL: Hope Publishing Company, 1981), No. 384.

10. Hastings, ed., *The Speaker's Bible*, vol. 16, p. 38.

11. Arthur W. Pink, *The Seven Sayings of the Saviour on the Cross* (Grand Rapids, MI: Baker, 1958), p. 110.

12. J. A. Motyer, *Philippian Studies: The Richness of Christ* (Downers Grove, IL: InterVarsity Press, 1966), p. 54.

13. Ibid., p. 55.

14. Thielman, *Philippians*, p. 80.

Chapter Seven: Worthy Citizens

1. James Montgomery Boice, *Philippians*, An Expositional Commentary (Grand Rapids, MI: Zondervan, 1971), p. 100.

2. Gordon D. Fee, *Paul's Letter to the Philippians*, The New International Commentary on the New Testament (Grand Rapids, MI: Eerdmans, 1995), p. 162.

3. Markus Bockmuehl, *The Epistle to the Philippians*, Black's New Testament Commentary (London: A & C Black Limited, 1998), p. 98.

4. Fee, *Paul's Letter to the Philippians*, p. 157.

5. Bockmuehl, *The Epistle to the Philippians*, p. 101.

6. Fee, *Paul's Letter to the Philippians*, pp. 164–166 makes four cogent arguments for this referring to the Holy Spirit.

7. Stephen E. Ambrose, *Comrades* (New York: Simon & Schuster, 1999), pp. 105, 106.

8. Peter T. O'Brien, *Commentary on Philippians*, New International Greek Testament Commentary (Grand Rapids, MI: Eerdmans, 1991), pp. 152, 153.

9. D. A. Carson, *Basics for Believers: An Exposition of Philippians* (Grand Rapids, MI: Baker, 1996), p. 55.

10. Frank Thielman, *Philippians*, The NIV Application Commentary (Grand Rapids, MI: Zondervan, 1995), p. 89, quoting *The Boston Globe* (July 6, 1994), p. 8.

11. O'Brien, *Commentary on Philippians*, p. 158.

12. Karl Barth, *Epistle to the Philippians*, trans. James W. Leitch (Louisville: Westminster/John Knox, 2002), p. 49.

13. John Calvin, *The Epistles of Paul the Apostle to the Galatians, Ephesians, Philippians and Colossians*, Calvin's Commentaries, trans. T. H. L. Parker (Grand Rapids, MI: Eerdmans, 1965), p. 243.

Chapter Eight: Living Worthily in the Church

1. J. Dwight Pentecost, *The Joy of Living: A Study of Philippians* (Grand Rapids, MI: Zondervan, 1973), p. 55.

2. Leslie Flynn, *Great Church Fights* (Wheaton, IL: Victor, 1976), p. 53.

3. Earl F. Palmer, *Integrity: A Commentary on the Book of Philippians* (Vancouver: Regent College Publishing, 1992), p. 86.

4. Peter T. O'Brien, *Commentary on Philippians*, New International Greek Testament Commentary (Grand Rapids, MI: Eerdmans, 1991), p. 179, explains:

> το ε φπονουντες (which stands in a chiastic relationship with ινα το αυτο φρονητε) is to be rendered 'intent on one purpose' and speaks of a life directed towards a single goal. το εν describes the one aim on which the readers ought to focus. K. Barth may be right when he claims that 'the concrete details are all hidden from us'. But in the light of : (1) the orientation of both Paul and the proclamation of Christ (vv. 14–18), (2) the suggestion that 'living worthily of the gospel' (1:27) is a comprehensive admonition that stands as a heading to the whole section 1:27—2:18 (styled 'The Situation of the Philippians'), and (3) the subsequent exhortations, it is possible to state what this goal is. το ε φπονουντες focuses on the need for the members of the congregation to be 'gospel oriented' as they relate to and care for one another.

5. Markus Bockmuehl, *The Epistle to the Philippians*, Black's New Testament Commentary (London: A & C Black Limited, 1998), p. 110.

6. Barbara W. Tuchman, *The Proud Tower, A Portrait of the World Before the War 1890–1914* (New York: Macmillan, 1966), p. 193.

7. Paul Johnson, *Intellectuals* (New York: Harper/Collins, 1988), p. 10.

8. Bockmuehl, *The Epistle to the Philippians*, pp. 110, 111.

9. Marvin R. O'Connell, *Blaise Pascal: Reasons of the Heart* (Grand Rapids, MI: Eerdmans, 1997), p. xii.

10. Bockmuehl, *The Epistle to the Philippians*, p. 114.

11. D. A. Carson, *Basics for Believers: An Exposition of Philippians* (Grand Rapids, MI: Baker, 1996), p. 60.

12. Bockmuehl, *The Epistle to the Philippians*, p. 114.

Chapter Nine: The Self-Humiliation of Christ

1. Leon Morris, *The Gospel According to John* (Grand Rapids, MI: Eerdmans, 1971), p. 616.

2. C. K. Barrett, *The Gospel According to St John* (London: S.P.C.K., 1975), pp. 366, 367.

3. Charles R. Swindoll, *Improving Your Serve: The Art of Unselfish Living* (Nashville: Word, 1981), pp. 94, 95.

4. Markus Bockmuehl, *The Epistle to the Philippians*, Black's New Testament Commentary (London: A & C Black Limited, 1998), p. 105.

5. Frank Thielman, *Philippians*, The NIV Application Commentary (Grand Rapids, MI: Zondervan, 1995), p. 115, explains:

> Paul says literally, however, "Think this in you," and the words "in you" (*en hymin*) are a common idiom in Greek for "among yourselves." Paul's primary concern, then, is social rather than cerebral: He wants the Philip-

pians to adopt in their mutual relations the same attitude that characterized Jesus.

6. J. A. Motyer, *Philippian Studies: The Richness of Christ* (Downers Grove,
IL: InterVarsity Press, 1966), p. 73.

7. John Calvin, *The Epistles of Paul the Apostle to the Galatians, Ephesians,
Philippians and Colossians*, Calvin's Commentaries, trans. T. H. L. Parker (Grand
Rapids, MI: Eerdmans, 1965), p. 247.

8. Peter T. O'Brien, *Commentary on Philippians*, New International Greek Testament Commentary (Grand Rapids, MI: Eerdmans, 1991), p. 216.

9. Ibid., p. 217, explains:

The meaning of εαυτό εκενωσεν is defined more precisely in the two par-
ticipial phrases that follow, namely μορφην δουλου λαβων ('taking the
form of a slave') and εν ομοιωματι ανθρωπων γενομενος ('being found
in human form'). The first three lines of v. 7 (7a, 7b, and 7c) should be
taken together. . . . V. 7b and c are formed in a parallel fashion to explicate
the main clause in v. 7a (εαυτό εκενωσεν), since the two aorist participles
λαβων and γενομενος are coincident with the finite verb εκενωσεν and
both are modal, describing the manner in which Christ 'emptied himself.'

10. Bockmuehl, *The Epistle to the Philippians*, p. 134.

11. O'Brien, *Commentary on Philippians*, pp. 225, 226.

12. J. B. Phillips, *New Testament Christianity* (New York: Macmillan, 1956),
p. 15.

13. O'Brien, *Commentary on Philippians*, p. 227.

14. Karl Barth, *Epistle to the Philippians*, trans. James W. Leitch (Louisville:
Westminster/John Knox, 2002), p. 64.

15. Bockmuehl, *The Epistle to the Philippians*, p. 138.

16. O'Brien, *Commentary on Philippians*, p. 231.

17. Bockmuehl, *The Epistle to the Philippians*, p. 139.

18. Calvin, *The Epistles of Paul the Apostle to the Galatians, Ephesians, Philippians and Colossians*, p. 249.

Chapter Ten: Christ's Super-Exaltation

1. James Montgomery Boice, *Philippians: An Expositional Commentary*
(Grand Rapids, MI: Zondervan, 1971), p. 160.

2. Peter T. O'Brien, *Commentary on Philippians*, New International Greek Testament Commentary (Grand Rapids, MI: Eerdmans, 1991), p. 238, explains:

The name (το ονομα is definite) greater than any other that God conferred
on Jesus as a gracious gift (εκαρισατο) is his own name, κυριος ('Lord'),
in its most sublime sense, that designation used in the LXX to represent the
personal name of the God of Israel, that is, *Yahweh*. The reasons for interpreting το ονομα as κυριος are: (1) in the ινα clause of vv. 10–11, which is
subordinate to the main clause in v. 9, Jesus is identified with κυριος (Yahweh), the one to whom universal homage is given (Is. 45:23); (2) it is best

to regard τω "Iησου and το ονομα το υππερ παν óoμα as juxtaposed; (3) for a Jew like Paul the superlative name was 'Yahweh.' Since the phrase in v. 10 can mean 'the name of Jesus' it is best to understand it as referring to the name 'Yahweh'; and (4) κυριος gives a symmetry to the hymn: θεος (2:6) becomes δουλος (v. 7) and is exalted to be κυριος (v. 11).

3. Ibid.

4. Frank Thielman, *Philippians*, The NIV Application Commentary (Grand Rapids, MI: Zondervan, 1995), p. 120.

5. O'Brien, *Commentary on Philippians*, p. 238.

6. Markus Bockmuehl, *The Epistle to the Philippians*, Black's New Testament Commentary (London: A & C Black Limited, 1998), p. 147.

7. O'Brien, *Commentary on Philippians*, p. 251.

Chapter Eleven: On Common Salvation

1. Gordon D. Fee, *Paul's Letter to the Philippians*, The New International Commentary on the New Testament (Grand Rapids, MI: Eerdmans, 1995), pp. 232, 233, n. 14.

2. D. A. Carson, *Basics for Believers: An Exposition of Philippians* (Grand Rapids, MI: Baker, 1996), p. 62.

3. Marvin R. O'Connell, *Blaise Pascal: Reasons of the Heart* (Grand Rapids, MI: Eerdmans 1997), p. 154.

4. Markus Bockmuehl, *The Epistle to the Philippians*, Black's New Testament Commentary (London: A & C Black Limited, 1998), pp. 155, 156.

5. Ibid., p. 156.

6. Tom Wright, *Paul for Everyone* (London: SPCK and John Knox Press, 2004), p. 107.

7. Fee, *Paul's Letter to the Philippians*, p. 248, explains:

But what suggests evangelism as the ultimate intent of their "holding firm" the gospel is (a) the word order ("*the word of life* holding firm," immediately following "in the world"); (b) the unique language for the gospel, "word *of life*," which occurs only here in Paul, and makes very little sense if it does not carry the thrust of bringing life to others; and (c) the context of Dan 12:3, in which the second line in the Hebrew reads: "and those who bring many to righteousness (shall shine) as the stars for ever and ever." Thus, it is not some kind of defensive posture that is in view (as in, "hold the gospel fast so that the enemy does not take it away from you"), but evangelism, that they clean up their internal act so that they may thereby "hold firm" the gospel.

8. Ibid., p. 249.

9. Bockmuehl, *The Epistle to the Philippians*, p. 162.

10. Fee, *Paul's Letter to the Philippians*, p. 253.

Chapter Twelve: Timothy: One Who Seeks Others' Interests

1. Anthony Trollope, *Barchester Towers* (London: Thomas Nelson & Sons, Ltd., 1942), p. 570.

2. Peter T. O'Brien, *Commentary on Philippians*, New International Greek Testament Commentary (Grand Rapids, MI: Eerdmans, 1991), p. 318, explains:

ισοψυχος, a rare poetic word that is found nowhere else in the NT and only once in the LXX (Ps. 54:14 [E.T. 55:13]), means 'of like soul or mind.'

3. Markus Bockmuehl, *The Epistle to the Philippians*, Black's New Testament Commentary (London: A & C Black Limited, 1998), p. 165.

4. Ibid.

5. Gail MacDonald, *High Call, High Privilege* (Wheaton, IL: Tyndale House, 1984), p. 86.

6. Guy H. King, *Joy Way: An Expositional Study of Philippians* (Fort Washington, PA: Christian Literature Crusade, 1973), p. 70.

7. Tim Stafford, "God's Missionary to Us," *Christianity Today*, 40, no. 4 (December 9, 1996), p. 29.

8. Dietrich Bonhoeffer, *Life Together* (San Francisco: HarperOne, 1954), p. 99.

9. Bockmuehl, *The Epistle to the Philippians*, p. 164.

10. Stephen E. Ambrose, *Comrades* (New York: Simon & Schuster, 1999), pp. 106, 107.

Chapter Thirteen: A Man to Honor

1. Markus Bockmuehl, *The Epistle to the Philippians*, Black's New Testament Commentary (London: A & C Black Limited, 1998), p. 278, n. 31 records that this is the view of G. B. Caird, *Paul's Letters from Prison*, New Clarendon Bible (Oxford, UK: Oxford University Press, 1976), p. 129; F. F. Bruce, *Philippians*, New International Biblical Commentary, 2nd ed. (Peabody, MA: Hendrickson, 1989), p. 96; and Moisés Silva, *Philippians*, 2nd ed., Baker Exegetical Commentary on the New Testament (Grand Rapids, MI: Baker Academic, 1992, 2005), p. 161.

2. Earl F. Palmer, *Integrity: A Commentary on the Book of Philippians* (Vancouver: Regent College Publishing, 1992), pp. 118, 119 gives poignant application of the Vietnam experience.

3. Gordon D. Fee, *Paul's Letter to the Philippians*, The New International Commentary on the New Testament (Grand Rapids, MI: Eerdmans, 1995), p. 276.

4. Frank Thielman, *Philippians*, The NIV Application Commentary (Grand Rapids, MI: Zondervan, 1995), p. 154.

5. Ibid.

6. Fee, *Paul's Letter to the Philippians*, p. 276, explains:

Epaphroditus thus served as an "apostle," one sent on behalf of the congregation to perform a given task. That task is then expressed with a metaphor from the sacrificial system: he "performed a priestly duty" on their behalf "for Paul's needs."

7. J. Dwight Pentecost, *The Joy of Living: A Study of Philippians* (Grand Rapids, MI: Zondervan, 1973), p. 113.

8. Peter T. O'Brien, *Commentary on Philippians*, New International Greek Testament Commentary (Grand Rapids, MI: Eerdmans, 1991), p. 335.

9. Fee, *Paul's Letter to the Philippians*, p. 279.
10. O'Brien, *Commentary on Philippians*, p. 337.
11. Fee, *Paul's Letter to the Philippians*, p. 283.
12. Bockmuehl, *The Epistle to the Philippians*, p. 174, explains:

Once again, those who stake their ambition on the example of Christ in 2.6–11 will find themselves in conflict with the values and presuppositions of the secular path to power. By saying that it is people like Epaphroditus whom the Philippians should hold in honour (*entimous*), Paul at once contradicts Graeco-Roman society's pervasive culture of rewarding the upwardly mobile quest for prestige and public recognition (*philotimia*). The Church instead will prize and value those who aspire to the mind of Christ.

Chapter Fourteen: Rejoicing and Warning

1. D. A. Carson, *Basics for Believers: An Exposition of Philippians* (Grand Rapids, MI: Baker, 1996), p. 80.
2. Peter T. O'Brien, *Commentary on Philippians*, New International Greek Testament Commentary (Grand Rapids, MI: Eerdmans, 1991), p. 348, referencing M. E. Thrall, *Greek Particles in the New Testament: Linguistic and Exegetical Studies*, New Testament Tools and Studies, III (Leiden: E.J. Brill, 1962), p. 28.
3. William Barclay, *The Letters to the Philippians, Colossians, and Thessalonians*, The Daily Study Bible (Philadelphia: The Westminster Press, 1957), p. 64.
4. Markus Bockmuehl, *The Epistle to the Philippians*, Black's New Testament Commentary (London: A & C Black Limited, 1998), p. 181. Note the author's well-reasoned arguments for this view on pp. 180–182.
5. Matthew Henry, *Matthew Henry's Commentary on the Whole Bible*, vol. 2 (Old Tappan, NJ: Revell, n.d.), p. 1096.
6. Moisés Silva, *Philippians*, 2nd ed., Baker Exegetical Commentary on the New Testament (Grand Rapids, MI: Baker Academic, 1992, 2005), p. 147, explains:

Hawthorne follows the view that the opponents were non-Christian Jews, but this is highly unlikely, because it has not been characteristic of Jewish people to pressure Gentiles to be circumcised. Moreover, as we shall see, the view that the Philippians' opponents were Judaizers (Jewish Christians who insisted that Gentile Christians submit to the Mosaic law, including circumcision) fits very well the contents of chapter 3 as a whole.

7. O'Brien, *Commentary on Philippians*, p. 354.
8. Karl Barth, *Epistle to the Philippians*, trans. James W. Leitch (Louisville: Westminster/John Knox, 2002), p. 93.
9. Bockmuehl, *The Epistle to the Philippians*, p. 188.
10. Silva, *Philippians*, p. 148.
11. O'Brien, *Commentary on Philippians*, p. 357.
12. Silva, *Philippians*, p. 148.
13. J. A. Motyer, *Philippian Studies: The Richness of Christ* (Downers Grove, IL: InterVarsity Press, 1966), pp. 118, 119. I have borrowed this expression from the author and expanded on the following quotation:

He is their Divine Obsession, the central concern of a one-track mind and a one-theme tongue. It bespeaks a complete satisfaction in Him, an over-mastering appreciation of what He has done (Gal. 6:14; 1 Cor. 2:2), and an unremitting presentation of Him to the world as worthy of all praise. At the centre of the three characteristics of the people of God there is the One who alone is worthy to be central—for is He not the centre of all heaven (Rev. 5:6)?

14. John Calvin, *The Epistles of Paul the Apostle to the Galatians, Ephesians, Philippians and Colossians*, Calvin's Commentaries, trans. T. H. L. Parker (Grand Rapids, MI: Eerdmans, 1965), p. 269 defines flesh as follows:

For in the term 'flesh' he includes everything external in man that he could glory in, as will appear from the context: or, to express it briefly, he calls 'flesh' everything that is outside Christ.

Chapter Fifteen: From Reveling to Revulsion

1. Peter T. O'Brien, *Commentary on Philippians*, New International Greek Testament Commentary (Grand Rapids, MI: Eerdmans, 1991), p. 365, quoting P. Bonnard, *L'ÈpÓtre de saint Paul aux Philippiens, et l'ÈpÓtre aux Colossiens*, CNT (Neuchâtel, Switzerland, 1950).

2. Markus Bockmuehl, *The Epistle to the Philippians*, Black's New Testament Commentary (London: A & C Black Limited, 1998), p. 196, referencing K. G. Kuhn, vol. 3, *Theological Dictionary of the New Testament*, pp. 359–365.

3. Josephus, *Antiquities*, 13:288; 17:42; 18:15.

4. O'Brien, *Commentary on Philippians*, p. 374.

5. In ibid. O'Brien explains:

The testimony of the book of Acts to Paul's persecution of the church is not inconsistent with this evidence in his letters (note Gal. 1:23, where Paul cites the report of others about his persecuting activity). Luke himself recounts it (Acts 7:58; 8:1; 9:1–2), the resurrected Jesus calls Paul to account for it in his heavenly appearance outside Damascus (9:4–5; 22:7–8; 26:14–15, where διωκω is used). Ananias speaks of Paul's persecuting activity (9:13–14), as do Jews and Christians who heard Paul preach in the synagogues of Damascus (9:21). Finally, Paul himself mentions it in two of his defense speeches (22:4–5; 26:9–11).

6. Bockmuehl, *The Epistle to the Philippians*, p. 202.

7. O'Brien, *Commentary on Philippians*, p. 380.

8. Tom Wright, *Paul for Everyone: The Prison Letters* (London: SPCK Westminster/John Knox, 2002), p. 118.

9. O'Brien, *Commentary on Philippians*, pp. 384, 385.

10. John Calvin, *The Epistles of Paul the Apostle to the Galatians, Ephesians, Philippians and Colossians*, Calvin's Commentaries, trans. T. H. L. Parker (Grand Rapids, MI: Eerdmans, 1965), p. 273.

11. Bockmuehl, *The Epistle to the Philippians*, pp. 210, 211 and O'Brien, *Commentary on Philippians*, pp. 398, 399 argue, as does most recent scholarship, that *dia pisteos Christou* is a subjective genitive.

12. O'Brien, *Commentary on Philippians*, pp. 399, 400.

13. D. A. Carson, *Basics for Believers: An Exposition of Philippians* (Grand Rapids, MI: Baker, 1996), p. 86.

Chapter Sixteen: Paul's Desire to Know Christ Fully

1. Gordon D. Fee, *Paul's Letter to the Philippians*, The New International Commentary on the New Testament (Grand Rapids, MI: Eerdmans, 1995), pp. 326, 327.

2. Mike Mason, *The Mystery of Marriage* (Portland: Multnomah, 1985), p. 26.

3. Peter T. O'Brien, *Commentary on Philippians*, New International Greek Testament Commentary (Grand Rapids, MI: Eerdmans, 1991), p. 403 explains:

Clearly the apostle intends to explain what is meant by knowing Christ (γνωναι αυτον) through this entire phrase (την δυναμιν της αναστασεὤ . . . παθηματων αυτου), and while each expression draws attention to separate facets of knowing him (and thus may be isolated in order to clarify their meaning), they are nevertheless to be regarded as a single entity.

See also Markus Bockmuehl, *The Epistle to the Philippians*, Black's New Testament Commentary (London: A & C Black Limited, 1998), p. 214.

4. O'Brien, *Commentary on Philippians*, p. 404.

5. Fee, *Paul's Letter to the Philippians*, p. 331.

6. James DeForest Murch, *Christian Minister's Manual* (Cincinnati: Standard, 1965), p. 137.

7. Karl Barth, *Epistle to the Philippians*, trans. James W. Leitch (Louisville: Westminster/John Knox, 2002), p. 103, writes:

To know Easter means, for the person knowing it, as stringently as may be: to be implicated in the events of Good Friday—to enter into the form of his death, or whatever may be the translation of the sinister *symmorphizesthai*.

8. Ibid., p. 49.

9. O'Brien, *Commentary on Philippians*, p. 410.

10. D. A. Carson, *Basics for Believers: An Exposition of Philippians* (Grand Rapids, MI: Baker, 1996), p. 88.

Chapter Seventeen: One Thing I Do

1. Frank Thielman, *Philippians*, The NIV Application Commentary (Grand Rapids, MI: Zondervan, 1995), p. 193.

2. Peter T. O'Brien, *Commentary on Philippians*, New International Greek Testament Commentary (Grand Rapids, MI: Eerdmans, 1991), pp. 422, 423.

3. Thielman, *Philippians*, p. 202, n. 17.

4. Ibid., p. 195, n. 3. The ancient historian Herodotus (ca. 490–425 B.C.) describes a Persian regiment's pursuit of their Greek opponents this way:

The Persian horse, meaning to continue their old harassing tactics, had found the enemy gone from the position they had occupied during the last few days, and had ridden in *pursuit*. Now, *having overtaken* the retreating columns, they renewed their attacks with vigour (9.58; see Herodotus, *The Histories* [Hammondsworth, Middlesex, UK: Penguin Books, 1972], 600.

5. O'Brien, *Commentary on Philippians*, p. 427.
6. Ibid., p. 429.
7. Ibid., pp. 430, 431 explains:

Only the term βραβειον is taken directly from the athletic imagery of the games. However, in this context οχοπος clearly describes the finish line of the race on which the athlete intently fixes his gaze, and thus διωξω must be interpreted in the sense of 'run.' οχοπος ('goal, mark') appears only here in the NT, although the cognate verb οχοπεω turns up six times in all, including two instances in Philippians: 2:4; 3:17. The noun refers to that on which one fixes one's gaze, whether it be a target at which an archer may shoot, metaphorically a goal or marker that controls a person's life, or as here the marker at the conclusion of the race upon which the runner fixes his gaze.

8. Ibid., p. 431, n. 64.
9. Ibid., p. 432.
10. In N. T. Wright, *Paul for Everyone: The Prison Letters* (London: SPCK Westminster John Knox Press, 2002), p. 122 the author suggests the event and application on which I have elaborated.
11. Markus Bockmuehl, *The Epistle to the Philippians*, Black's New Testament Commentary (London: A & C Black Limited, 1998), p. 222, explains:

On balance, then, we find underlying this passage a doctrine of both the Spirit and the Church which is remarkably hopeful and robust: Paul trusts the Spirit to bring the Church to a knowledge of the truth, and to reveal to it the areas where its thinking is 'out of step' (cf. v. 16) with the 'pattern' (v. 17) of life in Christ.

12. Ibid.
13. "Eric Liddell," at http://wikipedia.org/wiki/Eric_Liddell; last accessed September 8, 2006.
14. "Eric Liddell," *A Sporting Nation*, BBC; http://bbc.co.uk/Scotland/sport scotland/asportingnation/?id=0019; last accessed September 14, 2006.
15. "Eric Liddell," http://wikipedia.org/wiki/Eric_Liddell.

Chapter Eighteen: Stand Firm
1. Gordon D. Fee, *Paul's Letter to the Philippians*, The New International Commentary on the New Testament (Grand Rapids, MI: Eerdmans, 1995), p. 364 explains: "Only here does Paul use the compound 'fellow-imitators' . . . most likely Paul is calling on them to join together in imitating him."

2. Earl F. Palmer, *Integrity: A Commentary on the Book of Philippians* (Vancouver, Canada: Regent College Publishing, 1992), p. 145.

3. Peter T. O'Brien, *Commentary on Philippians*, New International Greek Testament Commentary (Grand Rapids, MI: Eerdmans, 1991), p. 454 explains:

In four short expressions the apostle provides a frightening description of the destiny and character of these enemies. Each of the four statements contains no finite verb. They are intentionally abrupt, even staccato-like, with sharp contrasts between the subjects and predicates of the first three and a clearly implied contrast in the fourth. So the nouns τελος ('destiny'), θεος ('god'), and δοξα ('glory') are set over against απωλεια ('eternal destruction'), χοιλια ('belly'), and αισχυνη ('shame'), while the verb φρονεω, which has previously been used in a positive sense, now has the negative τα επγεια as its object.

4. Markus Bockmuehl, *The Epistle to the Philippians*, Black's New Testament Commentary (London: A & C Black Limited, 1998), pp. 230, 231.

5. William F. Buckley Jr., *Nearer, My God* (New York: Harcourt Brace & Co., 1997), p. 201.

6. Bockmuehl, *The Epistle to the Philippians*, p. 232.

7. O'Brien, *Commentary on Philippians*, p. 458.

8. Ibid., p. 464, explains:

This wonderful transformation, which the Saviour will effect at the *parousia*, is of 'our weak mortal bodies' (GNB): το σωμα being a collective singular. This noun is employed in a variety of ways in Paul, not only as the instrument of human experience and suffering (2 Cor. 4:10; Gal. 6:17; Phil. 1:20) or the organ of human activity (1 Cor. 6:20; Rom. 12:1), but also as almost synonymous with the whole personality, in effect designating man as a totality (Rom. 8:23; 12:1; 1 Cor. 6:13–20).

9. Murray J. Harris, *Raised Immortal* (London: Marshall, Morgan & Scott, 1984), p. 121.

10. Ibid., p. 108.

Chapter Nineteen: Garrisoned by Peace

1. Markus Bockmuehl, *The Epistle to the Philippians*, Black's New Testament Commentary (London: A & C Black Limited, 1998), p. 258.

2. *Bengel's New Testament Commentary, Vol. 2: Romans—Revelation*, trans. Charlton T. Lewis and Marvin R. Vincent (Grand Rapids, MI: Kregel, 1981), p. 445.

3. D. A. Carson, *Basics for Believers: An Exposition of Philippians* (Grand Rapids, MI: Baker, 1996), p. 101.

4. Bockmuehl, *The Epistle to the Philippians*, p. 241.

5. Peter T. O'Brien, *Commentary on Philippians*, New International Greek Testament Commentary (Grand Rapids, MI: Eerdmans, 1991), p. 481 explains:

The verb appears also in the middle voice, with the meaning 'take hold of together, assist': at Lk. 5:7 with reference to physical help, and here at Phil. 4:3 of the assistance Paul's colleague will give to Euodia and Syntyche in reconciling their differences. The use of this verb συλλαμβανου in Paul's appeal may suggest that the two women were already attempting to overcome their discord.

6. Bockmuehl, *The Epistle to the Philippians*, p. 243 explains:

Here, Paul employs two fresh sets of crisply memorable imperatives to bring to a point the moral and spiritual message of his letter—quite possibly in deliberate contrast to the factious spirit displayed by Euodia and Syntyche. The first (vv. 4–7) encourages the readers to find the source of their peace and joy in God alone, who in Christ is 'near' and sustains them in every circumstance.

7. Karl Barth, *Epistle to the Philippians*, trans. James W. Leitch (Louisville: Westminster/John Knox, 2002), p. 120.
8. Bockmuehl, *The Epistle to the Philippians*, p. 59.
9. Emile Cailliet, *Pascal: The Emergence of Genius* (New York: Harper & Brothers, 1961), pp. 131, 132, which quotes from *Mémorial de Pascal, Oeuvres*, v. 12, 3–7 which is quoted here in full:

In the year of Grace, 1654,
On Monday, 23rd of November, Feast of St. Clement, Pope and Martyr,
        and of others in the Martyrology,
Vigil of Saint Chrysogonus, Martyr, and others,
From about half past ten in the evening until about half past twelve
FIRE
God of Abraham, God of Isaac, God of Jacob, not of the philosophers
        and scholars.
Certitude. Certitude. Feeling. Joy. Peace.
God of Jesus Christ.
Deum meum et Deum vestrum.
"Thy God shall be my God."
Forgetfulness of the world and of everything, except God.
He is to be found only by the ways taught in the Gospel.
Greatness of the human soul.
"Righteous Father, the world hath not known Thee, but I have
        known Thee."
Joy, joy, joy, tears of joy.
I have separated myself from Him.
Derelinquerunt me fontem aquae vivae.
"My God, wilt Thou leave me?"
Let me not be separated from Him eternally.
"This is eternal life, that they might know Thee, the only true God, and the
        one whom Thou has sent, Jesus Christ."

Jesus Christ.
Jesus Christ.
I have separated myself from Him: I have fled from Him, denied Him,
    crucified Him.
Let me never be separated from Him.
We keep hold of Him only by the ways taught in the Gospel.
Renunciation, total and sweet.
Total submission to Jesus Christ and to my director.
Eternally in joy for a day's exercise on earth.
Non obliviscar sermons tuos. Amen.

10. Ibid., p. 133.
11. Lloyd John Ogilvie, *Let God Love You: A Strikingly Perceptive View of the Christian Life Style As Seen Through Paul's Letter to Philippian Believers* (Nashville: Word Books, 1974), p. 137.
12. Carson, *Basics for Believers*, p. 106.
13. O'Brien, *Commentary on Philippians*, p. 488.
14. A. W. Tozer, *Born After Midnight* (Harrisburg, PA: Christian Publications, 1959), pp. 119, 120.
15. George Dana Boardman, *The Ten Commandments* (Philadelphia: Judson Press, 1952), pp. 48, 49, who quotes in full from Hildebert of Tours, *Alpha et Omega, Magna Deus!* as translated by Herbert Kenaston.
16. John R. W. Stott, *Christian Counter-Culture* (Downers Grove, IL: InterVarsity, 1978), p. 164.
17. O'Brien, *Commentary on Philippians*, p. 496.
18. Bockmuehl, *The Epistle to the Philippians*, p. 248.
19. O'Brien, *Commentary on Philippians*, p. 495.

Chapter Twenty: Good Thoughts
1. John Milton, *Paradise Lost*, Book I, lines 255–263.
2. Cornelius Plantinga Jr., "Pray the Lord My Mind to Keep," *Christianity Today*, 49, no. 9 (August 10, 1998), p. 50.
3. Markus Bockmuehl, *The Epistle to the Philippians*, Black's New Testament Commentary (London: A & C Black Limited, 1998), p. 250.
4. Peter T. O'Brien, *Commentary on Philippians*, New International Greek Testament Commentary (Grand Rapids, MI: Eerdmans, 1991), p. 502.
5. Ibid., p. 503.
6. Bockmuehl, *The Epistle to the Philippians*, p. 251.
7. Ibid., p. 252.
8. Gordon D. Fee, *Paul's Letter to the Philippians*, The New International Commentary on the New Testament (Grand Rapids, MI: Eerdmans, 1995), p. 418.
9. O'Brien, *Commentary on Philippians*, p. 504.
10. Bockmuehl, *The Epistle to the Philippians*, p. 253.
11. Fee, *Paul's Letter to the Philippians*, p. 418.
12. Ibid.
13. R. Kent Hughes, *Set Apart: Calling a Worldly Church to a Godly Life* (Wheaton, IL: Crossway Books, 2003), pp. 51–74.

14. A. T. Robertson, *Paul's Joy in Christ* (Grand Rapids, MI: Baker, 1979), p. 242.

15. Lehman Strauss, *Devotional Studies in Philippians* (Neptune, NJ: Loizeaux Brothers, 1959), p. 228.

16. Earl F. Palmer, *Integrity: A Commentary on the Book of Philippians* (Vancouver, Canada: Regent College Publishing, 1992), pp. 114, 115 suggests the application that I have put into my own words.

17. O'Brien, *Commentary on Philippians*, p. 512.

Chapter Twenty-one: Content in Christ

1. Gordon D. Fee, *Paul's Letter to the Philippians*, The New International Commentary on the New Testament (Grand Rapids, MI: Eerdmans, 1995), p. 431.

2. Peter T. O'Brien, *Commentary on Philippians*, New International Greek Testament Commentary (Grand Rapids, MI: Eerdmans, 1991), p. 521.

3. Ibid.

4. Markus Bockmuehl, *The Epistle to the Philippians*, Black's New Testament Commentary (London: A & C Black Limited, 1998), p. 260.

5. Ibid.

6. Fee, *Paul's Letter to the Philippians*, p. 427.

7. Ibid., p. 433.

8. Bockmuehl, *The Epistle to the Philippians*, p. 261.

9. John Calvin, *The Epistles of Paul the Apostle to the Galatians, Ephesians, Philippians and Colossians*, Calvin's Commentaries, trans. T. H. L. Parker (Grand Rapids, MI: Eerdmans, 1965), p. 292.

10. Bockmuehl, *The Epistle to the Philippians*, p. 261 explains:

> The verb translated learned (pass. *mueô*) originally meant to be inducted into the secret rites of a Hellenistic mystery cult (so also 3 Macc. 2.30); but like other mystery terminology it had come to adopt a transferred and more general meaning, not least in mystical and philosophical discourse (e.g., Philo, *Cher.* 49; *Sacr.* 62; Josephus *C. Ap.* 2.267). Initiation in the metaphorical sense may still be intended, in which case Paul's point is that Christian contentment remains unintelligible to those outside and can only be 'learned' from the God of peace (4.7, 9). Contentment is indeed a quiet secret known and cherished only by the few.

11. O'Brien, *Commentary on Philippians*, p. 257.

> The preposition εv has been taken in an instrumental sense to denote personal agency (= 'through [him who strengthens me]'), but, while this is possible, it is probably better to understand the phrase in an incorporative sense, that is 'in vital union with the one who strengthens me,' with the implication that the One who so strengthens Paul is Christ.

Similarly, Bockmuehl, *The Epistle to the Philippians*, p. 262, and Fee, *Paul's Letter to the Philippians*, pp. 434, 435.

Chapter Twenty-two: Assurances for the Generous

1. William Maxwell, *All the Days and Nights* (New York: Alfred K. Knopf, 1995), p. 274.

2. Gordon D. Fee, *Paul's Letter to the Philippians*, The New International Commentary on the New Testament (Grand Rapids, MI: Eerdmans, 1995), p. 438, n. 7 explains:

> Gk. χαλως (cf. Acts 10:33), for which the American slang, "you did good," offers a literal, if ungrammatical, "translation." καλως is the adverb of the adjective χαλως, which variously means "good, beautiful, pleasant, noble, splendid." The English equivalent "well" would lose too much of the sense of the Greek. The NIV chose to keep the sense of the adverb, but did so at the expense of the verb; "it was good of you" seems a bit bland for the Greek idiom.

3. Peter T. O'Brien, *Commentary on Philippians*, New International Greek Testament Commentary (Grand Rapids, MI: Eerdmans, 1991), p. 534 explains:

> However, in the light of contemporary usage 'the entire phrase, χοινωνειν εις λολον δοσεως χαι λημψεως, is an idiomatic expression indicating friendship.' Marshall concludes his lengthy discussion: 'Paul then is drawing upon familiar notions of friendship to acknowledge the recent gift and to express his gratitude. Rather than pointing to tension or embarrassment on Paul's part over the gift, the language implies the opposite. It reflects a warm and lasting relationship. He not only receives the gift gladly as a sign of their continuing concern, but also recalls the mutual exchange of services and affection which they had shared in the past.'

4. Ibid., pp. 538, 539.

5. Fee, *Paul's Letter to the Philippians*, p. 451.

6. Tom Wright, *Paul for Everyone: The Prison Letters* (London: SPCK Westminster/John Knox, 2002), p. 137.

7. Leland Ryken, ed., *The Christian Imagination: The Practice of Faith in Literature and Writing* (Colorado Springs: Shaw, 2002), p. 351, which quotes from Robert Siegel, *The Well at the World's End: Poetry, Fantasy, and the Limits of the Expressible*.

8. Fee, *Paul's Letter to the Philippians*, p. 453.

9. Ibid., p. 453, n. 16.

10. Ibid., pp. 453, 454, n. 16.

> Gk. εν δοζη, which I take to be locative here (as with the following εν χπιστω Ἰησου), not meaning "in heaven" as such (which is rightly objected to by most scholars), but referring to the ineffable and eternal "glory" in which God dwells, as the context within which God lavishes his riches on his own in Christ Jesus.

11. William W. How, "We Give Thee but Thine Own," *Hymns for the Living Church* (Carol Stream, IL: Hope Publishing House, 1974), no. 507.

Chapter Twenty-three: A Fond Farewell

1. See 1:5, *koinōnia*; 1:7, *synkoinōnos*; 2:1, *koinōnia*; 3:10, *koinōnia*; 4:14, *synkoinōnos*; 4:15, *koinōeō*.

2. J. A. Motyer, *Philippian Studies: The Richness of Christ* (Downers Grove, IL: InterVarsity Press, 1966), p. 26.

3. Frederick Langbridge, *A Cluster of Quiet Thoughts* (London: The Religious Tract Society, 1896).

4. John Calvin, *The Epistles of Paul the Apostle to the Galatians, Ephesians, Philippians and Colossians*, Calvin's Commentaries, trans. T. H. L. Parker (Grand Rapids, MI: Eerdmans, 1965), p. 295.

5. Markus Bockmuehl, *The Epistle to the Philippians*, Black's New Testament Commentary (London: A & C Black Limited, 1998), p. 271 explains:

NA[27] and most modern translations end here. There is, however, excellent and widespread early textual support for a concluding Amen (incl. p[46] a A D ψ as well as the Majority text and ancient versions), which is also found in the King James Version. While public reading in liturgical contexts does appear to favour scribal addenda of this kind (cf. the variant readings at the end of most Pauline letters), the manuscript support in this case is exceptionally strong and much of the dissenting evidence less reliable (with the sole exception of *Codex Vaticanus*). If anything, the undisputed earlier use of *amen* in 4.20 makes a later scribal omission here more likely than an insertion. Paul himself can use Amen to conclude his letters (Gal. 6.18; cf. Rom. 16.27) or to lend weight to important theological assertions (e.g. Rom. 1.25; 9.5; 11.36; 15.33; Gal. 1.5; Phil. 4.20; cf. Eph. 3.21). On balance, therefore, we should follow those like O'Brien, Hawthorne and R. P. Martin who take the textual evidence in favour of retaining the word here.

COLOSSIANS

Chapter Twenty-four: The Celebration of the Church

1. Ralph P. Martin, *Colossians and Philemon*, The New Century Bible (London: Oliphants, Marshall, Morgan & Scott, 1978), pp. 18, 19. Dr. Martin says:

In the Colossian church we appear to be in touch with a meeting-place where the free-thinking Judaism of the dispersion and the speculative ideas of Greek mystery-religion are in close contact. Out of this interchange and fusion comes a syncretism, which is both theologically novel (bringing Christ into a hierarchy and a system) and ethically conditioned (advocating a rigorous discipline and an ecstatic visionary reward). On both counts, in Paul's eyes, it is a deadly danger to the incipient church.

2. Alexander Maclaren, *The Epistles of St. Paul to the Colossians and Philemon*, The Expositor's Bible (New York: A. C. Armstrong, 1903), p. 17.

3. Martin, *Colossians and Philemon*, p. 46.

4. Peter T. O'Brien, *Colossians, Philemon*, Word Biblical Commentary, vol. 44 (Waco, TX: Word, 1982), p. 5.

5. John I. Durham, *Proclamation and Presence: Old Testament Essays in Honour of Gwynne Henton Davies* (Atlanta: John Knox Press, 1970), pp. 275–277 observes that in two-thirds of the instances of *shalom* in the Old Testament it is the result of the presence of God.

6. Eduard Schweizer, *The Letter to the Colossians*, trans. Andrew Chester (Minneapolis: Augsburg, 1982), p. 30.

7. Martin, *Colossians and Philemon*, p. 47 where he lists as examples 1 Thessalonians 1:3; 5:8; Romans 5:1–5; Galatians 5:5, 6; Ephesians 1:15, 18; 4:2–5; Hebrews 6:10–12; 10:22–24; 1 Peter 3:8, 21, 22; and Barnabas i:4; xi:8; Polycarp iii:2, 3.

8. R. C. Lucas, *Fullness and Freedom* (Downers Grove, IL: InterVarsity, 1980), p. 27.

9. Warren Wiersbe, *Be Complete* (Wheaton, IL: Victor, 1981), p. 24.

10. Charles Colson, *Born Again* (Old Tappan, NJ: Revell [Chosen Books], 1976), pp. 338, 339.

11. Eduard Lohse, *Colossians and Philemon*, trans. William R. Poehlmann and Robert J. Karris (Philadelphia: Fortress, 1971), p. 17 says:

> "Faith" and "love" are the hallmarks of the Christian life of the community, but "hope" refers to the content of the message which the community heard and accepted. This hope makes them capable of remaining firm in faith and practicing love to all the saints.

12. C. S. Lewis, *The Weight of Glory* (Grand Rapids, MI: Eerdmans, 1965), pp. 1, 2.

Chapter Twenty-five: The Prayer for the Church

1. Lois Neely, *Come Up to This Mountain* (Wheaton, IL: Tyndale, 1980), p. 65.

2. F. F. Bruce and E. K. Simpson, *Commentary on the Epistles to the Ephesians and the Colossians* (Grand Rapids, MI. Eerdmans, 1957), p. 185. Bruce quotes Bieltmann, which is here reproduced.

3. Eduard Lohse, *Colossians and Philemon* (Philadelphia: Fortress, 1971), p. 25 says:

> He has been making constant and earnest prayer for them, similar to 1 Thess. 1:2; 2:13; Rom. 1:9; and Eph. 1:16. This is also indicated by the use of both "to pray". . . and "to ask." This prayer is made to God with great intensity so that he may grant it.

4. Warren Wiersbe, *Be Complete* (Wheaton, IL: Victor, 1981), p. 35.

5. Harry Blamires, *The Christian Mind* (London: S.P.C.K., 1963), p. 43 says:

> . . . the Christian mind—a mind trained, informed, equipped to handle data of secular controversy within a framework of reference which is construct-

ed of Christian presuppositions. The Christian mind is the prerequisite of Christian action.

6. Lohse, *Colossians and Philemon*, p. 30.

7. Ralph P. Martin, *Colossians and Philemon*, The New Century Bible (London: Oliphants, Marshall & Scott, 1978), p. 53.

8. Wiersbe, *Be Complete*, p. 43.

9. C. S. Lewis, *The Weight of Glory* (Grand Rapids, MI: Eerdmans, 1965), p. 13.

10. Peter T. O'Brien, *Colossians, Philemon*, Word Biblical Commentary, vol. 44 (Waco, TX: Word, 1982), p. 27, which refers to Josephus, *Antiquities*, 9.235 where the same word is used of Tiglath-pileser's removal of the Transjordanian tribes to his own kingdom.

11. Bruce and Simpson, *Commentary on the Epistles to the Ephesians and the Colossians*, p. 190 where Bruce says:

> It appears that Paul tends to distinguish these two aspects of the heavenly kingdom by reserving the commoner expression "the kingdom of God" for its future consummation, while designating its present phase by some such term as "the kingdom of Christ." We may compare his language in 1 Cor. 15:24, where Christ, after reigning until all things are put under His feet, delivers the kingdom "to God, even the Father"; Christ's mediatorial sovereignty then gives place to the eternal dominion of God.

Chapter Twenty-six: The Preeminent Christ

1. Warren Wiersbe, *Be Complete* (Wheaton, IL: Victor, 1981), pp. 52, 53.

2. William Barclay, *The Letters to the Philippians, Colossians, and Thessalonians* (Philadelphia: Westminster, 1959), p. 142.

3. Peter T. O'Brien, *Colossians, Philemon*, Word Biblical Commentary, vol. 44 (Waco, TX: Word, 1982), p. 43.

4. Ralph P. Martin, *Colossians and Philemon*, The New Century Bible (London: Oliphants, Marshall & Scott, 1978), p. 57 where he says:

> The really significant point to observe, however, is that in ancient thought *eikon* was believed not only to be a plaster representation of the object so portrayed, but was thought in some way to participate in the substance of the object it symbolized. 'Image is not to be understood as a magnitude which is alien to the reality and present only in the consciousness. It has a share in the reality. Indeed, it is the reality.' (H. Klienknecht, TDNT ii, p. 389). Thus Christ as God's image means that he is not a copy of God, 'like him'; he is the objectivization of God in human life, the 'projection' of God on the canvas of our humanity and the embodiment of the divine in the world of men.

5. Phillip Edgecumbe Hughes, *A Commentary on the Epistle to the Hebrews* (Grand Rapids, MI: Eerdmans, 1977), p. 41.

6. Eduard Lohse, *Colossians and Philemon* (Philadelphia: Fortress, 1971), p. 50.

7. O'Brien, *Colossians, Philemon*, p. 46.

8. Ibid., p. 47.

9. H. Dermot McDonald, *Commentary on Colossians and Philemon* (Waco, TX: Word, 1980), p. 49.

10. From *The Collected Poems of Joseph Mary Plunket*, The Talbot Press, Dublin, as quoted in *The Interpreter's Bible*, vol. 2, ed. George Arthur Buttrick (New York: Abingdon Press, n.d.), p. 166.

Chapter Twenty-seven: The Supreme Reconciliation

1. Walter Lord, *A Night to Remember* (New York: Holt, Rinehart and Winston, 1976), pp. 70, 71.

2. F. F. Bruce and E. K. Simpson, *Commentary on the Epistles to the Ephesians and the Colossians* (Grand Rapids, MI: Eerdmans, 1957), pp. 206, 207.

3. William R. Nicholson, *Colossians—Oneness with Christ* (Grand Rapids, MI: Kregel, 1973), p. 90.

4. Clarence E. Macartney, *Macartney's Illustrations* (New York: Abingdon, 1946), p. 297.

5. Peter T. O'Brien, *Colossians and Philemon*, Word Biblical Commentary, vol. 44 (Waco, TX: Word, 1982), p. 66.

6. Arnold Dallimore, *George Whitefield*, vol. 1 (Wheaton, IL: Crossway Books), p. 132.

7. R. C. Sproul, *The Holiness of God* (Wheaton, IL: Tyndale, 1985), p. 214.

8. O'Brien, *Colossians and Philemon*, p. 69.

9. Clyde S. Fant Jr. and William M. Pinson., eds., *20 Centuries of Great Preaching*, vol. 6 (Waco, TX: Word), pp. 312, 313.

Chapter Twenty-eight: The Supreme Ministry

1. R. C. Sproul, *Tabletalk*, 9, no. 2 (April 1985), p. 12.

2. John R. W. Stott, *Between Two Worlds* (Grand Rapids, MI: Eerdmans, 1982), pp. 22, 23.

3. Warren Wiersbe, *Walking with the Giants* (Grand Rapids, MI: Baker, 1979), p. 269.

4. Stott, *Between Two Worlds*, p. 43.

5. Peter T. O'Brien, *Colossians, Philemon*, Word Biblical Commentary, vol. 44 (Waco, TX: Word, 1982), p. 75.

6. Ibid., pp. 78–81.

7. Wiersbe, *Walking with the Giants*, pp. 56, 57.

8. Gail MacDonald, *High Call, High Privilege* (Wheaton, IL: Tyndale, 1984), p. 86.

9. O'Brien, *Colossians, Philemon*, p. 90.

10. F. F. Bruce and E. K. Simpson, *Commentary on the Epistles to the Ephesians and the Colossians* (Grand Rapids, MI: Eerdmans, 1957), p. 221.

11. Ralph P. Martin, *Colossians and Philemon*, The New Century Bible (London: Oliphants, Marshall & Scott, 1978), p. 73.

12. G. Campbell Morgan, *The Westminster Pulpit*, Vols. 3, 4 (Old Tappan, NJ: Revell, n.d.), p. 160.

13. Maxie Dunnam, *Galatians, Ephesians, Philippians, Colossians, Philemon*, The Communicator's Commentary (Waco, TX: Word, 1982), pp. 363, 364.

Chapter Twenty-nine: The Supreme Concern

1. John R. W. Stott, *Between Two Worlds* (Grand Rapids, MI; Eerdmans, 1982), p. 285.

2. Clarence Edward Macartney, *Preaching Without Notes* (Grand Rapids, MI: Baker, 1976), p. 183.

3. W. E. Vine, *An Expository Dictionary of New Testament Words* (Old Tappan, NJ: Revell, 1966), p. 226.

4. Lyle W. Dorsett and Marjorie Lamp Mead, eds., *C. S. Lewis Letters to Children* (New York: Macmillan, 1985), p. 111.

5. F. F. Bruce and E. K. Simpson, *Commentary on the Epistles to the Ephesians and the Colossians* (Grand Rapids, MI: Eerdmans, 1957), p. 223.

6. Alexander Maclaren, *The Epistles of St. Paul to the Colossians and Philemon*, The Expositor's Bible (New York: A. C. Armstrong, 1903), pp. 165, 166.

7. Timothy Dwight, "I Love Thy Kingdom, Lord," 1800.

Chapter Thirty: The Supreme Charge

1. Peter T. O'Brien, *Colossians, Philemon*, Word Biblical Commentary, vol. 44 (Waco, TX: Word, 1982), p. 106.

2. *The Annals of America*, vol. 17, *1950–1960, Cold War in Nuclear Age*, 1968, p. 395.

3. Quoted by Ernest C. Reisinger, *Today's Evangelism: Its Message and Method* (Phillipsburg, NJ: Craig Press, 1982).

4. Hugh Evan Hopkins, *Charles Simeon of Cambridge* (Grand Rapids, MI: Eerdmans, 1977), p. 28.

5. R. C. Lucas, *Fullness and Freedom* (Downers Grove, IL: InterVarsity Press, 1980), p. 92.

6. Alexander Maclaren, *The Epistles of St. Paul to the Colossians and Philemon*, The Expositor's Bible (New York: A. C. Armstrong, 1903), pp. 183, 184.

Chapter Thirty-one: The Safeguard against Seduction

1. Donald Grey Barnhouse, *Let Me Illustrate* (Old Tappan. NJ: Revell, 1967), p. 86.

2. F. F. Bruce and E. K. Simpson, *Commentary on the Epistles to the Ephesians and the Colossians* (Grand Rapids, MI: Eerdmans, 1957), p. 230.

3. Edwin Newman, *Strictly Speaking* (New York: Warner Books, 1977), pp. 171, 172.

4. *The Arizona Republic*, January 7, 1986, p. A-2.

5. Bruce and Simpson, *Commentary on the Epistles to the Ephesians and the Colossians*, p. 230.

6. Peter T. O'Brien, *Colossians, Philemon*, Word Biblical Commentary, vol. 44 (Waco, TX: Word, 1982). p. 110.

7. Ibid.

8. Bruce and Simpson, *Commentary on the Epistles to the Ephesians and the Colossians*, p. 232.

9. O'Brien, *Colossians, Philemon*, p. 111.

10. R. E. O. White, *In Him the Fullness* (Old Tappan, NJ: Revell, 1973), p. 83.

11. Alexander Maclaren, *The Epistles of St. Paul to Colossians and Philemon*, The Expositor's Bible (New York: A. C. Armstrong, 1903), p. 198.

Chapter Thirty-two: The Fullness in Christ

1. F. F. Bruce and E. K. Simpson, *Commentary on the Epistles to the Ephesians and the Colossians* (Grand Rapids, MI: Eerdmans, 1957), p. 234 where Bruce says:

This "circumcision of Christ" is not primarily His circumcision as a Jewish infant of eight days old (Luke 2:21); it is rather his crucifixion, "the putting off the body of flesh," of which literal circumcision was at best a token anticipation.

2. Peter T. O'Brien, *Colossians, Philemon*, Word Biblical Commentary, vol. 44 (Waco, TX: Word, 1982), p. 118.

3. Ibid., p. 116.

4. Ibid., p. 119.

5. Plutarch, *The Lives of the Noble Grecians and Romans* (New York: The Modern Library, n.d.), pp. 340–342.

6. Ibid.

Chapter Thirty-three: The Guarding of Your Treasure

1. Adapted from Joy Davidman, *Smoke on the Mountain* (Philadelphia: Westminster Press, 1953), p. 13.

2. James S. Hewett, ed., *Parables, Etc.*, 6, no. 1 (March 1986), p. 1.

3. F. F. Bruce and E. K. Simpson, *Commentary on the Epistles to the Ephesians and the Colossians* (Grand Rapids, MI: Eerdmans, 1957), p. 250.

4. C. S. Lewis, *The Weight of Glory* (Grand Rapids, MI: Eerdmans, 1965), pp. 61–63.

5. R. E. O. White, *In Him the Fullness* (Old Tappan, NJ: Revell, 1973), pp. 90, 91.

6. Bruce and Simpson, *Commentary on the Epistles to the Ephesians and the Colossians*, p. 256.

Chapter Thirty-four: The Seeking of Things Above

1. F. F. Bruce and E. K. Simpson, *Commentary on the Epistles to the Ephesians and the Colossians* (Grand Rapids, MI: Eerdmans, 1957), p. 258, quoting *Weimar Ansgabe*, XXIII, p. 131.

2. Wesley H. Hager, *Conquering* (Grand Rapids, MI: Eerdmans, 1965), p. 16.

3. Ibid., p. 15.

4. Os Guinness, *The Gravedigger Files* (Downers Grove, IL: InterVarsity Press), p. 132, quoting Frank S. Mead, *Handbook of Denominations* (Nashville: Abingdon, 1970), p. 217.

Chapter Thirty-five: The Putting Off, Putting On, I

1. Warren Wiersbe, *Be Complete* (Wheaton, IL: Victor, 1981), p 103.

2. William Barclay, *The Letters to the Philippians, Colossians and Thessalonians* (Philadelphia: Westminster, 1959), p. 181.

3. Alexander Maclaren, *The Epistles of St. Paul to the Colossians and Philemon*, The Expositor's Bible (New York: A. C. Armstrong, 1903), p. 275.

4. William Barclay, *A New Testament Wordbook* (New York: Harper, n.d.), pp. 97–99.

5. Clarence E. Macartney, *Macartney's Illustrations* (New York: Abingdon, 1946), pp. 377, 378.

6. Maclaren, *The Epistles of St. Paul to the Colossians and Philemon*, p. 287.

7. Tertullian, *Apology*, 39.

Chapter Thirty-six: The Putting Off, Putting On, II

1. Peter T. O'Brien, *Colossians, Philemon*, Word Biblical Commentary, vol. 44 (Waco, TX: Word, 1982), p. 199.

2. William Barclay, *The Letters to the Philippians, Colossians, and Thessalonians* (Philadelphia: Westminster, 1959), p. 188.

3. John Perkins, *Let Justice Roll Down* (Ventura, CA: Regal, 1983), p. 203.

4. Barclay, *The Letters to the Philippians, Colossians, and Thessalonians*, pp. 188, 189.

5. F. W. Boreham, *The Heavenly Octave* (Grand Rapids, MI: Baker, 1978), p. 12.

6. Ibid., p. 17.

7. *Daily Bread*.

8. William Barclay, *A New Testament Wordbook* (New York: Harper, n.d.), pp. 103, 104.

9. R. E. O. White, *In Him the Fullness* (Old Tappan, NJ: Revell, 1973), p. 113.

10. Perkins, *Let Justice Roll Down*, pp. 162–166.

11. Ibid., pp. 205, 206.

12. F. F. Bruce and E. K. Simpson, *Commentary on the Epistles to the Ephesians and the Colossians* (Grand Rapids, MI: Eerdmans, 1957), p. 281.

Chapter Thirty-seven: The Fullness of His Peace, Word, and Name

1. F. F. Bruce and E. K. Simpson, *Commentary on the Epistles to the Ephesians and the Colossians* (Grand Rapids, MI: Eerdmans, 1957), p. 281.

2. Ibid., p. 284.

Chapter Thirty-eight: The Christian Family, I

1. Michael R. Tucker, *Live Confidently* (Wheaton, IL: Tyndale, 1976), p. 61.

2. William Barclay, *The Letters to the Philippians, Colossians, and Thessalonians* (Philadelphia: Westminster, 1959), pp. 192, 193.

3. Peter T. O'Brien, *Colossians, Philemon*, Word Biblical Commentary, vol. 44 (Waco, TX: Word, 1982), pp. 218, 219.

4. F. F. Bruce and E. K. Simpson, *Commentary on the Epistles to the Ephesians and the Colossians* (Grand Rapids, MI: Eerdmans, 1957), pp. 289, 290:

> This phrase has a thoroughly stoic ring about it; but the injunction ceases to be stoic when Paul baptizes it into Christ by adding the words, "in the Lord." By treating the relation between the sexes in the context, Paul (contrary to much popular opinion) places essential dignity of women in general and of wives in particular on an unshakable foundation.

5. Ibid., p. 289.

6. Eduard Lohse, *Colossians and Philemon* (Philadelphia: Fortress, 1971), p. 158, n. 28: "Pre-Christian antiquity knew of the terms 'to love/love' . . . but in the Hellenistic world these terms do not occur in rules for the household."

7. Richard Seizer, *Mortal Lessons: Notes on the Art of Surgery* (New York: Simon and Schuster, 1976), pp. 45, 46.

8. Charles Swindoll, *Think It Over*, "Love Without a Net," a publication of the First Evangelical Free Church of Fullerton, California.

Chapter Thirty-nine: The Christian Family, II

1. James Dobson, *Hide or Seek* (Old Tappan, NJ: Revell, 1974), pp. 9, 11.

2. Karl Barth and Carl Zuckmayer, *A Late Friendship*, trans. Geoffrey Bromiley (Grand Rapids, MI: Eerdmans, 1982), p. 47.

3. Dobson, *Hide or Seek*, pp. 82, 83.

4. In Hebrews 1:1 the word fathers (*pateron*) means "parents" in the context and is translated "parents" in many translations. Nevertheless, the specific nature of the three pairs of injunctions in 3:18—4:1 would argue for "fathers" here.

5. Peter T. O'Brien, *Colossians, Philemon*, Word Biblical Commentary, vol. 44 (Waco, TX: Word, 1982), p. 225.

6. William Barclay, *The Letters to the Philippians, Colossians, and Thessalonians* (Philadelphia: Westminster, 1959), p. 195.

Chapter Forty: The Christian Family, III

1. William Barclay, *The Letters to the Galatians and Ephesians* (Philadelphia: Westminster, 1958), pp. 212–214.

2. Ibid.

3. William MacDonald, *Ephesians, the Mystery of the Church* (Carol Stream, IL: Harold Shaw, 1968), p. 229.

4. Peter T. O'Brien, *Colossians, Philemon*, Word Biblical Commentary, vol. 44 (Waco, TX: Word, 1982), p. 229.

5. Humphrey House., ed., *Gerard Manley Hopkins, The Notebooks and Papers* (New York: Oxford, 1937), pp. 304, 305.

6. Alexander Maclaren, *The Epistles of St. Paul to the Colossians and Philemon*, The Expositor's Bible (New York: A. C. Armstrong, 1903), p. 352 .

7. R. E. O. White, *In Him the Fullness* (Old Tappan, NJ: Revell, 1973), p. 127.

Chapter Forty-one: The Fullness in Communication

1. Thomas R. Kelly, *A Testament of Devotion* (New York: Harper, 1941), p. 35.

2. Brother Lawrence, *The Practice of the Presence of God* (Old Tappan, NJ: Revell, 1958), pp. 30, 31.

3. R. C. Sproul, *The Holiness of God* (Wheaton, IL: Tyndale, 1985), p. 54.

4. Michael D. Aeschliman, *The Restitution of Man* (Grand Rapids, MI: Eerdmans, 1983), p. 5.

5. John R. W. Stott, *Between Two Worlds* (Grand Rapids, MI: Eerdmans, 1982), p. 128.

6. Joseph Bayly, *I Love to Tell the Story* (Elgin, IL: David C. Cook, 1978), p. 36.

7. *Tabletalk*, 10, no. 4 (August 1986), p. 7.

Chapter Forty-two: The Fullness in Fellowship, I

1. A. W. Tozer, *The Pursuit of God* (Wheaton, IL: Tyndale, 1982), pp. 119–123.

2. From the Department of Field Services, National Association of Evangelicals, January/February 1986 letter.

3. Lane T. Dennis, ed., *Letters of Francis A. Schaeffer* (Wheaton, IL: Crossway Books, 1985), p. 108.

Chapter Forty-three: The Fullness in Fellowship, II

1. Allen Emery, *A Turtle on a Fencepost* (Waco, TX: Word, 1979), pp. 75–78.

2. Warren Wiersbe, *Be Complete* (Wheaton, IL: Victor, 1981), p. 147.

3. Phillips Brooks, *The Influence of Jesus* (London: H. R. Allenson, 1875), p. 191.

Chapter Forty-four: The Fullness of Paul's Heart

1. Peter T. O'Brien, *Colossians, Philemon*, Word Biblical Commentary, vol. 44 (Waco, TX: Word, 1982), p. 257, where he says:

> The Epistles of the New Testament were from the first intended to be read aloud in the Christian assembly (showing that they ranked equally with the Old Testament), a point which is attested in one of Paul's earliest letters where he uses strong language in commanding that his letters be read aloud to all the brethren (1 Thessalonians 5:27 . . .).

2. Alexander Maclaren, *The Epistles of St. Paul to the Colossians and Philemon*, The Expositor's Bible (New York: A. C. Armstrong, 1903), p. 411.

PHILEMON

Chapter Forty-five: The Reconciling Wisdom

1. Andrew W. Blackwood, *Evangelical Sermons of Our Day* (New York: Harper and Bros., 1959), p. 338.

2. Ibid., p. 337.

3. H. Dermot McDonald, *Commentary on Colossians and Philemon* (Waco, TX: Word, 1980), p. 173, where he says:

> He has his own testimony to the sheer mercy of God. And if he already knows the content of Paul's letter, he will speak with thanksgiving to the Father who has qualified him to share in the inheritance of the saints in light, for his experience of deliverance (Colossians 1:12–14).

4. Charles Colson, *Who Speaks for God?* (Wheaton, IL: Crossway Books, 1985), p.153.

5. Ralph P. Martin, *Colossians and Philemon*, The New Century Bible (London: Oliphants, Marshall & Scott, 1978), p. 167, where he says:

The underlying assumption is that Paul knows the law by which a person harbouring a runaway slave was liable to the owner for the loss of work involved in the slave's defection, see Preiss, loco cit., p. 35. Oxrhynchus papyrus 1422 contains a notice that persons who gave shelter to escaped slaves were to be held accountable in law and could be prosecuted by the slaves' master.

6. William Wordsworth, *Ecclesiastical Sonnets*, Part 3, 43.

7. William Barclay, *The Letters to Timothy, Titus and Philemon* (Louisville: Westminster/John Knox, 1975), pp. 315, 316.

Scripture Index

General Index

Index of Sermon Illustrations

The PREACHING the
WORD SERIES

IS WRITTEN BY

PASTORS FOR PASTORS

AND THEIR CHURCHES